SCIENCE, PERCEPTION
AND REALITY

International Library of Philosophy and Scientific Method

EDITOR: TED HONDERICH
ADVISORY EDITOR: BERNARD WILLIAMS

A Catalogue of books already published in the
International Library of Philosophy and Scientific Method
will be found at the end of this volume.

SCIENCE, PERCEPTION AND REALITY

by

Wilfrid Sellars

LONDON

ROUTLEDGE & KEGAN PAUL

NEW YORK : THE HUMANITIES PRESS

First published 1963
by Routledge & Kegan Paul Ltd
Broadway House, 68-74 Carter Lane
London, E.C.4

Printed in Great Britain by
Compton Printing Ltd
London and Aylesbury

Second impression 1966
Third impression 1968

SBN 7100 3619 1

CONTENTS

v

ACKNOWLEDGEMENTS

'PHILOSOPHY and the Scientific Image of Man' consists of two lectures given at the University of Pittsburgh in December, 1960, as part of a series of lectures in the history and philosophy of science by various contributors. It was printed in *Frontiers of Science and Philosophy* (Robert Colodny, editor) and published by the University of Pittsburgh Press (Pittsburgh: 1962) which has kindly consented to its appearance in the present volume.

'Being and Being Known' is a lecture given at the St. Louis meeting of the American Catholic Philosophical Association in April, 1960, and is reprinted from the *Proceedings* of the Association by kind permission of the editor.

'Phenomenalism' was written in 1959 for inclusion in another volume, but was withdrawn and requires no acknowledgement.

'Empiricism and the Philosophy of Mind' consists of lectures delivered at the University of London in March, 1956, under the title, 'The Myth of the Given: Three Lectures on Empiricism and the Philosophy of Mind' from: Minnesota Studies in the Philosophy of Science, Vol. I, *The Foundations of Science and the Concepts of Psychology and Psychoanalysis*, edited by Herbert Feigl and Michael Scriven. University of Minnesota Press, Minneapolis. Copyright 1956 by the University of Minnesota.

'The Language of Theories' was read at the 1959 meeting of the American Association for the Advancement of Science (Section L) and was printed in *Current Issues in the Philosophy of Science*, (Herbert Feigl and Grover Maxwell, editors), published by Henry Holt, Rhinehart and Winston (New York: 1961) who have kindly consented to its appearance in the present volume.

'Truth and "Correspondence" ' was the opening paper in a symposium on Logic and Reality at the 1961 meeting of the Metaphysical Society. It was printed in the *Journal of Philosophy*, 59, 1962, and is reprinted by kind permission of the editors.

'Naming and Saying' was the opening paper in a symposium on Reference and Use at the 1961 meeting of the American Philosophical Association (Western Division). It was published in *Philosophy of Science*, 29, 1962, and is reprinted by kind permission of the editor.

ACKNOWLEDGEMENTS

'Grammar and Existence: a Preface to Ontology' consists of two lectures given at Yale University in March, 1958. It was published in *Mind*, 69, 1960, and is reprinted by kind permission of the editor.

'Particulars' originally appeared in *Philosophy and Phenomenological Research*, 13, 1952, and is reprinted by kind permission of the editor.

'Is there a Synthetic *A priori*?' is a revised version of a paper read at a symposium on this topic at the 1951 meeting of the American Philosophical Association (Eastern Division), and published in *Philosophy of Science*, 20, 1953. The present version appeared in *American Philosophers at Work* (Sidney Hook, editor), New York (Criterion Press, 1958), and is reprinted by kind permission of the publisher.

'Some Reflections on Language Games' was originally printed in *Philosophy of Science*, Vol. 21, 3 July 1954, pp. 204–228. Copyright © 1954 The Williams & Wilkins Co., Baltimore 2, Md., U.S.A. It appears here in a revised version prepared in 1955 for publication in Volume I of *Minnesota Studies in the Philosophy of Science*, but withdrawn to make room for 'Empiricism and the Philosophy of Mind'.

PHILOSOPHY AND THE
SCIENTIFIC IMAGE OF MAN

I. THE PHILOSOPHICAL QUEST

THE aim of philosophy, abstractly formulated, is to understand how things in the broadest possible sense of the term hang together in the broadest possible sense of the term. Under 'things in the broadest possible sense' I include such radically different items as not only 'cabbages and kings', but numbers and duties, possibilities and finger snaps, aesthetic experience and death. To achieve success in philosophy would be, to use a contemporary turn of phrase, to 'know one's way around' with respect to all these things, not in that unreflective way in which the centipede of the story knew its way around before it faced the question, 'how do I walk?', but in that reflective way which means that no intellectual holds are barred.

Knowing one's way around is, to use a current distinction, a form of 'knowing *how*' as contrasted with 'knowing *that*'. There is all the difference in the world between knowing *how* to ride a bicycle and knowing *that* a steady pressure by the legs of a balanced person on the pedals would result in forward motion. Again, to use an example somewhat closer to our subject, there is all the difference in the world between knowing *that* each step of a given proof in mathematics follows from the preceding steps, and knowing *how* to find a proof. Sometimes being able to find a proof is a matter of being able to follow a set procedure; more often it is not. It can be argued that anything which can be properly called 'knowing how to do something' presupposes a body of knowledge *that*; or, to put it differently, knowledge of truth or facts. If this were so, then the statement that 'ducks know *how* to swim' would be as metaphorical as the statement that they know *that* water supports them. However this may be, knowing how to do something at the level of characteristically human activity

1

presupposes a great deal of knowledge *that*, and it is obvious that the reflective knowing one's way around in the scheme of things, which is the aim of philosophy, presupposes a great deal of reflective knowledge of truths.

Now the subject-matter of this knowledge of truths which is presupposed by philosophical 'know-how', falls, in a sense, completely within the scope of the special disciplines. Philosophy in an important sense has no special subject-matter which stands to it as other subject-matters stand to other special disciplines. If philosophers did have such a special subject-matter, they could turn it over to a new group of specialists as they have turned other special subject-matters to non-philosophers over the past 2500 years, first with mathematics, more recently psychology and sociology, and, currently, certain aspects of theoretical linguistics. What is characteristic of philosophy is not a special subject-matter, but the aim of knowing one's way around with respect to the subject-matters of all the special disciplines.

Now the special disciplines know their way around in their subject-matters, and each learns to do so in the process of discovering truths about its own subject-matter. But each special discipline must also have a sense of how its bailiwick fits into the countryside as a whole. This sense in many cases amounts to a little more than the unreflective 'knowing one's way around' which is a common possession of us all. Again, the specialist must have a sense of how not only his subject-matter, but also the methods and principles of his thinking about it fit into the intellectual landscape. Thus, the historian reflects not only on historical events themselves, but on what it is to think historically. It is part of his business to reflect on his own thinking—its aims, its criteria, its pitfalls. In dealing with historical questions, he must face and answer questions which are not, themselves, in a primary sense historical questions. But he deals with these questions as they arise in the attempt to answer specifically historical questions.

Reflection on any special discipline can soon lead one to the conclusion that the *ideal* practitioner of that discipline would see his special subject-matter and his thinking about it in the light of a reflective insight into the intellectual landscape as a whole. There is much truth in the Platonic conception that the special disciplines are perfected by philosophy, but the companion conception that the philosopher must know his way around in each discipline as does the specialist, has been an ever more elusive ideal since the scientific revolution began. Yet if the philosopher cannot hope to know his way around in each discipline as does the specialist, there is a sense in which he can know his way around with respect to the subject-matter of that discipline, and must do so if he is to approximate to the philosophic aim.

2

The multiplication of sciences and disciplines is a familiar feature of the intellectual scene. Scarcely less familiar is the unification of this manifold which is taking place by the building of scientific bridges between them. I shall have something to say about this unification later in this chapter. What is not so obvious to the layman is that the task of 'seeing all things together' has itself been (paradoxically) broken down into specialities. And there *is* a place for specialization in philosophy. For just as one cannot come to know one's way around in the highway system as a whole without knowing one's way around in the parts, so one can't hope to know one's way around in 'things in general', without knowing one's way around in the major groupings of things.

It is therefore, the 'eye on the whole' which distinguishes the philosophical enterprise. Otherwise, there is little to distinguish the philosopher from the persistently reflective specialist; the philosopher of history from the persistently reflective historian. To the extent that a specialist is more concerned to reflect on how his work as a specialist joins up with other intellectual pursuits, than in asking and answering questions within his speciality, he is said, properly, to be philosophically-minded. And, indeed, one can 'have one's eye on the whole' without staring at it all the time. The latter would be a fruitless enterprise. Furthermore, like other specialists, the philosopher who specializes may derive much of his sense of the whole from the pre-reflective orientation which is our common heritage. On the other hand, a philosopher could scarcely be said to have his eye on the whole in the relevant sense, unless he has reflected on the nature of philosophical thinking. It is this reflection on the place of philosophy itself, in the scheme of things which is the distinctive trait of the philosopher as contrasted with the reflective specialist; and in the absence of this critical reflection on the philosophical enterprise, one is at best but a potential philosopher.

It has often been said in recent years that the aim of the philosopher is not to discover new truths, but to 'analyse' what we already know. But while the term 'analysis' was helpful in its implication that philosophy as such makes no *substantive* contribution to what we know, and is concerned in some way to improve the *manner* in which we know it, it is most misleading by its contrast to 'synthesis'. For by virtue of this contrast these statements suggest that philosophy is ever more myopic, tracing parts within parts, losing each in turn from sight as new parts come into view. One is tempted, therefore, to contrast the analytic conception of philosophy as myopia with the synoptic vision of true philosophy. And it must be admitted that if the contrast between 'analysis' and 'synthesis' were the operative connotation in the metaphor, then a purely analytic philosophy would

3

be a contradiction in terms. Even if we construe 'analysis' on the analogy of making ever smaller scale maps of the same overall terrain, which does more justice to the synoptic element, the analogy disturbs because we would have to compare philosophy to the making of small-scale maps from an original large-scale map; and a smaller scale map in this sense is a triviality.

Even if the analogy is changed to that of bringing a picture into focus, which preserves the synoptic element and the theme of working within the framework of what is already known while adding a dimension of gain, the analogy is disturbing in two respects. (*a*) It suggests that the special disciplines are confused; as though the scientist had to wait for the philosopher to clarify his subject-matter, bring it into focus. To account for the creative role of philosophy, it is not necessary to say that the scientist doesn't know his way around in his own area. What we must rather say is that the specialist knows his way around in his own neighbourhood, as his neighbourhood, but doesn't know his way around in it in the same way *as a part of the landscape as a whole.*

(*b*) It implies that the essential change brought about by philosophy is the standing out of detail within a picture which is grasped as a whole from the start. But, of course, to the extent that there is *one* picture to be grasped reflectively as a whole, the unity of the reflective vision is a task rather than an initial datum. The search for this unity at the reflective level is therefore more appropriately compared to the contemplation of a large and complex painting which is not seen as a unity without a prior exploration of its parts. The analogy, however, is not complete until we take into account a *second* way in which unity is lacking in the original datum of the contemporary philosopher. For he is confronted not by one picture, but, *in principle*, by *two* and, in fact, by *many*. The plurality I have in mind is not that which concerns the distinction between the fact finding, the ethical, the aesthetic, the logical, the religious, and other aspects of experience, for these are but aspects of one complex picture which is to be grasped reflectively as a whole. As such, it constitutes one term of a crucial duality which confronts the contemporary philosopher at the very beginning of his enterprise. Here the most appropriate analogy is stereoscopic vision, where two differing perspectives on a landscape are fused into one coherent experience.

For the philosopher is confronted not by one complex many-dimensional picture, the unity of which, such as it is, he must come to appreciate; but by *two* pictures of essentially the same order of complexity, each of which purports to be a complete picture of man-in-the-world, and which, after separate scrutiny, he must fuse into one vision. Let me refer to these two perspectives, respectively, as the *manifest* and the *scientific* images of man-in-the-world. And let me explain my terms. First, by calling them images I do not mean to deny to either or both of them the status of 'reality'. I am, to use Husserl's term, 'bracketing' them, transforming them from ways of experiencing the world into objects of philosophical reflection and evaluation. The term 'image' is usefully ambiguous. On the one hand it suggests the contrast between an object, e.g. a tree, and a projection of the object on a plane, or its shadow on a wall. In this sense, an image is as much an existent as the object imaged, though, of course, it has a dependent status.

In the other sense, an 'image' is something imagined, and that which is imagined may well not exist, although the imagining of it does—in which case we can speak of the image as *merely* imaginary or unreal. But the imagined *can* exist; as when one imagines that someone is dancing in the next room, and someone is. This ambiguity enables me to imply that the philosopher is confronted by two projections of man-in-the-world on the human understanding. One of these projections I will call the manifest image, the other the scientific image. These images exist and are as much a part and parcel of the world as this platform or the Constitution of the United States. But in addition to being confronted by these images as existents, he is confronted by them as images in the sense of 'things imagined'—or, as I had better say at once, *conceived*; for I am using 'image' in this sense as a metaphor for conception, and it is a familiar fact that not everything that can be conceived can, in the ordinary sense, be imagined. The philosopher, then, is confronted by two conceptions, equally public, equally non-arbitrary, of man-in-the-world and he cannot shirk the attempt to see how they fall together in one stereoscopic view.

Before I begin to explain the contrast between 'manifest' and 'scientific' as I shall use these terms, let me make it clear that they are both 'idealizations' in something like the sense in which a frictionless body or an ideal gas is an idealization. They are designed to illuminate the inner dynamics of the development of philosophical ideas, as scientific idealizations illuminate the development of physical systems. From a somewhat different point of view they can be compared to the 'ideal types' of Max Weber's sociology. The story is complicated by the fact that each image has a history, and while the main outlines of what I shall call the manifest image took shape in the mists of pre-history, the scientific image, promissory notes apart, has taken shape before our very eyes.

5

II. THE MANIFEST IMAGE

The 'manifest' image of man-in-the-world can be characterized in two ways, which are supplementary rather than alternative. It is, first, the framework in terms of which man came to be aware of himself as man-in-the-world. It is the framework in terms of which, to use an existentialist turn of phrase, man first encountered himself—which is, of course, when he came to be man. For it is no merely incidental feature of man that he has a conception of himself as man-in-the-world, just as it is obvious, on reflection, that 'if man had a radically different conception of himself he would be a radically different kind of man'.

I have given this quasi-historical dimension of our construct pride of place, because I want to highlight from the very beginning what might be called the paradox of man's encounter with himself, the paradox consisting of the fact that man couldn't be man until he encountered himself. It is this paradox which supports the last stand of Special Creation. Its central theme is the idea that anything which can properly be called conceptual thinking can occur only within a framework of conceptual thinking in terms of which it can be criticized, supported, refuted, in short, evaluated. To be able to think is to be able to measure one's thoughts by standards of correctness, of relevance, of evidence. In this sense a diversified conceptual framework is a whole which, however sketchy, is prior to its parts, and cannot be construed as a coming together of parts which are already conceptual in character. The conclusion is difficult to avoid that the transition from pre-conceptual patterns of behaviour to conceptual thinking was a holistic one, a jump to a level of awareness which is irreducibly new, a jump which was the coming into being of man.

There is a profound truth in this conception of a radical difference in level between man and his precursors. The attempt to understand this difference turns out to be part and parcel of the attempt to encompass in one view the two images of man-in-the-world which I have set out to describe. For, as we shall see, this difference in level appears as an irreducible discontinuity in the *manifest* image, but as, in a sense requiring careful analysis, a reducible difference in the *scientific* image.

I have characterized the manifest image of man-in-the-world as the framework in terms of which man encountered himself. And this, I believe, is a useful way of characterizing it. But it is also misleading, for it suggests that the contrast I am drawing between the manifest and the scientific images, is that between a pre-scientific, uncritical, naïve conception of man-in-the-world, and a reflected, disciplined, critical—in short a scientific—conception. This is not at all what I

6

have in mind. For what I mean by the manifest image is a refinement or sophistication of what might be called the 'original' image; a refinement to a degree which makes it relevant to the contemporary intellectual scene. This refinement or sophistication can be construed under two headings; (*a*) empirical; (*b*) categorial.

By empirical refinement, I mean the sort of refinement which operates within the broad framework of the image and which, by approaching the world in terms of something like the canons of inductive inference defined by John Stuart Mill, supplemented by canons of statistical inference, adds to and subtracts from the contents of the world as experienced in terms of this framework and from the correlations which are believed to obtain between them. Thus, the conceptual framework which I am calling the manifest image is, in an appropriate sense, itself a scientific image. It is not only disciplined and critical; it also makes use of those aspects of scientific method which might be lumped together under the heading 'correlational induction'. There is, however, one type of scientific reasoning which it, by stipulation, does *not* include, namely that which involves the postulation of imperceptible entities, and principles pertaining to them, to explain the behaviour of perceptible things.

This makes it clear that the concept of the manifest image of man-in-the-world is not that of an historical and bygone stage in the development of man's conception of the world and his place in it. For it is a familiar fact that correlational and postulational methods have gone hand in hand in the evolution of science, and, indeed, have been dialectically related; postulational hypotheses presupposing correlations to be explained, and suggesting possible correlations to be investigated. The notion of a purely correlational scientific view of things is both an historical and a methodological fiction. It involves abstracting correlational fruits from the conditions of their discovery, and the theories in terms of which they are explained. Yet it is a useful fiction (and hence no *mere* fiction), for it will enable us to define a way of looking at the world which, though disciplined and, in a limited sense, scientific, contrasts sharply with an image of man-in-the-world which is implicit in and can be constructed from the postulational aspects of contemporary scientific theory. And, indeed, what I have referred to as the 'scientific' image of man-in-the-world and contrasted with the 'manifest' image, might better be called the 'postulational' or 'theoretical' image. But, I believe, it will not be too misleading if I continue, for the most part, to use the former term.

Now the manifest image is important for our purpose, because it defines one of the poles to which philosophical reflection has been drawn. It is not only the great speculative systems of ancient and medieval philosophy which are built around the manifest image, but

7

also many systems and quasi-systems in recent and contemporary thought, some of which seem at first sight to have little if anything in common with the great classical systems. That I include the major schools of contemporary Continental thought might be expected. That I lump in with these the trends of contemporary British and American philosophy which emphasize the analysis of 'common sense' and 'ordinary usage', may be somewhat more surprising. Yet this kinship is becoming increasingly apparent in recent years and I believe that the distinctions that I am drawing in this chapter will make possible an understanding and interpretation of this kinship. For all these philosophies can, I believe, be fruitfully construed as more or less adequate accounts of the manifest image of man-in-the-world, which accounts are then taken to be an adequate and full description in general terms of what man and the world really are.

Let me elaborate on this theme by introducing another construct which I shall call—borrowing a term with a not unrelated meaning—the perennial philosophy of man-in-the-world. This construct, which is the 'ideal type' around which philosophies in what might be called, in a suitably broad sense, the Platonic tradition cluster, is simply the manifest image endorsed as real, and its outline taken to be the large-scale map of reality to which science brings a needle-point of detail and an elaborate technique of map-reading.

It will probably have occurred to you by now that there are negative over-tones to both constructs: the 'manifest image' and the 'perennial philosophy'. And, in a certain sense, this is indeed the case. I *am* implying that the perennial philosophy is analogous to what one gets when one looks through a stereoscope with one eye dominating. The manifest image dominates and mislocates the scientific image. But if the perennial philosophy of man-in-the-world is in this sense distorted, an important consequence lurks in the offing. For I have also implied that man is *essentially* that being which conceives of it-self *in terms of the image which the perennial philosophy refines and endorses*. I seem, therefore, to be saying that man's conception of himself in the world does not easily accommodate the scientific image; that there is a genuine tension between them; that man is not the sort of thing he conceives himself to be; that his existence is in some measure built around error. If this were what I wished to say, I would be in distinguished company. One thinks, for example, of Spinoza, who contrasted man as he falsely conceives himself to be with man as he discovers himself to be in the scientific enterprise. It might well be said that Spinoza drew a distinction between a 'mani-fest' and a 'scientific' image of man, rejecting the former as false and accepting the latter as true.

But if in Spinoza's account, the scientific image, as he interprets it,

8

dominates the stereoscopic view (the manifest image appearing as a tracery of explainable error), the very fact that I use the analogy of stereoscopic vision implies that as I see it the manifest image is not overwhelmed in the synthesis.

But before there can be any point to these comparisons, I must characterize these images in more detail, adding flesh and blood to the bare bones I have laid before you. I shall devote the remainder of this section and section III to developing the manifest image. In the concluding sections I shall characterize the scientific image, and attempt to describe certain key features of how the two images blend together in a true stereoscopic view.

I distinguished above between two dimensions of the refinement which turned the 'original' image into the 'manifest' image: the empirical and the categorial. Nothing has been said so far about the latter. Yet it is here that the most important things are to be said. It is in this connection that I will be able to describe the general structure of the manifest image.

A fundamental question with respect to any conceptual framework is 'of what sort are the basic objects of the framework?' This question involves, on the one hand, the contrast between an object and what can be true of it in the way of properties, relations, and activities; and, on the other, a contrast between the basic objects of the framework and the various kinds of groups they can compose. The basic objects of a framework need not be things in the restricted sense of perceptible physical objects. Thus, the basic objects of current theoretical physics are notoriously imperceptible and unimaginable. Their basic-ness consists in the fact that they are not properties or groupings of anything more basic (at least until further notice). The questions, 'are the basic objects of the framework of physical theory *thing-like*? and if so, to what extent?' are meaningful ones.

Now to ask, 'what are the basic objects of a (given) framework?' is to ask not for a *list*, but a *classification*. And the classification will be more or less 'abstract' depending on what the purpose of the inquiry is. The philosopher is interested in a classification which is abstract enough to provide a synoptic view of the contents of the framework but which falls short of simply referring to them as objects or entities. Thus we are approaching an answer to the question, 'what are the basic objects of the manifest image?' when we say that it includes persons, animals, lower forms of life and 'merely material' things, like rivers and stones. The list is not intended to be complete, although it is intended to echo the lower stages of the 'great chain of being' of the Platonic tradition.

The first point I wish to make is that there is an important sense in which the primary objects of the manifest image are *persons*. And to understand how this is so, is to understand central and, indeed, crucial themes in the history of philosophy. Perhaps the best way to make the point is to refer back to the construct which we called the 'original' image of man-in-the-world, and characterize it as a framework in which *all* the 'objects' are persons. From this point of view, the refinement of the 'original' image into the manifest image, is the gradual 'de-personalization' of objects other than persons. That something like this has occurred with the advance of civilization is a familiar fact. Even persons, it is said (mistakenly, I believe), are being 'depersonalized' by the advance of the scientific point of view.

The point I now wish to make is that although this gradual de-personalization of the original image is a familiar idea, it is radically misunderstood, if it is assimilated to the gradual abandonment of a superstitious belief. A primitive man did not *believe* that the tree in front of him was a person, in the sense that he thought of it both as a tree *and* as a person, as I might think that this brick in front of me is a doorstop. If this were so, then when he abandoned the idea that trees were persons, his concept of a tree could remain unchanged, although his beliefs about trees would be changed. The truth is, rather, that *originally* to be a tree was *a way of being a person*, as, to use a close analogy, to be a woman is a way of being a person, or to be a triangle is a way of being a plane figure. That a woman is a person is not something that one can be said to *believe*; though there's enough historical bounce to this example to make it worth-while to use the different example that one cannot be said to believe that a triangle is a plane figure. When primitive man ceased to think of what we called trees as persons, the change was more radical than a change in belief; it was a change in category.

Now, the human mind is not limited in its categories to what it has been able to refine out of the world view of primitive man, any more than the limits of what we can conceive are set by what we can imagine. The categories of theoretical physics are not essences distilled from the framework of perceptual experience, yet, if the human mind can conceive of *new* categories, it can also refine the old; and it is just as important not to over-estimate the role of creativity in the development of the framework in terms of which you and I experience the world, as it is not to under-estimate its role in the scientific enterprise.

I indicated above that in the construct which I have called the 'original' image of man-in-the-world, all 'objects' are persons, and all kinds of objects ways of being persons. This means that the sort of things that are said of objects in this framework are the sort of things that are said of persons. And let me make it clear that by 'persons', I do not mean 'spirit' or 'mind'. The idea that a man is a team of two things, a mind *and* a body, is one for which many reasons of different kinds and weights have been given in the course of human intellectual development. But it is obvious, on reflection, that whatever philosophers have made of the idea of a *mind*, the pre-philosophical conception of a 'spirit', where it is found, is that of a ghostly *person*, something analogous to flesh and blood persons which 'inhabits' them, or is otherwise intimately connected with them. It is, therefore, a development *within the framework of persons*, and it would be incorrect to construe the manifest image in such a way that persons are composite objects. On the other hand, if it is to do its work, the manifest framework must be such as to make meaningful the assertion that what we ordinarily call persons are composites of a person proper and a body—and, by doing so, make meaningful the contrary view that although men have many different types of ability, ranging from those he has in common with the lowest of things, to his ability to engage in scientific and philosophical reflection, he nevertheless is one object and not a team. For we shall see that the essential dualism in the manifest image is not that between mind and body as substances, but between two radically different ways in which the human individual is related to the world. Yet it must be admitted that most of the philosophical theories which are dominated by the manifest image are dualistic in the substantive sense. There are many factors which account for this, most of which fall outside the scope of this essay. Of the factors which concern us, one is a matter of the influence of the developing scientific image of man, and will be discussed in the following section. The other arises in the attempt to make sense of the manifest image in its own terms.

Now to understand the manifest image as a refinement or depersonalization of the 'original' image, we must remind ourselves of the range of activities which are characteristic of persons. For when I say that the objects of the manifest image are primarily persons, I am implying that what the objects of this framework, primarily *are* and *do*, is what persons are and do. Thus persons are 'impetuous' or 'set in their ways'. They apply old policies or adopt new ones. They do things from habit or ponder alternatives. They are immature or have an established character. For my present purposes, the most important contrasts are those between actions which are expressions of character and actions which are *not* expressions of character, on the one hand, and between habitual actions and deliberate actions, on the other. The first point that I want to make is that only a being capable of deliberation can properly be said to act, either impulsively or from habit. For in the full and non-metaphorical sense an action is the sort of thing that can be done deliberately. We speak of actions as *becoming* habitual, and this is no accident. It is important to realize

11

that the use of the term 'habit' in speaking of an earthworm as acquiring the habit of turning to the right in a T-maze, is a metaphorical extension of the term. There is nothing dangerous in the metaphor until the mistake is made of assuming that the habits of persons are the same sort of thing as the (metaphorical) 'habits' of earthworms and white rats.

Again, when we say that something a person did was an expression of his character, we mean that it is 'in character'—that it was to be expected. We do not mean that it was a matter of *habit*. To be *habitual* is to be 'in character', but the converse is not true. To say of an action that it is 'in character', that it was to be expected, is to say that it was predictable—*not*, however, predictable 'no holds barred', but predictable with respect to evidence pertaining to what the person in question has done in the past, and the circumstances as he saw them in which he did it. Thus, a person cannot, *logically* cannot, *begin* by acting 'in character', any more than he can *begin* by acting from habit.

It is particularly important to see that while to be 'in character' is to be predictable, the converse is not true. It does not follow from the fact that a piece of human behaviour is predictable, that it is an expression of character. Thus the behaviour of a burnt child with respect to the fire is predictable, but not an expression of character. If we use the phrase, 'the nature of a person', to sum up the predictabilities *no holds barred* pertaining to that person, then we must be careful not to equate the *nature* of a person with his *character*, although his character will be a 'part' of his nature in the broad sense. Thus, if everything a person did were predictable (in principle), given sufficient knowledge about the person and the circumstances in which he was placed, and was, therefore, an 'expression of his nature', it would not follow that everything the person did was an expression of his *character*. Obviously, to say of a person that everything that he does is an expression of his character is to say that his life is simply a carrying out of formed habits and policies. Such a person is a type only approximated to in real life. Not even a mature person always acts in character. And as we have seen, it cannot possibly be true that he has always acted in character. Yet, if determinism is true, everything he has done has been an expression of his 'nature'.

I am now in a position to explain what I mean when I say that the primary objects of the manifest image are persons. I mean that it is the modification of an image in which *all* the objects are capable of *the full range* of personal activity, the modification consisting of a gradual pruning of the implications of saying with respect to what *we* would call an inanimate object, that it *did* something. Thus, in the original image to say of the wind that it blew down one's house

12

would imply that the wind *either* decided to do so with an end in view, and might, perhaps, have been persuaded not to do it, *or* that it acted thoughtlessly (either from habit or impulse), or, perhaps, inadvertently, in which case other appropriate action on one's part might have awakened it to the enormity of what it was about to do.

In the early stages of the development of the manifest image, the wind was no longer conceived as acting deliberately, with an end in view; but rather from habit or impulse. Nature became the locus of 'truncated persons'; that which things could be expected to do, its habits; that which exhibits no order, its impulses. Inanimate things no longer 'did' things in the sense in which persons do them—not, however, because a *new* category of impersonal things and impersonal processes has been achieved, but because the category of *person* is now applied to these things in a pruned or truncated form. It is a striking exaggeration to say of a person, that he is a 'mere creature of habit and impulse', but in the early stages of the development of manifest image, the world includes truncated persons which *are* mere creatures of habit, acting out routines, broken by impulses, in a life which never rises above what ours is like in our most unreflective moments. Finally, the sense in which the wind 'did' things was pruned, save for poetic and expressive purposes—and, one is tempted to add, for philosophical purposes—of implications pertaining to 'knowing what one is doing' and 'knowing what the circumstances are'.

Just as it is important not to confuse between the 'character' and the 'nature' of a person, that is to say, between an action's being predictable with respect to evidence pertaining to prior action, and its being predictable no holds barred, so it is important not to confuse between an action's being *predictable* and its being *caused*. These terms are often treated as synonyms, but only confusion can arise from doing so. Thus, in the 'original' image, one person causes another person to do something he otherwise would not have done. But most of the things people do are not things they are *caused* to do, even if what they do is highly predictable. For example: when a person has well-established habits, what he does in certain circumstances is highly predictable, but it is not for that reason *caused*. Thus the category of causation (as contrasted with the more inclusive category of predictability) betrays its origin in the 'original' image. When all things were persons it was certainly not a framework conception that everything a person did was caused; nor, of course, was it a framework principle that everything a person did was predictable. To the extent that relationships between the truncated 'persons' of the manifest framework were analogous to the causal relationships between persons, the category itself continued to be used, although pruned of its implications with respect to plans, purposes, and policies. The most obvious analogue at the inanimate level of causation in the original sense is one billiard ball causing another to change its course, but it is important to note that no one who distinguishes between causation and predictability would ask, 'what *caused* the billiard ball on a smooth table to continue in a straight line?' The distinctive trait of the scientific revolution was the conviction that all events are predictable from relevant information about the context in which they occur, not that they are all, in any ordinary sense, caused.

III. CLASSICAL PHILOSOPHY AND THE MANIFEST IMAGE

I have characterized the concept of the manifest image as one of the poles towards which philosophical thinking is drawn. This commits me, of course, to the idea that the manifest image is not a mere external standard, by relation to which one interested in the development of philosophy classifies philosophical positions, but has in its own way an objective existence in philosophical thinking itself, and, indeed, in human thought generally. And it can influence philosophical thinking only by having an existence which transcends in some way the individual thought of individual thinkers. I shall be picking up this theme shortly, and shall ask how an image of the world, which, after all, is a way of thinking, *can* transcend the individual thinker which it influences. (The general lines of the answer must be obvious, but it has implications which have not always been drawn.) The point I wish to make now is that since this image has a being which transcends the individual thinker, *there is truth and error with respect to it, even though the image itself might have to be rejected, in the last analysis, as false.*

Thus, whether or not the world as we encounter it in perception and self-awareness is ultimately real, it is surely incorrect, for example, to say as some philosophers have said that the physical objects of the encountered world are 'complexes of sensations' or, equally, to say that apples are not *really* coloured, or that mental states are 'behavioural dispositions', or that one cannot intend to do something without knowing that one intends to do it, or that to say that something is good is to say that one likes it, etc. For there is a correct and an incorrect way to describe this objective image which we have of the world in which we live, and it is possible to evaluate the correctness or incorrectness of such a description. I have already claimed that much of academic philosophy can be interpreted as an attempt by individual thinkers to delineate the manifest image (not recognized, needless to say, as such) an image which is both immanent in and transcendent of their thinking. In this respect, a philosophy can be evaluated as perceptive or imperceptive, mistaken or correct, even though one is prepared to say that the image they delineate is but one way in which reality appears to the human mind. And it is, indeed, a task of the first importance to delineate this image, particularly in so far as it concerns man himself, for, as was pointed out before, man is what he is because he thinks of himself in terms of this image, and the latter must be understood before it is proper to ask, 'to what extent does manifest man survive in the synoptic view which does equal justice to the scientific image which now confronts us?'

I think it correct to say that the so-called 'analytic' tradition in recent British and American philosophy, particularly under the influence of the later Wittgenstein, has done increasing justice to the manifest image, and has increasingly succeeded in isolating it in something like its pure form, and has made clear the folly of attempting to replace it *piecemeal* by fragments of the scientific image. By doing so, it is made apparent, and has come to realize, its continuity with the perennial tradition.

Now one of the most interesting features of the perennial philosophy is its attempt to understand the status in the individual thinker of the framework of ideas in terms of which he grasps himself as a person in the world. How do individuals come to be able to think in terms of this complex conceptual framework? How do they come to have this image? Two things are to be noticed here: (1) The manifest image does not present conceptual thinking as a complex of items which, considered in themselves and apart from these relations, are not conceptual in character. (The most plausible candidates are images, but all attempts to construe thoughts as complex patterns of images have failed, and, as we know, were bound to fail.) (2) Whatever the ultimate constituents of conceptual thinking, the process itself as it occurs in the individual mind must echo, more or less adequately, the intelligible structure of the world.

There was, of course, a strong temptation not only to think of the constituents of thinking as qualitatively similar to the constituents of the world, but also to think of the world as causing constituents to occur in patterns which echo the patterns of events. The attempt, by precursors of scientific psychology, to understand the genesis of conceptual thinking in the individual in terms of an 'association' of elemental processes which were not themselves conceptual, by a direct action of the physical environment on the individual—the paradigm case being the burnt child fearing the fire—was a premature attempt to construct a scientific image of man.

The perennial tradition had no sympathy with such attempts. It recognized (*a*) that association of *thoughts* is not association of images, and, as presupposing a framework of conceptual thinking, cannot account for it; (*b*) that the direct action of perceptible nature, *as perceptible*, on the *individual* can account for associative connection, *but not the rational connections of conceptual thinking.*

Yet somehow the world *is* the cause of the individual's image of the world, and, as is well-known, for centuries the dominant conception of the perennial tradition was that of a direct causal influence of the world as intelligible on the individual mind. This theme, initiated by Plato, can be traced through Western thought to the present day. In the Platonic tradition this mode of causation is attributed to a being which is analogous, to a greater or lesser degree, to a person. Even the Aristotelian distinguishes between the way in which sensations make available the intelligible structure of things to man, and the way in which contingencies of perceptual experience establish expectations and permit a non-rational accommodation of animals to their environment. And there is, as we know today, a sound score to the idea that while reality is the 'cause' of the human conceptual thinking which represents it, this causal role cannot be equated with a conditioning of the individual by his environment in a way which could in principle occur without the mediation of the family and the community. The Robinson Crusoe conception of the world as generating conceptual thinking directly in the individual is too simple a model. The perennial tradition long limited itself to accounting for the presence in the individual of the framework of conceptual thinking in terms of a unique kind of action of reality as intelligible on the individual mind. The accounts differed in interesting respects, but the main burden remained the same. It was not until the time of Hegel that the essential role of the group as a mediating factor in this causation was recognized, and while it is easy for us to see that the immanence and transcendence of conceptual frameworks with respect to the individual thinker is a social phenomenon, and to find a recognition of this fact implicit in the very form of our image of man in the world, it was not until the nineteenth century that this feature of the manifest image was, however inadequately, taken into account.

The Platonic theory of conceptual abilities as the result of the 'illumination' of the mind by intelligible essences limited the role of the group and, in particular, the family to that of calling these abilities into play—a role which could, in principle, be performed by perceptual experience—and to that of teaching the means of giving verbal expression to these abilities. Yet the essentially social character of conceptual thinking comes clearly to mind when we recognize that there is no thinking apart from common standards of

16

correctness and relevance, which relate what *I do* think to what *anyone ought to* think. The contrast between '*I*' and 'anyone' is essential to rational thought.

It is current practice to compare the inter-subjective standards without which there would be no thinking, to the inter-subjective standards without which there would be no such a thing as a game; and the acquisition of a conceptual framework to learning to play a game. It is worth noting, however, that conceptual thinking is a unique game in two respects: (*a*) one cannot learn to play it by being told the rules; (*b*) whatever else conceptual thinking makes possible—and without it there is nothing characteristically human—it does so by virtue of containing a way of representing the world.

When I said that the individual as a conceptual thinker is essentially a member of a group, this does not mean of course, that the individual cannot exist apart from the group, for example as sole survivor of an atomic catastrophe, any more than the fact that chess is a game played by two people means that one can't play chess with oneself. A group isn't a group in the relevant sense unless it consists of a number of individuals each of which thinks of himself as '*I*' in contrast to 'others'. Thus a group exists in the way in which members of the group represent themselves. Conceptual thinking is not by accident that which is *communicated* to others, any more than the decision to move a chess piece is by accident that which finds an expression in a move on a board between two people.

The manifest image must, therefore, be construed as containing a conception of itself as a group phenomenon, the group mediating between the individual and the intelligible order. But any attempt to *explain* this mediation within the framework of the manifest image was bound to fail, for the manifest image contains the resources for such an attempt only in the sense that it provides the foundation on which scientific theory can build an explanatory framework; and while conceptual structures of this framework are *built on* the manifest image, they are not definable within it. Thus, the Hegelian, like the Platonist of whom he is the heir, was limited to the attempt to understand the relation between intelligible order and individual minds in analogical terms.

It is in the *scientific* image of man in the world that we begin to see the main outlines of the way in which man came to have an image of himself-in-the-world. For we begin to see this as a matter of evolutionary development as a group phenomenon, a process which is illustrated at a simpler level by the evolutionary development which explains the correspondence between the dancing of a worker bee and the location, relative to the sun, of the flower from which he comes. This correspondence, like the relation between man's 'original'

17

image and the world, is incapable of explanation in terms of a direct conditioning impact of the environment on the individual as such.

I have called attention to the fact that the manifest image involves two types of causal impact of the world on the individual. It is, I have pointed out, this duality of causation and the related irreducibility, within the manifest image of conceptual thinking in all its forms to more elementary processes, which is the primary and essential dualism of the perennial philosophy. The dualistic conception of mind and body characteristic of, but by no means an invariable feature of, *philosophia perennis*, is in part an inference from this dualism of causation and of process. In part, however, as we shall see, it is a result of the impact of certain themes present in even the smallest stages of the developing scientific image.

My primary concern in this essay is with the question, 'in what sense, and to what extent, does the manifest image of man-in-the-world survive the attempt to unite this image in one field of intellectual vision with man as conceived in terms of the postulated objects of scientific theory?' The bite to this question lies, we have seen, in the fact that man is that being which conceives of itself in terms of the manifest image. To the extent that the manifest does not survive in the synoptic view, to that extent man himself would not survive. Whether the adoption of the synoptic view would transform man in bondage into man free, as Spinoza believed, or man free into man in bondage, as many fear, is a question that does not properly arise until the claims of the scientific image have been examined.

IV. THE SCIENTIFIC IMAGE

I devoted my attention in the previous sections to defining what I called the 'manifest' image of man-in-the-world. I argued that this image is to be construed as a sophistication and refinement of the image in terms of which man first came to be aware of himself as man-in-the-world; in short, came to be man. I pointed out that in any sense in which this image, in so far as it pertains to man, is a 'false' image, this falsity threatens man himself, inasmuch as he is, in an important sense, the being which has this image of himself. I argued that what has been called the perennial tradition in philosophy—philosophia perennis—can be construed as the attempt to understand the structure of this image, to know one's way around in it reflectively with no intellectual holds barred. I analysed some of the main features of the image and showed how the categories in terms of which it approaches the world can be construed as progressive prunings of categories pertaining to the person and his relation to other persons and the group. I argued that the perennial tradition must be construed to include not only the Platonic tradition in its broadest sense, but philosophies of 'common sense' and 'ordinary usage'. I argued what is common to all these philosophies is an acceptance of the manifest image as the *real*. They attempt to understand the achievements of theoretical science in terms of this framework, subordinating the categories of theoretical science to its categories. I suggested that the most fruitful way of approaching the problem of integrating theoretical science with the framework of sophisticated common sense into one comprehensive synoptic vision is to view it not as a piecemeal task—e.g. first a fitting together of the common sense conception of physical objects with that of theoretical physics, and then, as a separate venture, a fitting together of the common sense conception of man with that of theoretical psychology—but rather as a matter of articulating two whole ways of seeing the sum of things, two images of man-in-the-world and attempting to bring them together in a 'stereoscopic' view.

My present purpose is to add to the account I have given of the manifest image, a comparable sketch of what I have called the scientific image, and to conclude this essay with some comments on the respective contributions of these two to the unified vision of man-in-the-world which is the aim of philosophy.

The scientific image of man-in-the-world is, of course, as much an idealization as the manifest image—even more so, as it is still in the process of coming to be. It will be remembered that the contrast I have in mind is not that between an *unscientific* conception of man-in-the-world and a *scientific* one, but between that conception which limits itself to what correlational techniques can tell us about perceptible and introspectible events and that which postulates imperceptible objects and events for the purpose of explaining correlations among perceptibles. It was granted, of course, that in point of historical fact many of the latter correlations were suggested by theories introduced to explain previously established correlations, so that there has been a dialectical interplay between correlational and postulational procedures. (Thus we might not have noticed that litmus paper turns red in acid, until this hypothesis had been suggested by a complex theory relating the absorption and emission of electromagnetic radiation by objects to their chemical composition; yet in principle this familiar correlation could have been, and, indeed, was, discovered before any such theory was developed.) Our contrast then, is between two ideal constructs: (*a*) the correlational and categorial refinement of the 'original image', which refinement I am calling the manifest image; (*b*) the image derived from the fruits of postulational theory construction which I am calling the scientific image.

It may be objected at this point that there is no such thing as *the*

19

image of man built from postulated entities and processes, but rather as many images as there are sciences which touch on aspects of human behaviour. And, of course, in a sense this is true. There *are* as many scientific images of man as there are sciences which have something to say about man. Thus, there is man as he appears to the theoretical physicist—a swirl of physical particles, forces, and fields. There is man as he appears to the biochemist, to the physiologist, to the behaviourist, to the social scientist; and all of these images are to be contrasted with man as he appears to himself in sophisticated common sense, the manifest image which even today contains most of what he knows about himself at the properly human level. Thus the conception of *the* scientific or postulational image is an idealization in the sense that it is a conception of an integration of a manifold of images, each of which is the application to man of a framework of concepts which have a certain autonomy. For each scientific theory is, from the standpoint of methodology, a structure which is built at a different 'place' and by different procedures within the intersubjectively accessible world of perceptible things. Thus 'the' scientific image is a construct from a number of images, each of which is *supported by* the manifest world.

The fact that each theoretical image is a construction on a foundation provided by the manifest image, and *in this methodological sense* pre-supposes the manifest image, makes it tempting to suppose that the manifest image is prior in a *substantive* sense; that the categories of a theoretical science are logically dependent on categories pertaining to its methodological foundation in the manifest world of sophisticated common sense in such a way that there would be an absurdity in the notion of a world which illustrated its theoretical principles *without also illustrating the categories and principles of the manifest world*. Yet, when we turn our attention to 'the' scientific image which emerges from the several images proper to the several sciences, we note that although the image is *methodologically* dependent on the world of sophisticated common sense, and in this sense does not stand on its own feet, yet it purports to be a *complete* image, i.e. to define a framework which could be the *whole truth* about that which belongs to the image. Thus although methodologically a development *within* the manifest image, the scientific image presents itself as a *rival* image. From its point of view the manifest image on which it rests is an 'inadequate' but pragmatically useful likeness of a reality which first finds its adequate (in principle) likeness in the scientific image. I say, 'in principle', because the scientific image is still in the process of coming into being—a point to which I shall return at the conclusion of this chapter.

To all of which, of course, the manifest image or, more accurately,

20

the perennial philosophy which endorses its claims, replies that the scientific image cannot replace the manifest without rejecting its own foundation.

But before attempting to throw some light on the conflicting claims of these two world perspectives, more must be said about the constitution of *the* scientific image from the several scientific images of which it is the supposed integration. There is relatively little difficulty about telescoping *some* of the 'partial' images into one image. Thus, with due precaution, we can unify the biochemical and the physical images; for to do this requires only an appreciation of the sense in which the objects of biochemical discourse can be equated with complex patterns of the objects of theoretical physics. To make this equation, of course, is not to equate the sciences, for as sciences they have different procedures and connect their theoretical entities via different instruments to intersubjectively accessible features of the manifest world. But diversity of this kind is compatible with intrinsic 'identity' of the theoretical entities themselves, that is, with saying that biochemical compounds are 'identical' with patterns of subatomic particles. For to make this 'identification' is simply to say that the *two* theoretical structures, each with its own connection to the perceptible world, could be replaced by *one* theoretical framework connected *at two levels of complexity* via different instruments and procedures to the world as perceived.

I distinguished above between the unification of the postulated *entities* of two sciences and the unification of the *sciences*. It is also necessary to distinguish between the unification of the theoretical *entities* of two sciences and the unification of the theoretical *principles* of the two sciences. For while to say that biochemical substances are complexes of physical particles is in an important sense to imply that the laws obeyed by biochemical substances are 'special cases' of the laws obeyed by physical particles, there is a real danger that the sense in which this is so may be misunderstood. Obviously a specific pattern of physical particles cannot obey different laws in biochemistry than it does in physics. It may, however, be the case that the behaviour of very complex patterns of physical particles is related in no simple way to the behaviour of less complex patterns. Thus it may well be the case that the only way in which the laws pertaining to those complex systems of particles which are biochemical compounds could be *discovered* might be through the techniques and procedures of biochemistry, i.e. techniques and procedures appropriate to dealing with biochemical substances.

There is, consequently, an ambiguity in the statement: The laws of biochemistry are 'special cases' of the laws of physics. It may mean: (*a*) biochemistry needs no variables which cannot be defined in terms

21

of the variables of atomic physics; (*b*) the laws relating to certain complex patterns of sub-atomic particles, the counterparts of bio-chemical compounds, are related in a simple way to laws pertaining to less complex patterns. The former, of course, is the only proposition to which one is committed by the identification of the theoretical objects of the two sciences in the sense described above.

Similar considerations apply, *mutatis mutandis*, to the physiological and biochemical images of man. To weld them into one image would be to show that physiological (particularly neurophysiological) entities can be equated with complex biochemical systems, and, there-fore, that in the weaker sense, at least, the theoretical principles which pertain to the former can be interpreted as 'special cases' of principles pertaining to the latter.

More interesting problems arise when we consider the putative place of man as conceived in behaviouristics in 'the' scientific image. In the first place, the term 'behaviouristic psychology' has more than one meaning, and it is important for our purpose to see that in at least one sense of the term, its place is not in the scientific image (in the sense in which I am using the term) but rather in the continuing correlational sophistication of the manifest image. A psychology is behaviouristic in the broad sense, if, although it permits itself the use of the full range of psychological concepts belonging to the manifest framework, it always confirms hypotheses about psychological events in terms of behavioural criteria. It has no anxieties about the con-cepts of sensation, image, feeling, conscious or unconscious thought, all of which belong to the manifest framework; but requires that the occurrence of a feeling of pain, for example, be asserted only on behavioural grounds. Behaviourism, thus construed, is simply good sense. It is not necessary to redefine the language of mental events in terms of behavioural criteria in order for it to be true that observ-able behaviour provides evidence for mental events. And, of course, even in the common sense world, even in [the manifest image, per-ceptible behaviour is the only *intersubjective* evidence for mental events.

Clearly 'behaviourism' in this sense does not preclude us from paying attention to what people say about themselves. For *using auto-biographical statements as evidence for* what a person is thinking and feeling is different from simply *agreeing with* these statements. It is part of the force of autobiographical statements in ordinary dis-course—not unrelated to the way in which children learn to make them —that, other things being equal, if a person says, 'I am in state ψ', it is reasonable to believe that he is in state ψ; the probability ranging from almost certainty in the case of, 'I have a toothache', to consider-ably less than certainty in the case of, 'I don't hate my brother'. The discounting of verbal and non-verbal behaviour as evidence is not limited to professional psychologists.

Thus, behaviourism in the first sense is simply a sophistication within the manifest framework which relies on pre-existent evidential connections between publicly observable verbal and non-verbal behaviour on the one hand and mental states and processes on the other, and should, therefore, be considered as belonging to the manifest rather than the scientific image as I have defined in these terms. Behaviourism in a second sense not only restricts its evidential base to publicly observable behaviour, but conceives of its task as that of finding correlations between constructs which it introduces and defines in terms of publicly accessible features of the organism and its environment. The interesting question in this connection is: 'Is there reason to think that a framework of correlation between constructs of this type could constitute a scientific understanding of human behaviour?' The answer to this question depends in part on how it is interpreted, and it is important to see why this is so.

Consider first the case of animal behaviour. Obviously, we know that animals are complex physiological systems and, from the standpoint of a finer-grained approach, biochemical systems. Does this mean that a science of animal behaviour has to be formulated in neurophysiological or biochemical terms? In one sense the answer is 'obviously not'. We bring to our study of animal behaviour a background knowledge of some of the relevant large-scale variables for describing and predicting the behaviour of animals in relation to their environments. The fact that these large-scale variables (the sort of thing that are grouped under such headings as 'stimulus', 'response', 'goal behaviour', 'deprivation', etc.) are such that we can understand the behaviour of the animal in terms of them is something which is not only suggested by our background knowledge, but is, indeed, *explained* by evolutionary theory. But the correlations themselves can be discovered by statistical procedures; and, of course, it is important to establish these correlations. Their discovery and confirmation by the procedures of behaviouristics must, of course, be distinguished from their *explanation* in terms of the postulated entities and processes of neurophysiology. And, indeed, while physiological considerations may *suggest* correlations be tested, the correlations themselves must be establishable independently of physiological consideration, if, and this is a 'definitional' point, they are to belong to a distinguishable science of behaviour.

Thus if we mean by 'earthworm behaviouristics' the establishing of correlations in large-scale terms pertaining to the earthworm and its environment, there may not be much to it, for a correlation does not belong to 'earthworm behaviouristics' unless it is a correlation in

23

these large-scale terms. On the other hand, it is obvious that not every scientific truth about earthworms is a part of earthworm behaviouristics, unless the latter term is so stretched as to be deprived of its distinctive sense. It follows that one cannot explain everything an earthworm does in terms of earthworm behaviouristics *thus defined.* Earthworm behaviouristics works within a background knowledge of 'standard conditions'—conditions in which correlations in terms of earthworm behaviour categories *are* sufficient to explain and predict what earthworms do in so far as it can be described in these categories. This background knowledge is obviously an essential part of the scientific understanding of what earthworms do, though not a part of earthworm behaviouristics, for it is simply the application to earthworms of physics, chemistry, parasitology, medicine, and neurophysiology.

We must also take into consideration the fact that most of the interesting constructs of correlational behaviouristics will be 'iffy' properties of organisms, properties to the effect that *if* at that time a certain stimulus *were* to occur, a certain response *would be* made. Thus, to use an example from another field, we are able to correlate the fact that a current has been run through a helix in which a piece of iron has been placed, with the 'iffy' property of being such that if an iron filing *were* placed near it, the latter *would be* attracted.

Now it may or may not be helpful at a given stage of scientific development, to suppose that 'iffy' properties of organisms are connected with states of a postulated system of entities operating according to certain postulated principles. It is helpful, if the postulated entities are sufficiently specific and can be connected to a sufficient diversity of large-scale behavioural variables to enable the prediction of new correlations. The methodological utility of postulational procedures for the behaviouristics of lower organisms has, perhaps, been exaggerated, primarily because until recently little was known in neurophysiology which was suited to throw much light on correlations at the large-scale level of behaviouristics. In human behaviouristics, however, the situation has been somewhat different from the start, for an important feature of characteristically human behaviour is that any two successive pieces of observable behaviour *essentially* involve complex, very complex, 'iffy' facts about what the person *would have said or done* at each intervening moment *if he had been asked certain questions*; and it happens that our background knowledge makes reasonable the supposition that these 'iffy' facts obtain *because an inner process is going on which is, in important respects, analogous to overt verbal behaviour, and each stage of which would find a natural expression in overt speech.* This is a point to which I shall return later on.

Thus it *does* prove helpful in human behaviouristics to postulate an inner sequence of events in order to interpret what could *in principle* be austerely formulated as correlations between behavioural states and properties, including the *very* important and, indeed, *essential* 'iffy' ones. But, and this is an important point, the postulated episodes are not postulated on neurophysiological grounds—at least this was not true until very recently, but because of our background knowledge that something analogous to speech goes on while people are sitting 'like bumps on a log'.

For our present purposes it does not make too much difference whether we say that human behaviouristics *as such* postulates inner speechlike processes, or that whatever their contribution to explanation or discovery, these processes fall by definition outside behaviouristics proper. Whether or not human behaviouristics, as a distinctive science, includes any statements about postulated entities, the correlations it establishes must find their counterparts in the postulational image, as was seen to be true in the case of the correlations established by earthworm behaviouristics. Thus, the scientific explanation of human behaviour must take account of those cases where the correlations characteristic of the organism in 'normal' circumstances break down. And, indeed, no behaviourist would deny that the correlations he seeks and establishes are in some sense the counterparts of neurophysiological and, consequently, biochemical connections, nor that the latter are special cases within a spectrum of *biochemical* connections (pertaining to human organisms), many of which are reflected in observable phenomena which, *from the standpoint of behaviouristics*, represent breakdowns in explanation. I shall, therefore, provisionally assume that although behaviouristics and neurophysiology remain distinctive sciences, the correlational content of behaviouristics points to a structure of postulated processes and principles which telescope together with those of neurophysiological theory, with all the consequences which this entails. On this assumption, if we trace out these consequences, the scientific image of man turns out to be that of a complex physical system.

V. THE CLASH OF THE IMAGES

How, then, are we to evaluate the conflicting claims of the manifest image and the scientific image thus provisionally interpreted to constitute *the* true and, in principle, *complete* account of man-in-the-world?

What are the alternatives? It will be helpful to examine the impact of the earlier stages of postulational science on philosophy. Some reflections on the Cartesian attempt at a synthesis are in order, for they bring out the major stresses and strains involved in any attempt at a synoptic view. Obviously, at the time of Descartes theoretical science had not yet reached the neurophysiological level, save in the fashion of a clumsy promissory note. The initial challenge of the scientific image was directed at the manifest image of inanimate nature. It proposed to construe physical things, in a manner already adumbrated by Greek atomism, as systems of imperceptible particles, lacking the perceptible qualities of manifest nature. Three lines of thought seemed to be open: (1) Manifest objects are identical with systems of imperceptible particles in that simple sense in which a forest is identical with a number of trees. (2) Manifest objects are what really exist; systems of imperceptible particles being 'abstract' or 'symbolic' ways of representing them. (3) Manifest objects are 'appearances' to human minds of a reality which is constituted by systems of imperceptible particles. Although (2) merits serious consideration, and has been defended by able philosophers, it is (1) and (3), particularly the latter, which I shall be primarily concerned to explore.

First, some brief remarks about (1). There is nothing immediately paradoxical about the view that an object can be both a perceptible object with perceptible qualities *and* a system of imperceptible objects, none of which has perceptible qualities. Cannot systems have properties which their parts do not have? Now the answer to this question is 'yes', if it is taken in a sense of which a paradigm example would be the fact that a system of pieces of wood can be a ladder, although none of its parts is a ladder. Here one might say that for the system as a whole to be a ladder is for its parts to be of such and such shapes and sizes and to be related to one another in certain ways. Thus there is no trouble about systems having properties which its parts do not have *if these properties are a matter of the parts having such and such qualities and being related in such and such ways.* But the case of a pink ice cube, it would seem clear, cannot be treated in this way. It does not seem plausible to say that for a system of particles to be a pink ice cube is for them to have such and such imperceptible qualities, and to be so related to one another as to make up an approximate cube. *Pink* does not seem to be made up of imperceptible qualities in the way in which being a ladder is made up of being cylindrical (the rungs), rectangular (the frame), wooden, etc. The manifest ice cube presents itself to us as something which is pink through and through, as a pink continuum, all the regions of which, however small, are pink. It presents itself to us as *ultimately homogeneous*; and an ice cube variegated in colour is, though not homogeneous in its specific colour, 'ultimately homogeneous', in the sense to which I am calling attention, with respect to the generic trait of being coloured.

26

Now reflection on this example suggests a principle which can be formulated approximately as follows:

> If an object is *in a strict sense* a system of objects, then every property of the object must consist in the fact that its constituents have such and such qualities and stand in such and such relations or, roughly,
>
> > every property of a system of objects consists of properties of, and relations between, its constituents.

With something like this principle in mind, it was argued that if a physical object is *in a strict sense* a system of imperceptible particles, then it cannot as a whole have the perceptible qualities characteristic of physical objects in the manifest image. It was concluded that manifest physical objects are 'appearances' *to human perceivers* of systems of imperceptible particles which is alternative (3) above.

This alternative, (3), however, is open to an objection which is ordinarily directed not against the alternative itself, but against an imperceptive formulation of it as the thesis that the perceptible things around us 'really have no colour'. Against *this* formulation the objection has the merit of calling attention to the fact that in the manifest framework it is as absurd to say that a visible object has no colour, as it is to say of a triangle that it has no shape. However, against the above formulation of alternative (3), namely, that *the very objects themselves* are appearances to perceivers of systems of imperceptible particles, the objection turns out on examination to have no weight. The objection for which the British 'common sense' philosopher G. E. Moore is directly or indirectly responsible, runs:

> Chairs, tables, etc., as we ordinarily think them to be, can't be 'appearances' of systems of particles lacking perceptible qualities, because we *know* that there are chairs, tables, etc., and it is a framework feature of chairs, tables, etc., that they have perceptible qualities.

It simply *disappears* once it is recognized that, properly understood, the claim that physical objects do not really have perceptible qualities is not analogous to the claim that something generally believed to be true about a certain kind of thing is actually false. It is not the denial of a belief *within a framework*, but a challenge to the framework. It is the claim that although the framework of perceptible objects, the manifest framework of everyday life, is adequate for the everyday purposes of life, it is ultimately inadequate and should not be accepted as an account of what there is *all things considered*. Once we see this, we see that the argument from 'knowledge' cuts no ice, for the reasoning:

> We know that there are chairs, pink ice cubes, etc. (physical objects). Chairs, pink ice cubes are coloured, are perceptible objects with perceptible qualities. Therefore, perceptible physical objects with perceptible qualities exist

operates *within* the framework of the manifest image and cannot *support* it. It fails to provide a point of view outside the manifest image from which the latter can be evaluated.

A more sophisticated argument would be to the effect that we successfully find our way around in life by using the conceptual framework of coloured physical objects in space and time, therefore, this framework represents things as they really are. This argument has force, but is vulnerable to the reply that the success of living, thinking, and acting in terms of the manifest framework can be accounted for by the framework which proposes to replace it, by showing that there are sufficient structural similarities between manifest objects and their scientific counterparts to account for this success.[1]

One is reminded of a standard move designed to defend the reality of the manifest image against *logically* rather than *scientifically* motivated considerations. Thus it has been objected that the framework of physical objects in space and time is incoherent, involving antinomies or contradictions, and that therefore this framework is unreal. The counter to this objection has often been, not a painstaking refutation of the arguments claiming to show that the framework is incoherent, but rather something along the following lines:

> *We know* that this collision occurred at a different place and time than that collision.
>
> Therefore, the statement that the first collision occurred at a different place and time from the other collision *is true*.
>
> Therefore, the statement that the two collisions occurred at different times and places *is consistent*.
>
> Therefore, statements about events happening at various times and places are, as such, consistent.

This argument, like the one we have already considered, does not prove what it sets out to prove, because it operates within the framework to be evaluated, and does not provide an external point of view from which to defend it. It makes the tacit assumption that if a framework is inconsistent, its incoherence must be such as to lead to retail and immediate inconsistencies, as though it would force people using it to contradict themselves on every occasion. This is surely false. The framework of space and time could be internally inconsistent, and yet be a successful conceptual tool at the retail level. We have examples

---

[1] It might seem that the manifest framework accounts for the success of the scientific framework, so that the situation is symmetrical. But I believe that a more penetrating account of theoretical explanation than I have been able to sketch in this chapter would show that this claim is illusory. I discuss this topic at some length in Chapter 4.

of this in mathematical theory, where inconsistencies can be present which do not reveal themselves in routine usage.

I am not, however, concerned to argue that the manifest image is unreal because ultimately incoherent in a narrowly conceived logical sense. Philosophers who have taken this line have either (*a*) left it at that (Hume; scepticism), or (*b*) attempted to locate the source of the inconsistency in features of the framework, and interpreted reality as an inadequately known structure *analogous* to the manifest image, but lacking just those features which are responsible for the inconsistency. In contrast to this, the critique of the manifest image in which we are engaged is based on logical considerations in a broader and more constructive sense, one which compares this image unfavourably with a *more* intelligible account of what there is.

It is familiar fact that those features of the manifest world which play no role in mechanical explanation were relegated by Descartes and other interpreters of the new physics to the minds of the perceiver. Colour, for example, was said to exist only in sensation; its *esse* to be *percipi*. It was argued, in effect, that what scientifically motivated reflection recognizes to be states of the perceiver are conceptualized in ordinary experience as traits of independent physical things, indeed that these supposed independent coloured things are actually conceptual constructions which ape the mechanical systems of the real world.

The same considerations which led philosophers to deny the reality of perceptible things led them to a dualistic theory of man. For if the human body is a system of particles, the body cannot be the subject of thinking and feeling, *unless thinking and feeling are capable of interpretation as complex interactions of physical particles*; unless, that is to say, the manifest framework of man as *one* being, a *person* capable of doing radically different kinds of things can be replaced without loss of descriptive and explanatory power by a postulational image in which he is a complex of physical particles, and all his activities a matter of the particles changing in state and relationship.

Dualism, of course, denied that either sensation or feeling or conceptual thinking could in this sense be construed as complex interactions of physical particles, or man as a complex physical system. They were prepared to say that a *chair* is really a system of imperceptible particles which 'appears' in the manifest framework as a 'colour solid' (cf. our example of the ice cube), but they were not prepared to say that man himself was a complex physical system which 'appears' to itself to be the sort of thing man is in the manifest image.

Let us consider in more detail the Cartesian attempt to integrate the manifest and the scientific images. Here the interesting thing to note is that Descartes took for granted (in a promissory-note-ish kind of way) that the scientific image would include items which would be the counterparts of the sensations, images, and feelings of the manifest framework. These counterparts would be complex states of the brain which, obeying purely physical laws, would resemble and differ from one another in a way which corresponded to the resemblances and differences between the conscious states with which they were correlated. Yet, as is well-known, he denied that there were brain states which were, in the same sense, the cerebral counterparts of conceptual thinking.

Now, if we were to ask Descartes, 'Why can't we say that sensations "really are" complex cerebral processes as, according to you, we *can* say that physical objects "really are" complex systems of imperceptible particles?' he would have a number of things to reply, some of which were a consequence of his conviction that sensation, images, and feelings belong to the same family as believing, choosing, wondering, in short are low-grade examples of conceptual thinking and share its supposed irreducibility to cerebral states. But when the chips are down there would remain the following argument:

> We have pulled perceptible qualities out of the physical environment and put them into sensations. If we now say that all there really is to sensation is a complex interaction of cerebral particles, then we have taken them out of our world picture altogether. We will have made it unintelligible how things could even *appear* to be coloured.

As for conceptual thinking, Descartes not only refused to identify it with neurophysiological process, he did not see this as a live option, because it seemed obvious to him that no complex neurophysiological process could be sufficiently analogous to conceptual thinking to be a serious candidate for being what conceptual thinking 'really is'. It is not as though Descartes granted that there might well be neurophysiological processes which are strikingly analogous to conceptual thinking, but which it would be philosophically incorrect to *identify* with conceptual thinking (as he had identified physical objects of the manifest world with systems of imperceptible particles). He did not take seriously the idea that there *are* such neurophysiological processes.

Even if he had, however, it is clear that he would have rejected this identification on the ground that we had a 'clear and distinct', well-defined idea of what conceptual thinking is before we even suspected that the brain had anything to do with thinking. Roughly: we know what thinking is without conceiving of it as a complex neurophysiological process, therefore, it cannot *be* a complex physiological process.

Now, of course, the same is true of physical objects. We knew what a physical object was long before we knew that there were imperceptible physical particles. By parity of reasoning we should conclude that a physical object cannot *be* a complex of imperceptible particles. Thus, if Descartes had had reason to think that neurophysiological processes strikingly analogous to conceptual thinking exist, it would seem that he should *either* have changed his tune with respect to physical objects *or* said that conceptual thinking *really is* neurophysiological process.

Now in the light of recent developments in neurophysiology, philosophers have come to see that there is no reason to suppose there can't be neurophysiological processes which stand to conceptual thinking as sensory states of the brain stand to conscious sensations. And, indeed, there have not been wanting philosophers (of whom Hobbes was, perhaps, the first) who have argued that the analogy should be viewed philosophically as an *identity*, i.e. that a world picture which includes *both* thoughts *and* the neurophysiological counterparts of thoughts would contain a redundancy; just as a world picture which included *both* the physical objects of the manifest image *and* complex patterns of physical particles would contain a redundancy. But to this proposal the obvious objection occurs, that just as the claim that 'physical objects are complexes of imperceptible particles' left us with the problem of accounting for the status of the perceptible qualities of manifest objects, so the claim that 'thoughts, etc., are complex neurophysiological processes' leaves us with the problems of accounting for the status of the *introspectable qualities* of thoughts. And it would seem obvious that there is a vicious regress in the claim that these qualities exist in introspective awareness of the thoughts which seem to have them, but not in the thoughts themselves. For, the argument would run, surely introspection is itself a form of thinking. Thus one thought (Peter) would be robbed of its quality only to pay it to another (Paul).

We can, therefore, understand the temptation to say that even if there are cerebral processes which are strikingly analogous to conceptual thinking, they are processes which *run parallel* to conceptual thinking (and cannot be identified with it) as the sensory states of the brain *run parallel* to conscious sensation. And we can, therefore, understand the temptation to say that all these puzzles arise from taking seriously the claim of *any* part of the scientific image to be *what really is*, and to retreat into the position that reality is the world of the manifest image, and that all the postulated entities of the scientific image are 'symbolic tools' which function (something like the distance-measuring devices which are rolled around on maps) to help us find our way around in the world, but do not themselves

31

describe actual objects and processes. On this view, the theoretical counterparts of *all* features of the manifest image would be *equally* unreal, and that philosophical conception of man-of-the-world would be correct which endorsed the manifest image and located the scientific image within it as a conceptual tool used by manifest man in his capacity as a scientist.

VI. THE PRIMACY OF THE SCIENTIFIC IMAGE: A PROLEGOMENON

Is this the truth of the matter? Is the manifest image, subject, of course, to continual emperical and categorial refinements, the measure of what there really is? I do not think so. I have already indicated that of the three alternatives we are considering with respect to the comparative claims of the manifest and scientific images, the first, which, like a child, says 'both', is ruled out by a principle which I am not defending in this chapter, although it does stand in need of defence. The second alternative is the one I have just reformulated and rejected. I propose, therefore, to re-examine the case against the third alternative, the primacy of the scientific image. My strategy will be to argue that the difficulty, raised above, which seems to stand in the way of the identification of thought with cerebral processes, arises from the mistake of supposing that in self-awareness conceptual thinking presents itself to us in a qualitative guise. Sensations and images *do*, we shall see, present themselves to us in a qualitative character, a fact which accounts for the fact that they are stumbling blocks in the attempt to accept the scientific image as real. *But* one scarcely needs to point out these days that however intimately conceptual thinking is related to sensations and images, it cannot be equated with them, nor with complexes consisting of them.

It is no accident that when a novelist wishes to represent what is going on in the mind of a person, he does so by 'quoting' the person's thoughts as he might quote what a person says. For thoughts not only are the sort of things that find overt expression in language, we conceive of them as analogous to overt discourse. Thus, *thoughts* in the manifest image are conceived not in terms of their 'quality', but rather as inner 'goings-on' which are analogous to speech, and find their overt expression in speech—though they can go on, of course, in the absence of this overt expression. It is no accident that one learns to think in the very process of learning to speak.

From this point of view one can appreciate the danger of misunderstanding which is contained in the term 'introspection'. For while there is, indeed, an analogy between the direct knowledge we have of our own thoughts and the perceptual knowledge we have of what is going on in the world around us, the analogy holds only in as much as both self-awareness and perceptual observation are basic forms of non-inferential knowledge. They differ, however, in that whereas in perceptual observation we know objects as being of a certain quality, in the direct knowledge we have of what we are thinking (e.g. I am thinking that it is cold outside) what we know non-inferentially is that *something analogous to and properly expressed by the sentence, 'It is cold outside', is going on in me.*

The point is an important one, for if the concept of a thought is the concept of an inner state analogous to speech, this leaves open the possibility that the inner state conceived in terms of this analogy is *in its qualitative character* a neurophysiological process. To draw a parallel: if I begin by thinking of the cause of a disease as a substance (to be called 'germs') which is analogous to a colony of rabbits, in that it is able to reproduce itself in geometrical proportion, but, unlike rabbits, imperceptible and, when present in sufficient number in the human body, able to cause the symptoms of disease, and to cause epidemics by spreading from person to person, there is no logical barrier to a subsequent identification of 'germs' thus conceived with the *bacilli* which microscopic investigation subsequently discovers.

But to point to the analogy between conceptual thinking and overt speech is only part of the story, for of equally decisive importance is the analogy between speech and what sophisticated computers can do, and finally, between computer circuits and conceivable patterns of neurophysiological organization. All of this is more or less speculative, less so now than even a few years ago. What interests the philosopher is the matter of principle; and here the first stage is decisive—the recognition that the concept of a thought is a concept by analogy. Over and above this all we need is to recognize the force of Spinoza's statement: 'No one has thus far determined what the body can do nor no one has yet been taught by experience what the body can do merely by the laws of nature insofar as nature is considered merely as corporeal and extended.' (*Ethics*, Part Three, Prop. II (note)).

Another analogy which may be even more helpful is the following: suppose we are watching the telegraphic report of a chess game in a foreign country.

White	Black
P—K3	P—QB3

And suppose that we are sophisticated enough to know that chess pieces can be made of all shapes and sizes, that chess boards can be horizontal or vertical, indeed, distorted in all kinds of ways provided that they preserve certain topological features of the familiar board.

Then it is clear that while we will think of the players in the foreign country as moving kings, pawns, etc., castling and check-mating, our concepts of the pieces they are moving and the moving of them will be simply the concept of items and changes which play a role analogous to the pieces and moves which take place when *we* play chess. We know that the items must have some intrinsic quality (shape, size, etc.), but we think of these qualities as 'those which make possible a sequence of changes which are structurally similar to the changes which take place on our own chess boards'.

Thus our concept of 'what thoughts are' might, like our concept of what a castling is in chess, be abstract in the sense that it does not concern itself with the *intrinsic* character of thoughts, *save as items which can occur in patterns of relationships which are analogous to the way in which sentences are related to one another and* to the contexts in which they are used.

Now if thoughts are items which are conceived in terms of the roles they play, then there is no barrier *in principle* to the identification of conceptual thinking with neurophysiological process. There would be no 'qualitative' remainder to be accounted for. The identification, curiously enough, would be even more straightforward than the identification of the physical things in the manifest image with complex systems of physical particles. And in this key, if not decisive, respect, the respect in which both images are concerned with conceptual thinking (which is the distinctive trait of man), *the manifest and scientific images could merge without clash in the synoptic view.*

How does the situation stand in respect to sensation and feeling? Any attempt at identification of these items with neurophysiological process runs into a difficulty to which reference has already been made, and which we are now in a position to make more precise. This difficulty accounts for the fact that, with few exceptions, philosophers who have been prepared to identify conceptual thinking with neuro-physiological process have *not* been prepared to make a similar identification in the case of sensation.

Before restating the problem let us note that curiously enough, there is more similarity between the two cases than is commonly recognized. For it turns out on reflection that just as conceptual thinking is construed in the manifest image by analogy with overt speech, so sensation is construed by analogy with its external cause, sensations being the states of persons which correspond, in their similarities and differences to the similarities and differences of the objects which, in standard conditions, bring them about. Let us assume that this is so. But if it is so, why not suppose that the inner-states which *as sensations* are conceived by analogy with their standard causes, are *in propria persona* complex neurophysiological episodes

34

in the cerebral cortex? To do so would parallel the conclusion we were prepared to draw in the case of conceptual thinking.

Why do we feel that there would be something extremely odd, even absurd, about such a supposition? The key to the answer lies in noticing an important difference between identifying thoughts with neurophysiological states and identifying sensations with neurophysiological states. Whereas both thoughts and sensations are conceived by analogy with publicly observable items, in the former case the analogy concerns the *role* and hence leaves open the possibility that thoughts are radically different *in their intrinsic character* from the verbal behaviour by analogy with which they are conceived. But in the case of sensations, the analogy concerns the quality itself. Thus a 'blue and triangular sensation' is conceived by analogy with the blue and triangular (facing) surface of a physical object which, when looked at in daylight, is its cause. The crucial issue then is this: can we define, in the framework of neurophysiology, states which are sufficiently analogous in their *intrinsic* character to sensations to make identification plausible?

The answer seems clearly to be 'no'. This is not to say that neurophysiological states cannot be defined (in principle) which have a high degree of analogy to the sensations of the manifest image. That this can be done is an elementary fact in psycho-physics. The trouble is, rather, that the feature which we referred to as 'ultimate homogeneity', and which characterizes the perceptible qualities of things, e.g. their colour, seems to be essentially lacking in the domain of the definable states of nerves and their interactions. Putting it crudely, colour expanses in the manifest world consist of regions which are themselves colour expanses, and these consist in their turn of regions which are colour expanses, and so on; whereas the state of a group of neurons, though it has regions which are also states of groups of neurons, has ultimate regions which are *not* states of groups of neurons but rather states of single neurons. And the same is true if we move to the finer grained level of biochemical process.

Nor do we wish to say that the ultimate homogeneity of the sensation of a red rectangle is a matter of each physical particle in the appropriate region of the cortex *having* a colour; for whatever other difficulties such a view would involve, it doesn't make sense to say of the particles of physical theory that they are coloured. And the principle of reducibility, which we have accepted without argument, makes impossible the view that groups of particles can have properties which are not 'reducible to' the properties and relations of the members of the group.

It is worth noting that we have here a recurrence of the essential features of Eddington's 'two tables' problem—the two tables being, in our terminology, the table of the manifest image and the table of the scientific image. There the problem was to 'fit together' the manifest table with the scientific table. Here the problem is to fit together the manifest sensation with its neurophysiological counterpart. And, interestingly enough, the problem in both cases is essentially the same: *how to reconcile the ultimate homogeneity of the manifest image with the ultimate non-homogeneity of the system of scientific objects.*

Now we are rejecting the view that the scientific image is a mere 'symbolic tool' for finding our way around in the manifest image; and we are accepting the view that the scientific account of the world is (in principle) the adequate image. Having, therefore, given the perceptible qualities of manifest objects their real locus in sensation, we were confronted with the problem of choosing between dualism or identity with respect to the relation of conscious sensations to their analogues in the visual cortex, and the above argument seems to point clearly in the dualistic direction. The 'ultimate homogeneity' of perceptible qualities, which, among other things, prevented *identifying* the perceptible qualities of physical objects with complex properties of systems of physical particles, stands equally in the way of *identifying*, rather than *correlating*, conscious sensations with the complex neural processes with which they are obviously connected.

But such dualism is an unsatisfactory solution, because *ex hypothesi* sensations are essential to the explanation of how we come to construct the 'appearance' which is the manifest world. They are essential to the explanation of how there even *seem* to be coloured objects. But the scientific image presents itself as a closed system of explanation, and *if the scientific image is interpreted as we have interpreted it up to this point the* explanation will be in terms of the constructs of neurophysiology, which, according to the argument, *do not involve the ultimate homogeneity, the appearance of which in the manifest image is to be explained.*

We are confronted, therefore, by an antinomy, *either,* (*a*) the neurophysiological image is *incomplete,* i.e. and must be supplemented by new objects ('sense fields') which do have ultimate homogeneity, and which somehow make their presence felt in the activity of the visual cortex as a system of physical particles; or, (*b*) the neurophysiological image is complete and the ultimate homogeneity of the sense qualities (and, hence, the sense qualities, themselves) is *mere appearance* in the very radical sense of not existing in the spatiotemporal world at all.

Is the situation irremediable? Does the assumption of the reality of the scientific image lead us to a dualism of particles and sense fields? of matter and 'consciousness'? If so, then, in view of the obviously intimate relation between sensation and conceptual thinking (for example, in perception), we must surely regress and take back the identification or conceptual thinking with neurophysiological process which seemed so plausible a moment ago. We could then argue that although in the absence of other considerations it would be plausible to equate conceptual thinking with neurophysiological process, when the chips are *all* down, we must rather say that although conceptual thinking and neurophysiological process are each analogous to verbal behaviour as a public social phenomenon (the one by virtue of the very way in which the very notion of 'thinking' is formed; the other as a scientifically ascertained matter of fact), they are also *merely* analogous to one another and cannot be identified. If so, the manifest and the scientific conception of *both* sensations *and* conceptual thinking would fit into the synoptic view as parallel processes, a dualism which could only be avoided by interpreting the scientific image *as a whole* as a 'symbolic device' for coping with the world as it presents itself to us in the manifest image.

Is there any alternative? As long as the ultimate constituents of the scientific image are particles forming ever more complex systems of particles, we are inevitably confronted by the above choice. But the scientific image is not yet complete; we have not yet penetrated all the secrets of nature. And if it should turn out that particles instead of being the primitive entities of the scientific image could be treated as singularities in a space-time continuum which could be conceptually 'cut up' without significant loss—*in inorganic contexts, at least*—into interacting particles, then we would not be confronted at the level of neurophysiology with the problem of understanding the relation of *sensory consciousness* (with its ultimate homogeneity) to *systems of particles*. Rather, we would have the alternative of saying that although for many purposes the central nervous system can be construed without loss as a complex system of physical particles, *when it comes to an adequate understanding of the relation of sensory consciousness to* neurophysiological process, we must penetrate to the non-particulate foundation of the particulate image, and recognize that in this non-particulate image the qualities of sense are a dimension of natural process which occurs only in connection with those complex physical processes which, when 'cut up' into particles in terms of those features which are the least common denominators of physical process—present in inorganic as well as organic processes alike—become the complex system of particles which, in the current scientific image, *is* the central nervous system.

VII. PUTTING MAN INTO THE SCIENTIFIC IMAGE

Even if the constructive suggestion of the preceding section were capable of being elaborated into an adequate account of the way in which the scientific image could recreate in its own terms the sensations, images, and feelings of the manifest image, the thesis of the primacy of the scientific image would scarcely be off the ground. There would remain the task of showing that categories pertaining to man as a *person* who finds himself confronted by standards (ethical, logical, etc.) which often conflict with his desires and impulses, and to which he may or may not conform, can be reconciled with the idea that man is what science says he is.

At first sight there would seem to be only one way of recapturing the specifically human within the framework of the scientific image. The categories of the person might be reconstructed without loss in terms of the fundamental concepts of the scientific image in a way analogous to that in which the concepts of biochemistry are (in principle) reconstructed in terms of sub-atomic physics. To this suggestion there is, in the first place, the familiar objection that persons as responsible agents who make genuine choices between genuine alternatives, and who could on many occasions have done what in point of fact they did not do, simply *can't* be construed as physical systems (even broadly interpreted to include sensations and feelings) which evolve in accordance with laws of nature (statistical or non-statistical). Those who make the above move can be expected to reply (drawing on distinctions developed in section I) that the concepts in terms of which we think of a person's 'character', or the fact that 'he could have done otherwise', or that 'his actions are predictable' would appear in the reconstruction as extraordinarily complex defined concepts not to be confused with the concepts in terms of which we think of the 'nature' of NaCl, or the fact that 'system X would have failed to be in state S given the same initial conditions' or that 'it is predictable that system X will assume state S given these initial conditions'. And I think that a reply along these lines could be elaborated which would answer *this* objection to the proposed reconstruction of categories pertaining to persons.

But even if the proposed reconstruction could meet what might be called the 'free will' objection, it fails decisively on another count. For it can, I believe, be conclusively shown that such a reconstruction is *in principle* impossible, the impossibility in question being a strictly logical one. (I shall not argue the point explicitly, but the following remarks contain the essential clues.) If so, that would seem to be the end of the matter. Must we not return to a choice between (*a*) a dualism in which men as scientific objects are contrasted with the 'minds' which are the source and principle of their existence as persons; (*b*) abandoning the reality of persons as well as manifest physical objects in favour of the exclusive reality of scientific objects; (*c*) returning once and for all to the thesis of the merely 'calculational' or 'auxiliary' status of theoretical frameworks and to the affirmation of the primacy of the manifest image?

Assuming, in accordance with the drift of the argument of this chapter, that none of these alternatives is satisfactory, is there a way out? I believe there is, and that while a proper exposition and defence would require at least the space of this whole volume, the gist can be stated in short compass. To say that a certain person desired to do A, thought it his duty to do B but was forced to do C, is not to *describe* him as one might describe a scientific specimen. One does, indeed, describe him, but one does something more. And it is this something more which is the irreducible core of the framework of persons.

In what does this something more consist? First, a relatively superficial point which will guide the way. To think of a featherless biped as a person is to think of it as a being with which one is bound up in a network of rights and duties. From this point of view, the irreducibility of the personal is the irreducibility of the 'ought' to the 'is'. But even more basic than this (though ultimately, as we shall see, the two points coincide), is the fact that to think of a featherless biped as a person is to construe its behaviour in terms of actual or potential membership in an embracing group each member of which thinks of itself as a member of the group. Let us call such a group a 'community'. Once the primitive tribe, it is currently (almost) the 'brotherhood' of man, and is potentially the 'republic' of rational beings (cf. Kant's 'Kingdom of Ends'). An individual may belong to many communities, some of which overlap, some of which are arranged like Chinese boxes. The most embracing community to which he belongs consists of those with whom he can enter into meaningful discourse. The scope of the embracing community is the scope of 'we' in its most embracing non-metaphorical use. 'We', in this fundamental sense (in which it is equivalent to the French '*on*' or English '*one*') is no less basic than the other 'persons' in which verbs are conjugated. Thus, to recognize a featherless biped or dolphin or Martian as a person is to think of oneself and it as belonging to a community.

Now, the fundamental principles of a community, which define what is 'correct' or 'incorrect', 'right' or 'wrong', 'done' or 'not done', are the most general common *intentions* of that community with respect to the behaviour of members of the group. It follows that to recognize a featherless biped or dolphin or Martian as a person requires that one think thoughts of the form, 'We (one) shall do (or abstain from doing) actions of kind A in circumstances of kind C'. To think thoughts of this kind is not to *classify* or *explain*, but to *rehearse an intention*.[1]

Thus the conceptual framework of persons is the framework in which we think of one another as sharing the community intentions which provide the ambience of principles and standards (above all, those which make meaningful discourse and rationality itself possible) within which we live our own individual lives. A person can almost be defined as a being that has intentions. Thus the conceptual framework of persons is not something that needs to be *reconciled with* the scientific image, but rather something to be *joined* to it. Thus, to complete the scientific image we need to enrich it *not* with more ways of saying what is the case, but with the language of community and individual intentions, so that by construing the actions we intend to do and the circumstances in which we intend to do them in scientific terms, we *directly* relate the world as conceived by scientific theory to our purposes, and make it *our* world and no longer an alien appendage to the world in which we do our living. We can, of course, as matters now stand, realize this direct incorporation of the scientific image into our way of life only in imagination. But to do so is, if only in imagination, to transcend the dualism of the manifest and scientific images of man-of-the-world.

[1] Community intentions ('One shall . . .') are not just private intentions (I shall . . .') which everybody has. (This is another way of putting the above-mentioned irreducibility of 'we'.) There is, however, a logical connection between community and private intentions. For one does not really share a community intention unless, however often one may rehearse it, it is reflected, where relevant, in the corresponding private intention.

2

BEING AND BEING KNOWN

THE purpose of this chapter is to explore what I conceive to be the profound truth contained in the Thomistic thesis that the senses in their way and the intellect in its way are informed by the natures of external objects and events. But while I shall be defending the thesis that knowledge involves an isomorphism of the knower with the known at both the sensuous and intellectual levels, I shall argue that the Thomistic tradition has an oversimplified conception of this isomorphism. Since many of the characteristic theses of this tradition, e.g. the immateriality of the intellect, are grounded in its interpretation of the isomorphism of knower and known, the question as to whether this interpretation is correct is central to the evaluation of the Thomistic system.

2. Let me begin by contrasting the Thomistic account of intellectual acts with two other accounts—in my opinion radically mistaken— which have successively dominated the philosophical scene since the Renaissance. The first of these found its classic expression in the philosophy of Descartes; the second in the early stages of contemporary British and American realism. These erroneous views are interesting both for what they have in common and for their differences.

3. They have in common the idea that intellectual acts differ *not* in their intrinsic character as acts, but by virtue of being directly related to different relata. Thus the thought of X differs from the thought of Y not *qua* act of thought, but *qua* related to X as opposed to Y. The two positions construe the status of these immediate relata differently. For the Cartesian, the immediate relatum is an item having being-for-mind ('objective' reality). Thus the thought of a golden mountain is a thought which is related to a golden mountain *qua* having being-for-mind, being for the mind that is thinking of it. This relation is often metaphorically expressed by saying that the thought has a golden mountain (in the 'objective' mode of being) as its 'content'. In this

terminology we can say that for the Cartesian acts of the intellect differ not *qua* acts, but *qua* having different contents. To use Arnauld's analogy, acts are like similar purses which differ only *qua* containing different kinds and numbers of coin.

4. It is not my purpose to develop the Cartesian position and discuss how Descartes and his successors were tempted to construe these contents as the immediate and primary objects of knowledge, and found themselves on the road to scepticism and idealism. This is a sad story with which you are all familiar, for it is one of the outstanding merits of the Thomistic tradition that it steadfastly refused to make this mistake, and correctly diagnosed it as a cancer at the heart of modern philosophy.

5. Now whereas the Cartesians postulated a domain of contents to mediate between the intellect and the real order, the extreme realists of the early decades of the present century expanded the real order to include all the items which had puzzled previous philosophers into the theory of contents. Thus non-existent objects and states of affairs found their place in the real order by means of a distinction between existence and subsistence and such other devices as Russell's theory of descriptions. The act of thinking that Socrates is mortal was construed as a direct relation between two reals: (1) an act of the intellect; (2) a state of affairs. The act of thinking that Socrates is foolish was also construed as a relation between an act of the intellect and a state of affairs in the real order. The difference by virtue of which the one thought was true and the other false was simply that the latter state of affairs, though a *subsistent* real, did not *exist*. But my concern is not to elaborate the characteristic doctrines of this new extreme realism, but simply to emphasize that like the Cartesians it interpreted the difference between intellectual acts as *extrinsic*, a matter of having different relata.

6. Now one can sympathize with the Neo-realistic rejection of contents. As has often been pointed out, to say that an object or state of affairs acquires 'objective' being as a content of thought when we think about it seems less an *explanation* than a metaphorical *restatement* of the fact that we are thinking about it. But if we dispense with 'contents', are we not forced to expouse extreme realism? The answer, of course, is No. For it is only if we assume that intellectual acts are identical in species, differing only extrinsically by virtue of their different relata, that we are committed to this alternative. And once we look this assumption in the face, we see how odd it is. As a matter of fact the notion that acts of the intellect are *intrinsically* alike regardless of what they are about is so odd that one can understand the temptation of many recent realists to abandon the

very notion of intellectual acts, and to flirt with naïve forms of sensationalism and behaviourism.

7. But what is the alternative? In general terms it is to hold that acts of the intellect differ intrinsically *qua* acts in a way which systematically corresponds to what they are about, i.e. their subject-matter. And of the approaches along these lines which take seriously the category of intellectual act, the one which seems to me most fruitful is the doctrine of the mental word.

8. There are many forms which the doctrine of the mental word can take, and, indeed, has taken in the history of the philosophy of mind. I shall be concerned to contrast two of these forms, one of them the Thomistic doctrine (to the extent that I understand it), the other a view which has its roots in Wittgenstein's *Tractatus*, and which I am prepared to defend. But first some general considerations are in place, considerations common to all theories of the mental word. (*a*) We must distinguish between mental words, mental statements, mental questions, etc. (*b*) We must distinguish between varieties of mental word: names, predicates, logical words, abstract singular terms, etc. (*c*) But above all we must distinguish between mental words as *acts* and mental words as *dispositions* or *propensities*. This last distinction corresponds to that drawn by Thomists between the intellect in *second* act and the intellect in *first* act. The intellect is in first act with respect to a certain mental word, e.g. ·man·,[1] when it has this word in its 'vocabulary', i.e. is able and disposed to think in terms of it. When the intellect is in second act with respect to the word ·man· it is by virtue of actually thinking of something as a man. If the intellect is in first act with respect to this word, we shall say that it has the concept ·man·.

9. Theories of the mental word characteristically hold that the intellect at birth is devoid of concepts, i.e. is not in first act with respect to any mental words. The view that the intellect is innately in first act with respect to some mental words is not an absurd one. Indeed, as I shall argue, the classical ('abstractive') account of concept formation runs into trouble as soon as it leaves the haven of concepts pertaining to the proper sensibles—and only *seems* to account for them. But fortunately the view that the intellect at birth has no concepts does not require a commitment to the abstractive theory of concept formation, and one can reject the latter without rejecting the former.

10. It will have been noticed that I have as yet said nothing specific about what a mental word is. More accurately, I have limited myself to characterizing mental words (by implication) as forms of the

[1] I shall form the names of mental words by putting the corresponding English expressions within dot-quotes.

intellect which are *analogous* to words in the ordinary sense of the term, i.e. to words as they occur in meaningful speech. Different theories of the mental word give different accounts of this analogy. How this analogy is to be understood will be a central theme in the second half of my argument. In discussing the Thomistic position the analogy is of less interest, because, according to this position, in contrast to the position I shall defend, the nature of a mental word can be understood independently of this analogy.

11. The three basic questions which any theory of the mental word must answer are: (1) What is a mental word? (2) How do we come by them? i.e. how do we acquire our mental vocabulary? (3) How are mental words related to the real order? These questions, as I see it, are answered by the Thomist along the following lines.

12. The mental word ·triangular· is the nature or form *triangular* as informing the possible intellect, i.e. as putting the possible intellect in *first* act. The possible intellect is informed in a unique way. A piece of wax becomes triangular through being informed by the nature *triangular*. One is tempted to say that the possible intellect does not become triangular, but since to be informed by the nature *triangular* is to become triangular, what one says instead is that the possible intellect becomes triangular *in the immaterial mode*.

13. The above is an account of the mental word ·triangular· *qua* disposition or *habitus*. A mental word as second act of the intellect would be, for example, the nature *triangular* as informing the intellect in second act, i.e. as informing an act of the intellect in that narrower sense in which acts are contrasted with dispositions or propensities.[1] It will be useful at this point to extend to mental words the familiar distinction drawn by C. S. Peirce between word *tokens* and word *types*. In this terminology each particular act of the intellect which is informed by the nature *triangular* will be said to be a token of the mental word ·triangular· as type. Thus, the mental word ·triangular· as type would be the nature *triangular qua* capable of informing (immaterially) the possible intellect. The nature *triangular* as that which is capable of informing both pieces of wax and intellects, i.e. considered in abstraction from its role as word and its role as physical form, will be referred to as the absolute nature *triangular*.

14. The existence in the intellect of the word ·triangular· as *habitus* is, to continue our exposition, grounded in the immaterial existence of the absolute nature *triangular* in the faculty of sense. The heart of the theory is the idea that sense is already a cognitive faculty, acts of which belong to the intentional order, the order of signification. Sensations are sign events—*natural* signs if by this is meant that they

[1] When I speak in an unqualified way of an intellectual act, I shall mean it in the sense of second act.

are not conventional, though they are not (or, better, not merely) natural signs in the sense of *symptoms* or *signals*. The act of sense does not need to be noticed in order to play its role as sign. In one terminology, acts of sense and intellect are *intrinsic* signs as contrasted with such *extrinsic* signs as smoke (of fire) and lightning (of thunder).

15. To give the bare bones of the abstractive theory in terms of an example, *white* and *triangular* exist materially in the external white and triangular thing. Then, by action of the thing on the open eyes of a man who is not blind, the absolute natures *white* and *triangular* come to exist immaterially in the organ of sight. By virtue of this fact the organ in act *signifies* the white triangular thing. Hitherto when speaking of the mental word we have had in mind the mental word as in the intellect, the *intellectual* word. But since acts of sense belong to the order of signification, there is equal appropriateness in speaking of the *sensitive* word. Thus we might reformulate the above by saying that the act of the visual organ is a token of the sensitive word (or phrase) ·white triangular thing· by virtue of being (immaterially) informed by the determinate nature of the external object *qua* visible.

16. In the case of both sense and intellect the word ·triangular· is in the faculty by virtue of the faculty being immaterially informed by the absolute nature *triangular*. What, then, are the distinctive features of the vocabulary of sense (if I may so call it) as contrasted with the vocabulary of the intellect? One might well expect to find some such distinctions as the following:

(*a*) The vocabulary of sense contains only such predicative words as stand for the proper sensibles.

(*b*) The vocabulary of sense does not include abstract singular terms (formal universals), e.g. ·triangularity·. The intellect somehow forms these words from their predicative counterparts.

(*c*) The vocabulary of sense does not contain such mental words as ·mental word· or ·signifies·. Query: does ·mental word· belong to the vocabulary of inner sense? of the reflexive awareness of intellective acts?

I postpone for the moment the question as to whether the vocabulary of sense contains such basic logical words as ·and·, ·or·, ·not·, ·if . . . , then . . .· And I mention, for future reference, that according to the Thomistic position although sense belongs to the intentional order, it does not judge, i.e. the 'language' of sense contains no statements or assertions. Apparently sense can signify *this white thing*, but not *this thing is white* nor *this white thing exists*.

17. The abstractive theory of concept formation rests on this conception of sense as belonging to the order of intentionality or signification. To put it simply, the intellect can get its basic vocabulary

from sense because this basic vocabulary already exists in the faculty of sense where it has been brought about by the action of external things. I shall therefore begin my critical discussion of the Thomistic doctrine of the mental word by attacking this assimilation of sense to the intentional order. My thesis will be that sense is a cognitive faculty only in the sense that it makes knowledge possible and is an essential element in knowledge, and that of itself it knows nothing. It is a necessary condition of the intentional order, but does not of itself belong to this order. This thesis was first advanced by Kant, but can, fortunately, be separated from other, less attractive, features of the Kantian system.

18. There are many reasons for the plausibility of the idea that sense belongs to the intentional order: the ease with which sensation can be confused with the unreflective perceptual judgement which is built upon it; the fact, noted above, that sense makes knowledge possible and is a necessary condition of the intentional order. It is primarily due, however, to the fact that sensations have what I shall call a *pseudo-intentionality* which is easily mistaken for the genuine intentionality of the cognitive order.

19. The first thing to note is that the expressions by which we refer to and characterize sensations do show a remarkable analogy to the expressions by which we refer to and characterize items belonging to the intentional or cognitive order. Thus we speak of

a sensation of a white triangular thing

and this shows a striking grammatical similarity to the language by which we refer to and characterize thoughts; thus we speak of

a thought of a white triangular thing.

And since we are construing the latter as an act of the intellect which signifies a white triangular thing by virtue of being a token of the mental phrase ·(such and such a) white triangular thing·, there is a strong temptation to construe the former as an act of sense which signifies a white triangular thing by virtue of being a token of the mental (sensitive) phrase ·(this) white triangular thing·.

20. But it is doubtful if this temptation would be strong enough to carry the day if it were not for the considerations which generate the idea that the natures *white* and *triangular* inform the act of sense in an *immaterial* way. For this amounts to the idea that sense in act is *isomorphic* in the *immaterial* mode with the object of sense, and I shall be arguing subsequently (*a*) that there is a sense in which sensations *are* isomorphic with objects of sense, (*b*) that sensations are not white and triangular in the way in which *material* objects are white and triangular, and (*c*) in § 56 below, that there are plausible,

if mistaken, considerations which point to an equation of intentionality with isomorphism in the immaterial mode, considerations which are the very source of the latter conception.

21. Now it certainly must be granted that the sensation of a white triangular thing is neither white nor triangular (nor, for that matter, a thing) in the way in which its external cause is a white triangular thing. And, I believe, it must also be granted that unless the sensation of a white triangular thing were *in some way* isomorphic with its external cause, knowledge of the physical world would be impossible. Finally, I believe, it must be granted that whiteness and triangularity are *somehow* involved in the form or species of the act of sense. It is, unfortunately, only too easy to suppose that these admissions add up to the Thomistic theory of sensation. It is therefore important to see that all of these theses can be accounted for in a radically different way which involves no attribution of intentionality to sense.

22. According to this alternative account, our concept of a sensation of a white triangular thing is the concept of a state of the perceiving organism which

(*a*) is of a kind which is normally brought about by white and triangular objects,

(*b*) is of a kind which differs systematically from those states which are normally brought about by objects of other colours and shapes,

(*c*) is a kind which is brought about in abnormal circumstances by objects of other colours and shapes, and hence contributes to the explanation of the fact that objects viewed in abnormal circumstances seem to be other than they are.

23. Thus although the sensation is not literally white and triangular, it is of a kind which can be called white and triangular *in a derivative sense of these predicates*. In Thomistic terminology, the act of sense which is a sensation *of* a white triangular thing must indeed, have a form or species *qua* act, but this form or species does not consist of the *white* and *triangular* appropriate to material things though immaterially received; it consists of *white* and *triangular* in a different sense of these terms. By this I do not, of course, mean that 'white' as in 'a white sensation' and 'white' as in 'a white elephant' are mere homonyms. They have different but related meanings, as, in a different way, do 'healthy' as in 'healthy food' and the same word as in 'healthy man'. Thus, instead of saying that the act of sense is informed *immaterially* by the natures *white* and *triangular* in the primary sense of these terms, we can simply say that the act of sense is informed by the natures *white* and *triangular* in the derivative sense characterized in paragraph 22 above.

47

24. This can also be put by saying that the concepts of the various kinds of sensation are concepts formed by analogy. The Thomistic tradition makes significant use of the idea that certain of our concepts are analogical concepts; and contemporary philosophies of science stress the role of analogy in the conceptual structures of scientific theory. What is, perhaps, new in the account I am proposing is the idea that direct self-knowledge may essentially involve analogical concepts, i.e. that the concepts in terms of which we have what is often called 'reflexive knowledge' of our mental acts are analogical extensions of concepts pertaining to the public or intersubjective world of things and persons.

25. This thesis certainly runs counter to the Cartesian interpretation of the reflexive awareness of a mental act as an adequate (i.e. among other things, non-analogical) grasp of the act as being of a certain determinate kind or species. But, I think we must say, so much the worse for Descartes. It is a serious mistake to suppose that merely by virtue of having sensations we experience sensations *as* sensations (do animals experience sensations as being sensations?), and that from this experience, by an act of so-called abstraction, the intellect can acquire a non-analogical understanding of what it is to be a sensation. I shall shortly be arguing that the same situation obtains in the case of our concepts of intellectual acts, which I shall also construe as analogical concepts the *fundamentum* of which are concepts pertaining to meaningful speech.

26. I suggested a moment ago that the concept of a sensation of a white triangular thing is the concept of an act which is white and triangular in a derivative sense of these terms. It is, to repeat, a white and triangular act *not* by being immaterially white and triangular in the sense of 'white' and 'triangular' appropriate to material things, but by simply being white and triangular in a derivative sense.[1] Let me now remind you that on the account I am proposing, the analogy between the two *whites* and the two *triangulars* involved the idea that the various species of visual sensation form a family of resemblances and differences which corresponds to the family of resemblances and differences which is the system of sensible qualities in the basic sense, the sense which pertains to material things. It is in this way that the isomorphism of acts of sense and material things is to be understood. The place of *derivative white* and *derivative triangular* in the system of the species of sense acts is isomorphic in the *structural* sense (explained by contemporary relation theory) with the place of *basic white* and

---

[1] It is perhaps worth noting that the above account of the derivation omits an essential step, in that the expression 'white and triangular sensation' presupposes the expression 'sensing whitely and triangularly' so that the introduction of the adverbs 'whitely' and 'triangularly' would be the basic analogical move.

basic triangular in the system of the perceptible qualities of material things.

27. I won't stay to criticize in detail the abstractive theory of concept formation, for once the supposed intentionality of acts of sense has been exposed as a pseudo-intentionality, i.e. once it is clearly recognized that acts of sense are intrinsically non-cognitive and do not present anything to us as being of a kind—e.g. white or triangular —the abstractive theory has been undercut, and can be left to wither on the vine. One or two points are worth making, however, which supplement the above argument, and lead into the second half of this essay.

28. The first is that the intellect in first act has logical words in its vocabulary. Some of these logical words are, in the contemporary phrase, 'truth-functional connectives' (e.g. ·and· and ·not·), the most significant feature of which is that if a sentence or group of sentences is about the real order, the sentence which is formed from them by the use of these connectives is also about the real order. Thus Socrates is *not* wise· is as much about the real order as ·Socrates is wise·. Other logical words, e.g. ·implies· in the sense of logical implication, are such that sentences involving them are about the logical order, as is shown by the fact that these sentences require abstract singular terms (e.g. ·Triangularity implies trilaterality·).

29. Now, abstractive theories notoriously have trouble with both kinds of logical word. The idea that acts of sense are informed by *not* as well as by *white*, by *implies* as well as *triangular* is rooted in the fact that whiteness is what it is by virtue of belonging to a family of competing qualities (what is white is *ipso facto* not red) and that triangularity is what it is by virtue of implying trilaterality. Thus *if* the mental words ·white· and ·triangular· are in the act of sense so also must be ·not· and ·implies·. The alternative I am recommending is to say that *none* of these words are present in the act of sense, for it does not belong to the intentional order. To which it can be added that the predicative word ·white· doesn't make sense apart from statement; ·white and triangular thing· presupposes ·(this) thing is triangular·. Predicates cannot be in sense unless judgement is there also.

30. One cannot have one intellectual word in one's vocabulary without having *many*, including logical as well as non-logical words. The possible intellect is put in first act by virtue of being informed by a whole, if rudimentary, language. Philosophers have been fascinated by the fact that one can't have the concept of white without being able to see things *as white*, indeed, until one has actually seen something as white. But this can be explained without assuming that sensation is a consciousness, for example, of white things as white. For it demands only that the coming-to-be in the intellect of the

49

word ·white· coincides with a second act of the intellect which is the perceptual judgement that some (perceived) object is white. And this is compatible with the idea that a complicated process of language training (involving the exhibition of objects of many colours and shapes) is a necessary condition of both.

II. THE ISOMORPHISM OF THE INTELLECT AND THE REAL

31. I have argued above that there is a sound core in the Thomistic contention that the act of sense is isomorphic with its external cause, but that rightly understood both terms of this isomorphism belong to the real order, i.e. neither term, and specifically the act of sense, belongs to the intentional order. My present purpose is to argue that there is an isomorphism in the real order between the developed intellect and the world, an isomorphism which is a necessary condition of the intellect's intentionality as signifying the real order, but is to be sharply distinguished from the latter.

32. In other words, I shall draw a sharp distinction between what I shall *initially* characterize as two dimensions of isomorphism between the intellect and the world:

    (*a*) an isomorphism in the real order,
    (*b*) an isomorphism in the logical order.

I shall use the verb 'to picture' for the first of these 'dimensions' and the verb 'to signify' for the second. I shall argue that a confusion between *signifying* and *picturing* is the root of the idea that the intellect as *signifying* the world is the intellect as informed in a unique (or immaterial) way by the natures of things in the real order.[1]

33. I claimed above that although the intellect *signifies* the world by virtue of *picturing* it, nevertheless signifying and picturing are radically different relations, to which I will now add that they take radically different terms. Thus, when we say

    X pictures Y

both X and Y belong to the real order, i.e. neither belongs to the order of intentionality; and when we say

    X signifies Y

both X and Y belong to the logical order, i.e. the order of intentionality.

[1] I argue in Chapter 6 that this same confusion is the source of some of the more obscure features of Wittgenstein's *Tractatus*.

34. Thus the two statements

(*a*) The intellect *pictures* the world
(*b*) The intellect *signifies* the world

though closely related, belong to different orders of discourse; and while the terms 'intellect' and 'world' as they occur in (*a*) are not mere homonyms by simple ambiguity with the same expressions as they occur in (*b*), they nevertheless have different (though related) meanings in the two statements.

35. As I pointed out above, a basic feature of the position I wish to defend is the idea that the concept of a mental word, or, better, of a mental language, is a derivative concept formed by analogy from the concept of the spoken word. The exact nature of this analogical extension of the concept of meaningful speech is a topic for a separate chapter of at least equal length. It is discussed, in general terms, in Chapter 3[1] and there is to be found such cash as I can muster to back up what for the present must remain a promissory note. Fortunately, the main point I wish to make can be appreciated without subscribing to my views on this particular matter, for my primary purpose is to explore the distinction between picturing and signifying as it applies to the spoken word. For, I would argue, just as the concept of the mental word is an extension by analogy of the concept of the spoken word, so the distinction between picturing and signifying as it applies to the mental word is an extension by analogy of the corresponding distinction as it applies to the spoken word.

36. But this is not the end of the liberties I shall take. For instead of proceeding directly to a discussion of the spoken word, I shall present the distinctions I have in mind as they appear when projected into discourse about computing machines, guided missiles, and robots. There are many facets to the question 'Can machines think?' on which I shall not touch; indeed, strictly speaking, I shall not discuss it at all. I shall simply sketch two different ways in which we would be willing (in one case with a certain measure of reluctance) to talk about the anthropoid robots of the future, as a means of throwing light on what I mean by the contrast between signifying and picturing in connection with human speech, and, therefore (promissory-note-wise) in connection with the mental word.

37. Suppose such an anthropoid robot to be 'wired' in such a way

---

[1] See also 'Intentionality and the Mental' (a correspondence with Roderick Chisholm) in the second volume of the series, *Minnesota Studies in the Philosophy of Science*, edited by Herbert Feigl, Michael Scriven and Grover Maxwell and published by the University of Minnesota Press (Minneapolis, 1958). For a similar approach see Peter Geach's *Mental Acts*, published by Blackwell (Oxford, 1956).

that it emits high frequency radiation which is reflected back in ways which project the structure of its environment (and its 'body'). Suppose that it responds to different patterns of returning radiation by printing such 'sentences' as 'Triangular object at place p, time t' on a tape which it is able to play over and over and to scan.[1] Suppose that, again by virtue of its wiring diagram, it makes calculational moves from 'sentences' or sets of 'sentences' to other 'sentences' in accordance with logical and mathematical procedures (and some system of priorities) and that it prints these 'sentences' on the tape. Suppose, furthermore, that in addition to logical and mathematica moves the robot is able to make inductive moves, i.e. if its tape contains several 'sentences' pairs of the form

> lightning at p, t   thunder at $p + \Delta p$, $t + \Delta t$

and no 'sentence' pair of the form

> lightning at p, t   peace at $p + \Delta p$, $t + \Delta t$

it prints the 'sentence'

> whenever lightning at p, t; thunder at $p + \Delta p$, $t + \Delta t$.

Clearly the wiring diagram must provide for the cancelling of such 'inductive generalizations' when a subsequent pair of 'observation sentences' turns up which is inconsistent with it.[2]

38. Let us suppose, finally, that the wiring diagram provides for the printing of certain general resolutive 'sentences'—'sentences' of the form 'Whenever I am in circumstances C, I shall do A', and that whenever the robot prints 'I shall now do A' it is so set up that it proceeds to 'do' A.[3]

[1] This scanning will be analogous to the robot's scanning of its external environment. It will involve a printing on the tape of higher order sentences, i.e. sentences which record the presence of first order sentences on the tape. I shall not attempt to characterize the 'programming' and the role of this tape scanning save by stressing the fundamental analogy of tape scanning to environment scanning, and the analogy between the way in which environment (and 'body') scanning is involved in the robot's 'actions'. and the way in which tape scanning is involved in the robot's 'computing actions'. The reader will find a discussion of some related issues in Chapter 11.

[2] Actually the matter is far more complicated than this, as is ordinary inductive reasoning. For sometimes we keep the generalization and reject the observation. Indeed, the above account of the robot's 'observations' is equally over simplified, for whether it responds to a certain stimulus with 'Triangular object at p, t' or with '*Apparently* triangular object at p, t' will be a function of what it already has on the tape, e.g. it will record the latter if it has recorded 'Mirror at p+p, t'. But my aim is not to give directions for making an anthropoid robot, but to suggest a piece of science fiction which each of you can write.

[3] As was suggested in f.n. 1, some of these 'resolutives' will concern circumstances which are the presence of first order 'sentences' on its tape and 'actions' which are the printing of further 'sentences' on the tape.

39. Suppose such a robot to wander around the world, scanning its environment, recording its 'observations', enriching its tape with deductive and inductive 'inferences' from its 'observations' and guiding its 'conduct' by 'practical syllogisms' which apply its wired in 'resolutions' to the circumstances in which it 'finds itself'. It achieves an ever more adequate adjustment to its environment, and if we permitted ourselves to *talk* about it in human terms (as we have been) we would say that it *finds out* more and more about the world, that it *knows* more and more *facts* about what took place and where it took place, some of which it *observed*, while it *inferred* others from what it did *observe* by the use of *inductive generalizations* and deductive *reasoning*.

40. But let us stop talking about the robot in human terms, in terms of what it thinks or knows—in short in terms of the framework of intentionality—and let us consider it from the standpoint of the electronic engineer. For while we can talk about the items on the tape as 'sentences' and assimilate them by analogy (and with hesitation) to the logical order, we can also consider the states of the robot in mechanical and electronic terms; and the point I wish to make is that in these terms it makes perfectly good sense to say that as the robot moves around the world the record on the tape contains an ever more complete and perfect map of its environment. In other words, the robot comes to contain an increasingly adequate and detailed *picture* of its environment in a sense of 'picture' which is to be explicated in terms of the logic of relations. This picturing cannot be abstracted from the mechanical and electronic processes in which the tape is caught up. The patterns on the tape do not picture the robot's environment merely by virtue of being patterns on the tape. In Wittgenstein's phrase, the 'method of projection' of the 'map' involves the manner in which the patterns on the tape are added to, scanned, and responded to by the other components of the robot. It is a map only by virtue of the physical *habitus* of the robot, i.e. by virtue of mechanical and electronic propensities which are rooted, ultimately, in its wiring diagram. A distant analogy to this picturing is the way in which the wavy groove of a phonograph record pictures the music which it can reproduce. This picturing also cannot be abstracted from the procedures involved in making and playing the record.

41. Now it must be confessed that the above account of the isomorphism between the physical state of the robot and his environment is meagre and metaphorical. The task of characterizing the robot in such a way that you would really be prepared to say that it was 'almost human', that it could 'almost' be said to observe, think, reason, deliberate, decide, and act, would not only take far more

time than I have at my disposal, it would take me out of my depth. My purposes, however, will have been served if you can conceive of such a robot, and if you can see in general terms what would be meant by saying that the robot contained a 'picture' of the world. For the important philosophical point is that this 'picturing' would be an isomorphism in the real order.

42. Thus the robot would contain a picture of the occurrence of a particular flash of lightning *not* by virtue of the absolute nature *lightning* existing immaterially in the robot's electronic system, but by virtue of the correspondence of the 'place' of a certain pattern[1] on the tape in the system of patterns on the tape to the 'place' of the flash of lightning in the robot's spatiotemporal environment. Since this isomorphism is an isomorphism in the sense of contemporary relation theory which falls completely within the real order, there would be no temptation to say that the robot's environment had 'immaterial being' in the physical *habitus* of the robot.

43. Suppose it to be granted, then, that the robot is isomorphic in the real order with its environment (and, for that matter, with itself, for it can picture itself—within certain limits—and must do so if it is to be as like a rational being as we want it to be). The point I now wish to make is that there is another way in which we can come to think of certain items on the robot's tape record as isomorphic with the real. And even if this line of thought involves an analogical extension to the robot of categories appropriate to rational beings proper, the drawing of the distinction between these two isomorphisms in the case of the robot will prepare the way for a corresponding distinction in the case of rational beings proper.

44. The isomorphism we have been considering has been defined in the framework of electronic theory. Let us now abandon this austere approach and succumb to the tendency to think of the robot as almost a human being; let us permit ourselves to talk about it in terms of the categories of logic and intentionality. In this context we might say, for example, that the tape pattern ': :' signifies *lightning*; that the more complex pattern ': :, 9, 15' *signifies* lightning at place 9 and time 15. Let us suppose, in short, that we talk about patterns on the tape as *symbols* which have meaning, which belong to the order of signification, and that we can say what they signify.

45. But instead of exploring this way of talking about patterns on the robot's tape, I shall explore instead the way of talking about

---

[1] It is, strictly speaking, the 'singular sentences' on the tape, whether printed in 'observation' or by 'inference' which picture the environment. A discussion of the way in which the robot pictures what is printed on its tape would require additional distinctions. The central theme would be that the 'language' of picturing is truth-functional.

human speech which is being stretched to cover the robot. Thus, instead of discussing what it means to say that

in Robotese ': :' signifies *lightning*

let us consider

in German 'Mensch' signifies *man*

for if we can give a correct account of the latter, we will understand what we are doing when we extend this way of talking to the robot. Once again I shall give promissory notes instead of hard cash. Since the task I have set myself is to draw a large scale contrast between two interpretations of knowledge as involving an isomorphism of the intellect and the real, the hard core of a theory of signification will suffice.

46. It is tempting to suppose that

'Mensch' signifies man

asserts a relation between an item in the order of signification (the German word 'Mensch') and an item in the real order (the—supposed —absolute nature *man*). Actually nothing (according to the theory of signification I am prepared to defend) could be further from the truth. The statement in question is about *two* items in the order of signification, the German word 'Mensch' and the English word 'man', and says that the one is the counterpart of the other. It says, in effect, that the German word 'Mensch' has the same use as the English word 'man'.

47. Actually this won't *quite* do, and to see why it won't do is to understand the temptation to suppose that the statement in question affirms a relation between a word and an absolute nature. For there is an obvious difference between

'Mensch' signifies *man*

and

'Mensch' has the same use as 'man'.

This difference is that the former won't achieve its purpose of ex-plaining the 'Mensch' unless the hearer knows the use of the word 'man', whereas the latter can be fully appreciated by one who does not know this use. Thus these two statements are not equivalent. This, however, can be remedied by interpreting the former state-ment as presupposing that the word 'man' is in the hearer's vocabulary, and hence as equivalent (roughly) to

'Mensch' (in German) has the same use as *your* word 'man'.

48. It is this asymmetry between the ways in which the words 'Mensch' and 'man' are referred to which is misinterpreted as the

difference between 'Mensch' as German word and *man* as absolute nature. The word 'man' is either *used predicatively*[1] or *mentioned*. There is no such thing as its use to stand for an absolute nature in the real (extra-linguistic) order.

49. Another source of this misconception lies in the fact that 'signifies' is not univocal. For we can say not only that

'Mensch' signifies *man*

but that

'Mensch' signifies (the formal universal) Manhood

which I shall not discuss on this occasion, and, which is of more direct concern,

'Mensch' signifies Socrates, Plato, etc.

Since Socrates, Plato, etc., belong to the real order, the temptation to construe ' "Mensch" signifies *man*' as affirming a relation between something in the logical order and something in the real order is reinforced. But can we not construe

'Mensch' signifies Socrates, Plato, etc.

as an ellipsis for

'Mensch' signifies *man*, and Socrates, Plato, etc., are men?[2]

50. The heart of my contention, thus, is that the basic role of signification statements is to say that two expressions, at least one of which is in our own vocabulary, have the same use.[3]

51. Now all this is not only sketchy, but highly controversial. I believe that I could elaborate the above remarks into a fairly persuasive theory of signification, but for present purposes I hope the reader will grant for the sake of argument that it could be done. For if what I am saying is correct, some interesting consequences follow, consequences which throw new light on the idea that in cognition we have an assimilation of the intellect to the real.

52. The primary consequence is that whereas what we have called *picturing* is a relation between items both of which belong to the real order, *signification* is a relation between items both of which belong

---

[1] The statement 'Man is mortal' can be interpreted as having the force of 'Men *as such* are mortal', an explication of which might show it to involve *both* a use and a mention of the word 'man'.

[2] A more accurate account would read:

'Mensch' signifies something which is true of Socrates, Plato, etc., where ' "man" is true of Plato' is to be understood in terms of ' "Plato is a man" is true', and hence in terms of 'Plato is a man'.

[3] This is often misleadingly put by saying that 'the meaning of a term is its use'.

to the order of signification.[1] Let me elaborate this point by returning to the robot. In the framework of physical theory we can say that a subset of the patterns on the tape constitute a picture of the robot's environment. Here is an isomorphism between physical realities. If, now, we make such statements as

the tape pattern ': :' signifies *lightning*,

etc., another isomorphism is being elaborated, this time between the tape patterns *accepted as a language* and *our own language*.

53. And if this is so, we see that even though these two isomorphisms are quite distinct and belong to two universes of discourse, there is nevertheless an intimate connection between them which can be put by saying that our willingness to treat the pattern ': :' as a symbol which *translates* into our word 'lightning' rests on the fact that we recognize that there is an isomorphism in the real order between the place of the pattern ': :' in the functioning of the robot and the place of lightning in its environment. In this sense we can say that isomorphism *in the real order* between the robot's electronic system and its environment is a presupposition of isomorphism *in the order of signification* between robotese and the language we speak.

54. Let me conclude this chapter by applying these considerations to the mental word. I have suggested that the notion of mental words is an extension by analogy of the notion of the spoken word, or, to put it somewhat differently, that acts of the intellect (thoughts) are conceived by analogy with speech, i.e. as something which is *like* speech but, as we say, 'goes on inside'. That the analogy is not perfect —involves disanalogies—is as essential to the notion of an *act of the intellect* as the fact that it is an analogy. Thoughts, after all, are not patterns of 'inner sounds' produced by the wagging of a hidden tongue; nor are they verbal imagery—though they may be reflected in verbal imagery. On the other hand, they are conceived to be analogous to patterns of overt speech and related to the give and take of

---

[1] (Added in proof) From a more penetrating point of view, signification statements are of the form

The design '***' (in L_1) plays the role played in L_2—our language—by the design '——'

and refer to two designs as role-players. Thus in the case of signification statements about intellectual acts, we would have

The kind of inner state which finds its overt expression in an utterance which signifies ——, plays a role in 'inner speech' which is analogous to that played by the design '——' in our language.

Thus, the 'relationship' of the logical to the real order is, in the last analysis, a matter of certain items in the real order playing roles. Compare the 'relationship' of the chess order to descriptive matter of fact. What the items might be which play the role of 'words' in 'inner speech' is discussed in the concluding sections of this chapter.

man's relation to himself and his environment as are the patterns of overt speech.

55. It must be granted that we *explain* the correspondence between overt speech and the real order in terms of the idea that overt speech is but the manifestation at the overt level of inner patterns and connections, but this is compatible with the idea that we conceive of these inner patterns and connections in terms of their manifestations. After all, we explain the behaviour of perceptible things in terms of imperceptible objects (electrons, positrons, etc.); but this is compatible with the fact that we conceive of the imperceptible by analogy with the perceptible.

56. Now if one confuses *picturing* with *signifying* and if one takes signifying to be a relation between a word and a real—to use a simple illustration, if one confuses between

> tokens of the word 'man' *picture* men

(more accurately, are constuents of statements which picture men) and

> tokens of the word 'man' *signify men*

and take the latter to involve a relation between the word 'man' and the absolute nature *man*, then, since both signifying and picturing are isomorphisms, one will think of the actualities which token the *word* as isomorphic *in the Aristotelian sense* with the physical actualities which embody the absolute nature *man*, i.e. individual men. And one will put this by saying that the actualities which token the word embody the absolute nature *man*—though in a unique way ('immaterially'); and while this would be a puzzling view with respect to the spoken word, the fact that the concept of the mental word is a concept by analogy leaves enough logical space to make it plausible with respect to the mental word. The spoken word would then be said to be informed in a derivative sense by the absolute nature *man* by virtue of expressing a mental word which is this nature as (immaterially) informing acts of the intellect. This conception of the mental word is, of course, the primary ground for the Thomistic contention that the intellect is immaterial.

57. What of the Cartesian arguments to prove that the intellect is immaterial? I pointed out above that Descartes assumed that if we have direct (non-inferential) knowledge of an inner state, e.g. the sensation of a white triangle, then this something must present itself *in propria persona*, i.e. in a non-analogical guise. In Cartesian language we must have an adequate idea of it. I argued that this principle is without foundation, and that our direct, 'reflexive' knowledge of our sensations (when we have it) involves concepts which are formed

in a complicated way from concepts pertaining to the perceptible qualities of physical things. Let me make the same point in the present context. Our direct knowledge that the thought that it is raining has occurred to us involves the concept of an occurrent which is analogous to the statement that it is raining, i.e. it involves the concept of the mental sentence ·It is raining· and of a certain act as a token of the mental sentence as a statement event is a token of the English sentence 'It is raining'.

58. Now if this is correct, we can see that the concept of the mental word carries with it both dimensions of isomorphism. Thus we can say that the mental sentences which inform the intellect in its first and second acts are the counterparts of sentences in the vocabulary of overt speech. Thus the mental sentence ·It is raining· is the inner counterpart of our English sentence 'It is raining'. This is an isomorphism in the order of signification and is the analogue of translation. And if the argument to date is sound, this isomorphism implies that *qua* belonging to the real order the intellect *pictures* the world, i.e. is related to the real order as the electronic state of the anthropoid robot is related.

59. But what sort of thing is the intellect as belonging to the real order? I submit that as belonging to the real order it is the central nervous system, and that recent cybernetic theory throws light on the way in which cerebral patterns and dispositions picture the world. Descartes argued that the intellect cannot be a physiological entity because we can have direct knowledge *that* we are thinking and *of what* we are thinking without knowing that there is such a thing as a nerve. This argument presupposes, as was pointed out above, that direct knowledge must present what is shown *in propria persona*. Once this principle is abandoned, there is no absurdity in the idea that what we know *directly* as *thoughts* in terms of *analogical* concepts may *in propria persona* be neurophysiological states. To show that this is not only *not* absurd, but is actually the case, however, is a task for another occasion. And with the addition of this promissory note to the many I have already issued, I bring this large scale contrast between two theories of the mental word to a close.

3

PHENOMENALISM

THE trend in recent epistemology away from what I shall call classical phenomenalism ('physical objects are patterns of actual and possible sense contents') has become almost a stampede. Once again, as so often in the history of philosophy, there is a danger that a position will be abandoned before the reasons for its inadequacy are fully understood, with the twin results that: (*a*) it will not be noticed that its successor, to all appearances a direct contrary, shares some of its mistakes; (*b*) the truths contained in the old position will be cast aside with its errors. The almost inevitable result of these stampedes has been the 'swing of the pendulum' character of philosophical thought; the partial truth of the old position reasserts itself in the long run and brings the rest of the tangle with it.

I believe that this is exactly what is happening with respect to the phenomenalistic account of physical objects. On the other hand, I also believe that the tools are at hand for a decisive clarification of traditional puzzles about perceptual knowledge, and that the pendulum can be brought to a stop. This chapter is an attempt to do just that by submitting phenomenalism to a thorough review in the light of recent achievements in the logic of conceptual frameworks. I hope to isolate the important insights contained in recent phenomenalism, so that they can remain as abiding philosophical achievements no longer periodically obscured by the confusions with which they have been associated.

In the early stages of the argument, devoted to an initial survey of the ground, I shall be distinguishing a number of 'phenomenalisms' all of which are variations on a common theme. This theme is the idea that the physical objects and processes of the 'common sense' world (i.e. physical objects as contrasted with 'scientific objects' such as electrons and electro-magnetic fields) actually do have the kinds of quality they seem to have. Some physical objects *are* red, even though other physical objects, viewed in abnormal circumstances,

merely seem to be red. Notice that this common theme is an ontological one. It says nothing about the 'direct' or 'indirect', 'inferential'
or 'non-inferential', character of perceptual experience. On the other
hand, the reasons which philosophers have offered to support one or
other variation on this ontological theme (or which have led them to
reject it *in toto*) have stemmed largely from perceptual epistemology,
meaning theory, and reflection on the bearing of the sciences, in
particular physics and psychology, on the problem of what there
really is.

The simplest form of phenomenalism would be that 'naïve' realism
which holds that while the verb 'to see' has many uses—including
perhaps, that in which Macbeth 'saw' a dagger which was not there—
its primary use is one in which a person is said to see a physical
object and to see that it is of a certain colour, e.g. green, where this
implies that the physical object in question exists and that it is in fact
green. According to 'naïve' realism, seeing that a leaf is green is a
special case of knowing that a leaf is green. Indeed, it is a special case
of direct, i.e. non-inferential, knowing. One *can* infer from the fact
that the leaf looks black when one is viewing it in a red light that the
leaf is green. To do so, however, is not to *see* that the leaf is green.
Nor does seeing that the leaf is green consist in inferring that it is
green from the fact, say, that it looks green and one knows oneself
to be viewing it in daylight. This is not to say that such an inference
cannot occur, but simply that it is not an analysis of seeing that the
leaf is green.

'Naïve' realism, thus understood, is not committed to the paradoxical view that 'O appears red to S' has the force of 'S knows (sees)
that O is red'—thus implying that things are everything they seem to
be—though the label 'naïve realism' has often been used in this sense.
To avoid confusion—and the paradox of calling anything as sophisticated as an ably defended philosophical position 'naïve'—I will use
the phrase 'direct realism' instead. According to direct realism, then,
seeing that a leaf is green is not a matter of seeing that it looks green
and inferring from this, together with the character of the circumstances of perception, that it is green. Nor, the direct realist goes on
to say, is seeing that the leaf is green a matter of (directly) seeing that
a certain item, not a physical object, is green and inferring (or taking
for granted) that the item 'belongs to' a green leaf. My immediate
purpose, however, is not to explore the merits of direct realism—
though I shall be doing so shortly. For before this increasingly
popular view can be evaluated, we must turn to the announced task
of examining classical phenomenalism.

Direct realism and classical phenomenalism share what I have
referred to as the 'phenomenalistic theme'. For both are inclined to

say that physical objects and processes actually do have the various sorts of quality which they can also merely seem to have. The extent of this agreement, however, must not be exaggerated, since, of course, they give quite different accounts of what it is for a physical object or process to have (or, for that matter, to seem to have) a certain quality, e.g. red. The point is a familiar one. Direct realism takes as the basic grammar of colour predicates,

O is (was, will be) red at place p

e.g. 'This apple is red on the surface (but white inside)'. It faces the problems of explaining statements of the form 'O looks (looked, will look) red at place p to S' in terms of this 'basic' statement form. Classical phenomenalism, on the other hand, introduces in one way or another a set of entities, not themselves physical objects, which are more 'basic' than physical objects and characterized by colour in a sense more basic than that in which physical objects are coloured.[1] Let us call these entities, following Ayer, 'sense contents'. We can then say that according to the classical phenomenalist the fact that a physical object is red in the appropriate sense of 'red'—red_p—is constituted by the fact that the actual sense contents which would 'belong' to it if it were viewed in standard conditions are red in the appropriate sense of 'red'—red_s. On the other hand, the object merely looks red_p to S if the red_s sense contents which S is directly seeing occur under relevantly abnormal circumstances of perception.

Another way of looking at the difference between the two positions is to note that according to classical phenomenalism, whenever an object *looks* ϕ_p to someone, whether or not it is ϕ_p, a ϕ_s sense content exists; also that all sense contents the direct seeing of which is ingredient in the seeing of a physical object whether as it is (say, red_p) or as it merely seems to be (say, $black_p$) are constituents of the object. Thus a $black_s$ sense content can be a constituent of an object which is red_p through and through and through (e.g. a piece of sealing wax). By contrast, the direct realist typically holds that the only entities characterized by colour which are involved in the perception of physical objects are the physical objects themselves and their *publicly observable* parts and that only those colours belong to a physical object or one of its parts which it would be seen to have by a standard observer in standard conditions. He may be prepared to say, as we shall see, that for a physical object to *be* red is for its 'surface' to *be*

[1] What, exactly, is meant by 'more basic than' in this connection is by no means clear. Certainly it is not claimed that expressions for these entities and the colours which characterize them are learned before expressions for physical objects and their colours. Whether or not the same is true of the corresponding 'concepts' or 'recognitional capacities' is less clear.

red in a more basic sense (not, of course, red$_s$), and that for a physical object to *look* red is for its 'surface' to *look* red. But, as is well known, he rejects the inference from 'x looks ϕ' to '(Ex) x is ϕ' with its correlative distinction between 'ϕ_p' and 'ϕ_s'.

I pointed out above that according to the direct realist (*dit* 'naïve') the basic grammar of colour predicates is illustrated by

This apple is red on the surface, but white inside.

We can, indeed, say 'the surface of the apple is red'; but if by 'surface' is meant, e.g. the skin, we would merely have another statement about the colour of a physical object. Perhaps we wish to say that the skin itself is red 'on the surface' (and pinkish underneath). Well and good; we can still handle this in terms of the proposed basic grammar. We can even introduce in terms of this form the idea that however thin a 'skin' we take, that 'skin' would be red. We must, however, beware of making the move (which has often been made) from

This apple is red at the surface because it has a skin which is red

to

This apple (or skin) is red at the surface because it has a 'surface' which is red

where the quoted 'surface' no longer means a physical object (e.g. a skin) nor sums up a reference to 'no matter how thin a paring were taken', but introduces an entity of a new category, a particular without thickness. If one makes this move, he is committing himself to the idea that

O is red at the surface

entails

O has x and x is red

where x is a 'surface' or 'expanse', and while this is an ontological thesis, it is difficult, in view of the fact that we do not see inside things (most things, that is), to avoid concluding that 'seeing' an apple consists in *seeing* the 'surface' of the apple and 'believing in' the rest.

Notice that the 'colour surfaces' of the philosopher who makes the above move from an initial position of direct realism are not yet the counterparts of the sense contents of the classical phenomenalist. For these 'surfaces', like the physical objects to which they belong, are *public* entities which presumably can *look* other than they *are*. In other words, a direct realist could reasonably be expected to apply to them the distinction between *being* of a certain colour and *seeming to be* of that colour which was originally drawn in connection with physical objects, and to do the same with the numberless colour surfaces which would be exposed by slicing the apple in all possible ways. The direct realist who has embarked on this path might use some such formula as 'the object consists of actual and potential colour "surfaces"'—which has a verbal similarity to the thesis of classical phenomenalism. Yet there would remain one essential difference. The direct realist would insist that each 'surface' is a public object which can look other than it is. Thus, a certain exposed 'surface' could be red and yet, because of differing circumstances of perception, look red to S, black to S', and purple to S''. For classical phenomenalism, on the other hand, there would be as many actual sense contents as there were experiences of the exposed surface: a red one sensed by S, a black one sensed by S', and a purple one sensed by S''.

It is worth pausing to note that the direct realist can scarcely hold that the remainder of the apple, over and above its exposed 'surface', consists of actual 'surfaces' waiting, so to speak, to be disclosed. After all, the apple can be sliced in many ways, and the resulting 'surfaces' have claim to be 'the' constituents of the apple. Surely the only plausible forms of the view that physical objects *qua* coloured 'consist of actual colour through and through' are those which either think of objects *qua* coloured as 'colour solids' and of 'surfaces' as dependent coloured particulars which have a merely potential existence until the object is 'sliced', or conceive of colour points as basic realities, physical objects *qua* coloured being 3-dimensional and 'colour surfaces' being 2-dimensional sets of colour points. Of these two views the second alone would be fully consistent with the idea that 'O is red at the surface' is analysable into 'O has a "surface" which is red', for one who thinks of colour solids as the basic mode of being of colour is unlikely to make the mistake of thinking of the surfaces of such solids as particulars. The idea, however, that our common sense conception of physical objects is analysable into that of a 3-dimensional (solid) continuum of colour points is a dubious one, to say the least. While if 'surfaces' are highly derived abstractions pertaining to the solids of which they are the 'surfaces', then so far from 'O is red at the surface' being explained in terms of 'O has a "surface" which is red' the converse would have to be true.

Not only is his move an ill-considered one, the direct realist who analyses the red apple into a red 'surface' the seeing of which involves no supplementation by 'belief', and a 'core' which is 'believed in', has stepped on the slippery slope which leads to classical phenomenalism. For if the 'surface' is one particular related to others, there is no contradiction in supposing it to exist without the others. Why, then, should not there be *unattached* colour 'surfaces'? And if the object of *pure*-seeing (seeing which contains no 'supplementing belief') is always 'surfaces', what *inductive* reason could there be for supposing that there are 'cores' to which they belong? Is it, perhaps, a synthetic *a priori* truth that every 'surface' covers a 'core'? At this point the existence of hallucinations and double vision is likely to suggest that it isn't even true.

Here we must be careful. The direct realist who eschews 'surfaces' will simply say that there seemed to Macbeth to be a dagger in front of him or that it seems to Jones that there are two candles on the table. But one who is sliding down the slippery slope will be tempted to say that although there *merely seemed* to Macbeth to be a *dagger*, there *really was* a dagger-shaped 'surface' which Macbeth was pure-seeing, and that although it merely seems to Jones as if there were two candles on the table, there really are two curved white 'surfaces' which Jones is pure-seeing. He *need* not, of course, make this move. It is open to him to say that there merely seemed to Macbeth to be a dagger-shaped 'surface'; that there merely seem to Jones to be two curved white 'surfaces'. These would be the 'existential seeming' counterparts of the 'qualitative seeming' he has already extended to his 'surfaces'. He could, in other words, stop his drift in the direction of classical phenomenalism by keeping his 'surfaces' what they were to begin with, namely *publicly observable closed* 'surfaces' only part of which can be seen at one time (without the use of mirrors) and which always contain a 'core' though one may be mistaken as to just what kind of 'core' it is. Where there is no 'core', he will insist, there merely seems to be a 'surface'. 'Surfaces' as originally introduced include *back* 'surfaces' as well as *front* or *facing* 'surfaces'. To limit 'surfaces' to facing 'surfaces' is to take a decisive step in the direction of equating 'surface' with 'seen colour surface', preparing the way for the identification of 'surfaces' with the sense contents of classical phenomenalism.

Perhaps the most important single outcome of the above discussion is the recognition that there are *two* radically different trains of thought which might lead one to distinguish between a 'basic' and a 'derivative' sense of 'seeing x', and, correspondingly, of 'seeing that x is ϕ'. One of them is rooted in a distinction between physical objects and their public 'surfaces'. It is, in essence, a misinterpretation of the fact that we can see a book without seeing its back cover or its insides, and amounts to a distinction between what we see without supplementation by belief or taking for granted (i.e. a public 'surface') and what we see in a sense (see$_2$) which consists of seeing in the former (see$_1$) a 'surface' and believing or taking it to belong to a physical object of a certain kind. It is worth insisting once again that this reification of surfaces into objects of perception is a mistake. It is simply not the case that we *see* 'surfaces' and *believe in* physical

65

objects. Rather, what we see is the physical object, and if there is a sense in which 'strictly speaking' what we see *of* the physical object is that it is red on the facing part of its surface and rectangular on the facing side, nevertheless the physical object as having *some* colour all around (and all through) and *some* shape on the other side is the object seen, and not an entity called a 'surface'. This mistake, however, has been endemic in modern perception theory, and has led to a distinction between two senses of 'see' each with an appropriate kind of object, the 'see$_1$' and 'see$_2$' characterized above. Notice that according to the above train of thought, items which are seen$_1$ (public 'surfaces') as well as items which are seen$_2$ (physical objects) can seem to be other than they are.

On the second train of thought, what is basically-seen (seen$_1$) is a sense content, sense contents being *private* and at least as numerous as the facts of the form 'there seems to S to be a physical object in a certain place', with which they are supposed to have an intimate, but variously construed, connection. Here, also, seeing$_2$ a physical object is explicated in terms of seeing$_1$ an item—in this case a sense content —and 'believing' or 'taking' it to 'belong' in an appropriate sense to a physical object.

If one confuses between these two ways of distinguishing (correctly or not) between a 'basic' and a 'derivative' sense of 'see', melting them into a single contrast between what is *directly* seen and what is *seen but not directly seen*, one is bound to be puzzled (as was, for example, Moore) as to whether or not what is directly seen can be the surface of a physical object, and as to whether or not what is directly seen can look other than it is.

Before embarking on the next stage of my argument, let me pause to emphasize that I do not intend to deny that when Macbeth saw (i.e. seemed to see, thought he saw) a dagger, there existed as an element in his visual experience something that might well be called a dagger-shaped colour expanse. Indeed, I think, (and shall argue) that *all things considered* it is as certain as anything can be that there was. The point I wish to stress, however, is that unless one locates correctly the idea that there are such 'expanses', one runs the risk of other mislocations and confusions, the net result being to lessen seriously the chances of getting out of the morass of traditional perception theory.

II. SENSE CONTENTS

My exploration of classical phenomenalism will be built around a study of the key terms in the slogan 'physical objects are patterns of actual and possible sense contents'. I shall begin by examining the ways in which philosophers have used the expression 'sense content' and related technical terms. I think that three major traditions can be distinguished which differ radically in spite of verbal similarities in their formulations. I shall begin by considering the approach which is in many respects the simplest of the three, a virtue which springs from its use of a thoroughly familiar model for its technical language. This model is ordinary perception talk. Such perception-theoretical expressions as 'directly see', 'directly hear', etc., are given a logic which parallels, in significant respects, the logic of the verbs 'to see', 'to hear', etc., as they occur in everyday perceptual discourse. Thus, to such statements as

Jones *saw* a book and *saw that* it was blue

there correspond such statements as

Jones *directly saw* a bulgy red expanse and *directly saw that* it was bulgy and red.

And just as *seeing that* is a specific form of *knowing that*, a variety of observational knowledge, of *observing* or *perceiving that*, so *directly seeing that* is construed as a variety of *directly observing* or *perceiving that*, and, hence, as a specific form of *directly knowing that*. Again, just as *seeing x* is a form of *perceiving x*, so *directly seeing x* is introduced as a specific form of *directly perceiving x*, or, as the term is introduced, *sensing x*.

The fact that 'sensing x' is introduced on the model of 'perceiving x' as ordinarily used brings with it a number of implicit commitments not all of which can be dodged without cutting the theory off from the roots of its meaning. One such commitment rests on the fact that in ordinary perceptual discourse the consequence from

Jones saw a book

to

There was a book (i.e. the one that Jones saw)

is valid. The theory, thus introduced, brings with it, therefore, a commitment to the consequence from

Jones sensed a red and triangular expanse

to

There was a red and triangular expanse (i.e. the one that Jones sensed).

Another commitment rests on the fact that in ordinary perceptual discourse the objects of perception typically exist before they are noticed and after we have turned away; in short they can and do exist unperceived. The theory, introduced on this model, brings with it the implication that the red and triangular item which Jones sensed is capable of existing unsensed. Other implications are that items which are sensed can appear to be other than they are, and that the fact that a sensed item is red and triangular can no more depend on the fact that someone *senses that* it is red and triangular, than the fact that a table is round and brown depends on the fact that someone *perceives that* it is round and brown.

But before further exploration of this first approach, it will be useful to describe the second approach, which has a quite different background and orientation. It is a sophisticated approach, and if the influence of ordinary perception talk is clearly there, it is often curiously indirect, mediated by the influence of a certain interpretation of conceptual thinking. Indeed, it would not be amiss to say that the fundamental model of this second approach is the framework of categories traditionally used to explain the status of the objects of thought. But the point of saying this will emerge as the view itself is described.

According to this second approach, then, the *esse* of the red and triangular item of which one has an 'idea' or 'impression' on a particular occasion is *percipi*. By this is meant, fundamentally, that the inference from

S has a sensation of a red and triangular expanse

to

There exists a red and triangular expanse

is illegitimate. Why it should be construed as invalid will be taken up shortly. For the moment it will be useful to set down beside it as a supposed parallel the invalidity of the inference from

S has an idea of (i.e. is thinking of) a golden mountain

to

There exists a golden mountain.

Notice that the thesis we are considering is to the effect that the *esse* of the red and triangular expanse of which one is having a sensation, *qua being that of which one is having a sensation*, is *percipi*. This must not be confused with the claim that the *esse* of colour expanses *in general and without qualification* is *percipi*. It is perfectly possible to claim that the *esse* of a triangular expanse of which one is having a sensation is *percipi*, while insisting that there are triangular expanses the *esse* of which is not *percipi*. Thus, Locke would surely have agreed with Berkeley that the *esse* of the (red) triangular expanse of which, on a particular occasion, he is having a perception is *percipi*, while denying that the *esse* of all triangular expanses is *percipi*. And a

Locke who avoided bifurcating nature would say the same of *red* triangular expanses as well.

In this second framework, the general claim that the *esse* of all colour expanses is *percipi* might be formulated—somewhat anachronistically—as the claim that expressions such as 'a red triangle'[1]— in the sense in which they refer to what is 'immediately' or 'directly' perceived—can properly occur only in the context

S has a sensation of . . .

thus, 'S has a sensation of a red triangle', or, as we shall see, in derivative contexts which are introduced in terms of it. This is a stronger thesis than the above, according to which 'S has a sensation of a red triangle' does not entail 'There exists a red triangle'. For, with a qualification to be developed in a moment, it insists that the latter statement is ill-formed.

In the material mode of speech, this more radical thesis might be put by saying that there are no red triangles, only sensations of red triangles. It is easy to see, however, that if one were to introduce the term 'sense content' in such a way that

There exists a red and triangular sense content

had the force of

Someone is having the sensation of a red triangle

then, of course, one could say

There are red and triangular *sense contents*

as well as

There are sensations of red triangles.

But, then, these would be simply two ways of saying the same thing, and the inference from

S is having a sensation of a red triangle

to

There exists a red and triangular sense content

would be analytic.

We are now in a position to see that whereas a philosopher who takes the *first* approach might claim that red triangles cannot exist unsensed, and put this by saying that their *esse* is *percipi*, he would

---

[1] To avoid clumsiness, as well as to join up with customary philosophical usage, I shall abbreviate 'a red and triangular expanse' into 'a red triangle'.

(in addition to doing violence to his model) be making a quite different claim from the above. He would, indeed, be claiming that

(Ex) x is a red triangle

entails

(ES) S senses x

and this claim would be a puzzling one, for it is difficult to see why the existence of an item (a red triangle) should entail a relational fact about it which is not included in its definition. The entailment would have to be *synthetic*, and either *a priori* or *inductive*, and both alternatives are not without their difficulties. However this may be, the point I wish to stress for the moment is that on the *second* approach, the idea that the *esse* of colour expanses is *percipi* is not the claim that 'x is red' entails '(ES) S has a sensation of x'. Rather it is the claim that 'x is red'—unless it has the sense of 'x is a red *sense content*'—is ill-formed. And however paradoxical it may seem to say that 'red triangle' does not properly occur apart from the context 'sensation of (a red triangle)' it must be remembered that the second approach does not have as its model our ordinary perception talk. For it would indeed be paradoxical to make the parallel claim with respect to 'green tree' and the context 'perception of (a green tree)' as ordinarily used.

Another significant difference between the second and first approaches concerns the fact that whereas on the first approach *sensing x* has a close logical connection with *sensing that-p*—a connection which parallels the connection in its model between statements of the form 'S saw x' (e.g. 'Jones saw the table') and statements of the form 'S saw that-p' (e.g. 'Jones saw that the table was brown') —the *second* approach does not even contain the form

S has a sensation *that . . .*

This difference accounts for the fact that proponents of the *first* approach characteristically speak of sensing as a form of *knowing*, whereas those who take the *second* line characteristically deny that having a sensation is a form of knowing. They grant, of course, that one may know that he is having a sensation of a red triangle. But this knowing is supervenient to the sensation, whereas on the *first* approach

S senses that x is red and triangular

is a special case of

S knows that-p.

And just as in the model (ordinary perception talk)

Jones sees x

implies that Jones has singled out x in terms of some *fact* about it
and is in a position to ascertain by vision *more facts* about it (*see
that* x is f, g, h, etc.), so in the approach built on this model there is a
commitment to regard the form 'sensing x' as logically tied to the
form 'sensing that x is f'.

Let us leave the first and second approaches for a moment, and
turn our attention to a third. A relative newcomer to the scene, it
equates

S has a sensation of a red triangle

with

There appears to S to be a red and triangular physical object
in a certain place.

It follows immediately that it agrees with the second approach that

S has a sensation of a red triangle

does not entail

A red triangle exists

for the 'appears-' statement to which it is equivalent in sense does
not entail the latter. Once again, however, it must be noted that the
category expression 'sense content' can be so introduced that

A red and triangular *sense content* exists

has the force of

(ES) (Ex) S has a sensation of x · and x is a red triangle

in which case

S has a sensation of a red triangle

does entail

A red and triangular *sense content* exists.

But the important thing about this *third* approach is that according
to it, while the fact that there appears to me to be a red and triangular physical object over there is not itself a *knowing*, it is facts
of this kind which are *directly known* in sense perception.[1] Or, to put

---

[1] Notice that whereas on the *second* approach having a sensation does not seem
to imply (as it does on the *first* account) that the subject has any knowledge, this
does not seem to be true of the account we are now exploring. For while the fact
that there appears to someone to be a red and triangular physical object in a
certain place is not itself a *knowing*, it does seem to imply that the person in
question has *some* knowledge (knowledge that-p). But this point will be discussed
shortly.

the same point in the language of sensation, what one directly knows in perception is that one is having sensations (e.g. of a red triangle).

Now facts of the form 'there appears to x to be a red and triangular physical object over there' entail (or, perhaps, presuppose) the existence of x and of *there* (and hence Space). Of these commitments the latter is, for our purposes, the more interesting, in as much as it implies that whereas there may *merely* appear to be a red and triangular object in a certain place, the place itself is not something which might *merely* appear to be. This commitment can, however, be eliminated by rephrasing the above form to read

> There appears to x to be a Space (or, perhaps, a spatial system) at a certain place in which a red and triangular physical object is located.

But if we leave aside this refinement, and others which might be introduced, the essence of the third account can be stated as the claim that to know that one is having a sensation of a red triangle is to know that there appears to one to be a red and triangular *physical* object at a certain place. And while there is nothing absurd in the idea that one could directly know such a fact, it does seem absurd to combine this third conception of *sensation* with the thesis of classical phenomenalism. For, one is inclined to expostulate, how can physical objects be patterns of actual and possible sense contents, if to say that a ϕ sense content exists is to say that there appears to someone to be a ϕ physical object somewhere?

It would seem clear that if classical phenomenalism is to get off the ground, it must give a different interpretation of sense contents than that offered by the third approach. It is surely reasonable to say that

> Whenever there appears to S to be a red and triangular physical object somewhere, then it is also true that S has a sensation of a red triangle

But if classical phenomenalism is to be a live option, this cannot be taken to express an identity of sense.

Now I want to suggest that once the above indented statement is taken as synthetic, it is true (though, as we shall see, its converse is not). Whether or not its truth gives support to phenomenalism will emerge in the course of the discussion. But if sensations are not 'existential appearings' what are they? Let me say at once that it is a form of the *second* approach which I wish to defend. I shall begin to sharpen distinctions by exploring the differences between approaches *two* and *three*. On neither approach is *having a sensation* a form of *knowing*. On the third approach, however, *but not on the second as I propose to defend it, having a sensation* is a form of *thinking*. For having it appear to one that there is a red and triangular physical object over there is a case of thinking in that broad sense in which *wondering*, *wishing*, *resolving*, etc., as well as *judging*, *reasoning*, etc., are modes of thought.

Thus, just as *resolving to do A* is a mode of thought, even though it is not a mere matter of thinking that something is the case, so *its appearing to me that there is a red and triangular physical object over there* is a form of thinking, even though it is not a mere matter of thinking that something is the case. Just as *resolving to do A* involves having the idea of oneself doing A, so the *appearing* requires that the person appeared to have the idea of there being a red and triangular physical object in that place. Clearly the resolving isn't simply the having the idea of oneself doing A. Equally clearly the appearing isn't simply a matter of having the idea that there is a real and triangular object in a certain place. *Being appeared to* is a *conceptual*—though not a merely conceptual—state of affairs. One can't be appeared to unless one has the conceptual framework of physical objects in Space and Time.

Now on the second view, in the form in which I wish to defend it, having a sensation is *not* a conceptual fact.[1] Nor does the ability to have sensations presuppose the possession of a conceptual framework. To bring out the force of this claim, let us consider the following objection. 'How', it might be asked, 'can

S has a sensation of a red triangle

fail to entail

There is a red triangle

unless having a sensation of a red triangle is a matter of there *appearing to be* (and hence, possibly, *merely* appearing to be) a red triangle?' To this challenge the answer, in general terms, is that if

S has a sensation of a red triangle

had the sense of

S is in that state which is brought about *in normal circumstances by the action on the eyes of a red and triangular physical object* .

then

S has a sensation of a red triangle

---

[1] Knowing that one has a sensation would, of course, be a conceptual fact. I would agree with Kant that one couldn't know that one has a sensation unless one had not only the conceptual framework of *persons* and *sensations*, but also that of physical objects in Space and Time. My grounds for saying this will come out later.

would not entail

There is a red triangle

though it would, of course, entail that there are such things as red and triangular physical objects. This fact enables me to make the additional point that if the second approach to the status of sensations made the above move, it would be precluded from holding that the *esse* of red and triangular items *generally* is *percipi*, for the status of 'red triangle' in 'sensation of a red triangle' would be derivative from that of 'red and triangular' in the context of statements about physical objects.

Let us suppose, however, that instead of contextually defining 'sensation of a red triangle' in terms of 'red and triangular physical object' as suggested above, and by so doing *explaining* the failure of the existential inference,[1] we simply said that it is an *irreducible fact* about sensations that the existential inference is invalid.[2] Classically the 'non-extensionality' of the context 'S has a sensation of (a red triangle)', the irreducible impropriety of the 'existential inference', was interpreted on the model of the logical non-extensionality of the context 'x is thinking of a red triangle'. With a proper commentary, one which discounts the *conceptual* character of the latter context while highlighting its non-extensionality, the model is a useful one. Unfortunately, in its classical use the conceptual character of the model was *not* discounted.[3] Thus it is worth noting that Aristotle seems to have conceived of sensation as, for example, the awareness of this white thing *as white* (and *as a thing*) thus introducing into sensation the 'form of judgement' *S is P*. To do this, of course, is to treat sensation as cognitive and conceptual, and to construe the difference between sense and intellect not as that between a 'raw material' which involves *no* consciousness of anything *as thus and so* on the one hand, and any consciousness of something *as thus and so* on the other, but rather between perceptual consciousness of *individual* things as *determinately thus and so*, and consciousness in terms of the general (*All S is P*), the generic (*S is an animal*) and the abstract (*Triangularity is complex*).

---

[1] The inference, that is, from 'S has a sensation of a red triangle' to '(Ex) x is red and triangular'.

[2] It will be remembered that the inference from 'S has a sensation of a red triangle' to '(Ex) x is a red and triangular *sense content*' would be valid, but trifling.

[3] *Vide* the Cartesian classification of sensations, feelings, images, etc., as *cogitationes*. The influence of this model can readily be traced through seventeenth and eighteenth century thought (and subsequently) in both 'empiricism' and 'rationalism'. Kant's rejection of this assimilation of the manifold of sense to the conceptual was part and parcel of his Copernican revolution.

Whether or not the 'irreducible non-extensionality' form of the second approach is lured by its model into conceptualizing sensation, it is not precluded, as was the form discussed above which defined sensations of red triangles as states brought about in normal circumstances by the action of red and triangular physical objects on the eyes, from holding that the *esse* of all red triangles is *percipi*, and that except in *derivative* senses, thus as referring to the powers of physical objects to cause sensations of red triangles, 'red triangle' occurs properly only in the context 'S has a sensation of (a red triangle)' or contexts which unpack into this.

Such a view would be closely related to the claim, so characteristic of modern philosophy, that the *esse* of colours is *percipi*. The distinction between 'primary' and 'secondary' qualities would turn on the idea that whereas colours have *only* 'being-for-sense', shapes, in addition to having 'being-for-sense' *qua* immediately perceived would have unqualified being in the physical world as well.

But the idea that it is a basic or underivative fact about sensations that the 'existential inference' is invalid need not be combined with the idea that the *esse* of all colours or shapes is *percipi*.[1] And if it is not, then we get a version of the second approach to sensation according to which the statement

Sensations of red triangles are those states of perceivers which are brought about in normal circumstances by the action of red and triangular physical objects on the eyes

would not be an analytic statement, resting on a contextual definition of 'sensation of a red triangle', but would either be a *synthetic* statement, or, if *analytic*, would be so by virtue of the definability of 'red and triangular physical object' as the sort of physical object which in normal circumstances causes perceivers to have sensations of red triangles.

A few paragraphs back I made the point that if sensation talk is logically—and not merely historically or genetically—built upon the framework of physical objects, then classical phenomenalism cannot get off the ground. This consideration eliminates, as materials for a phenomenalist construction, sense contents as construed by the third

---

[1] The idea that colours have only being-for-sense was grounded in the idea that mechanics doesn't need to mention the colours of things in explaining why they move as they do. Berkeley saw that no object, *pace* Descartes, can have merely the metrical and structural properties studied by geometry. Either these non-geometrical qualities are such sense qualities as colour, or we must postulate qualities which we do not sense. Classical concept empiricisms precluded the latter alternative; and taking the former, Berkeley was committed to either abandoning the *esse-percipi* principle for colours, or extending it, as he did, to geometrical properties.

—or 'appearing'—approach to sensation. It also eliminates that form of the second approach which *equates*

S has a sensation of a red triangle

with

S is in that state which is brought about in normal circumstances, etc.

Of the alternatives we have examined, then, the phenomenalist is left with (*a*) the form of the second approach which rejects the above equation and takes the category of sensation to be an *irreducible* category for which the inference from 'S has a sensation of a red triangle' to '(Ex) x is a red triangle' does not obtain; (*b*) the first approach, i.e. the sense datum theory.

According to the first approach, it will be remembered, there simply are such things as red and triangular expanses. They are 'directly perceived' and it is directly perceived *that* they are *thus-and-so*, i.e. red and triangular. (That it may take skill and a special 'set' to discriminate these expanses and the direct perception of them within the larger context of naïve experience is granted.) It has already been pointed out above that this approach, having as it does ordinary perception talk as its model, does not readily permit of an *esse est percipi* interpretation of the objects of direct perception. The closest approximation to such a principle it can accommodate would involve a distinction between

S directly sees x; S directly sees that-p

as *cognitive* facts and, to stipulate a new use for the verb 'to sense',

S senses x

which would stand for the fact that x stands in a certain *non-cognitive* relation to S. To say that the *esse* of sense contents is *being sensed* would be to say that sense contents occur only in this *non-cognitive* relation to S. Thus, it might be held that sense contents occur only in the context of a certain kind of cortical process, or only as elements of a system of sense contents, for example in what H. H. Price has called 'somato-centric bundles'. Notice that the claim that the *esse* of sense contents is in either of these ways *being sensed* is compatible with the idea that there are or might be sense contents which are not directly perceived or 'sensed' in a *cognitive* use of this term.

III. POSSIBLE SENSE CONTENTS

Let us grant, then, provisionally, that there is available for the phenomenalist an account of sense contents which does not rule out his enterprise *ab initio*. The next step, as specified by our programme, is to explore what might be meant by the phrase 'possible sense content'. Here the essential point can be made quite briefly, though its implications will require careful elaboration. A 'possible' sense content in the desired meaning of 'possible' would be more aptly referred to as a *conditional* or (to use Mill's term[1]) *contingent* sense content. The logical structure of this concept can best be brought by an analogy. Suppose we use the phrase 'conditional skid' to refer to a skid which *would* take place if a certain driver *were* to do something, e.g. swerve. A beginning driver is constantly aware of the 'existence' of conditional skids, collisions, etc., relatively few of which, fortunately, become actualized.

Notice that the contrasting term to 'possible skid' in the sense of *conditional* or *contingent skid* will be 'actual skid' *not* in the sense of *actually existing skid*, but simply as used to refer to skids *in the ordinary sense of the term* as contrasted with the conditional skids which are contextually defined in terms of them. Thus 'actual skid' differs from 'skid' only by calling attention to the contrast between skids and conditional skids.

Let us, therefore, explore what it would mean to say that at a certain time and place there was a conditional skid. Obviously a conditional skid does not exist merely by virtue of the fact that the statement 'such and such a motion of such and such a car on such and such a surface occurred at this time and place' is both logically and physically self-consistent. 'Conditional' involves a reference to *existing circumstances*, to *alternative courses of action* and to the *outcome* of these courses of action in the existing circumstances. The sense of 'possible' (='conditional') which we are exploring must also be carefully distinguished from the *epistemic* sense of 'possible' illustrated by

It is possible that it will rain tomorrow

This sense, like the one we are defining, is also not simply a matter of the logical and physical self-consistency of the statement 'It will rain tomorrow'. It is a cousin of 'probable' and the above statement has, roughly, the sense of

The presently available evidence is compatible with the idea that it will rain tomorrow.

The sense we have in mind, on the other hand, is, so to speak, ontological rather than epistemic. It says how things stand, not how we stand with respect to evidence about how things stand.

[1] J. S. Mill, *An Examination of Sir William Hamilton's Philosophy*, 3rd Edition, Appendix to Chapters XI and XII. This appendix is such a clear formulation and defence of the phenomenalistic position that it fails by a hairsbreadth to refute it along the lines of the following argument.

Consider the following statements, where x is a piece of salt:

x is soluble
It is possible that x will shortly dissolve
A possible dissolving of x exists.

The first statement says simply that if x were put in water it would dissolve. It is compatible with the idea that x is in an inaccessible place miles away from water. The second statement, which involves the *epistemic* sense of 'possible' claims that the available evidence is compatible with the idea that x will shortly dissolve, and hence rules out the idea that *the evidence points to* the above description of the circumstances. The third statement—a contrived one, obviously, *but so is the language of possible sense contents*—claims that the circumstances of x are such as to leave open to us at least one course of action which would eventuate in the dissolving of x, and hence rules out the above description of the circumstances.

Notice that in statements of the kind we are considering agents and circumstances do not come into the picture in the same way. Roughly circumstances come in as *actualities*, agents come in as *having powers*. Thus, returning to the example of the skid, we have

The circumstances of the driver are such, and his capacities to move his limbs are such, that there is at least one move he can make which would result in a skid.

We are clearly in the region of difficult problems pertaining to the conceptual framework of *conduct*. What is an action? What is the scope of 'circumstances'? Could a person ever have done something other than what he actually did? etc., etc.[1] Fortunately these problems are tangential to our investigation. For our purpose the significant feature of the above analysis of a 'possible' or 'conditional' skid is the implied reference to general principles (laws of nature) about what circumstances are consistent with the performance of what actions and about

---

[1] It is perhaps relevant to note that the idea that determinism is incompatible with 'could have done otherwise' rests on a confusion between
    It could not have been the case that x did A at t
and
    x was not able to do A at t.
The former has the sense of
    That x did A at t is physically impossible relative to the antecedent state of the universe.
In the case of minimal actions (roughly, bodily actions under voluntary control) 'x was able to do A at t' means, roughly,
    If x had willed at t to do A, then x would have done A
and neither it nor its denial makes reference to the antedecent state of the universe.

78

what would eventuate if the agent were to do an action of a certain kind which he is able to do in his circumstances. For, to bring the matter to a head, to say that E would eventuate if X, who is in circumstances C, were to do A, is to imply that it is a general truth that

When A is done in C, E eventuates

This general truth may be either 'strictly universal' or 'statistical'. The important thing is that it is *factual*, i.e. that it is not *logically* true. Thus, if the belief in such a generalization is to be a *reasonable* one, the reasons must be of an inductive character. This points to inductive arguments of the form

In observed cases of A being done in C, E has invariably (usually) eventuated

So, (in all probability) doing A in C invariably (usually) eventuates in E.

If we transfer these considerations from the case of the possible skid to the case of the possible sense content, a number of points can be made at once. To begin with, we must distinguish between

(*a*) the fact that the circumstances of perception are of kind C;

(*b*) the fact that the perceiver can do A; and

(*c*) the fact that doing A in C (usually) eventuates in having a sense content of the kind in question

Now we can readily imagine that someone who, though a friend of sensations and sense contents, is not engaged in defending classical phenomenalism might well illustrate these distinctions by putting himself in a position in which he can truthfully say

(*a'*) I am standing, eyes closed, facing a fireplace in which a fire is burning.

(*b'*) I am not blind and can open my eyes.

(*c'*) Opening my eyes when facing a fire usually eventuates in my having toothy orange and yellow sense contents.

He might well say in these circumstances that a possible or conditional toothy orange and yellow sense content exists.

Suppose, however, that he undertakes to defend the idea that 'physical objects are patterns of actual and conditional sense contents' where 'conditional sense content' has the sense we have been explicating. What moves can he be expected to make? The simplest move would be to start with the above model for interpreting the existence of conditional sense contents, but claim that each of the three statements, (*a'*), (*b'*), and (*c'*), can be reformulated in terms of sense contents. *But what sort of sense contents? Actual? or both actual* and *conditional*?[1] This question probes to the heart of the matter. For if the presuppositions of statements asserting the existence of conditional sense contents are such as are ordinarily formulated in terms of physical objects, persons, sense organs, etc., as above, then the claim that physical objects are patterns of actual *and conditional* sense contents implies that when reformulated in terms of sense contents, these presuppositions refer to conditional as well as actual sense contents which *in their turn* presuppose generalizations, and if these generalizations are also such as are ordinarily formulated in terms of physical objects, persons, sense organs, etc., then we are faced with the absurdity of generalizations which are such that their own truth is presupposed by the very meaning of their terms. This vicious circularity finds its partial expression in the fact that if the reformulation from the language of physical objects to the language of sense contents were carried on step by step it would not only be an endless regress, but would involve a *circulo in definiendo*, 'eye', for example, being explicated in terms of 'eye'.

The assumption that the general truths presupposed by the existence of conditional sense data are such as are ordinarily formulated in terms of physical objects, eyes, etc., also has for a consequence that those generalizations could never be supported by instantial inductions the premises of which referred to actual sense data only. For since the terms of the supported generalizations refer to actual *and conditional* sense contents, the premises would have to do so as well. Indeed, the truth of the premises for such a generalization would presuppose the truth of such generalizations.

The preceding argument has been based on the assumption that the general truths presupposed by the existence of conditional sense contents are such as are formulated in ordinary language by statements relating sensations to the physical and physiological conditions of perception. This consideration suggests that all the classical phenomenalist need do by way of reply is to insist that there are *independent*[2] general truths about sense contents the terms of which involve no reference to conditional sense contents, and which can therefore be supported by instantial inductive arguments the premises of which refer to actual sense contents only. To probe more deeply into classical phenomenalism we must, therefore, examine this new claim. Are there inductively establishable generalizations about the occurrence

---

[1] See the opening paragraph of this section for an explication of the sense of 'actual' in the phrase 'actual (as contrasted with conditional) sense content'. I take it that it is obvious from what has been said that the existence of conditional entities presupposes the existence of actual entities.

[2] By calling them 'independent' I mean simply that they are not supposed to be the 'translated' counterparts of common sense or scientific propositions about perception.

of sense contents which make no reference to either physical objects or conditional sense contents? Can we, in short, explain conditional sense contents in terms of actual sense contents?

Now there is no contradiction in the idea that there are (perhaps statistical) uniformities which specify the circumstances in which sense contents of a certain kind occur in terms of actual (i.e. not conditional) sense contents. Are there any such? Here we must be careful to distinguish between two radically different kinds of generalization.[1] Let us call them *accidentally autobiographical* (A-generalizations) and *essentially autobiographical* (E-generalizations) respectively. If one fails to distinguish between them, the fact that there are true generalizations of one kind may deceive him into thinking that there are true generalizations of the other.

The difference between the two kinds of generalization is that between

Whenever (or for the most part whenever) I have such and such a pattern of sense contents, I have a sense content of the kind in question

(1) where it makes good sense to suppose that the generalization remains true if 'anybody' is substituted for 'I', and (2) statements of the same form where it is clear that the generalization would not remain true if the substitution were made. The former are A-generalizations; the latter E-generalizations.

Now it is reasonably clear that there have been uniformities in my immediate sense history. It is notorious that the antecedents must be very complex in order to discount the circumstances (e.g. blinks, getting one's hand in the way, etc., etc.) which upset simple applecarts. But if I am guarded enough in my conception of the antecedent, it will indeed have been followed (for the most part) by the consequent in my past experience. Before we ask ourselves whether such uniformities in a person's sense history can serve as premises for an inductive argument, and whether, if they can, the evidenced generalizations can do the job required of them by the phenomenalist, let us imagine someone, Mr. Realist, to comment on the above as follows:

I grant that such past uniformities can be discovered, but surely I have come to discover them while conceiving of myself as a person, having a body, and living in an environment consisting of such and such physical

---

[1] For present purposes it is unnecessary to break up the antecedents of these generalizations into a phenomenally characterized circumstance and a (supposed) phenomenal act of the perceiver (e.g. a setting oneself to open one's eyes) which jointly eventuate in the sense content in question.

objects (my house, this fireplace, the road out front, the wallpaper, etc.). I cannot even imagine what it would be like to discover them without operating within this conceptual framework.

To which we can imagine someone, Mr. Phenomenalist, to reply:

I grant that in the 'context of discovery' your coming to notice these uniformities transpired within the framework you mention; but surely in the 'context of justification' these uniformities stand on their own feet as evidence for inductive generalizations about sense contents.

Mr. Realist is likely to retort:

Surely it is paradoxical to grant that the noticing of the uniformities occurs within the conceptual framework of persons and things in space and time, while insisting that this framework is one in which physical objects are patterns of actual and conditional sense contents. For, *ex hypothesi*, the notion of a conditional sense content is to be explicated in terms of the kind of uniformity which is discovered while using the framework.

and Mr. Phenomenalist to counter with:

The *historical* or *genetic* fact that a child is taught the conceptual framework of persons and things in space and time and later uses this framework in the discovery of the complex uniformities which are presupposed by conditional sense contents is not incompatible with the *logical* claim that this framework is reducible to the framework of sense contents, actual and conditional. Surely the intersubjective conceptual framework which is the common heritage of countless generations can embody a wisdom which the individual must scratch to acquire. . . .

It is at this point that the distinction drawn above between the two kinds of generalization about actual sense contents becomes relevant. For if we ask, 'Are the uniformities we have found to obtain in our past experience such that if they could serve as inductive evidence for sense content generalizations, the conditional sense contents they would make available would serve the phenomenalist's purposes?' the answer must be a simple 'No'. For the uniformities each of us finds are not only autobiographical, they are expressions of the fact that each of us lives among *just these individual physical objects*. The uniformities I find are bound up with the fact that my environment has included wallpaper of such and such a pattern, a squeaky chair, this stone fireplace, etc., etc. My having had *this* pattern of sense contents has usually eventuated in my having had *that* sense content, because having *this* pattern of sense contents guarantees, for example, that I am awake, not drugged, wearing my glasses and looking at the fireplace. And a generalization which is an expression of the contingencies of my existence can scarcely be one of the generalizations which, in the intersubjective conceptual heritage of the race, support the phenomenally conditional sense contents postulated by the phenomenalist. Thus, even granting that there are inductively warranted generalizations which permit the definition of phenomenally conditional sense contents, the latter will be logically tied to the peculiarities of my environment in such a way that they cannot be transferred to other things in other places.

What the phenomenalist obviously wants are generalizations which will serve the same purpose as the familiar principles about what people generally experience in various kinds of circumstances, but which will not lead to circularity or vicious regress when put to phenomenalistic use. But these principles are *impersonal*, applying, with qualifications which allow for individual, but in principle repeatable, differences, to all perceivers. In other words, what the phenomenalist wants are generalizations, in sense content terms, which are *accidentally* autobiographical, generalizations in which the antecedent serves to guarantee *not* that I am in the presence of *this individual* thing, e.g. my fireplace, but rather that my circumstances of perception are of a certain *kind*. What he *wants* for his antecedents are patterns of sense contents which are the actual sense content counterparts of the kinds of perceptual circumstances which common sense expresses in the language of persons, sense organs, and physical things. The best he can *get*, however, are essentially autobiographical uniformities in which the antecedents, however complex, are the actual sense content counterparts of the presence to *this* perceiver of *these individual things*.

In pinpointing our argument to the effect that the phenomenal uniformities we actually can put our fingers on cannot serve the phenomenalist's purpose, we have had to neglect equally telling considerations. Thus, we have permitted the phenomenalist to refer to perceivers and their personal identity in stating his phenomenal uniformities, without raising the objection that these concepts are part and parcel of the framework of physical things in space and time. We could do this because it is clear that the phenomenalist would simply retreat to the idea of an actual-phenomenal counterpart of a person, and there would have been no point in criticizing this notion until we had explored his account of the framework of persons and physical things alike. We are now in a position to press our offensive on a broader front. For if we are correct in asserting that autobiographical generalizations of the sort which could find support in the uniformities which have occurred in our sense histories could not authorize the conditional sense contents required by the phenomenalist's analysis, we can now make the stronger point that these uniformities are precluded from serving as instantial evidence for these putative autobiographical generalizations. For these uniformities come, so to speak, with dirty hands. Once it is granted that the framework of physical things is not reducible to that of actual and conditional sense contents, and, in effect, this is the burden of our argument to date, we see that the very selection of the complex patterns of actual sense contents in our past experiences which are to serve as the antecedents of the generalizations in question presuppose our common sense knowledge of ourselves as perceivers, of the specific physical environment in which we do our perceiving and of the general principles which correlate the occurrence of sensations with bodily and environmental conditions. We select those patterns which go without being in a certain perceptual relation to a particular object of a certain quality, where we know that being in this relation to an object of that quality normally eventuates in our having the sense content referred to in the consequent. Thus, the very principles in terms of which the uniformities are selected carry with them the knowledge that these uniformities are *dependent* uniformities *which will continue only as long as these particular objects constitute one's environment*, and hence preclude the credibility of the generalization in sense content terms which abstract consideration might lead us to think of as instantly confirmed by the past uniformities.

The fact that the noticing of complex uniformities within the course of one's sense history presupposes the conceptual picture of oneself as a person having a body and living in a particular environment of physical things will turn out, at a later stage of the argument, to be but a special case of the logical dependence of the framework of private sense contents on the public, inter-subjective, logical space of persons and physical things.

One final remark before closing this section. It should be noticed that although the uniformities we have been considering are biographical facts about individual persons, there is a sense in which they imply impersonal truths about all perceivers. For we know that if *anybody* with a similar perceptual equipment were placed in our environment, (roughly) the same uniformities would obtain in his immediate experience. As is made clear by the preceding argument, however, this knowledge is not an induction from uniformities found in our immediate experience, but simply one more consequence of our framework knowledge about persons, physical things, and sense perception.

IV. THE NEW PHENOMENALISM

The view we have been discussing, and which we have called classical phenomenalism, has fallen from its high estate of a few short years ago. It has been explicitly abandoned by many of its most ardent proponents, including most of those who brought it to its present state of intricate sophistication by their successive attempts to strengthen it against ever more probing criticism. And these defections have by no means been offset by new recruits. One might therefore be tempted to conclude that the above tortuous argument was a waste of time, and that the task of exploring the whys and wherefores of classical phenomenalism should be left to the historian. There might be something to this contention if philosophers had abandoned classical phenomenalism for the right reasons and with a clear understanding of its inadequacies. That this is not the case is the burden to the present section.

The point can best be introduced by noticing that the decline of the claim that the framework of physical objects is 'in principle' *translatable* into the framework of sense contents has been accompanied by the rise of the claim, often by the same philosophers, that even if such a translation is 'in principle' impossible, nevertheless there is a sense in which only sense contents *really* exist. This new phenomenalism can best be understood by comparing it with a form of realism which is almost its twin.

In the early years of the century, certain philosophers in the Lockean tradition were wont to argue that the framework of physical objects is analogous to a *theory*. Just as it is reasonable to suppose that there are molecules although we don't *perceive* them, because the hypothesis that there are such things enables us to explain why perceptible things (e.g. balloons) behave as they do, so, they argued, it is reasonable to suppose that physical objects exist although we do not *directly perceive* them, because the hypothesis that there are such things enables us to understand why our sense contents occur in the order in which they do.

This neo-Lockean approach responded to the venerable challenge, 'How can evidence in terms of sensations alone provide inductive reasons for supposing that sensations are caused by material things?' by granting that *instantial* induction cannot do the trick and appealing, instead, to that other mode of inductive argument, so central to modern physical science, the 'hypothetico-deductive method'. I shall shortly be arguing that this appeal was in principle misguided, and that, to put the matter in the form of a paradox, a necessary condition of the success of the appeal is the viability of classical phenomenalism; which would mean, of course, that it only *seems* to get off the ground.

But before making a frontal attack on Hypothetico-Deductive Realism, I shall first show how closely it is related to what I have called the New Phenomenalism. The point is a simple one. The New Phenomenalism can be regarded as that variant of Hypothetico-Deductive Realism which accepts the claim, characteristic of positivistic philosophies of science, that theoretical entities are 'calculational devices' and do not exist in the full-blooded sense in which observables exist. Just as certain philosophers of science were prepared to say that

> atoms, electrons, etc. don't really exist. Frameworks of so-called scientific objects are pieces of conceptual machinery which enable us to derive observational conclusions from observational premises. Frameworks of scientific objects cannot be translatable into the framework of observable fact, not, however, because they refer to *unobservable* entities, but because the very idea that they refer to *anything* is an illegitimate extension to theoretical terms of semantical distinctions appropriate to the language of observable fact

so there is a current tendency, particularly among ex-phenomenalists of the 'classical' variety to argue that

> although the framework of physical objects is not translatable into the framework of sense contents, this is not because it refers to entities over and above sense contents. It is merely a conceptual device which enables us to find our way around in the domain of what we directly observe in a manner analogous to the role played by scientific objects with respect to the domain of the observable in a less stringent sense of this word.

It is my purpose to argue that this won't do, *not* however, on the ground that 'real existence' should not be denied to theoretical entities—though, indeed, I agree that it should not[1]—but rather on the ground that the relation of the framework of physical objects to the framework of sense contents cannot be assimilated to that of a micro-theory to its observation base. To see that this is so requires no more than a bringing together of certain themes from the preceding section of the paper with the standard account[2] of the relationship between theoretical and observational frameworks.[3]

According to what I have referred to as the 'standard' account of the role of theories, a theoretical framework is an uninterpreted deductive system which is co-ordinated with a certain sector of the framework of observable things in such a way that *to each inductively established generalization in this sector there corresponds a theorem in the calculus, and that to no theorem in the calculus does there*

---

[1] See Chapter 4.

[2] This 'standard' account is the one associated with the names of N. Campbell, H. Reichenbach, R. Carnap, and many others. A clear presentation is contained in C. G. Hempel's monograph on 'Concept Formation in the Empirical Sciences', in the *International Encyclopedia of Unified Science* published by the University of Chicago Press.

[3] For our purposes it will be sufficient to note certain formal features of the relationship. That the standard philosophical commentary on these formal features involves serious mistakes is the burden of Chapter 4.

correspond a disconfirmed inductive generalization in the observation framework. The co-ordination is done by 'correspondence rules' which are in certain respects analogous to definitions in that they correlate defined expressions in the theoretical framework (e.g. 'average momentum of a population of molecules') with empirical constructs in the framework of observation ('e.g. pressure of a gas'). The correspondence rules provide only a partial co-ordination (a 'partial interpretation') in that they are not strong enough to permit the derivation of rules co-ordinating the primitive expressions of the theory (e.g. 'molecule') with observational counterparts.

There are many interesting facets to this account of the tie between theoretical and observational discourse. The one which is directly relevant to our argument, however, is expressed by that part of the above summary statement which has been put in italics, according to which the tie between theoretical and observational discourse is a matter of co-ordinating *inductive generalizations* in the latter with theorems in the former. The significance of this point should be obvious. To claim that the relationship between the framework of sense contents and that of physical objects can be construed on the above model is to commit oneself to the idea that there are inductively confirmable generalizations about sense contents which are 'in principle' capable of being formulated without the use of the language of physical things. If the argument of the preceding section was successful, this idea is a mistake.

A few paragraphs ago I made the point that the New Phenomenalism can be construed as that form of Hypothetico-Deductive Realism which denies that theoretical entities 'really exist'. To this it can now be added that the success of the New Phenomenalism presupposes the success of the old. Hence the New Phenomenalism is either mistaken or superfluous; and if it is mistaken neither Classical Phenomenalism nor Hypothetico-Deductive Realism is available as an alternative.

V. DIRECT REALISM: CAUSAL VERSUS EPISTEMIC MEDIATION

What, then, is the alternative? Surely to scrap the premises that led to this impasse by affirming that physical objects are really and directly perceived, and that there is no more basic form of (visual) knowledge than *seeing* physical objects[1] and *seeing that* they are, for example, red and triangular on this side. But to make this affirmation stick it is essential to realize that it does not commit one to the view that the only items in visual experience which can be *directly known* are

[1] Including public flashes of light, and other publicly perceptible visual phenomena.

physical matters of fact. Thus it is perfectly compatible with the idea that people can *directly know* that there seems to be a red and triangular physical object in a certain place, and, I shall argue, with the idea that people can *directly know* that they are having a certain visual impression (e.g. an impression of a red triangle).

What can properly be meant by speaking of a knowing as 'direct'? Clearly the use of the modifier is intended to imply that the knower has not *inferred* what he knows. But this is no mere psychological point. For one only knows what one has a right to think to be the case. Thus to say that someone directly knows that-p is to say that his right to the conviction that-p essentially involves the fact that the idea that-p occurred to the knower in a specific way. I shall call this kind of credibility 'trans-level credibility', and the inference schema

X's thought that-p occurred in manner M
So, (probably) p

to which it refers, as trans-level inference. The problem of spelling out the principles of trans-level inference and explaining their authority is a difficult one which far transcends the scope of this chapter. The above remarks are at best an indication of the direction in which a discussion of the 'directness' of direct knowledge would move. I cannot pass up the opportunity, however, to emphasize once again the inextricable mutual involvement of trans-level and same-level inference in the justification of empirical statements.[1]

The distinction within visual perception between what is directly known and what is not must be carefully drawn if one is not to backslide into representationalism. Thus the fact that there is a sense in which my knowledge that this is a book and in all probability red and rectangular on the *other* side is an *inference* from my perception that this *physical object* is red and rectangular on *this* side, must not be confused with the idea that my knowledge that this is a book, etc., is an inference from a 'direct seeing' of a red, flat, and rectangular 'surface'. We saw in Section I that the perception that this physical object is red, flat, and rectangular on this side is a direct but limited perception of a *physical object*. Its limitations are characteristic of most visual perception, though they are minimized in such cases as the perception of a cube of pink ice.

Again, the fact that my knowledge that I am having a sensation of a red triangle, or that there seems to me to be a red and triangular object over there, is more *secure* than my perception that this physical object is red and rectangular on this side does not impugn the latter's status as direct knowledge. For (*a*) the fact that on occasion I *can* infer that there *is* a physical object in front of me which *is* red and

---

[1] I discuss these matters at length in Chapter 5.

triangular on this side from the fact that there *seems* to me to be a physical object in front of me which is red and triangular on the facing side, or from the fact that I am having a sensation of a red triangle, by no means requires that such knowledge is always a conclusion from such premises; and (*b*) the frameworks of qualitative and existential appearings and of sense impressions are parasitical upon discourse concerning physical things. The latter is obvious in the case of the framework of appearings; it is equally true, if less obviously so, in the case of the framework of sense impressions, as I shall shortly attempt to show.

But before reviewing the status of sense impressions and sense contents in the light of the above remarks, let us remind ourselves that while the direct realist rejects the view we have called classical phenomenalism, he is nevertheless phenomenalistic in the broad sense characterized in the opening paragraphs of this paper. For it holds that although things frequently appear other than they are, they *are* as they appear to be under advantageous circumstances. Thus, to take an example we have already used, a pink ice cube is a directly perceived, public, cold, solid, smooth, pink physical object having the familiar thermal and mechanical causal properties of ice. In advantageous circumstances it.

(*a*) appears to perceivers to be pink and cubical;
(*b*) is responsible for the fact that there appears to these perceivers to be a pink and cubical physical object in front of them;
(*c*) causes these perceivers to have impressions of a pink cube.[1]

Again, the phenomenal world, thus conceived, of public physical objects, sounds, flashes, etc., exhibits a lawfulness which is formulable in phenomenal terms, i.e. in terms of the directly perceptible qualities and relations of these objects. (Generalizations which are in this sense phenomenal must not, of course, be confused with the generalizations in sense content terms which we found to be snares and delusions.) And since there are such generalizations, it is here, rather than at the level of sense contents, that we find a *pou sto* for the apparatus of hypothetico-deductive explanation, the introduction of

---

[1] Much can be learned about the grammar of sense impression talk by reflecting on the fact that we speak of Jones and Smith as having impressions of *a* red triangle. Could it be the *same* red triangle? The fact that it doesn't make sense to say that their impressions are of the *same* red triangle (except as an odd way of saying that they are having impressions of the same kind) is partly responsible for the doctrine of essences. We shall see that the logical form of impressions is not, to use a crude schematism,

xRy, i.e. (impression) R (red triangle)

but

fx, i.e. impression of the *of-a-red-triangle* kind.

theoretical entities to explain why observable (phenomenal) objects behave as they do.

At this point it is imperative that our direct realism be sufficiently critical. And to make it so requires three steps which will be seen to be closely related as the argument proceeds. The *first* step is the abandonment of the abstractive theory of concept formation in all its disguises. In its simplest form this theory tells us that we acquire our basic equipment of concepts from the direct perception of physical objects as determinately red, triangular, etc. Thus, we come to be able to think of an *absent* object as red by virtue of having directly perceived *present* objects *as* red. Having the concept of red pre-supposes the direct perception of one or more objects *as* red, the direct perception *that they are red*. This is at best a misleading half-truth. For while one does not have the concept of red until one has directly perceived something *as* red, *to be* red,[1] the coming to see something as red is the culmination of a complicated process which is the slow building up of a multi-dimensional pattern of linguistic responses (by verbal expressions to things, by verbal expressions to verbal expressions, by meta-linguistic expressions to object-language expressions, etc.) the fruition of which as conceptual occurs when all these dimensions come into play in such direct perceptions as that this physical object (not that one) over here (not over there) is (rather than was) red (not orange, yellow, etc.). Thus, while the coming to be of a basic empirical concept coincides with the coming to be of a direct perception that something is the case, the abstractive theory, as Kant saw, makes the mistake of supposing that the logical space of the concept simply transfers itself from the objects of direct perception to the intellectual order, or better, is transferred by the mind as Jack Horner transferred the plum. The idea that this logical space is an evolutionary development, culturally inherited, is an adaptation rather than a rejection of Kant's contention that the forms of experience are *a priori* and innate.

We are now able to see that his conception of the forms of ex-perience was too narrow, and that non-formal patterns of inference are as essential to the conceptual order as the patterns explored by formal logic, Aristotelian *or* mathematical.

To nail down this point, we must take the *second* step towards an adequately critical direct realism. This step consists in the recognition that the direct perception of physical objects is mediated by the occurrence of sense impressions which latter are, in themselves,

---

[1] A more careful formulation would be 'unless it has appeared *that* there is a red object in front of one': for a child *could* be taught the use of colour words by showing him objects of the wrong colours under conditions of abnormal illumination.

thoroughly non-cognitive. Step *three:* this mediation is causal rather than epistemic. Sense impressions do not mediate by virtue of being known. With these remarks, we pick up once again the discussion of sensations and sense contents which was interrupted that we might lay the ghost of classical phenomenalism.

VI. SENSE IMPRESSIONS AGAIN

From the point of view we have now reached, sense impressions can, *as a first approximation,* be construed as entities postulated by a theory (at first common-sensical, then more and more refined) the aim of which is to explain such general truths as that when people look in mirrors in front of which there is a red object, there seems to them to be a red object 'behind the mirror', and other facts of this kind.

The significance of the phrase 'as a first approximation' will come out in a moment. But before I make any other moves, I must emphasize that the following argument presupposes that the 'calculational device' interpretation of theoretical entities is mistaken.[1] As I see it, to have good reason for holding a theory is *ipso facto* to have good reason for holding that the entities postulated by the theory exist. Thus, when I say that, as a first approximation, sense impressions can be construed as theoretical entities, I am not implying that sense impressions do not 'really' exist. Indeed, I should argue, not only do they really exist (since the theory is a good one), we can *directly* know (not merely infer by using the theory) on particular occasions that we are having sense impressions of such and such kinds. This ability directly to know that one is having a sense impression of a certain kind, however, presupposes the inter-subjective logical space of sense impressions as an explanation of such perceptual phenomena as those referred to in the first paragraph of this section. This fact about the logic of sense impressions also finds its expression in the fact that the training of people to respond conceptually to states of themselves which are not publicly observable requires that trainer and trainee alike (they may be identical) share *both* the intersubjective framework of public objects and the intersubjective theory of private episodes, autobiographical sentences of which (in the present tense) are to acquire the additional role of *Konstatierungen* by becoming symptoms (through conditioning) of inner episodes and recognized as such.[2]

[1] I argue this point in Chapter 4.

[2] A fuller treatment of this topic would tie it in with the discussion of trans-level inference in the preceding section. Furthermore, since the 'theory' of sense-impressions presupposes not only the framework of public physical objects, but also that of perceivers and perceptual episodes, it is clear that an adequate account of the logical status of sense impressions and our knowledge of them

The crucial move in understanding the logic of sense impressions talk, however, is a reprise of a point made early in the chapter when, in the course of discussing the 'of-ness' of sense impressions, it was pointed out that if

(a) S has an impression of a red triangle

had the sense of

(b) S is in that state brought about in normal circumstances by the influence of red and triangular physical objects on the eyes

then the truth of (a) would not entail the existence of anything red and triangular.[1] Even if, as will become clear, this account of the meaning of (a) won't do as it stands, the logical point that (a) has the form

S is in a state of kind ϕ, i.e. ϕ (S)

rather than

(S) R (y)

remains true when it has been corrected.

What, then, is a visual impression (e.g. of a red triangle), if it is not simply that state of a perceiver which is normally brought about by the influence of a red and triangular physical object on the eye? The answer is implicit in the above characterization of the framework of sense impressions as a 'theory' certain sentences of which have been enriched by a reporting role. For even where a theoretical state of affairs can be given a definite description (in Russell's sense) in terms of the phenomena it is introduced to explain, this definite description cannot exhaust the sense of the relevant theoretical expression. If it did, the theory would be no theory at all, but at most the claim that a theory can be found. Clearly what gives sense to the primitive expressions of a formalized theory are in the first place the postulates which connect theoretical states of affairs with one another and in the second place the correspondence rules which connect the deductive system with the phenomena to be explained. Thus, to grasp the sense of the phrase 'impression of a red triangle', we must see how

[1] Though, as was also pointed out, if the locution 'a red and triangular sense content exists' were introduced as the equivalent of 'Someone has a sensation of a red triangle' then we could say that the truth of (a) entails the existence of something red and triangular. But what he would be saying would be exciting only if misunderstood.

presupposes an account of such private episodes as seeing or seeming to see that there is a red and triangular physical object in front of one. There is a discussion of these topics in Chapter 5.

this phrase functions in the 'postulates' of the framework of sense impressions.

Here we run up against the obvious fact that the framework of sense impressions is *not* a formalized theory. Its 'postulates' are formulated in terms of analogies the force and limitations of which must be tickled out piecemeal by exploring the logic of sample uses of the framework. Such an explanation, which, if it were not for the danger of terminological confusion, might be called the phenomenology of sense impressions, is an arduous and time-consuming task which lies beyond the scope of this discussion. In any case, my concern is with broad issues of philosophical strategy, and even a large-scale map of the jungle of perceptual epistemology can bring decisive clarification. I shall therefore limit myself to a summary statement of what I take to be the outcome of such an exploration.

One item stands out above all others. Analysis reveals a *second* way in which the sense of 'impression of a red triangle' is related to the sense of 'red and triangular physical object'. The first has already been characterized by relating 'S has an impression of a red triangle' to 'S is in that state, etc.' The second consists in the fact that visual impressions of red triangles are conceived as items which are analogous *in certain respects* to physical objects which are red and triangular on the facing side.[1] Here it is essential to note that the analogy is between sense impressions and physical objects and not between sense impressions and *perceptions of* physical objects. Failure to appreciate this fact reinforces the temptation to construe impressions as *cognitive* and *conceptual* which arises from the misassimilation of the 'of-ness' of sensation to the 'of-ness' of thought.[2] It is also essential to note that the analogy is a trans-category analogy, for it is an analogy between a state and a physical thing. Failure to appreciate this fact reinforces the temptation to construe

S has an impression of a red triangle

as having the form 'xRy', where y is a strange kind of particular[3] analogous in certain respects to the facing side of a red and triangular physical object.

[1] That only one side is relevant to the analogy accounts for the fact that the red triangle of an impression of a red triangle has no back side.

[2] The correct interpretation of the 'of-ness' of thought does resemble, in an important respect the 'of-ness' of sense impressions as analysed above. To oversimplify, a thought *of* p turns out to have the form a thought of the ·p· kind, where the latter are episodes which, whatever their character as scientific objects, play a role analogous to that played in English by tokens of 'p'. This similarity, however, highlights rather than obscures the essential difference between the intentionality of thought and the pseudo-intentionality of sense impressions.

[3] See the previous footnote but one.

With these warnings out of the way, we can turn our attention to the positive analogy. It has two parts:

(*a*) Impressions of red, blue, yellow, etc., triangles are implied to resemble-and-differ in a way which is formally analogous to that in which physical objects which are triangular and (red or blue or yellow, etc.) on the facing side resemble-and-differ; and similarly *mutatis mutandis* in the case of other shapes.

(*b*) Impressions of red triangles, circles, squares, etc., are implied to resemble-and-differ in a way which is formally analogous to that in which physical objects which are red and (triangular or circular or square, etc.), on the facing side resemble-and-differ; and similarly *mutatis mutandis* in the case of other colours.

In effect, these analogies have the force of postulates implicitly defining two families of predicates, 'ϕ_1' . . . 'ϕ_n' and 'ψ_1' . . . 'ψ_n', applicable to sense impressions, one of which has a logical space analogous to that of colours, the other a logical space analogous to that of the spatial properties of physical things.

In addition to these analogies, the framework of sense impressions involves a causal hypothesis, the general character of which can be indicated by saying that the fact that blue objects appear in certain circumstances to be green, and that in certain circumstances there appear to be red and triangular objects in front of people when there is no object there at all, are explained by postulating that in these circumstances impressions are brought about of the kinds which are normally brought about by blue objects (in the first case) and by red and triangular objects (in the second).

It has sometimes been suggested that the basic mode of existence of colours is 'adverbial', i.e. that the basic mode of existence of blue is expressed by the context 'S senses bluely'. This suggestion is typically developed into the idea that physical blue is the power to cause normal perceivers to sense bluely. From our standpoint this suggestion, although it contains an important insight, puts the cart before the horse and misconstrues as basic a 'colour' concept which is derived by analogy from colour concepts pertaining to physical objects. The violence done by this construction is reflected both by its paradoxical ring, and the reluctance of its sponsors to extend the same interpretation of the way in which shapes are involved in the impressions of sense.

The sound core of the adverbial interpretation of perceptible qualities consists in the fact that verbal nouns relating to inner episodes presuppose the corresponding verbs. Thus:

x has a circular$_s$ impression

(where 'circular$_s$' is the analogical predicate corresponding to 'circular$_p$') would, from the standpoint of a rational reconstruction, presuppose the form

> x is impressed circularly$_s$

or, in the active voice,

> x senses circularly$_s$

Notice that these analogical adverbs are not adverbs of manner comparable to 'quickly', 'clearly' etc. They combine with 'senses' or 'is impressed' to constitute the verb, thus 'senses-circularly$_s$', and 'is-impressed-circularly$_s$'.

VII. BEYOND DIRECT REALISM: A KANTIAN CRITIQUE

The argument to date has been an attempt to spell out the relations which exist between the framework of sense impressions and the framework of physical objects, and by so doing to show exactly why neither classical phenomenalism nor hypothetico-deductive phenomenalism (let alone hypothetico-deductive realism) is a tenable position. But though the primary aim of the argument has been negative, it is clear that the argument up to this point can be more positively construed as a defence of direct realism, and therefore of a position which is phenomenalistic in that broad sense which amounts to the idea that things are, in standard circumstances, what they seem to be. It must now be pointed out, however, that if the argument to date is sound, it has a momentum which must sweep away even this broad sense of phenomenalism. If it were halted at this point, it would be inconsistent with its presuppositions.

A review of the later stages of the argument discloses that on two occasions essential use was made of premises concerning the status of theoretical frameworks. On the first occasion, the point was made that the correspondence rules of a theory correlate 'theorems' in the language of the theory with inductive generalizations in the framework of the phenomena the theory is designed to explain. Since the point to be made was simply that if there are no inductive generalizations in sense content terms, then the framework of physical objects cannot be construed as a theory analogous to the theories of microphysics, a closer scrutiny of just what it is that theories accomplish by correlating theorems with inductions and just what this correlation amounts to was not called for. On the second occasion, however, an additional theme was introduced, namely, the idea that to have good reasons for espousing a theory which postulates the existence of unobservable entities is to have good reason for saying that these entities really exist. And this idea, as we have noted, runs up against the objection that the entities postulated by theories of this type are and can be nothing but 'computational devices' for deriving observation framework conclusions from observation framework premises, and that even this role is 'in principle' dispensable. For, it is argued, every success achieved by the theory has the form

$$T \rightarrow (O_i \supset O_j)$$

where '$O_i \supset O_j$' is a generalization which relates two kinds of situation definable in the observation framework, and which, though derivable from the theory (including its correspondence rules), must in principle be capable of *independent* inductive confirmation or disconfirmation. Now, in my opinion, it must be admitted that *if* the observation framework permits the formulation of inductive generalizations—statistical or non-statistical—which hold within limits which can be accounted for in terms of such concepts as accuracy of measurement and experimental error, i.e. the variance of which is purely 'epistemic', then the positivistic interpretation of theoretical entities is inescapable. But must we grant the antecedent of this hypothetical? Of course, if we knew that the conceptual framework of perceptible physical objects in space and time had an absolute authenticity, i.e. that the physical objects of the perceptible macroworld as conceived by the direct realist really existed, we would know that any testable consequences to which a theory could call attention would be law-like uniformities, statistical or otherwise, in the behaviour of physical objects. *But do we know that the physical objects of the perceptible world really exist? and is the behaviour of macro-objects even statistically lawful in a way which leaves to theories only the job of deriving these laws from its postulates and correspondence rules?* I argue in Chapter 4 that the answer to both these questions is no, and that the negative answer to the *second*, together with the fact that *theories explain why physical objects come as close as they do to conforming to statistical laws which have a purely 'epistemic' variance*, is what justifies the negative answer to the *first*.

On the view I propose, the assertion that the micro-entities of physical theory really exist goes hand in hand with the assertion that *the macro-entities of the perceptible world do not really exist*. This position can be ruled out of court only by showing that the framework of perceptible physical objects in space and time has an authenticity which guarantees a parasitical status for the subtle and sophisticated framework of physical theory. I argue in Chapter 5 that the very conception of such absolute authenticity is a mistake. And if this contention is correct, the premise to the effect that theoretical entities really exist,[1] which was used in explaining the status of sense impressions, requires us to go one step further, once its presuppositions are made explicit, and argue that the physical objects, the perception of which they causally (but not epistemically) mediate, are unreal. It commits us, in short, to the view that the perceptual world is phenomenal in something like the Kantian sense, the key difference being that the real or 'noumenal' world which supports the 'world of appearances' is not a *metaphysical* world of unknowable things in themselves, but simply the world as construed by scientific theory.

To say that there are no such things as the physical objects of the perceptible world is, of course, to make a point *about* the framework of physical objects, not *in* it. In this respect it differs from the assertion that there are no centaurs. As long as we are *in* the framework of physical objects, of course, we evaluate statements about particular physical objects and the perception of them in terms of the criteria provided by the framework. Direct Realism gives an excellent reconstruction of the ways in which physical things, perceivers, sense impressions, perceptions *of* physical objects, perceptions *that* they are thus and so, privileged access to one's own thoughts, feelings, and sense impressions, etc., etc., fit together to make one framework of entities and knowledge about these entities. To say that the framework is phenomenal in a quasi-Kantian sense, as I am doing, is to say that science is making available a more adequate framework of entities which *in principle*, at least, could serve all the functions, and, in particular, the perceptual functions of the framework we actually employ in everyday life. It is not, of course, to say that there is good reason to put it to this use. Indeed, there are sound methodological reasons for not teaching ourselves to respond to perceptual situations in terms of constructs in the language of theoretical physics. For while this could, in principle, be done, the scientific quest is not yet over, and even granting that the main outlines are blocked in, the framework of physical objects in space and time, shaped over millenia of social evolution, provides, when accompanied by correct philosophical commentary, a firm base of operations with which to correlate the developing structure of scientific theory, refusing to embrace any stage without reserve as our very way of perceiving the world, *not* because it wouldn't be a *better* way, but because the better is the enemy of the best.

---

[1] i.e. that to have good reason for espousing a theory is *ipso facto* to have good reason for saying that the entities postulated by the theory really exist.

VIII. BEYOND SENSE IMPRESSIONS

Let me bring this already overloaded chapter to a close by discussing a topic which will bring all of its main themes into one focus. Suppose someone to raise the following objection, 'I can understand the temptation to say that there really are such things as clouds of electrons, etc., but why conclude from this that the physical objects of ordinary perceptual experience don't really exist? Why not simply say that we must revise our conception of them and recognize that while *as perceptible physical objects* they have the qualities of sense, *as systems of imperceptible particles* they have the properties ascribed to them by scientific theory?' I reply that this won't do at all. The attempt to melt together Eddington's two tables does violence to both and justice to neither. It requires one to say that one and the same thing is both the *single* logical subject of which an *undefined* descriptive predicate (e.g. 'red') is true,[1] and a *set of logical subjects* none of which is truly characterized by this predicate, thus raising all the logical puzzles of 'emergence'. And if, as is often done, 'red' as predicable of physical objects is tacitly shifted from the category of *primitive* descriptive predicates (where it properly belongs) to the category of *defined* descriptive predicates by being given the sense of 'power to cause normal observers to have impressions of red', then the very stuffing has been knocked out of the framework of physical objects, leaving not enough to permit the formulation of the very laws which are implied by the existence of these powers, and which are pre-supposed by the micro-theory which might be invoked to explain them.

The point I have in mind is essentially the same as that on which our critique of classical phenomenalism was based. For to suppose that the qualities of physical things are *powers* is to overlook the fact that the occurrent properties of physical objects are presupposed by the laws which authorize *both* the ascription to 'circumstances'[2] of powers to manifest themselves in the sense contents of percipients (stressed by power phenomenalism) *and* the assertion of subjunctive conditionals about the sense contents which would eventuate for a perceiver were such and such (phenomenal) conditions to be satisfied (stressed by classical phenomenalism).[3] As a matter of fact, the

[1] That the form of predication is complex ('O is now red at place p') does not impugn the undefined or primitive character of 'red'.

[2] The concept of the 'circumstances of perception' is eviscerated by Power Phenomenalism. 'Circumstances' serve merely as the logical subjects of powers and have no other actuality.

[3] Indeed, we saw, the 'uniformities' which do obtain presuppose not only the general principles which relate impressions of sense to impact of the physical environment on the sense organs, but also *particular* matters of fact concerning the physical environment and sensory equipment of the perceiver in question.

subjunctive conditionals of classical phenomenalism can be reformulated in the language of 'powers' as the 'passive' counterparts of the 'active' powers of 'circumstances' to manifest themselves in the immediate experience of perceivers, i.e. as the powers of perceivers to be appeared to by the 'circumstances'.[1]

But if the alternative to saying that physical objects are both single logical subjects for primitive predicates like 'red' and sets of logical subjects for micro-theoretical predicates is the position, defended in the preceding section, that physical objects with their occurrent qualities don't really exist, where do their qualities, e.g. colour, really exist? What really exists and has them, if physical objects do not? This question requires an answer in three stages.

The *first* stage consists in the statement that *nothing* really has them. The logic of the colour predicates of the framework of physical objects is such that only a physical object[2] *could* have colour in this sense of the term, and *ex hypothesi* there are none.

The *second* stage consists in pointing out that our argument has led us to the idea that while visual sense impressions are not, of course, coloured in the sense in which physical objects are coloured, they do have intrinsic properties which have a logical space formally similar to the logical space of the colours of physical things. And this suggests that in the scientific picture of the world the counterparts of the colours of the physical object framework will turn out to be aspects, in some sense, of the percipient organism.

The *third* stage begins with the reminder that when we abandon the framework of physical objects, our conception of a *person* cannot remain inviolate. In the pre-theoretical framework of physical objects, living things, and persons, the situation is much as presented in classical philosophy at its best. A person is a single logical subject, not a set of logical subjects. The Aristotelian includes the physical aspects of persons in this single logical subject by attributing only a 'virtual' existence to the physical parts of the body construed as logical subjects. This requires that statements about what the legs, hands, etc., of a person are doing be construed as expressible in terms which mention no logical subject other than the person as a whole.

---

[1] Needless to say, only a realistic interpretation of this manifesting is entitled to the ordinary connotation of the terms 'active' and 'passive' as expressing ways of looking at causal transactions. In power phenomenalism they are to be interpreted in terms of the difference between the active and passive voices of the verb 'C manifests itself to S in (sense content) x' (i.e. 'C manifests itself to S in x', and 'S is manifested to by C in x'. Since, as was pointed out above, the circumstance, C, is merely the logical subject of the 'active' powers, power phenomenalism is in immediate danger of collapsing into solipsism.

[2] The existence of public flashes of red light complicates this point, but changes nothing of principle.

For the Aristotelian, the term 'leg' as referring to a part of a person, and the term 'leg' as referring to amputated limbs would have radically different *logical* grammars. The Platonist, for a number of reasons into which we need not enter, prefers a framework in which a person consists of a person and a body, thus permitting the latter to be an actual plurality of logical subjects.[1] The Platonist hesitates as to whether sense impressions belong to the body or to the *psyche*. On the whole, he takes the latter course, though constantly tempted to divide the *psyche* into a team consisting of a rational, a sentient, and (perhaps) a vital *psyche*. The former course, as is implied by the preceding footnote, would require an Aristotelian approach to the sentient body.

The purpose of the above quasi-historical remarks is to remind the reader that in the common sense framework of persons and physical objects as we have described it, thoughts and sense impressions are adjectival to single logical subjects (as contrasted with sets of logical subjects). What are we to make of these single logical subjects in the light of scientific theory? And, in particular, is there any reason to suppose that in a new synthesis there will be logical subjects for yet other analogues of the colour predicates (and geometrical predicates) of the framework of physical objects? If so, these counterparts twice removed would not be *adverbial* (as in the last analysis are the predicates of sense impressions)[2] and we could say with good conscience that it is these logical subjects which 'really have the colours and shapes which physical objects seem to have'. But what a difference there would be between what we would mean by saying this, and the sense it has as usually advanced.

The basic roadblock is the unity of the person as the subject of conceptual activities. To do justice to this unity we must, it would seem, take it to be ultimate and irreducible, and, in effect, commit ourselves to either a Platonic or an Aristotelian ontology of the 'I'. That this is not so is the fruit of a line of thought initiated by Kant.[3] As in the case of the status of the framework of physical objects, he sketched the *form* of a solution, giving it, however, a *metaphysical* content which must be replaced by scientific considerations. The

---

[1] A consistent development of this position requires that all the primitives of the conceptual framework to which the body belongs be such as to apply to the ultimate logical subjects of the frame. A set of logical subjects can have a property (e.g. *juxtaposed*) which the elements do not and cannot have, but the attribution of the property to the set must be explicable, in principle, in terms of predicates applicable to the members of the set. In other words, predicates applicable to the set cannot be primitive.

[2] See the concluding paragraph of Section VI.

[3] Cf. his treatment of the 'I think' in the *Transcendental Deduction of the Categories* and in the *Paralogisms*.

heart of the matter is the fact that the irreducibility of the 'I' within the framework of first person discourse (and, indeed, of 'you' and 'he' as well) is compatible with the thesis that persons can (in principle) be exhaustively described in terms which involve no reference to such an irreducible logical subject. For the description will *mention* rather than *use* the framework to which these logical subjects belong. Kant saw that the transcendental unity of apperception is a form of experience rather than a disclosure of ultimate reality. If persons are 'really' multiplicities of logical subjects, then unless these multiplicities used the conceptual framework of persons there would be no persons. But the idea that persons 'really are' such multiplicities does not require that concepts pertaining to persons be *analysable into* concepts pertaining to sets of logical subjects. Persons may 'really be' bundles, but the concept of a person is not the concept of a bundle.

Suppose, then, we take a neo-Hobbesian line with respect to the conceptual activities of persons, and construe these activities on the model of the computational activities of an electronic robot, one, however, which is capable of responding to its own computational activities in the language of persons.[1] What would be the implications of this line for the status of sense impressions? The immediate consequence is obvious. By 'identifying' in the above manner a person with a plurality of logical subjects, i.e. the constituent parts of the 'computer', we have undermined the logic of sense impressions. For whether these parts be construed as material particles or as nerve cells, the fact that they are a plurality precludes them from serving either jointly or separately as the subjects of the verb 'to sense red-triangle-wise'. We must therefore either introduce another logical subject (an immaterial substance) to do this work, or turn each sensing into a logical subject in its own right, i.e. introduce a new category of entity ('phantasms' or 'sensa' we might call them) with predicates the logical space of which is modelled on that of visual impressions, as the latter was modelled on that of coloured and shaped physical objects. To one who is confronted by these alternatives, the

[1] The philosophical problems involved in reconciling such a neo-Hobbesian line with the meaningfulness of human speech, with the Cartesian argument that thinking cannot be a physical process because we can clearly and distinctly understand what we mean by a thought without thinking of thoughts as physical processes, and with the fact that thinking involves the recognition of standards or norms, are far too complex to be more than mentioned in this chapter. I have, however, discussed them at length in Chapters 5 and 11, and in a correspondence with Roderick Chisholm which appears as an appendix to Volume II of the *Minnesota Studies in the Philosophy of Science*, edited by Herbert Feigl, Michael Scriven, and Grover Maxwell and published by the University of Minnesota Press (Minneapolis: 1958).

familiar facts about the dependence of sense impressions on brain processes are bound to point in the second direction, which is, in effect, that of the epiphenomenalism of Hobbes.

Epiphenomenalism is a far more radical dualism than the Cartesian dualism of matter and mind. For the latter is, at least in intention, a dualism of interacting substances. Phantasms, being the counterparts of the having of sense impressions, are fleeting particulars with none of the attributes of thinghood. They neither act nor are acted on, but simply occur. Their impotence is logical, rather than a puzzling empirical fact. They are the prototype of the 'events' into which modern philosophers have been prone to analyse things and the interactions of things. And if these analyses reflect a misunderstanding of the place of events in the framework of things, they have far more merit if they are viewed as attempts to construct a framework alternative to the framework of interacting things; alternative, yet, in the last analysis, equivalent, a different, but philosophically illuminating mode of representation.[1] In such a framework, changing things become genidentical patterns of 'events' and those irreducible metrical *Undinge*, Space and Time, become abstract forms of order.

These considerations suggest that epiphenomenalism, with its disparate categories of *things* (whether the material particles of Hobbes or the nerve cells of modern Neuro-physiology) and 'phantasms', is a half-way house; that a unified picture requires a translation of the physiological context in which epiphenomena occur into the framework of 'events'. With this in mind, let us strain our feeling for conceptual possibilities to the limit by raising the question which more than any other must fascinate the philosopher who takes science seriously and has not succumbed to any of the reductive fallacies exposed in earlier sections of this chapter. How are we to conceive the relationship between the sequence of micro-physical 'events' which constitute a brain's being in the physical state appropriate to the occurrence of a red and triangular sensum, and the sequence of 'events' which is the sensum? or, to put it somewhat differently, what would be the relation between terms for sensa and the primitive vocabulary of a micro-physics capable of dealing with inorganic phenomena? To ask this question is to realize that it is a disguised demand for the general lines of a completed scientific theory of sentient organisms. The philosopher's task can only be that of clearing the way by exposing mistaken presuppositions and metaphysical assumptions. I shall bring this chapter to a close by examining some relevant dogmas.

[1] For a detailed comparison of the framework of things and the framework of 'events' see my essay on 'Time and the World Order' in Volume III of the *Minnesota Studies in the Philosophy of Science*.

In the first place, there is the dogma that sensa cannot be in physical space. This conviction seems to be a misinterpretation of the logical truths that *impressions* are not in physical space (which is clear) and that the pseudo-objects 'of' which we 'have' impressions are not in physical space. But if sensa are in physical space—not, of course, the space of physical objects, but of their micro-theoretical counterparts—*where* are they? They are, we have seen, the counterparts of impressions, those states of perceivers which are postulated to explain certain familiar facts of perception and misperception. The obvious, but crude, answer, then, is that they are 'in the brain'. A better answer is that they are where the relevant brain *events* are, for the phrase 'in the brain' has the logical grammar of 'thing inside thing', e.g. lump of sugar in a sugar bowl. If it is retorted that sensa do not *seem* to be where these brain events are, the answer is twofold: (*a*) Brain events are not perceived, so that nothing could *seem* to stand in *any* relation to them. (*b*) If there is a sense in which sensa can be said to 'seem' to be on the surfaces of physical things, it is a highly derived and meta-phorical sense which must not be confused with that in which red objects can seem to be black, or there can seem to be a book behind the mirror. Strictly speaking, sensa do not *seem*. They belong to a highly sophisticated account of the world, and simply do not belong to the framework of perceptual consciousness. It is, indeed, true, from the standpoint of this sophisticated framework that when a person sees that a physical object is red and triangular on the facing side, part of what is 'really' going on is that a red and triangular sensum exists where certain micro-theoretically construed cortical processes are going on; but it would be a mixing of frameworks to say, with some philosophers, that people 'mistake sensa for physical objects', or 'take sensa to be *out there*'. For these latter ways of putting it sug-gest that sensa belong to the conceptual framework in terms of which people experience the world.

Another familiar line of thought which requires close scrutiny is the move from the premise that where there is metrical *form* there must be *content*, to the conclusion that the 'qualities of sense' are the content of physical things. The premise is true. The conclusion is true of the physical world of common experience, though awkwardly formulated. But the argument is obviously invalid unless a premise is added to the effect that the 'qualities of sense' are the *only* contents available to embody metrical form. Certainly they are the only contents which play this role in the framework of perceptible things. But what of the framework of physical theory? Granted that the metrical properties of the framework of perceptible things are anchored in the qualities of touch and sight (a fact which Berkeley saw, but put to bad use), must the metrical forms of micro-physical process be similarly embodied in colours and other qualities of sense? Are nuclear events 'patterns of colour which obey the laws of micro-physics' as physical objects are colour solids which obey the laws of macro-physics? Must the colour predicates of the framework of perceptible things be tacitly present (though with modified grammar) as primitive predicates of the micro-theory of inorganic things? (We have granted that they will be present in the micro-theory of sentient organisms.) To ask these questions is to answer them in the negative. A primitive predicate in a theory is meaningful if it does its theoretical job; and to do this job, as we have seen, it does not have to stand for a perceptible feature of the world.

The phrase 'partial interpretation', often used in explaining the status of micro-theories, plays into the hands of 'structuralism' by suggesting that a theory falls short of complete meaningfulness to the extent that the correspondence rules fall short of enabling a complete translation of the theory into the observation framework with which it is correlated. The picture is that of a skeleton which has some flesh on its bones. A philosopher who subscribes to the realistic interpretation of theories, but is taken in by this picture, will be tempted to cover the bones which science leaves uncovered with the qualities of sense, supplementing the 'partial interpretation' of theoretical terms given by science with a *metaphysical* interpretation. But all such moves rest on a failure to distinguish between correspondence rules, which do *not* stipulate identities of sense, and definitions, which do. Only if correspondence rules were (partial) definitions, would the meaning of theoretical terms be incomplete. It is perhaps not too misleading to say that the meaning of a theoretical term is its use; and that if there is a sense in which there are degrees of meaningfulness for theoretical terms, it is a matter of the extent to which the theory satisfies the criteria of a good theory, rather than of degrees of translatability into the observation language.

If these contentions are sound, then there is no *a priori* reason to suppose that the content for the metrical forms of micro-physical process must be the sensa of sophisticated perception theory. And to say that this content must be *like* sensa is *false* if it means that they must be colours which nobody has seen, and *trivial* if it simply means that they are like colours in being dimensions of content.

The third and final point I wish to make is that while it would be a category mistake to suppose that sensa can be construed as a dimension of neural process as long as one is working within a framework of thing-like particulars, whether nerve cells, organic compounds, or micro-physical particles, the same considerations do not rule out the possibility that when an ideally completed neurophysiology interprets the physical concepts it employs in terms of the spatio-temporally punctiform particulars of an ideally completed micro-physics, sensa might fall into place as one qualitative dimension among others, one, however, which exists only in neurophysiological contexts.[1] Needless to say, the idea that colours might in this sense be a dimension of neural process must not be confused with the idea that nerves are coloured inside like chocolate candies.

To sum up this final section, the scientist, in his attempt to understand perception, must oscillate between the 'Aristotelian' framework in which his problems are initially posed, and in which one logical subject, the person, has sense impressions, and a working 'Hobbesian' framework in which, the unity of the person having been broken down into a plurality of logical subjects, the impressions become logical subjects in their own right, though of an attenuated and epiphenomenal kind. A unified picture of the perceiver can be found only at the beginning and at the end of the scientific quest. It has been my purpose to show that we are not without some glimpse of the end.

[1] For an elaboration of this, and related, themes, see 'The Concept of Emergence', by Paul Meehl and Wilfrid Sellars, in Volume I of *Minnesota Studies in the Philosophy of Science*.

4

THE LANGUAGE OF
THEORIES[1]

I. INTRODUCTION

1. MY purpose is to see what fresh light, if any, is thrown on old familiar puzzles about the empirical (or factual) meaningfulness of theoretical statements and the reality of theoretical entities by certain views on related topics which I have sketched in Chapters 5, 8, and 11 and in a recent paper.[2] These views concern (a) the interpretation of basic semantical categories; (b) the role of theories in scientific explanation.

2. The term 'theory', it is generally recognized, covers a wide variety of explanatory frameworks resembling one another by that family resemblance which is easy to discern but most difficult to describe. Each type of theory presents its own problems to the philosopher of science, and although current literature shows an increasing tendency to reflect the realities of scientific practice rather than antecedent epistemological commitments, the type of theory with which I shall be concerned—namely, that which postulates unobserved entities to explain observable phenomena—is still suffering from the effects of a Procrustean treatment by positivistically oriented philosophies of science.

3. I shall assume, at least to begin with, that *something* like the standard modern account of this type of theory is correct. And in

[1] I wish to acknowledge the invaluable assistance I have received from friends and colleagues who gave me their comments on an earlier draft of this chapter. I am particularly grateful to Professor Adolf Grünbaum for a page by page critique with respect to both exposition and substance, without which this chapter would have fallen far shorter than it does of saying what I wanted it to say.

[2] 'Counterfactuals, Dispositions and the Causal Modalities', in Volume II of *Minnesota Studies in the Philosophy of Science*, edited by H. Feigl, M. Scriven, and G. Maxwell, and published by the University of Minnesota Press (Minneapolis: 1958).

view of the distinguished names associated with this account, it would be most surprising if it were not close to the truth. It is built upon a distinction between: (*a*) the vocabulary, postulates, and theorems of the theory as an uninterpreted calculus; (*b*) the vocabulary and inductively testable statements of the observation framework; (*c*) the 'correspondence rules' which correlate, in a way which shows certain analogies to inference and certain analogies to translations, statements in the theoretical vocabulary with statements in the language of observation. Each of these categories calls for a brief initial comment.

4. The theoretical language contains, in addition to that part of vocabulary which ostensibly refers to unobserved entities and their properties, (*a*) logical and mathematical expressions which have their ordinary sense, and (*b*) the vocabulary of space and time. (Query: can we say that the latter part of the theoretical vocabulary, too, has its ordinary sense? to use the material mode, are the space and time of kinetic theory the same as the space and time of the observable world, or do they merely 'correspond' to them? In relativity physics it is surely the latter.)

5. The nontheoretical language with which a given theory is connected by means of correspondence rules may itself be a theory with respect to some other framework, in which case it is nontheoretical only in a relative sense. This calls up a picture of levels of theory and suggests that there is a level which can be called nontheoretical in an absolute sense. Let us assume for the moment that there is such a level and that it is the level of the observable things and properties of the everyday world and of the constructs which can be explicitly defined in terms of them. If following Carnap we call the language appropriate to this level the *physical-thing language*, then the above assumption can be formulated as the thesis that the physical-thing language is a nontheoretical language in an absolute sense. The task of theory is then construed to be that of explaining inductively testable generalizations formulated in the physical-thing language, which task is equated with *deriving* the latter from the theory by means of the correspondence rules.

6. Correspondence rules typically connect defined expressions in the theoretical language with definable expressions in the language of observation. They are often said to give a 'partial interpretation' of the theory in terms of observables, but this is at best a very misleading way of talking; for whatever may be true of 'correspondence rules' in the case of physical geometry,[1] it is simply not true, in the case of

---

[1] The case of geometry is not independent, for geometrical concepts must be defined for micro-entities. Even if abstraction is made from this, there remains the problems of extending idealized congruences to situations in which the congruences are physically impossible—for example, the centre of the sun.

theories which postulate unobserved micro-entities, that a correspondence rule stipulates that a theoretical expression is to *have the same sense* as the correlated expression in the observation language. The phrase 'partial interpretation' suggests that the only sense in which the interpretation fails to be a translation is that it is partial; that is, that while *some* stipulations of identity of sense are laid down, they do not suffice to make possible a complete translation of the theoretical language into the language of observation. It is less misleading to say that while the correspondence rules *co-ordinate* theoretical and observational sentences, neither they nor the derivative rules which are their consequences place the primitives of the theory into one-man correspondence with observation language counterparts. This way of putting it does not suggest, as does talk of 'partial interpretation', that if the partial correlation could be made complete, it would *be* a translation. (That in some cases a 'complete correlation' might be *transformed* into a translation by reformulating correspondence rules as semantical stipulations is beside the point.)

7. For the time being, then, we shall regard the correspondence rules of theories of the kind we are examining as a special kind of verbal bridge taking one from statements in the theoretical vocabulary to statements in the observation vocabulary and vice versa. The term 'correspondence rule' has the advantage, as compared with 'bridge law', 'co-ordinating definition', or 'interpretation', of being neutral as between various interpretations of the exact role played by these bridges in different kinds of theory.

8. Puzzles about the meaning of theoretical terms and the reality of theoretical entities are so intimately bound up with the status of correspondence rules that to clarify the latter would almost automatically resolve the former. This fact is the key to my strategy in this chapter. But before attempting to develop a suitable framework for this analytical task, a few remarks on contemporary treatments of correspondence rules are in order. Until recently it was customary, in schematic representations of theories, to keep the postulates and theorems of the theory, the empirical generalizations of the observation framework, and the correspondence rules linking theory with observation in three distinct compartments. This had the value of emphasizing the methodologically distinct roles of these three different types of statement. On the other hand this mode of representation carried with it the suggestion of an *ontological* (as contrasted with methodological) dualism of theoretical and observational universes of discourse which a more neutral presentation might obviate. Thus it has recently been the tendency to list the correspondence rules with the postulates of the theory, distinguishing them simply as those postulates which include observational as well as theoretical expres-

sions.[1] This procedure can do no harm if the relevant methodological and semantical distinctions ultimately find adequate expression in some other way.

II. SOME SEMANTICAL DISTINCTIONS[2]

9. That 'meaning' has many meanings is an axiom of contemporary philosophy. Of these, some are logical in a narrow sense of the term—thus, naming, denoting, connoting. Others are logical in a somewhat more inclusive sense. Thus there is the methodological sense in which a meaningful expression may be scientifically meaningless, have no scientific point—thus an arbitrarily defined function of measurable quantities. Still other varieties of meaning, though 'semantical' in a broad sense of the term, are the concern of psychology and rhetoric rather than of logic in even the most inclusive sense of this term.

10. It is with those senses of meaning which directly pertain to logical theory in a narrow sense that I shall be concerned in this part of my argument. I shall attempt to sketch a coherent treatment of basic semantical categories which may throw light on questions of meaning and existence pertaining to theoretical discourse. I shall make no attempt to provide a formalized theory of meaning elegantly reduced to a minimum of primitive notions and propositions. Such attempts are premature and dangerous in any area if they are based on misinterpretations of the initial explicanda. Nowhere, in my opinion, have these dangers been realized more disastrously than in some recent theories of meaning.[3]

11. Thus, instead of attempting to explicate the various logical

---

[1] This method of presentation is in certain respects analogous to that of drawing no formal distinction between definitions, on the one hand, and postulates and theorems of the form 'a = b' on the other in the development of a calculus, leaving it to subsequent reflection to determine how the latter are to be parcelled out into definitional and nondefinitional identities.

[2] The substantive argument of the chapter resumes with Section III. The present section draws semantical distinctions which are later used to give a precise formulation to the problem of the reality of theoretical entities and its correct solution. It may, however, be omitted without prejudice to the main thrust of the argument, and should, perhaps, in any case be omitted on a first reading.

[3] I have in mind (*Introduction to Semantics*) Carnap's formalization of semantical theory in terms of a primitive relation of designation which holds between words and *extralinguistic* entities. This reconstruction commits one to the idea that if a language is meaningful, there exists a domain of entities (the *designata* of its names and predicates) which exist independently of any human concept formation. Of course, Carnap's semantical theory as such involves no commitment as to what this domain includes, but if one adds the premise that the physical thing *language* is meaningful, one is committed to the idea that the framework of observable physical things and their properties has an absolute reality which, if the argument of the present paper is sound, it does not have.

senses of 'meaning' in terms of a single primitive notion—for example, *the designation relation* or *denotes*—I shall simply give what I hope is a defensible account of the various kinds or modes of meaning and of how they are inter-related. I shall distinguish the following:

(*a*) Meaning as translation
(*b*) Meaning as sense
(*c*) Meaning as naming
(*d*) Meaning as connotation
(*e*) Meaning as denotation

12. The expression 'means' as a translation rubric is easily confused with its other uses. The essential feature of this use is that whether the translation be from one language to another, or from one expression to another in the same language, the translated expression and the expression into which it translates must have the same use.[1] Thus if we are to use 'means' in this sense we must say *not*

(1) (The English adjective) 'round' means *circularity*

but

(2) (The English adjective) 'round' means *circular*

where 'round' and 'circular' are both *predicative* expressions having the same sense. The essential difference between (2) and

(3) (The English adjective) 'round' has the same use as (the English adjective) 'circular'

is that to say of two expressions in a language that they have the same use—as in (3)—is not to *give* that use; (2) gives the use of 'round' by presupposing that 'circular' is in the active vocabulary of the person to whom the statement is made and, normally, of the person making the statement, whereas (3) does not.

13. The translation use of 'means' gives expression to the fact that the same linguistic role can be played by different expressions. It should perhaps be added that since statements involving this sense of 'means' are used to *explain* the use of one expression in terms of the use of others, they are usually not reversible. Thus,

(4) 'triangle' means *plane figure bounded by three straight lines*

and

(5) 'plane figure, etc.' means *triangle*

are not equally appropriate. With this qualification, to say that an expression has meaning in this sense is to commit oneself to explaining

[1] To speak of two expressions as having the same use is to presuppose a criterion of sameness of use which separates relevant from irrelevant differences in use. Clearly, differences which are irrelevant to one context of inquiry may be relevant to another.

THE LANGUAGE OF THEORIES

its use by means of another expression with the same use. Such a statement as

(6) 'Red' means *red*

can perhaps be construed as a limiting case which gets its sense by implying that 'red' *has* a use, and by implying that this use is not capable of explanation in terms of more basic expressions.

14. Closely related to 'means' as a translation rubric is 'means' in the sense of 'expresses the concept . . .' In this case we must say not

(2) (The English adjective) 'round' means *circular*

but

(1) (The English adjective) 'round' means *circularity*

or, as I shall put it,

(7) (The English adjective) 'round' *expresses the concept* circularity.[1]

Notice that it would be incorrect to put this by saying that

(8) 'Round' *names* the concept Circularity

for this is done by 'roundness'. Thus we have

(9) 'Round' means[2] *circular*.

(10) 'Round' expresses the concept Circularity
(11) 'Roundness' names the concept Circularity.

15. Again,

(12) (The Italian word) 'Parigi' *means* Paris

in the translation sense of 'means'. But here, of course, it is also true that

(13) (The Italian word) 'Parigi' *names* Paris

It is even true that

(14) (The Italian word) 'Parigi' *expresses the concept* Paris or, to use a medieval locution, Pariseity.

---

[1] In what follows, I shall choose my examples of meaning statements of the first two kinds without regard to whether they would be good explanations of usage in standard conditions. I shall also drop the explicit reference to the language to which an expression belongs when the context makes it clear which language is intended.

[2] From now on I shall use 'means' in examples only in the sense of the translation rubric.

For, as we shall see, we must recognize individual concepts as well as universal concepts (and, indeed, other kinds of concept as well), and can do so without ontological discomfort.

16. Again, we shall say that

(15) 'Parigi' *connotes* the property of being the capital of France and, in general, names connote those properties the possession of which are criteria for being properly referred to by the name in question. The distinction between the concept expressed by a name and the concepts or properties connoted by the name is of the utmost importance as illustrations will shortly make evident. The concept can, within limits, remain the same although the criteria change or become differently weighted.[1] Let me give two further sets of illustrations for the distinctions I have been drawing.

(16) (The Italian word) 'Icaro' means *Icarus*

(17) (The Italian word) 'Icaro' *names* nothing real (or actual)

(18) (The Italian word) 'Icaro' expresses the concept Icarus (or Icaruseity)

(19) (The Italian word) 'Icaro' connotes the property of being the son of Daedalus.

An illustration in terms of a common rather than a proper name would be

(20) 'Cheval' means *horse*

(21) 'Cheval' expresses the concept Horsekind

(22) 'Cheval' connotes the property of having four legs

(23) 'Cheval' names Man o' War, Zev, etc.

17. Finally, denoting must be distinguished from naming. Thus, we can say that

(24) 'round' *denotes* circular things

but does not name them. The closest thing to a name of circular things *qua* circular would be the common noun expression 'circular thing'. Again, for 'round' to denote, in this sense, circular things is not the same as for it to denote the class of circular things. If we wish to use the term 'denotes' in such a way that

(25) 'round' denotes the class of circular things,

we must be careful to distinguish between *naming* a class and *denoting* a class, for 'circular' is not the name of anything, let alone a class.

[1] See Wittgenstein's discussion of essentially the same point in *Philosophical Investigations*, § 79. See also § 47 of my essay 'Counterfactuals, Dispositions and the Causal Modalities', op. cit.

18. I shall return to the task of distinguishing and relating the above modes of meaning shortly. But first I want to point out that nothing would seem to be less controversial nor more trivial than that theoretical terms can be said to have meaning or be meaningful where the sense of 'meaning' envisaged is that which pertains to translation. Surely in the sense in which

(9) 'Round' means *circular*

so that there is something which 'round' means—that is, *circular*—it is equally true that

(26) (The German word) 'Molekuel' means *molecule,*

so that there is something which 'Molekuel' means—that is, *molecule.* All that would seem to be required is that such statements as (26) be made to people who have the theoretical expression which serves as *explicans* in their active vocabulary.

19. Notice, however, that he must have it in his active vocabulary as an expression which belongs to a theoretical language. Thus if theoretical expressions functioned *merely* as expressions in a *purely* syntactical game, which they obviously do not, it would be patently incorrect to bring them into *meaning* statements, whether as *explicandum* or as *explicans.*

20. But to make this point, sound though it be, is not to prove that theoretical terms in established theories 'have meaning' in any more interesting sense than that they are translatable. Nor, strictly, does it establish that they have meaning in even this limited sense. For we are immediately faced by the new question: When is an expression in what is prima facie a language functioning enough unlike a *mere* counter to warrant saying that we have *translated* it, as opposed to merely correlating it with another counter which we know how to deploy? For even if we were to decide that theoretical expressions were too much like pieces in a game to be properly talked about in terms of meaning, we could explain their use by means of a rubric which might also be used in explaining an oddly shaped chess piece by correlating it with this piece in our set. We would then say that the use of translation talk in connection with theoretical expressions is best regarded as a metaphorical extension of the translation rubric to contexts which resemble translations in certain respects, but are not translations proper.

21. Thus the fact that it would be odd to deny that expressions in a French formulation of kinetic theory translate into their English equivalents is by no means a conclusive reason for holding that the language of kinetic theory is a language in the full-blooded sense of

113

the term. Might not theoretical terms have meaning in the translational mode, without having it in any of the other modes we have distinguished? After all, even such a properly linguistic expression as the French 'helas!' translates into 'alas!' but certainly names nothing, has no connotation, and expresses no concept.[1] And 'oui' translates into 'yes'.

22. If we turn first to meaning as expressing a concept, we must face the question as to what exactly is conveyed by such a statement as

(10) 'Round' expresses the concept Circularity

or

(26) 'Socrates' expresses the individual concept Socrateity.

Without further ado, I shall propose a straightforward, if radical, thesis to the effect that the sense of (10) is but little different from that of the translation statement

(9) 'Round' means *circular*.

The difference consists essentially in the fact that whereas in (9) the adjective 'circular' is used to *give* the role shared by 'round' and 'circular' and does not mention the role by means of a *name* (though it implicitly describes it as the role played in our language by 'circular'),[2] in (10) we find a *name* for this role, a name which is formed in a special way from a sign design which plays the named role in our language.[3]

23. But if this account is correct, then to say that

(27) 'Molekuel' expresses the concept of a molecule

and, in general, to makes statements of the form

(28) '. . . .' expresses the concept—

about theoretical expressions is simply another way of drawing upon the fact that theory-language roles, like observation-language roles,

---

[1] It may, nevertheless, be said to express a sense. See below, § 23.

[2] See 12 above.

[3] See my 'Quotation Marks, Sentences and Propositions', in Volume X of *Philosophy and Phenomenological Research*, 1950. (Added in proof) Strictly speaking 'circularity' is not the name of the role played by 'circular' in English, but is rather to be construed as a singular term formed from a metalinguistic common noun for items which play this role (e.g. there are several 'circular's on this page), as 'the pawn' is formed from an object language common noun for items which play a certain role in chess. 'Circularity', then, is the name of a linguistic type in the sense in which 'the pawn' is the name of a chess piece. Similar considerations apply to other abstract singular terms, e.g. 'that Chicago is large'. For an elaboration of this interpretation of abstract singular terms, see my 'Abstract Entities', in the June 1963 issue of *The Review of Metaphysics*.

can be played by more than one set of sign designs. We must, however, be a bit more discriminating than in our discussion of the translation rubric, in view of the fact that not all properly linguistic roles are *conceptual*. Thus, while it makes sense to say that 'round' expresses the concept [property] Roundness, that 'and' expresses the concept [operation] of Conjunction and that '*notwendig*' (in German) expresses the concept [modality] Necessity, etc., we can scarcely say that 'Hélas!' (in French) expresses the concept Alas, though we *can* say

(29) 'Hélas!' (in French) expresses the sense Alas

For this gives expression to the fact that 'Hélas!' plays in French the role that is played by the English word 'Alas!' and is equivalent to

(30) 'Hélas!' (in French) plays the role played by 'Alas!' in our language.

Just where we are to draw the line between expressions which express concepts, and those which, though properly linguistic, do not, is a nice question which I shall make no systematic attempt to answer.[1]

24. The above remarks may reconcile us to the idea that theoretical expressions can correctly be said to express concepts. But do they *name* anything? Do they *denote* anything?

25. Names, we have seen, connote criteria and name the objects which satisfy these criteria. We have distinguished between two radically different kinds of object which we may illustrate, respectively, by Socrates and by Roundness. Roughly the distinction is between those objects which are concepts and those which are not.[2]

---

[1] If one begins by listing a variety of types of expression which can without too much discomfort be said to express concepts—noun expressions, predicative expressions, logical connectives, quantifiers—one is likely to conclude that to express a concept is to be relevant to inferences which can be drawn from statements in which the expression occurs; and to note that 'All men are mortal, alas!' has no more inferential force (pragmatic implications aside) than 'All men are mortal'. It would be because 'good', 'bad', 'right', 'wrong', etc., do play roles in practical reasoning that they could properly be said to express concepts. I think that this approach is sound, but to be carefully worked out it would require a precise account of the difference between such an obviously nonconceptual expression as a left-hand parenthesis, and logical operators, such as 'and'. Ordinary distinctions between 'categorematic' and 'syncrategorematic' expressions lump together a distinction of kind with distinctions of degree.

[2] (Added in proof) My use of 'concept' corresponds closely to Frege's use of 'sense'. It is the predicative subset of concepts, as I am using this term, which correspond (differences of theory aside) for Frege's concepts. My 'concepts' are distributive objects in the sense in which the pawn is a distributive object. See footnote 3 on p. 114 above and the articles to which it refers.

26. Nonconceptual objects can be roughly divided into *basic* and *derivative*. Derivative objects can be informally characterized as those which are referred to by noun expressions that can be eliminated by contextual definition. In this sense events are derivative objects in the physical-thing framework. Statements about the events in which physical things participate can be reduced to statements in which all the nonpredicative expressions refer to physical things.[1] In the framework of kinetic theory, as classically presented, the basic objects (granted that we *can* speak of theoretical objects) would be individual molecules.

27. To know that a name names something is to know that some object satisfies the connotation of the name and by doing so satisfies the concept which is expressed by the name. To know this is to know that which is expressed by the existence statement formed from the name and the verb 'to exist'. Thus, in the case of common names, with which we shall primarily be concerned,

(31) Ns exist

(32) (Ex) x satisfies the criteria connoted by 'N'

(33) (Ex) x satisfies the concept of an N

(34) (Ex) 'N' names x

are different ways of making the same statement.

28. It will be clear from the above that I am committing myself to the view that *only those existentially quantified statements in which the quantified variable takes names of objects as its substituends have the force of existence statements*. The fact that its substituends are names of objects correlates the variable with a range of objects. On this account

(35) (Ef) Socrates is f

would not be an existence statement; for the variable 'f' does not in the above sense have a range of objects. The substituends for 'f' are not *names*, but *predicates*. The variable 'f' may indeed be said to have a *meaning range*, that is, the range expressed by

red, circular, wise, mortal, etc.

But *meanings unlike concepts are not objects*, and talk of meanings springs from the purely translational sense of 'means'.[2]

29. Notice that there is, of course, an object in the neighbourhood of 'wise', but its name is 'Wisdom', and it falls in the range of

---

[1] See my essay 'Time' in Volume III of the *Minnesota Studies in the Philosophy of Science*. Minneapolis: University of Minnesota Press. 1962.

[2] This point is elaborated in Chapter 8.

the concept variable 'f-ness'. Unlike (35), the closely related statement

(36) (E f-ness) Socrates exemplifies f-ness

does satisfy the above mentioned necessary condition for being an existence statement. But if the preceding account is correct, expressions of the form 'f-ness' name linguistic objects; and while, given that a language is rich enough to express the sense of 'Socrates exemplifies wisdom' as well as 'Socrates is wise', these two statements are necessarily equivalent, it would be simply a mistake to assume that the quantified *object language* statement

(35) (Ef) Socrates is f

has the sense of an existence statement asserting the existence of an extralinguistic abstract entity.

30. As a parenthetical remark it may be noted that it follows from the above that the Ramsey sentence of a theory is not an existence statement. (The Ramsey sentence of a formalized theory is, roughly, the sentence formed from the conjunction of its postulates by replacing all theoretical predicates by variables and prefixing the conjunction by these variables quantified 'existentially'.) Even though the Ramsey sentence does imply—given that we are willing to talk about the concepts expressed by theoretical terms—the existence of concepts or properties satisfying the conditions expressed by the postulates of the theory, the question whether these concepts or properties are *theoretical* or *observational* is simply the question whether constants substituted for the variables quantified in the Ramsey sentence can be construed, *salva veritate*, as belonging to the observational vocabulary.

31. According to the above analysis, then, to know that molecules exist is to know that

(37) (Ex) x is $\phi_1 \ldots \phi_n$

where being $\phi_1 \ldots \phi_n$ is a sufficient condition in the framework of the theory for somebody to satisfy the concept of a molecule. The question arises, under what circumstances can we be said to know this? Note that while (37) is a statement in the language of the theory, it need not be construed as either a postulate or a theorem of the theory. What the theory does is provide us with a licence to move from statements in the observation language asserting the existence of a certain physical state of affairs at a certain time and place to statements asserting the presence of a group of molecules at that time and place. To know that molecules exist is to be entitled to the observational premises, and to be entitled to the licence to move from this premise to the theoretical conclusion. To be entitled to this licence is for the theory to be a good theory.

32. Carnap's distinction[1] between internal and external questions of existence is relevant here. For even if the question, 'Are there molecules?' is one which cannot be answered without going outside the language of the theory in the narrow sense of this phrase, it *is* internal to the framework provided by the functioning of a theory as a theory. And as such it can be contrasted with the 'external' question, 'Is there good reason to adopt the framework of molecules?'

III. MICROTHEORETICAL EXPLANATION

33. It would seem, then, that if kinetic theory is a *good* theory, we are entitled to say that molecules exist. This confronts us with a classical puzzle. For, it would seem, we can also say that if our observation framework is a *good* one, we are entitled to say that horses, chairs, tables, etc., exist. Shall we then say that *both* tables and molecules exist? If we do, we are immediately faced with the problem as to how theoretical objects and observational objects 'fit together in one universe'. To use Eddington's well-worn example, instead of the one table with which pretheoretical discourse was content, we seem forced to recognize two tables of radically different kinds. Do they both *really* exist? Are they, perhaps, *really* the same table? If only one of them *really* exists, which?

34. It has frequently been suggested that a theory might be a *good* theory, and yet be *in principle* otiose. (Not otiose; *in principle* otiose.) By this is meant that theory might be known on general grounds to be the sort of thing which, in the very process of being perfected, generates a *substitute* which, in the limiting case of perfection, would serve all the scientific purposes which the perfected theory could serve. The idea is, in brief, that the cash value at each moment of a developing theory is a set of propositions in the observation framework known as *the observational consequences of the theory*, and that once we separate out the heuristic or 'pragmatic' role of a theory from its role in explanation, we see that the observational consequences of an ideally successful theory would serve all the scientific purposes of the theory itself.

35. If we knew that theories of the kind we are considering were *in principle* otiose, we might well be inclined to say that there *really* are no such things as molecules, and even to abandon our habit of

---

[1] See his essay on 'Empiricism, Semantics, and Ontology', printed as an appendix in his *Meaning and Necessity*, 2nd Edition, Chicago: University of Chicago Press, 1959,

talking about theoretical expressions in semantical and quasi-semantical terms. We might refuse to say that theoretical terms express concepts, or name or denote objects; we might refuse to say that theoretical objects exist. And we might well put this by claiming that theoretical languages are *mere* calculational devices. This resolution of the initial puzzle has at least the merit of being neat and tidy. It seems to carve theoretical discourse at a joint, and to cut off a superfluous table with no loss of blood.

36. I shall argue that this is an illusion. But what is the alternative? One possible line of thought is based on the idea that perhaps the observational level of physical things (which includes one of the tables) has been mistakenly taken to be an 'absolute'. It points out that if the framework of physical things were in principle subject to discard, the way would be left open for the view that perhaps there is only one table after all; this time, however, the table construed in theoretical terms.

37. I think that this suggestion contains the germ of the solution to the puzzle; but only if it is developed in such a way as to free it from the misleading picture—the levels picture—which generates the puzzle. It is, I believe, a blind alley if, accepting this picture, it simply argues that the observational framework *is itself a theory*, and that the relation of the framework of microphysical theory to it is implicitly repeated in its relation to a more basic level—the level, say, of sense contents. For though this account might well enable one to dispense in principle with the physical objects which serve as mediating links between sense contents and molecules (the latter two being capable, in principle, of being directly connected), nevertheless we should still be left with *two* tables, a cloud of molecules on the one hand, and a pattern of actual and possible sense contents on the other.

38. My line will be that the true solution of our puzzle is to be found by rejecting as in paragraph 36 the unchallengeable status of the physical-thing framework, *without, however, construing this framework as a theory with respect to a mere basic level.* My strategy will be to bring out the misleading and falsifying nature of the *levels* picture of theories. Thus I shall not be concerned, save incidentally and by implication, with the widespread view that the relation of physical-object discourse to sense-impression discourse is analogous to that of micro-theories in physics to the framework of physical things.

39. There are two main sources of the temptation to talk of theories in terms of levels: (i) In the case of microtheories, there is the difference of size between macro- and micro-objects. With respect to this I shall only comment that the entities postulated by a theory need not be smaller than the objects of which the behaviour is to be explained.

Thus, it is logically possible that physical objects might be theoretically explained as singularities arising from the interference of waves of cosmic dimensions. (ii) The more important source of the plausibility of the *levels* picture is the fact that we not only explain *singular matters of empirical fact* in terms of *empirical generalizations*; we also, or so it seems, explain these generalizations themselves by means of *theories*. This way of putting it immediately suggests a hierarchy at the bottom of which are

Explained Nonexplainers,

the intermediate levels being

Explained Explainers

and the top consisting of

Unexplained Explainers

Now there is clearly *something* to this picture. But it is radically misleading if (*a*) it finds too simple—too simple in a sense to be given presently—a connection between explaining an explanandum and finding a defensible general proposition under which it can either be subsumed,[1] or from which it can be derived with or without the use of correspondence rules; (*b*) it is supposed that whereas in the observation framework inductive generalizations serve as principles of explanation for particular matters of fact, microtheoretical principles are principles of explanation *not* (*directly*) *for particular matters of fact in the observation framework but for the inductive generalizations in this framework* (*the explaining being equated with deriving the latter from the former*) *which in their turn serve as principles of explanation for particular matters of fact.*[2]

40. This latter point is the heart of the matter; for to conceive of the *explananda* of theories as, simply, *empirical laws* and to *equate* theoretical explanation with the derivation of empirical laws from theoretical postulates by means of logic, mathematics, and correspondence rules is to sever the vital tie between theoretical principles and particular matters of fact in the framework of observation.

[1] For a sustained critique of the subsumption picture of scientific explanation from a somewhat different point of view, see Michael Scriven's papers in Volumes I and II of the *Minnesota Studies in the Philosophy of Science*, and his unpublished doctoral dissertation (Oxford) on explanation.

[2] From a purely formal point of view, of course, one could derive ('explain') the observational consequence (C) of an observational antecedent (A) by using the theoretical theorem '$A_T \longrightarrow C_T$' and the correspondence rules '$A \longleftrightarrow A_T$' and '$C \longleftrightarrow C_T$' without using the inductive generalization '$A \longrightarrow C$'. This, however, would only disguise the commitment to the autonomous or 'absolute' (*not* unrevisible) status of inductive generalizations in the observation framework.

Indeed, the idea that the aim of theories is to explain *not* particular matters of fact *but rather* inductive generalizations is nothing more nor less than the idea that theories are in principle dispensable. For to suppose that particular observable matters of fact are the proper *explananda* of inductive generalizations in the observation framework and of these only, is to suppose that, even though theoretical considerations may lead us to formulate new hypotheses in the observational framework for inductive testing and may lead us to modify, subject to inductive confirmation, such generalizations as have already received inductive support, the *conceptual framework* of the observation level is autonomous and immune from theoretical criticism.

41. The truth of the matter is that the idea that microtheories are designed to explain empirical laws and explain observational matters of fact only in the derivative sense that they explain explainers of the latter rests on the above-mentioned confusion between explanation and derivation. To avoid this confusion is to see that theories about observable things *do not 'explain' empirical laws in the manner described, they explain empirical laws by explaining why observable things obey to the extent that they do, these empirical laws*;[1] that is, they explain why individual objects of various kinds and in various circumstances in the observation framework behave in those ways in which it has been inductively established that they do behave. Roughly, it is because a gas is—in some sense of 'is'—a cloud of molecules which are behaving in certain theoretically defined ways, that it obeys the *empirical* Boyle–Charles law.

42. Furthermore, theories not only explain why observable things obey certain laws, they also explain why in certain respects their behaviour obeys no inductively confirmable generalization in the observation framework. This point can best be introduced by contriving an artificially simple example. It might, at a certain time, have been discovered that gold which has been put in *aqua regia* sometimes dissolves at one rate, sometimes at another, even though as far as can be observationally determined, the specimens and circumstances are identical. The microtheory of chemical reactions current at that time might admit of a simple modification to the effect that there are two structures of microentities each of which 'corresponds' to gold as an observational construct, but such that pure samples of one dissolve, under given conditions of pressure, temperature, etc., at a different rate from samples of the other. Such a modification of the theory would explain the observationally unpredicted variation in the rate of dissolution of gold by saying that samples of observational

---

[1] The same is true in principle—though in a way which is methodologically more complex—of micro-microtheories about microtheoretical objects.

gold are mixtures of these two theoretical structures in various proportions, and have a rate of dissolution which varies with the proportion. Of course, if the correspondence rules of the theory enables one to derive observational criteria for distinguishing between observational golds of differing theoretical compositions, one would be in a position to replace the statement that gold dissolves in *aqua regia* sometimes at one rate, sometimes at another, by laws setting fixed rates for two *varieties* of observational gold and their mixtures. But it is by no means clear that the correspondence rules (together with the theory) *must* enable one to do this in order for the theory to be a good theory. The theory must, of course, explain why observational chemical substances do obey *some* laws, and the theoretical account of the variation in the rate at which gold dissolves in *aqua regia* must cohere with its general explanation of chemical reactions, and not simply postulate that there is an unspecified dimension of variation in the microstructure of gold which corresponds to this observed variation. But this is a far cry from requiring that the theory lead to a confirmable set of empirical laws by which to replace the initial account of random variations.

43. Thus, microtheories not only explain why observational constructs obey inductive generalizations, they explain what, as far as the observational framework is concerned, is a random component in their behaviour, and, in the last analysis it is by doing the latter that microtheories establish their character as indispensable elements of scientific explanation and (as we shall see) as knowledge about what *really* exists. Here it is essential to note that in speaking of the departure from lawfulness of observational constructs I do not have in mind simply departure from all-or-none lawfulness ('strict universality'). Where microexplanation is called for, correct macroexplanation will turn out (to eyes sharpened by theoretical considerations) to be in terms of 'statistical' rather than strictly universal generalizations. But this is only the beginning of the story, for the distinctive feature of those domains where microexplanation is appropriate is that in an important sense such regularities as are available are not statistical *laws*, because they are unstable, and this instability is explained by the microtheory.

The logical point I am making can best be brought out by imagining a domain of inductive generalizations about observables to be idealized by discounting errors of measurement and other forms of experimental error. For once these elements in the 'statistics' have been discounted, our attention can turn to the logico-mathematical structure of these idealized statistical statements. And reflection makes clear that where microtheoretical explanation is to be appropriate, these statements must have (and this is a logical point) a

122

mathematical structure which is not only compatible with, but calls for, an explanation in terms of 'microvariables' (and hence *micro-initial conditions*: the nonlawlike element adumbrated in the preceding paragraph) such as the microtheory provides. This point is but the converse of the familiar point that the irreducibly and lawfully statistical ensembles of quantum-mechanical theory are mathematically inconsistent with the assumption of hidden variables.

To sum up the above results, microtheories explain why inductive generalizations pertaining to a given domain *and any refinement of them within the conceptual framework of the observation language* are at best approximations to the truth. To this it is anticlimatic to add that theories explain why inductive generalizations hold only within certain boundary conditions, accounting for discontinuities which, as far as the observation framework is concerned, are brute facts.

44. My contention, then, is that the widespread picture of theories which equates theoretical explanation with the derivation of empirical laws is a mistake, a mistake which cannot be corrected by extending the term 'law' to include a spectrum of inductively established statistical uniformities ranging from 100 per cent to 50-50. Positively put, my contention is that theories explain laws by explaining why the objects of the domain in question obey the laws that they do to the extent that they do.

IV. CORRESPONDENCE RULES AGAIN

45. Suppose it to be granted that this contention is correct. What are its implications for the puzzles with which we began? The first point to be made is that if the basic schema of (micro-) theoretical explanation is,

> Molar objects of such and such kinds obey (approximately) such and such inductive generalizations because they *are* configurations of such and such theoretical entities.

then our puzzles are focused, as it were, into the single puzzle of the force of the italicized word 'are', *Prima facie* it stands for identity, but how is this identity to be understood? Once again we are led to ask the methodological counterpart question, that is, what *is* a correspondence rule?

46. One possible but paradoxical line of thought would be that an effective microtheory for a certain domain of objects for which inductive generalizations exist is from the standpoint of a philosopher interested in the ontology of science, a framework which aspires to *replace* the observation framework. The observation framework

would be construed as a poorer explanatory framework with a better one available to replace it. But thus boldly conceived, this replacement would involve dropping both the empirical generalizations and the individual observational facts to be explained by the theory, and would seem to throw out the baby with the bath. The observation framework would be construed as a poorer explanatory framework with a better one available to replace it. Before we ask what could be meant by 'replacing an observation framework by a theoretical framework', let us note one possible reaction to this suggestion. It might be granted that this is the sort of thing that is done when one theoretical framework is 'reduced' to another, and that the notion of the replaceability of a microframework by a micro-microframework is a reasonable explanation of the force of such a statement as

Ions behave as they do because they *are* such and such configurations of subatomic particles.

Yet the parallel explanation of the force of 'are' where the identity relates not theoretical entities with other theoretical entities, but theoretical entities with observational entities might be ruled out of court. Once again we would have run up against the thesis of the inviolability of observation concepts on which the rejection of the replacement idea is ultimately grounded. This thesis, however, is false.

47. Nor is it satisfactory to interpret the proposal in paragraph 46 as follows: The framework of physical things is a candidate for replacement *on the ground that* it is actually a common sense theoretical framework, and *qua* theoretical framework may be replaced by another. For unless the conception of the framework of physical things as a replaceable explanatory framework goes hand in hand with an abandonment of the levels picture of explanation, it leads directly to the idea that below the level of physical-thing discourse is a level of observation in a stricter sense of this term, and of confirmable inductive generalizations pertaining to the entities thus observed.

48. The notion of such a level is a myth. The idea that sense contents exhibit a lawfulness which can be characterized without placing them in a context either of persons and physical things or of micro-neurological events is supported only by the conviction that it must be so if we are not to flaunt 'established truths' about meaning and explanation. Since my quarrel on this occasion is with these 'established truths', I shall not argue directly against the idea that there is an autonomous level of sense contents with respect to which the framework of physical things plays a role analogous to that of a theory in the levels of explanation sense.

49. My answer to the question of paragraph 45 requires that

we distinguish between two interpretations of the idea that the framework of physical things is an explanatory framework capable in principle of being replaced by a better explanatory framework. One of these interpretations is the view on which I have just been commenting. The alternative, in general terms, will clearly be a view according to which the framework of physical things is a replaceable theory-like structure in a sense that does not involve a commitment to a deeper 'level' of observation and explanation.

50. The groundwork for such a view has already been laid with the above rejection of identification of theoretical explanations with derivation. But what is a correspondence rule if it is *not* simply a device for deriving laws from theoretical postulates? We have seen that a correspondence rule is not a partial definition of theoretical terms by observation terms. Nor, obviously, is it a definition of observation terms as currently used by means of theoretical terms. But might it not be construed as a *redefinition* of observation terms? Such a redefinition would, of course, be a dead letter unless it were actually carried out in linguistic practice. And it is clear that to be fully carried out in any interesting sense, it would not be enough that sign designs which play the role of observation terms be borrowed for use in the theoretical language as the defined equivalents of theoretical expressions. For this would simply amount to making these sign designs ambiguous. In their new use they would no longer be *observation* terms. The force of the 'redefinition' must be such as to demand not only that the observation-sign design correlated with a given theoretical expression by syntactically interchangeable with the latter, *but that the latter be given the perceptual or observational role of the former so that the two expressions become synonymous by mutual readjustment.* And to this there is an obvious objection: *the meaningful use of theories simply does not require this usurpation of the observational role by theoretical expressions.* Correspondence rules thus understood would remain dead letters.

51. But if the above conception of correspondence rules as 'redefinitions' will not do as it stands, it is nevertheless in the neighbourhood of the truth; for if correspondence rules cannot be regarded as implemented redefinitions, can they not be regarded as statements to the effect that certain redefinitions of observation terms would be in principle acceptable. This would be compatible with the fact that the redefinitions in question are implemented only in the syntactical dimension, no theoretical expressions actually acquiring the observational-perceptual roles they would have to have if they were to be synonyms of other expressions playing this role. This view has at least the merit of accounting for the peculiar character of correspondence rules as expressing more than a factual equivalence but less than an

identity of sense. It would explain how theoretical complexes can be unobservable, yet 'really' identical with observable things.

52. On one classical interpretation, correspondence rules would appear in the material mode as statements to the effect that the same objects which have observational properties also have theoretical properties, thus identifying the denotation, but not the sense, of certain observational and theoretical expressions. On another classical interpretation, correspondence rules would appear in the material mode as asserting the coexistence of two sets of objects, one having observational properties, the other theoretical properties, thus identifying neither the denotation nor the sense of theoretical and observational expressions. According to the view I am proposing, correspondence rules would appear in the material mode as statements to the effect that the objects of the observational framework *do not really exist—there really are no such things*. They envisage the *abandonment* of a sense and its denotation.

53. If we put this by saying that to offer the theory is to claim that the theoretical language could beat the observation language *at its own game* without loss of scientific meaning, our anxieties are aroused. Would not something be *left out* if we taught ourselves to use the language of physical theory as a framework in terms of which to make our perceptual responses to the world? I do not have in mind the role played by our observational concepts in our practical life, our emotional and aesthetic responses. The repercussions here of radical conceptual changes such as we are envisaging would no doubt be tremendous. I have in mind the familiar question: would not the abandonment of the framework of physical things mean the abandonment of the *qualitative* aspects of the world?

54. To this *specific* question, of couse, the answer is yes. But it would be a mistake to generalize and infer that *in general* the replacement of observation terms by theoretical constructs must 'leave something out'. Two points can be touched on briefly. (*a*) I have suggested elsewhere[1] that the sensible qualities of the common sense world, omitted by the physical theory of material things, might reappear in a new guise in the microtheory of sentient organisms. This claim would appear in the material mode as the claim that the sensible qualities of things *really* are a dimension of neural activity. (*b*) There is an obvious sense in which scientific theory cannot leave out qualities, or, for that matter, relations. Only the most pythagoreanizing philosopher of science would attempt to dispense with descriptive (that is, nonlogical) predicates in his formulation of the scientific picture of the world.

---

[1] Chapter 1, section VI; also Chapter 3, section VII.

5

EMPIRICISM AND THE PHILOSOPHY OF MIND

I. AN AMBIGUITY IN SENSE-DATUM THEORIES

I PRESUME that no philosopher who has attacked the philosophical idea of givenness or, to use the Hegelian term, immediacy, has intended to deny that there is a difference between *inferring* that something is the case and, for example, *seeing* it to be the case. If the term 'given' referred merely to what is observed as being observed, or, perhaps, to a proper subset of the things we are said to determine by observation, the existence of 'data' would be as noncontroversial as the existence of philosophical perplexities. But, of course, this just is not so. The phrase 'the given' as a piece of professional—epistemological—shoptalk carries a substantial theoretical commitment, and one can deny that there are 'data' or that anything is, in this sense, 'given' without flying in the face of reason.

Many things have been said to be 'given': sense contents, material objects, universals, propositions, real connections, first principles, even givenness itself. And there is, indeed, a certain way of construing the situations which philosophers analyse in these terms which can be said to be the framework of givenness. This framework has been a common feature of most of the major systems of philosophy, including, to use a Kantian turn of phrase, both 'dogmatic rationalism' and 'sceptical empiricism'. It has, indeed, been so pervasive that few, if any, philosophers have been altogether free of it; certainly not Kant, and, I would argue, not even Hegel, that great foe of 'immediacy'. Often what is attacked under its name are only specific varieties of 'given'. Intuited first principles and synthetic necessary connections were the first to come under attack. And many who today attack 'the whole idea of givenness'—and they are an increasing number—are really only attacking sense data. For they transfer to other items, say physical objects or relations of appearing, the characteristic features

127

of the 'given'. If, however, I begin my argument with an attack on sense-datum theories, it is only as a first step in a general critique of the entire framework of givenness.

2. Sense-datum theories characteristically distinguish between an *act* of awareness and, for example, the colour patch which is its *object*. The act is usually called *sensing*. Classical exponents of the theory have often characterized these acts as 'phenomenologically simple' and 'not further analysable'. But other sense-datum theorists—some of them with an equal claim to be considered 'classical exponents'— have held that sensing is analysable. And if some philosophers seem to have thought that if sensing is analysable, then it cannot be an *act*, this has by no means been the general opinion. There are, indeed, deeper roots for the doubt that sensing (if there is such a thing) is an act, roots which can be traced to one of two lines of thought tangled together in classical sense-datum theory. For the moment, however, I shall simply assume that however complex (or simple) the fact that x is sensed may be, it has the form, whatever exactly it may be, by virtue of which for x to be sensed is for it to be the object of an act.

Being a sense datum, or sensum, is a relational property of the item that is sensed. To refer to an item which is sensed in a way which does not entail that it *is* sensed, it is necessary to use some other locution. *Sensibile* has the disadvantage that it implies that sensed items could exist without being sensed, and this is a matter of controversy among sense-datum theorists. *Sense content* is, perhaps, as neutral a term as any.

There appear to be varieties of sensing, referred to by some as *visual sensing, tactual sensing*, etc., and by others as *directly seeing, directly hearing*, etc. But it is not clear whether these are species of sensing in any full-blooded sense, or whether 'x is visually sensed' amounts to no more than 'x is a colour patch which is sensed', 'x is directly heard' than 'x is a sound which is sensed', and so on. In the latter case, being a *visual sensing* or a *direct hearing* would be a relational property of an act of sensing, just as being a sense datum is a relational property of a sense content.

3. Now if we bear in mind that the point of the epistemological category of the given is, presumably, to explicate the idea that empirical knowledge rests on a 'foundation' of non-inferential knowledge of matter of fact, we may well experience a feeling of surprise on noting that according to sense-datum theorists, it is *particulars* that are sensed. For what is *known*, even in non-inferential knowledge, is *facts* rather than particulars, items of the form *something's being thus-and-so* or *something's standing in a certain relation to something else*. It would seem, then, that the sensing of sense contents *cannot* constitute knowledge, inferential *or* non-inferential; and if so, we may well ask,

what light does the concept of a sense datum throw on the 'foundations of empirical knowledge'? The sense-datum theorist, it would seem, must choose between saying:

(a) It is *particulars* which are sensed. Sensing is not knowing. The existence of sense data does not *logically* imply the existence of knowledge, or

(b) Sensing *is* a form of knowing. It is *facts* rather than *particulars* which are sensed.

On alternative (a) the fact that a sense content was sensed would be a *non-epistemic* fact about the sense content. Yet it would be hasty to conclude that this alternative precludes *any* logical connection between the sensing of sense contents and the possession of non-inferential knowledge. For even if the sensing of sense contents did not logically imply the existence of non-inferential knowledge, the converse might well be true. Thus, the non-inferential knowledge of particular matter of fact might logically imply the existence of sense data (for example, *seeing that a certain physical object is red* might logically imply *sensing a red sense content*) even though the sensing of a red sense content were not itself a cognitive fact and did not imply the possession of non-inferential knowledge.

On the second alternative, (b), the sensing of sense contents would logically imply the existence of non-inferential knowledge for the simple reason that it would *be* this knowledge. But, once again, it would be facts rather than particulars which are sensed.

4. Now it might seem that when confronted by this choice, the sense-datum theorist seeks to have his cake and eat it. For he characteristically insists *both* that sensing is a knowing *and* that it is particulars which are sensed. Yet his position is by no means as hopeless as this formulation suggests. For the 'having' and the 'eating' can be combined without logical nonsense provided that he uses the word *know* and, correspondingly, the word *given* in two senses. He must say something like the following:

The non-inferential knowing on which our world picture rests is the knowing that certain items, e.g. red sense contents, are of a certain character, e.g. red. When such a fact is non-inferentially known about a sense content, I will say that the sense content is sensed *as being*, e.g. *red*. I will then say that a sense content is *sensed* (full stop) if it is *sensed as being* of a certain character, e.g. red. Finally, I will say of a sense content that it is *known* if it is sensed (full stop), to emphasize that sensing is a *cognitive* or *epistemic* fact.

Notice that, given these stipulations, it is logically necessary that if a sense content be *sensed*, it be *sensed as being of a certain character*, and that if it be *sensed as being of a certain character*, the *fact that it is*

129

of this character be *non-inferentially known.* Notice also that the being sensed of a sense content would be *knowledge* only in a stipulated sense of *know.* To say of a *sense content*—a colour patch, for example —that it was 'known' would be to say that *some fact about it* was non-inferentially known, e.g. that it was red. This *stipulated* use of *know* would, however, receive aid and comfort from the fact that there is, in ordinary usage, a sense of *know* in which it is followed by a noun or descriptive phrase which refers to a particular, thus

> Do you know John?
> Do you know the President?

Because these questions are equivalent to 'Are you acquainted with John?' and 'Are you acquainted with the President?' the phrase 'knowledge by acquaintance' recommends itself as a useful metaphor for this stipulated sense of *know* and, like other useful metaphors, has congealed into a technical term.

5. We have seen that the fact that a sense content is a *datum* (if, indeed, there are such facts) will logically imply that someone has non-inferential knowledge *only* if to say that a sense content is given is contextually defined in terms of non-inferential knowledge of a fact about this sense content. If this is not clearly realized or held in mind, sense-datum theorists may come to think of the givenness of sense contents as the *basic* or *primitive* concept of the sense-datum framework, and thus sever the logical connection between sense data and non-inferential knowledge to which the classical form of the theory is committed. This brings us face to face with the fact that in spite of the above considerations, many if not most sense-datum theorists *have* thought of the givenness of sense contents as the basic notion of the sense-datum framework. What, then, of the logical connection in the direction *sensing sense contents → having non-inferential knowledge*? Clearly it is severed by those who think of sensing as a unique and unanalysable act. Those, on the other hand, who conceive of sensing as an *analysable* fact, while they have prima facie severed this connection (by taking the sensing of sense contents to be the basic concept of the sense-datum framework), will nevertheless, in a sense, have maintained it, if the result they get by analysing *x is a red sense datum* turns out to be the same as the result they get when they analyse *x is non-inferentially known to be red.* The entailment which was thrown out the front door would have sneaked in by the back.

It is interesting to note, in this connection, that those who, in the classical period of sense-datum theories, say from Moore's 'Refutation of Idealism' until about 1938, analysed or sketched an analysis of sensing, did so in *non-epistemic* terms. Typically it was held that for a sense content to be sensed is for it to be an element in a certain kind of relational array of sense contents, where the relations which constitute the array are such relations as spatiotemporal juxtaposition (or overlapping), constant conjunction, mnemic causation—even real connection and belonging to a self. There is, however, one class of terms which is conspicuous by its absence, namely *cognitive* terms. For these, like the 'sensing' which was under analysis, were taken to belong to a higher level of complexity.

Now the idea that epistemic facts can be analysed without remainder—even 'in principle'—into non-epistemic facts, whether phenomenal or behavioural, public or private, with no matter how lavish a sprinkling of subjunctives and hypotheticals is, I believe, a radical mistake—a mistake of a piece with the so-called 'naturalistic fallacy' in ethics. I shall not, however, press this point for the moment, though it will be a central theme in a later stage of my argument. What I do want to stress is that whether classical sense-datum philosophers have conceived of the givenness of sense contents as analysable in non-epistemic terms, or as constituted by acts which are somehow both irreducible *and* knowings, they have without exception taken them to be fundamental in another sense.

6. For they have taken givenness to be a fact which presupposes no learning, no forming of associations, no setting up of stimulus-response connections. In short, they have tended to equate *sensing sense contents* with *being conscious*, as a person who has been hit on the head is *not* conscious, whereas a new-born babe, alive and kicking, *is* conscious. They would admit, of course, that the ability to know that a *person*, namely oneself, is *now*, at a certain time, feeling a pain, *is* acquired and does presuppose a (complicated) process of concept formation. But, they would insist, to suppose that the simple ability to *feel a pain* or *see a colour*, in short, to sense sense contents, is *acquired* and involves a process of concept formation, would be very odd indeed.

But if a sense-datum philosopher takes the ability to sense sense contents to be unacquired, he is clearly precluded from offering an analysis of *x senses a sense content* which presupposes acquired abilities It follows that he could analyse *x senses red sense content s* as *x non-inferentially knows that s is red* only if he is prepared to admit that the ability to have such non-inferential knowledge as that, for example, a red sense content is red, is itself unacquired. And this brings us face to face with the fact that most empirically minded philosophers are strongly inclined to think that all classificatory consciousness, all knowledge *that something is thus-and-so*, or, in logicians' jargon, all subsumption of particulars under universals, involves learning, concept formation, even the use of symbols. It is clear from the above analysis, therefore, that *classical* sense-datum theories—I

131

emphasize the adjective, for there are other, 'heterodox', sense-datum theories to be taken into account—are confronted by an inconsistent triad made up of the following three propositions:

A. *X senses red sense content s* entails *x non-inferentially knows that s is red.*

B. The ability to sense sense contents is unacquired.

C. The ability to know facts of the form *x is ϕ* is acquired.

A and B together entail not-C; B and C entail not-A; A and C entail not-B.

Once the classical sense-datum theorist faces up to the fact that A, B, and C do form an inconsistent triad, which of them will he choose to abandon?

(1) He can abandon A, in which case the sensing of sense contents becomes a noncognitive fact—a noncognitive fact, to be sure which may be a necessary condition, even a *logically* necessary condition, of non-inferential knowledge, but a fact, nevertheless, which cannot *constitute* this knowledge.

(2) He can abandon B, in which case he must pay the price of cutting off the concept of a sense datum from its connection with our ordinary talk about sensations, feelings, after-images, tickles and itches, etc., which are usually thought by sense-datum theorists to be its common sense counterparts.

(3) But to abandon C is to do violence to the predominantly nominalistic proclivities of the empiricist tradition.

7. It certainly begins to look as though the classical concept of a sense datum were a mongrel resulting from a crossbreeding of two ideas:

(1) The idea that there are certain inner episodes—e.g. sensations of red or of C♯ which can occur to human beings (and brutes) without any prior process of learning or concept formation; and without which it would *in some sense* be impossible to see, for example, that the facing surface of a physical object is red and triangular, or *hear* that a certain physical sound is C♯.

(2) The idea that there are certain inner episodes which are the non-inferential knowings that certain items are, for example, red or C♯; and that these episodes are the necessary conditions of empirical knowledge as providing the evidence for all other empirical propositions.

And I think that once we are on the lookout for them, it is quite easy to see how these two ideas came to be blended together in traditional epistemology. The *first* idea clearly arises in the attempt to explain the facts of sense perception in scientific style. How does it happen that people can have the experience which they describe by saying, 'It is as though I were seeing a red and triangular physical object', when either there is no physical object there at all, or, if there is, it is neither red nor triangular? The explanation, roughly, posits that in every case in which a person has an experience of this kind, whether veridical or not, he has what is called a 'sensation' or 'impression' 'of a red triangle'. The core idea is that the proximate cause of such a sensation is *only for the most part* brought about by the presence in the neighbourhood of the perceiver of a red and triangular physical object; and that while a baby, say, can have the 'sensation of a red triangle' without either *seeing* or *seeming to see that the facing side of a physical object is red and triangular*, there usually *looks*, to adults, *to be* a physical object with a red and triangular facing surface, when they are caused to have a 'sensation of a red triangle'; while *without* such a sensation, no such experience can be had.

I shall have a great deal more to say about this kind of 'explanation' of perceptual situations in the course of my argument. What I want to emphasize for the moment, however, is that, as far as the above formulation goes, there is no reason to suppose that having the sensation of a red triangle is a *cognitive* or *epistemic* fact. There is, of course, a temptation to assimilate 'having a sensation of a red triangle' to 'thinking of a celestial city' and to attribute to the former the epistemic character, the 'intentionality' of the latter. But this temptation *could* be resisted, and it *could* be held that having a sensation of a red triangle is a fact *sui generis*, neither epistemic nor physical, having its own logical grammar. Unfortunately, the idea that there are such things as sensations of red triangles—in itself, as we shall see, quite legitimate, though not without its puzzles—seems to fit the requirements of another, and less fortunate, line of thought so well that it has almost invariably been distorted to give the latter a reinforcement without which it would long ago have collapsed. This unfortunate, but familiar, line of thought runs as follows:

> The seeing that the facing surface of a physical object is red and triangular is a *veridical* member of a class of experiences—let us call them 'ostensible seeings'—some of the members of which are non-veridical; and there is no inspectible hallmark which guarantees that *any* such experience is veridical. To suppose that the non-inferential knowledge on which our world picture rests consists of such ostensible seeings, hearings, etc., as *happen* to be veridical is to place empirical knowledge on too precarious a footing—indeed, to open the door to scepticism by making a mockery of the word *knowledge* in the phrase 'empirical knowledge'.

Now it is, of course, possible to delimit subclasses of ostensible seeings, hearings, etc., which are progressively less precarious, i.e. more reliable, by specifying the circumstances in which they occur, and the vigilance of the perceiver. But the possibility that any given ostensible seeing, hearing, etc., is non-veridical can never be entirely eliminated. Therefore, given that the foundation of empirical *knowledge* cannot consist of the veridical members of a class not all the members of which are veridical, and from which the non-veridical members cannot be weeded out by 'inspection', this foundation cannot consist of such items as *seeing that the facing surface of a physical object is red and triangular*.

Thus baldly put, scarcely anyone would accept this conclusion. Rather they would take the contrapositive of the argument, and reason that *since* the foundation of empirical knowledge *is* the non-inferential knowledge of such facts, it *does* consist of members of a class which contains non-veridical members. But before it is thus baldly put, it gets tangled up with the first line of thought. The idea springs to mind that *sensations of red triangles* have exactly the virtues which *ostensible seeings of red triangular physical surfaces* lack. To begin with, the grammatical similarity of 'sensation of a red triangle' to 'thought of a celestial city' is interpreted to mean, or, better, gives rise to the presupposition, that *sensations* belong in the same general pigeonhole as *thoughts*—in short, are cognitive facts. *Then*, it is noticed that sensations are *ex hypothesi* far more intimately related to mental processes than external physical objects. It would seem easier to 'get at' a red triangle of which we are having a sensation, than to 'get at' a red and triangular physical surface. But, above all, it is the fact that it *does not make sense* to speak of unveridical sensations which strikes these philosophers, though for it to strike them as it does, they must overlook the fact that if it makes sense to speak of an experience as *veridical* it must correspondingly make sense to speak of it as *unveridical*. Let me emphasize that not *all* sense-datum theorists—even of the classical type—have been guilty of *all* these confusions; nor are these *all* the confusions of which sense-datum theorists have been guilty. I shall have more to say on this topic later. But the confusions I have mentioned are central to the tradition, and will serve my present purpose. For the upshot of blending all these ingredients together is the idea that a sensation of a red triangle is the very paradigm of empirical knowledge. And I think that it can readily be seen that this idea leads straight to the orthodox type of sense-datum theory and accounts for the perplexities which arise when one tries to think it through.

II. ANOTHER LANGUAGE?

8. I shall now examine briefly a heterodox suggestion by, for example, Ayer[1] to the effect that discourse about sense data is, so to speak, another language, a language contrived by the epistemologist, for situations which the plain man describes by means of such locutions as 'Now the book looks green to me' and 'There seems to be a red and triangular object over there'. The core of this suggestion is the idea that the vocabulary of sense data embodies no increase in the content of descriptive discourse, as over and against the plain man's language of physical objects in Space and Time, and the properties they have and appear to have. For it holds that sentences of the form

X presents S with a ϕ sense datum

are simply *stipulated* to have the same force as sentences of the form

X looks ϕ to S.

Thus 'The tomato presents S with a bulgy red sense-datum' would be the contrived counterpart of 'The tomato looks red and bulgy to S' and would mean exactly what the latter means for the simple reason that it was stipulated to do so.

As an aid to explicating this suggestion, I am going to make use of a certain picture. I am going to start with the idea of a *code*, and I am going to enrich this notion until the codes I am talking about are no longer *mere* codes. Whether one wants to call these 'enriched codes' codes at all is a matter which I shall not attempt to decide.

Now a code, in the sense in which I shall use the term, is a system of symbols each of which represents a complete sentence. Thus, as we initially view the situation, there are two characteristic features of a code: (1) Each code symbol is a unit; the parts of a code symbol are not themselves code symbols. (2) Such logical relations as obtain among code symbols are completely parasitical; they derive entirely from logical relations among the sentences they represent. Indeed, to speak about logical relations among code symbols is a way of talking which is introduced in terms of the logical relations among the sentences they represent. Thus, if ' ○ ' stands for 'Everybody on board is sick' and ' △ ' for 'Somebody on board is sick', then ' △ ' would follow from ' ○ ' in the sense that the sentence represented by ' △ ' follows from the sentence represented by ' ○ '.

Let me begin to modify this austere conception of a code. There is no reason why a code symbol might not have parts which, without

---

[1] Ayer, A. J., *Foundations of Empirical Knowledge*, London: Macmillan, 1940, and 'The Terminology of Sense Data' in *Philosophical Essays*, pp. 66–104, London: Macmillan, 1954. (Also in *Mind*, 54, 1945, pp. 289–312.)

becoming full-fledged symbols on their own, do play a role in the system. Thus they might play the role of *mnemonic devices* serving to put us in mind of features of the sentences represented by the symbols of which they are parts. For example, the code symbol for 'Someone on board is sick' might contain the letter S to remind us of the word 'sick', and, perhaps, the reversed letter E to remind those of us who have a background in logic of the word 'someone'. Thus, the flag for 'Someone on board is sick' might be 'ƎS'. Now the suggestion at which I am obviously driving is that someone might introduce so-called sense-datum sentences as code symbols or 'flags', and introduce the vocables and printables they contain to serve the role of reminding us of certain features of the sentences in ordinary perceptual discourse which the flags as wholes represent. In particular, the role of the vocable or printable 'sense datum' would be that of indicating that the symbolized sentence contains the context '. . . looks . . .', the vocable or printable 'red' that the correlated sentence contains the context '. . . looks red . . .', and so on.

9. Now to take this conception of sense-datum 'sentences' seriously is, of course, to take seriously the idea that there are no independent logical relations between sense-datum 'sentences'. It *looks* as though there were such independent logical relations, for these 'sentences' look like *sentences*, and they have as proper parts vocables or printables which function *in ordinary usage* as *logical words*. Certainly if sense-datum talk is a code, it is a code which is easily mistaken for a language proper. Let me illustrate. At first sight it certainly seems that

    A. The tomato presents S with a red sense datum

entails both

    B. There are red sense data

and

    C. The tomato presents S with a sense datum which has some specific shade of red.

This, however, on the kind of view I am considering, would be a mistake. (B) would follow—even in the inverted commas sense of 'follows' appropriate to code symbols—from (A) only because (B) is the flag for (β), 'Something looks red to somebody', which *does* follow from (α) 'The tomato looks red to Jones' which is represented in the code by (A). And (C) would 'follow' from (A), in spite of appearances, only if (C) were the flag for a *sentence* which *follows* from (α).

I shall have more to say about this example in a moment. The point to be stressed now is that to carry out this view consistently one must

136

deny to such vocables and printables as 'quality', 'is', 'red', 'colour', 'crimson', 'determinable', 'determinate', 'all', 'some', 'exists', etc. etc., *as they occur in sense-datum talk*, the full-blooded status of their counterparts in ordinary usage. They are rather *clues* which serve to remind us which sense-datum 'flag' it would be proper to fly along with which other sense-datum 'flags'. Thus, the vocables which make up the two 'flags'

(D) All sense data are red

and

(E) Some sense data are not red

remind us of the genuine logical incompatibility between, for example,

(F) All elephants are grey

and

(G) Some elephants are not grey,

and serve, therefore, as a clue to the impropriety of flying these two 'flags' together. For the sentences they symbolize are, presumably,

(δ) Everything looks red to everybody

and

(ε) There is a colour other than red which something looks to somebody to have,

and these *are* incompatible.

But one would have to be cautious in using these clues. Thus, from the fact that it is proper to infer

(H) Some elephants have a determinate shade of pink

from

(I) Some elephants are pink

it would clearly be a mistake to infer that the right to fly

(K) Some sense data are pink

carries with it the right to fly

(L) Some sense data have a determinate shade of pink.

9. But if sense-datum sentences are really sense-datum 'sentences' —i.e. code flags—it follows, of course, that sense-datum talk neither *clarifies* nor *explains* facts of the form *x looks φ to S* or *x is φ*. That it would appear to do so would be because it would take an almost superhuman effort to keep from taking the vocables and printables

which occur in the code (and let me now add to our earlier list the vocable 'directly known') to be *words* which, if homonyms of words in ordinary usage, have their ordinary sense, and which, if invented, have a meaning specified by their relation to the others. One would be constantly tempted, that is, to treat sense-datum flags as though they were sentences in a *theory*, and sense-datum talk as a *language* which gets its use by co-ordinating sense-datum sentences with sentences in ordinary perception talk, *as molecule talk gets its use by co-ordinating sentences about populations of molecules with talk about the pressure of gases on the walls of their containers.* After all,

x looks red to S · ≡ · there is a class of red sense data which
belong to x, and are sensed by S

has at least a superficial resemblance to

g exerts pressure on w · ≡ · there is a class of molecules which
make up g, and which are bouncing
off w,

a resemblance which becomes even more striking once it is granted that the former is not an *analysis* of *x looks red to S* in terms of sense data.

There is, therefore, reason to believe that it is the fact that both codes and theories are contrived systems which are under the control of the language with which they are co-ordinated, which has given aid and comfort to the idea that sense-datum talk is 'another language' for ordinary discourse about perception. Yet although the logical relations between sentences in a theoretical language are, in an important sense, under the control of logical relations between sentences in the observation language, nevertheless, within the framework of this control, the theoretical language has an *autonomy* which contradicts the very idea of a code. If this essential difference between theories and codes is overlooked, one may be tempted to try to eat his cake and have it. By thinking of sense-datum talk as *merely another language*, one draws on the fact that codes have no surplus value. By thinking of sense-datum talk as *illuminating* the 'language of appearing', one draws on the fact that theoretical languages, though *contrived*, and depending for their meaningfulness on a co-ordination with the language of observation, have an explanatory function. Unfortunately, these two characteristics are incompatible; for it is just because theories have 'surplus value' that they can provide explanations.

No one, of course, who thinks—as, for example, does Ayer—of the existence of sense data as entailing the existence of 'direct knowledge', would wish to say that sense *data* are theoretical entities. It could scarcely be a theoretical fact that I am directly knowing that a certain sense content is red. On the other hand, the idea that sense *contents* are theoretical entities is not *obviously* absurd—so absurd as to preclude the above interpretation of the plausibility of the 'another-language' approach. For even those who introduce the expression 'sense content' by means of the context '. . . is directly known to be . . .' may fail to keep this fact in mind when putting this expression to use—for example, by developing the idea that physical objects and persons alike are patterns of sense contents. In such a specific context, it is possible to forget that sense *contents*, thus introduced, are essentially sense *data* and not merely items which exemplify sense qualities. Indeed, one may even lapse into thinking of the *sensing* of sense contents, the givenness of sense *data*, as *non-epistemic* facts.

I think it fair to say that those who offer the 'another-language' interpretation of sense data find the illumination it provides to consist primarily in the fact that in the language of sense data, physical objects are patterns of sense contents, so that, viewed in this framework, there is no 'iron curtain' between the knowing mind and the physical world. It is to elaborating plausible (if schematic) translations of physical-object statements into statements about sense contents, rather than to spelling out the force of such sentences as 'Sense content *s* is directly known to be red', that the greater part of their philosophical ingenuity has been directed.

However this may be, one thing can be said with confidence. If the language of sense data *were* merely a code, a notational device, then the cash value of any philosophical clarification it might provide must lie in its ability to illuminate logical relations *within* ordinary discourse about physical objects and our perception of them. Thus, the fact (if it were a fact) that a code can be constructed for ordinary perception talk which 'speaks' of a 'relation of identity' between the components ('sense data') of 'minds' and of 'things', would presumably have as its cash value the insight that ordinary discourse about physical objects and perceivers could (in principle) be constructed from sentences of the form, 'There looks to be a physical object with a red and triangular facing surface over there' (the counterpart in ordinary language of the basic expressions of the code). In more traditional terms, the clarification would consist in making manifest the fact that persons and things are alike logical constructions out of *lookings* or *appearings* (*not* appearances!). But any claim to this effect soon runs into insuperable difficulties which become apparent once the role of 'looks' or 'appears' is understood. And it is to an examination of this role that I now turn.

III. THE LOGIC OF 'LOOKS'

10. Before turning aside to examine the suggestion that the language of sense data is 'another language' for the situations described by the so-called 'language of appearing', I had concluded that classical sense-datum theories, when pressed, reveal themselves to be the result of a mismating of two ideas: (1) The idea that there are certain 'inner episodes', e.g. the sensation of a red triangle or of a C♯ sound, which occur to human beings and brutes without any prior process of learning or concept formation, and without which it would—in *some* sense —be impossible to see, for example, that the facing surface of a physical object is red and triangular, or *hear* that a certain physical sound is C♯; (2) The idea that there are certain 'inner episodes' which are the non-inferential knowings that, for example, a certain item is red and triangular, or, in the case of sounds, C♯, which inner episodes are the necessary conditions of empirical knowledge as providing the evidence for all other empirical propositions. If this diagnosis is correct, a reasonable next step would be to examine these two ideas and determine how that which survives criticism in each is properly to be combined with the other. Clearly we would have to come to grips with the idea of *inner episodes*, for this is common to both.

Many who attack the idea of the given seem to have thought that the central mistake embedded in this idea is exactly the idea that there are inner episodes, whether thoughts or so-called 'immediate experiences', to which each of us has privileged access. I shall argue that this is just not so, and that the Myth of the Given can be dispelled without resorting to the crude verificationisms or operationalisms characteristic of the more dogmatic forms of recent empiricism. Then there are those who, while they do not reject the idea of inner episodes, find the Myth of the Given to consist in the idea that knowledge of these episodes furnishes *premises* on which empirical knowledge rests as on a foundation. But while this idea has, indeed, been the most widespread form of the Myth, it is far from constituting its essence. Everything hinges on *why* these philosophers reject it. If, for example, it is on the ground that the learning of a language is a *public* process which proceeds in a domain of *public* objects and is governed by *public* sanctions, so that *private* episodes—with the exception of a mysterious nod in their direction—must needs escape the net of rational discourse, then, while these philosophers are immune to the form of the myth which has flowered in sense-datum theories, they have no defence against the myth in the form of the givenness of such facts as that *physical object x looks red to person S at time t*, or that *there looks to person S at time t to be a red physical object over there.* It will be useful to pursue the Myth in this direction for a while before more general issues are raised.

11. Philosophers have found it easy to suppose that such a sentence as 'The tomato looks red to Jones' says that a certain triadic relation, *looking* or *appearing,* obtains among a physical object, a person, and a quality,[1] 'A looks ϕ to S' is assimilated to 'x gives y to z'—or, better, since giving is, strictly speaking, an action rather than a relation—to 'x is between y and z', and taken to be a case of the general form 'R(x,y,z)'. Having supposed this, they turn without further ado to the question, 'Is this relation analysable?' Sense-datum theorists have, on the whole, answered 'Yes', and claimed that facts of the form *x looks red to X* are to be analysed in terms of sense data. Some of them, without necessarily rejecting this claim, have argued that facts of this kind are, at the very least, to be *explained* in terms of sense data. Thus, when Broad[2] writes 'If, in fact, nothing elliptical is before my mind, it is very hard to understand why the penny should seem *elliptical* rather than of any other shape (p. 240),' he is appealing to sense data as a means of *explaining* facts of this form. The difference, of course, is that whereas if *x looks ϕ to S* is correctly *analysed* in terms of sense data, then no one could believe that x looks ϕ to S without believing that S has sense data, the same need not be true if *x looks ϕ to S* is explained in terms of sense data, for, in the case of some types of explanation, at least, one can believe a fact without believing its explanation.

On the other hand, those philosophers who reject sense-datum theories in favour of so-called theories of appearing have characteristically held that facts of the form *x looks ϕ to S* are ultimate and irreducible, and that sense data are needed neither for their analysis nor for their explanation. If asked, 'Doesn't the statement "x looks red to S" have as part of its meaning the idea that s stands in some relation to something that *is* red?' their answer is in the negative, and, I believe, rightly so.

12. I shall begin my examination of 'X looks red to S at t' with the simple but fundamental point that the sense of 'red' in which things *look* red is, on the face of it, the same as that in which things *are* red. When one glimpses an object and decides that it looks red (to *me, now,* from here) and wonders whether it really *is* red, one is surely wondering whether the colour—red—which it looks to have is the one it really does have. This point can be obscured by such verbal

---

[1] A useful discussion of views of this type is to be found in Roderick Chisholm's 'The Theory of Appearing', in Max Black (ed.), *Philosphical Analysis,* pp. 102–18. Ithaca: Cornell Univ. Pr., 1950 and in H. H. Price's *Perception.* London: Methuen, 1932.

[2] Broad, C. D., *Scientific Thought,* London: Kegan Paul, 1923.

manipulations as hyphenating the words 'looks' and 'red' and claiming that it is the insoluble unity 'looks-red' and not just 'looks' which is the relation. In so far as this dodge is based on insight, it is insight into the fact that *looks* is not a relation between a person, a thing, and a quality. Unfortunately, as we shall see, the reason for this fact is one which gives no comfort at all to the idea that it is *looks-red* rather than *looks* which is the relation.

I have, in effect, been claiming that *being red* is logically prior, is a logically simpler notion, than *looking red*; the function 'x is red' to 'x looks red to y'. In short, that it just won't do to say that *x is red* is analysable in terms of *x looks red to y*. But what, then, are we to make of the necessary truth—and it is, of course, a necessary truth —that

$$x \textit{ is } \text{red} \cdot \equiv \cdot x \text{ would } \textit{look} \text{ red to standard observers in standard conditions?}$$

There is certainly some sense to the idea that this is at least the schema for a definition of *physical redness* in terms of *looking red*. One begins to see the plausibility of the gambit that *looking-red* is an insoluble unity, for the minute one gives 'red' (on the right-hand side) an independent status, it becomes what it obviously is, namely 'red' as a predicate of physical objects, and the supposed definition becomes an obvious circle.

13. The way out of this troubling situation has two parts. The *second* is to show how 'x *is* red' can be necessarily equivalent to 'x would *look* red to standard observers in standard situations' without this being a definition of 'x is red' in terms of 'x looks red'. But the *first*, and logically prior, step is to show that 'x looks red to S' does not assert either an unanalysable triadic relation to obtain between x, red, and S, or an unanalysable dyadic relation to obtain between x and S. Not, however, because it asserts an *analysable* relation to obtain, but because *looks* is not a relation at all. Or, to put the matter in a familiar way, one can say that *looks* is a relation if he likes, for the sentences in which this word appears show some grammatical analogies to sentences built around words which we should not hesitate to classify as relation words; but once one has become aware of certain other features which make them very unlike ordinary relation sentences, he will be less inclined to view his task as that of *finding the answer* to the question 'Is looks a relation?'

14. To bring out the essential features of the use of 'looks', I shall engage in a little historical fiction. A young man, whom I shall call John, works in a necktie shop. He has learned the use of colour words in the usual way, with this exception: I shall suppose that he has never looked at an object in other than standard conditions. As he examines

his stock every evening before closing up shop, he says, 'This is red', 'That is green', 'This is purple', etc., and such of his linguistic peers as happen to be present nod their heads approvingly.

Let us suppose, now, that at this point in the story, electric lighting is invented. His friends and neighbours rapidly adopt this new means of illumination, and wrestle with the problems it presents. John, however, is the last to succumb. Just after it has been installed in his shop, one of his neighbours, Jim, comes in to buy a necktie.

'Here is a handsome green one,' says John.

'But it *isn't* green,' says Jim, and takes John outside.

'Well,' says John, 'it was green in there, but now it is blue.'

'No,' says Jim, 'you know that neckties don't change their colour merely as a result of being taken from place to place.'

'But perhaps electricity changes their colour and they change back again in daylight?'

'That would be a queer kind of change, wouldn't it?' says Jim.

'I suppose so,' says bewildered John. 'But we saw that it was green *in there.*'

'No, we didn't see that it was green in there, because it wasn't green, and you can't see what isn't so!'

'Well, this is a pretty pickle,' says John. *'I just don't know what to say.'*

The next time John picks up this tie in his shop and someone asks what colour it is, his first impulse is to say 'It is green'. He suppresses this impulse, and, remembering what happened before, comes out with 'It is blue'. He does not *see* that it is blue, nor would he say that he sees it to be blue. What does he see? Let us ask him.

'I don't know *what* to say. If I didn't know that the tie is blue—and the alternative to granting this is odd indeed—I would swear that I was seeing a green tie and seeing that it is green. It is *as though* I were seeing the necktie to be green.'

If we bear in mind that such sentences as 'This is green' have both a *fact-stating* and a *reporting* use, we can put the point I have just been making by saying that once John learns to stifle the *report* 'This necktie is green' when looking at it in the shop, there is no other *report* about colour and the necktie which he knows how to make. To be sure, he now says 'This necktie is blue'. But he is not making a *reporting* use of this sentence. He uses it as the conclusion of an inference.[1]

---

[1] (Added 1963) When John has mastered looks talk he will be able to say not only 'The tie looks green' but 'The tie looks to be blue', where the latter has the sense of '. . . looks as blue ties look in these circumstances'. The distinction between 'looks ø' and 'looks to be ø' corresponds to Chisholm's distinction between non-comparative and comparative 'appears'—statements.

15. We return to the shop after an interval, and we find that when John is asked, 'What is the colour of this necktie?' he makes such statements as, 'It looks green, but take it outside and see.' It occurs to us that perhaps in learning to say 'This tie *looks* green' when in the shop, he has learned to make a new kind of report. Thus, it might seem as though his linguistic peers have helped him to notice a new kind of *objective* fact, one which, though a relational fact involving a perceiver, is as logically independent of the beliefs, the conceptual framework of the perceiver, as the fact that the necktie is blue; but a *minimal* fact, one which it is safer to report because one is less likely to be mistaken. Such a minimal fact would be the fact that the necktie looks green to John on a certain occasion, and it would be properly reported by using the sentence, 'This necktie *looks* green.' It is this type of account, of course, which I have already rejected.

But what is the alternative? If, that is, we are not going to adopt the sense-datum analysis. Let me begin by noting that there certainly seems to be something to the idea that the sentence 'This looks green to me now' has a reporting role. Indeed, it would seem to be essentially a report. But if so, *what* does it report, if not a minimal objective fact, and if what it reports is not to be analysed in terms of sense data?

16. Let me next call attention to the fact that the experience of having something look green to one at a certain time is, in so far as it is an experience, obviously very much like that of seeing something to be green, in so far as the latter is an experience. But the latter, of course, is not *just* an experience. And this is the heart of the matter. For to say that a certain experience is a *seeing that* something is the case, is to do more than describe the experience. It is to characterize it as, so to speak, making an assertion or claim, and—which is the point I wish to stress—to *endorse* that claim. As a matter of fact, as we shall see, it is much more easy to see that the statement 'Jones sees that the tree is green' ascribes a propositional claim to Jones's experience and endorses it, than to specify how the statement *describes* Jones's experience.

I realize that by speaking of experiences as containing propositional claims, I may seem to be knocking at closed doors. I ask the reader to bear with me, however, as the justification of this way of talking is one of my major aims. If I am permitted to issue this verbal currency now, I hope to put it on the gold standard before concluding the argument.

16. It is clear that the experience of seeing that something is green is not *merely* the occurrence of the propositional claim 'this is green' —not even if we add, as we must, that this claim is, so to speak, evoked or wrung from the perceiver by the object perceived. Here Nature—to turn Kant's simile (which he uses in another context) on

its head—puts us to the question. The something more is clearly what philosophers have in mind when they speak of 'visual impressions' or 'immediate visual experiences'. What exactly is the logical status of these 'impressions' or 'immediate experiences' is a problem which will be with us for the remainder of this argument. For the moment it is the propositional claim which concerns us.

I pointed out above that when we use the word 'see' as in 'S sees that the tree is green' we are not only ascribing a claim to the experience, but endorsing it. It is this endorsement which Ryle has in mind when he refers to *seeing that something is thus and so* as an *achievement*, and to 'sees' as an *achievement word*. I prefer to call it a 'so it is' or 'just so' word, for the root idea is that of *truth*. To characterize S's experience as a *seeing* is, in a suitably broad sense—which I shall be concerned to explicate—to apply the semantical concept of truth to that experience.

Now the suggestion I wish to make is, in its simplest terms, that the statement 'X looks green to Jones' differs from 'Jones sees that x is green' in that whereas the latter both ascribes a propositional claim to Jones's experience *and endorses it*, the former ascribes the claim but does not endorse it. This is the essential difference between the two, for it is clear that two experiences may be identical *as experiences*, and yet one be properly referred to as a *seeing that* something is green, and the other *merely* as a case of something's *looking* green. Of course, if I say 'X *merely looks* green to S' I am not only failing to endorse the claim, I am rejecting it.

Thus, when I say 'X looks green to me now' I am *reporting* the fact that my experience is, so to speak, intrinsically, *as an experience*, indistinguishable from a veridical one of seeing that x is green. Involved in the report is the ascription to my experience of the claim 'x is green'; and the fact that I make this report rather than the simple report 'X is green' indicates that certain considerations have operated to raise, so to speak in a higher court, the question 'to endorse or not to endorse'. I may have reason to think that x may not after all be green.

If I make at one] time the report 'X looks green'—which is not only a report, but the withholding of an endorsement—I may later, when the original reasons for withholding endorsement have been rebutted, endorse the original claim by saying, 'I saw that it was green, though at the time I was only sure that it looked green.' Notice that I will only say 'I see that x is green' (as opposed to 'X is green') when the question 'to endorse or not to endorse' has come up. 'I see that x is green' belongs, so to speak, on the same level as 'X looks green' and 'X merely *looks* green'.

17. There are many interesting and subtle questions about the

dialectics of 'looks talk', into which I do not have the space to enter. Fortunately, the above distinctions suffice for our present purposes. Let us suppose, then, that to say that 'X looks green to S at t' is, in effect, to say that S has that kind of experience which, if one were prepared to endorse the propositional claim it involves, one would characterize as *seeing x to be green at t*. Thus, when our friend John learns to use the sentence 'This necktie looks green to me' he learns a way of reporting an experience of the kind which, as far as any categories I have yet permitted him to have are concerned, he can only characterize by saying that as an experience it does not differ from seeing something to be green, and that evidence for the proposition 'This necktie is green' is *ipso facto* evidence for the proposition that the experience in question is *seeing that the necktie is green*.

Now one of the chief merits of this account is that it permits a parallel treatment of 'qualitative' and 'existential' seeming or looking. Thus, when I say 'The tree looks bent' I am endorsing that part of the claim involved in my experience which concerns the existence of the tree, but withholding endorsement from the rest. On the other hand, when I say 'There looks to be a bent tree over there' I am refusing to endorse any but the most general aspect of the claim, namely, that there is an 'over there' as opposed to a 'here'. Another merit of the account is that it explains how a necktie, for example, can look red to S at t, without looking scarlet or crimson or any other determinate shade of red. In short, it explains how things can have a *merely generic* look, a fact which would be puzzling indeed if looking red were a *natural* as opposed to *epistemic* fact about objects. The core of the explanation, of course, is that the propositional claim involved in such an experience may be, for example, either the more determinable claim 'This is red' or the more determinate claim 'This is crimson'. The complete story is more complicated, and requires some account of the role in these experiences of the 'impressions' or 'immediate experiences' the logical status of which remains to be determined. But even in the absence of these additional details, we can note the resemblance between the fact that x can look red to S, without it being true of some specific shade of red that x looks to S to have that shade, and the fact that S can believe that Cleopatra's Needle is tall, without its being true of some determinate number of feet that S believes it to be that number of feet tall.

18. The point I wish to stress at this time, however, is that the concept of *looking green*, the ability to recognize that something *looks green*, presupposes the concept of *being green*, and that the latter concept involves the ability to tell what colours objects have by looking at them—which, in turn, involves knowing in what circumstances to place an object if one wishes to ascertain its colour by looking at it.

146

Let me develop this latter point. As our friend John becomes more and more sophisticated about his own and other people's visual experiences, he learns under what conditions it is as though one were seeing a necktie to be of one colour when in fact it is of another. Suppose someone asks him, 'Why does this tie look green to me?' John may very well reply, 'Because it is blue, and blue objects look green in this kind of light.' And if someone asks this question when looking at the necktie in plain daylight, 'John may very well reply, 'Because the tie *is* green'—to which he may add, 'We are in plain daylight, *and in daylight things look what they are.*' We thus see that

x is red $\cdot \equiv \cdot$ x looks red to standard observers in standard conditions

is a necessary truth *not* because the right-hand side is the definition of 'x is red', but because 'standard conditions' means conditions in which things look what they are. And, of course, *which* conditions are standard for a given mode of perception is, at the common sense level, specified by a list of conditions which exhibit the vagueness and open texture characteristic of ordinary discourse.[1]

19. I have arrived at a stage in my argument which is, at least prima facie, out of step with the basic presuppositions of logical atomism. Thus, as long as *looking green* is taken to be the notion to which *being green* is reducible, it could be claimed with considerable plausibility that fundamental concepts pertaining to observable fact have that logical independence of one another which is characteristic of the empiricist tradition. But now, at first sight, the situation is *quite* disquieting. For if the ability to recognize that x looks green presupposes the concept of *being green*, and if this in turn involves knowing in what circumstances to view an object to ascertain its colour, then, since one can scarcely determine what the circumstances are without noticing that certain objects have certain perceptible characteristics—including colours—it would seem that one could not form the concept of *being green*, and, by parity of reasoning, of the other colours, unless he already had them.

Now, it just won't do to reply that to have the concept of green, to know what it is for something to be green, it is sufficient to respond, when one is *in point of fact* in standard conditions, to green objects with the vocable 'This is green'. Not only must the conditions be of a sort that is appropriate for determining the colour of an object by

---

[1] (Added 1963) Standard circumstances are, indeed, the circumstances in which things look as they are. But the non-trivial character of the above formula emerges when we replace 'standard circumstances' by the mention of a specific kind of circumstance (e.g. daylight) and add that daylight is the standard circumstance of perception, i.e. the condition in which colour words have their primary perceptual use.

looking, the subject must *know* that conditions of this sort *are* appropriate. And while this does not imply that one must have concepts before one has them, it does imply that one can have the concept of green only by having a whole battery of concepts of which it is one element. It implies that while the process of acquiring the concept of green may—indeed does—involve a long history of acquiring *piecemeal* habits of response to various objects in various circumstances, there is an important sense in which one has *no* concept pertaining to the observable properties of physical objects in Space and Time unless one has them all—and, indeed, as we shall see, a great deal more besides.[1]

20. Now, I think it is clear what a logical atomist, supposing that he found any merit at all in the above argument, would say. He would say that I am overlooking the fact that the logical space of physical objects in Space and Time rests on the logical space of sense contents, and he would argue that it is concepts pertaining to sense contents which have the logical independence of one another which is characteristic of traditional empiricism. 'After all,' he would point out, 'concepts pertaining to theoretical entities—molecules, for example —have the mutual dependence you have, perhaps rightly, ascribed to concepts pertaining to *physical* fact. But,' he would continue, 'theoretical concepts have empirical content because they rest on—are co-ordinated with—a more fundamental logical space. Until you have disposed, therefore, of the idea that there is a more fundamental logical space than that of physical objects in Space and Time, or shown that it too is fraught with coherence, your incipient *Meditations Hegeliènnes* are premature.'

And we can imagine a sense-datum theorist to interject the following complaint: 'You have begun to write as though you had shown not only that *physical redness* is not to be analysed in terms of *looking red*—which I will grant—but also that physical redness is not to be analysed at all, and, in particular, not to be analysed in terms of the redness of red sense contents. Again, you have begun to write as though you had shown not only that observing that x *looks* red is not more basic than observing that x *is* red, but also that there is *no* form of visual noticing more basic than seeing that x is red, such as the sensing of a red sense content. I grant', he continues, 'that the tendency of sense-datum theorists has been to claim that the *redness* of physical objects is to be analysed in terms of *looking red*, and *then* to

---

[1] (Added 1963) The argument can admit a distinction in principle between a rudimentary concept of 'green' which could be learned without learning the logical space of looks talk, and a richer concept of 'green' in which 'is green' can be challenged by 'merely looks green'. The essential point is that even to have the more rudimentary concept presupposes having a battery of other concepts.

claim that *looking red* is itself to be analysed in terms of *red sense contents*, and that you may have undercut this line of analysis. But what is to prevent the sense-datum theorist from taking the line that the properties of physical objects are *directly* analysable into the qualities and phenomenal relations of sense contents?'

Very well. But once again we must ask, How does the sense-datum theorist come by the framework of sense contents? and, How is he going to convince us that there are such things? For even if *looking red* does not enter into the analysis of physical redness, it is by asking us to reflect on the experience of having something look red to us that he hopes to make this framework convincing. And it therefore becomes relevant to note that my analysis of *x looks red to S at t* has not, at least as far as I have pushed it to date, revealed any such items as sense contents. And it may be relevant to suggest that once we see clearly that physical redness is not to be given a dispositional analysis in terms of *looking red*, the idea that it is to be given *any* kind of dispositional analysis loses a large measure of its plausibility. In any event, the next move must be to press further the above account of qualitative and existential looking.

IV. EXPLAINING LOOKS

21. I have already noted that sense-datum theorists are impressed by the question, 'How can a physical object look red to S, unless something in that situation *is* red and S is taking account of it? If S is not experiencing something red, how does it happen that the physical object looks *red*, rather than green or streaky?' There is, I propose to show, *something* to this line of thought, though the story turns out to be a complicated one. And if, in the course of telling the story, I shall be led to make statements which resemble *some* of the things sense-datum theorists have said, this story will amount to a sense-datum theory only in a sense which robs this phrase of an entire dimension of its traditional epistemological force, a dimension which is characteristic of even such heterodox forms of sense-datum theory as the 'another language' approach.

Let me begin by formulating the question: 'Is the fact that an object looks to S to be red and triangular, or that there looks to S to be a red and triangular object over there, to be explained in terms of the idea that Jones has a sensation—or impression, or immediate experience —of a red triangle?' One point can be made right away, namely that if these expressions are so understood that, say, the immediate experience of a red triangle implies the existence of something—not a physical object—which *is* red and triangular, and if the redness which this item has is the same as the redness which the physical object *looks* to have, then the suggestion runs up against the objection that the redness physical objects *look* to have is the same as the redness physical objects actually *do* have, so that items which *ex hypothesi* are not physical objects, and which radically, even categorially, differ from physical objects, would have the same redness as physical objects. And while this is, perhaps, not entirely out of the question, it certainly provides food for thought. Yet when it is claimed that 'obviously' physical objects cannot *look* red to one unless one is experiencing something that *is* red, is it not presumed that the redness which the *something* has is the redness which the physical object *looks to have*?

Now there are those who would say that the question, 'Is the fact that an object looks red and triangular to S to be explained—as opposed to notationally reformulated—in terms of the idea that S has an impression of a red triangle?' simply does not arise, on the ground that there are perfectly sound explanations of qualitative and existential lookings which make no reference to 'immediate experiences' or other dubious entities. Thus, it is pointed out, it is perfectly proper to answer the question, 'Why does this object look red?' by saying, 'Because it is an orange object looked at in such and such circumstances.' The explanation is, in principle, a good one, and is typical of the answers we make to such questions in everyday life. But because these explanations are good, it by no means follows that explanations of other kinds might not be equally good, and, perhaps, more searching.

22. On the face of it there are at least two ways in which additional but equally legitimate explanations *might* be forthcoming for such a fact as that *x looks red*. The first of these is suggested by a simple analogy. Might it not be the case that just as there are two kinds of good explanation of the fact that this balloon has expanded, (*a*) in terms of the Boyle–Charles laws which relate to empirical concepts of volume, pressure, and temperature pertaining to gases, and (*b*) in terms of the kinetic theory of gases; so there are two ways of explaining the fact that this object looks red to S: (*a*) in terms of empirical generalizations relating the colours of objects, the circumstances in which they are seen, and the colours they look to have, and (*b*) in terms of a theory of perception in which 'immediate' experiences' play a role analogous to that of the molecules of the kinetic theory.

Now there is such an air of paradox to the idea that 'immediate experiences' are *mere* theoretical entities—entities, that is, which are postulated, along with certain fundamental principles concerning them, to explain uniformities pertaining to sense perception, as molecules, along with the principles of molecular motion, are postulated to explain the experimentally determined regularities pertaining to gases—that I am going to lay it aside until a more propitious context of thought may make it seem relevant. Certainly, those who have thought that qualitative and existential lookings are to be explained in terms of 'immediate experiences' thought of the latter as the most untheoretical of entities, indeed, as *the* observables *par excellence.*

Let us therefore turn to a second way in which, at least prima facie, there might be an additional, but equally legitimate explanation of existential and qualitative lookings. According to this second account, when we consider items of this kind, we *find* that they contain as components items which are properly referred to as, for example, 'the immediate experience of a red triangle'. Let us begin our exploration of this suggestion by taking another look at our account of existential and qualitative lookings. It will be remembered that our account of qualitative looking ran, in rough and ready terms, as follows:

> 'x looks red to S' has the sense of 'S has an experience which involves in a unique way the idea *that x is red* and involves it in such a way that if this idea were true,[1] the experience would correctly be characterized as a seeing that x is red'.

Thus, our account implies that the three situations

(*a*) Seeing that x, over there, is red
(*b*) Its looking to one that x, over there, is red
(*c*) Its looking to one as though there were a red object over there

differ primarily in that (*a*) is so formulated as to involve an endorsement of the idea that x, over there, is red, whereas in (*b*) this idea is only partially endorsed, and in (*c*) not at all. Let us refer to the idea *that x, over there, is red* as the *common propositional content* of these three situations. (This is, of course, not strictly correct, since the propositional content of (*c*) is *existential*, rather than about a presupposedly designated object x, but it will serve my purpose. Furthermore, the common propositional content of these three experiences is much more complex and determinate than is indicated by the sentence we use to describe our experience to others, and which I am using to represent it. Nevertheless it is clear that, subject to the first of these qualifications, the propositional content of these three experiences *could* be identical.)

The propositional content of these three experiences is, of course, but a part of that to which we are logically committed by characterizing them as situations of these three kinds. Of the remainder, as we have seen, part is a matter of the extent to which this propositional content is endorsed. It is the residue with which we are now concerned. Let us call this residue the *descriptive content*. I can then point

---

[1] (Added 1963) . . . and if S knew that the circumstances were normal.

out that it is implied by my account that not only the *propositional content* but also the *descriptive content* of these three experiences may be identical. I shall suppose this to be the case, though that there must be some factual difference in the *total* situations is obvious.

Now, and this is the decisive point, in characterizing these three experiences, as respectively, a *seeing that x, over there, is red, its looking to one as though x, over there, were red*, and *its looking to one as though there were a red object over there*, we do not specify this common *descriptive* content save *indirectly*, by implying that *if the common propositional content were true,*[1] then all these three situations would be cases of *seeing* that x, over there, is red. Both existential and qualitative lookings are experiences that would be *seeings* if their propositional contents were true.

Thus, the very nature of 'looks talk' is such as to raise questions to which it gives no answer: What is the *intrinsic* character of the common descriptive content of these three experiences? and, How are they able to have it in spite of the fact that whereas in the case of (*a*) the perceiver must be in the presence of a red object over there, in (*b*) the object over there need not be red, while in (*c*) there need be no object over there at all?

23. Now it is clear that if we were required to give a more direct characterization of the common descriptive content of these experiences, we would begin by trying to do so in terms of the quality *red*. Yet, as I have already pointed out, we can scarcely say that this descriptive content is itself something red unless we can pry the term 'red' loose from its prima-facie tie with the category of physical objects. And there is a line of thought which has been one of the standard gambits of perceptual epistemology and which seems to promise exactly this. If successful, it would convince us that *redness* —in the most basic sense of this term—is a characteristic of items of the sort we have been calling sense contents. It runs as follows:

> While it would, indeed, be a howler to say that we do not see chairs, tables, etc., but only their facing surfaces, nevertheless, although we see a table, say, and although the table has a back as well as a front, we do not see the back of the table as we see its front. Again, although we see the table, and although the table has an 'inside', we do not see the inside of the table as we see its facing outside. Seeing an object entails seeing its facing surface. If we are seeing that an object is red, this entails seeing that its facing surface is red. A red surface is a two-dimensional red expanse—two-dimensional in that though it may be *bulgy*, and in *this* sense three-dimensional, it has no *thickness*. As far as the analysis of perceptual consciousness is concerned, a red physical object is one that has a red expanse as its surface.

[1] (Added 1963) . . , *and if the subject knew that the circumstances were normal.*

152

Now a red expanse is not a physical object, nor does the existence of a red expanse entail the existence of a physical object to which it belongs. (Indeed, there are 'wild' expanses which do not belong to any physical object.) The 'descriptive content'—as you put it—which is common to the three experiences (*a*), (*b*) and (*c*) above, is exactly this sort of thing, a bulgy red expanse.

Spelled out thus baldly, the fallacy is, or should be, obvious; it is a simple equivocation on the phrase 'having a red surface'. We start out by thinking of the familiar fact that a physical object may be of one colour 'on the surface' and of another colour 'inside'. We may express this by saying that, for example, the 'surface' of the object is red, but its 'inside' green. But in saying this we are *not* saying that there is a 'surface' in the sense of a bulgy two-dimensional particular, a red 'expanse' which is a component particular in a complex particular which also includes green particulars. The notion of two-dimensional bulgy (or flat) particulars is a product of philosophical (and mathematical) sophistication which can be *related to* our ordinary conceptual framework, but does not belong in an *analysis* of it. I think that in its place it has an important contribution to make. (See below, Section 61 (5), pp. 193–4.) But this place is in the logical space of an ideal *scientific* picture of the world and not in the logical space of ordinary discourse. It has nothing to do with the logical grammar of our ordinary colour words. It is just a mistake to suppose that as the word 'red' is actually used, it is ever surfaces in the sense of two-dimensional particulars which are red. The only particular involved when a physical object is 'red on the outside, but green inside' is the physical object itself, located in a certain region of Space and enduring over a stretch of Time. The fundamental grammar of the attribute *red* is *physical object x is red at place p and at time t*. Certainly, when we say of an object that it is red, we commit ourselves to no more than that it is red 'at the surface'. And sometimes it is red at the surface by having what we would not hesitate to call a 'part' which is red through and through—thus, a red table which is red by virtue of a layer of red paint. But the red paint is not itself red by virtue of a component—a 'surface' or 'expanse'; a particular with no thickness—which is red. There may, let me repeat, turn out to be some place in the total philosophical picture for the statement that there 'really are' such particulars, and that they are elements in perceptual experience. But this place is not to be found by an analysis of ordinary perceptual discourse, any more than Minkowski four-dimensional Space–Time worms are an *analysis* of what we mean when we speak of physical objects in Space and Time.

V. IMPRESSIONS AND IDEAS: A LOGICAL POINT

24. Let me return to beating the neighbouring bushes. Notice that the common descriptive component of the three experiences I am considering is itself often referred to (by philosophers, at least) as an *experience*—as, for example, an *immediate experience*. Here caution is necessary. The notorious 'ing-ed' ambiguity of 'experience' must be kept in mind. For although *seeing that x, over there, is red* is an *experiencing*—indeed, a paradigm case of experiencing—it does not follow that the descriptive content of this experiencing is itself an experien*cing*. Furthermore, because the fact that *x, over there, looks red to Jones* would be a *seeing*, on Jones's part, *that x, over there, is red*, if its propositional content were true, and because if it *were* a seeing, it *would be* an experiencing, we must beware of concluding that the fact that *x, over there, looks red to Jones* is itself an *experiencing*. Certainly, the fact that something looks red to me can itself be *experienced*. But it is not itself an experiencing.

All this is not to say that the common descriptive core may not turn out to be an experien*cing*,[1] though the chances that this is so appear less with each step in my argument. On the other hand, I can say that it is a component in states of affairs which are experien*ced*, and it does not seem unreasonable to say that it is itself experien*ced*. But what kind of experience (in the sense of experien*ced*) *is* it? If my argument to date is sound, I cannot say that it is a *red* experience that is, a red experienced item. I could, of course, introduce a new use of 'red' according to which to say of an 'immediate experience' that it was red, would be the stipulated equivalent of characterizing it as that which could be the common descriptive component of a *seeing* that something is red, and the corresponding qualitative and existential *lookings*. This would give us a *predicate* by which to describe and report the experience, but we should, of course, be only verbally better off than if we could only refer to this kind of experience as *the kind which* could be the common descriptive component of a *seeing* and a qualitative or existential *looking*. And this makes it clear that one way of putting what we are after is by saying that we want to have a *name* for this kind of experience which is truly a *name*, and not just shorthand for a definite description. Does ordinary usage have a *name* for this kind of experience?

I shall return to this quest in a moment. In the meantime it is important to clear the way of a traditional obstacle to understanding

---

[1] (Added 1963) The term 'experiencing' in the question 'Is the common descriptive component an experiencing?' is used in an epistemic sense. In the non-epistemic sense of an 'undergoing', the common descriptive component is, of course, an experiencing.

the status of such things as *sensations of red triangles*. Thus, suppose I were to say that while the experience I am examining is not a red experience, it is an experience *of red*. I could expect the immediate challenge: 'Is "sensation of a red triangle" any better off than "red and triangular experience"? Does not the existence of a sensation of a red triangle entail the existence of a red and triangular item, and hence, *always on the assumption that red is a property of physical objects*, of a red and triangular physical object? Must you not, therefore, abandon this assumption, and return to the framework of sense contents which you have so far refused to do?'

One way out of dilemma would be to assimilate 'Jones has a sensation of a red triangle' to 'Jones believes in a divine Huntress'. For the truth of the latter does not, of course, entail the existence of a divine Huntress. Now, I think that most contemporary philosophers are clear that it is possible to attribute to the context

. . . sensation of . . .

the *logical* property of being such that 'There is a sensation of a red triangle' does not entail 'There is a red triangle' without assimilating the context '. . . sensation of . . .' to the context '. . . believes in . . .' in any closer way. For while mentalistic verbs characteristically provide nonextensional contexts (when they are not 'achievement' or 'endorsing' words), not all nonextensional contexts are mentalistic. Thus, as far as the purely *logical* point is concerned, there is no reason why 'Jones has a sensation of a red triangle' should be assimilated to 'Jones believes in a divine Huntress' rather than to 'It is possible that the moon is made of green cheese' or to any of the other nonextensional contexts familiar to logicians. Indeed there is no reason why it should be assimilated to any of these. '. . . sensation of . . .' or '. . . impression of . . .' could be a context which, though sharing with these others the logical property of nonextensionality, was otherwise in a class by itself.

25. Yet there is no doubt but that *historically* the contexts '. . . sensation of . . .' and '. . . impression of . . .' *were* assimilated to such mentalistic contexts as '. . . believes . . .', '. . . desires . . .', '. . . chooses . . .', in short, to contexts which are either themselves 'propositional attitudes' or involve propositional attitudes in their analysis. This assimilation took the form of classifying sensations with *ideas* or *thoughts*. Thus Descartes uses the word 'thought' to cover not only *judgements, inferences, desires, volitions*, and (occurrent) *ideas of abstract qualities*, but also *sensations, feelings*, and *images*. Locke, in the same spirit, uses the term 'idea' with similar scope. The apparatus of Conceptualism, which had its genesis in the controversy over universals, was given a correspondingly wide application. Just as

155

objects and situations were said to have 'objective being' in our *thoughts*, when we think of them, or judge them to obtain—as contrasted with the 'subjective' or 'formal being' which they have in the world—so, when we have a sensation of a red triangle, the red triangle was supposed to have 'objective being' in our sensation.

In elaborating, for a moment, this conceptualistic interpretation of sensation, let me refer to that which has 'objective being' in a *thought* or *idea* as its *content* or *immanent object*. Then I can say that the fundamental difference between occurrent *abstract ideas* and *sensations*, for both Locke and Descartes, lay in the *specificity* and, above all, the *complexity* of the content of the latter. (Indeed, both Descartes and Locke assimilated the contrast between the simple and the complex in ideas to that between the generic and the specific.) Descartes thinks of sensations as confused thoughts of their external cause; Spinoza of sensations and images as confused thoughts of bodily states, and still more confused thoughts of the external causes of these bodily states. And it is interesting to note that the conceptualistic thesis that abstract entities have only *esse intentionale* (their *esse* is *concipi*) is extended by Descartes and, with less awareness of what he is doing, Locke, to include the thesis that colours, sounds, etc., exist 'only in the mind' (their *esse* is *percipi*) and by Berkeley to cover all perceptible qualities.

Now, I think we would all agree, today, that this assimilation of sensations to thoughts is a mistake. It is sufficient to note that if 'sensation of a red triangle' had the sense of 'episode of the kind which is the common descriptive component of those experiences which *would be* cases of seeing that the facing surface of a physical object is red and triangular if an object *were* presenting a red and triangular facing surface' then it would have the nonextensionality, the noticing of which led to this mistaken assimilation. But while we have indeed escaped from this blind alley, it is small consolation. For we are no further along in the search for a 'direct' or 'intrinsic' characterization of 'immediate experience'.

VI. IMPRESSIONS AND IDEAS: AN HISTORICAL POINT

26. There are those who will say that although I have spoken of exploring blind alleys, it is really I who am blind. For, they will say, if that which we wish to characterize intrinsically is an *experience*, then there *can* be no puzzle about knowing *what kind* of experience it is, though there may be a problem about how this knowledge is to be communicated to others. And, indeed, it is tempting to suppose that if we *should* happen, at a certain stage of our intellectual development, to be able to classify an experience *only* as *of the kind which*

could be common to a *seeing* and corresponding qualitative and existential *lookings*, all we would have to do to acquire a 'direct designation' for this kind of experience would be to pitch in, 'examine' it, locate the kind which it exemplifies and which satisfies the above description, name it—say 'ϕ'—and, in full possession of the concept of ϕ, classify such experiences, from now on, as ϕ experiences.

At this point, it is clear, the concept—or, as I have put it, the myth—of the given is being invoked to explain the possibility of a direct account of immediate experience. The myth insists that what I have been treating as one problem really subdivides into two, one of which is really no problem at all, while the other may have no solution. These problems are, respectively

(1) How do we become aware of an immediate experience as of one sort, and of a simultaneous immediate experience as of another sort?

(2) How can I know that the labels I attach to the sorts to which my immediate experiences belong, are attached by you to the same sorts? May not the sort I call 'red' be the sort you call 'green'—and so on systematically throughout the spectrum?

We shall find that the second question, to be a philosophical perplexity, presupposes a certain answer to the first question—indeed the answer given by the myth. And it is to this first question that I now turn. Actually there are various forms taken by the myth of the given in this connection, depending on other philosophical commitments. But they all have in common the idea that the awareness of certain *sorts*—and by 'sorts' I have in mind, in the first instance, determinate sense repeatables—is a primordial, non-problematic feature of 'immediate experience'. In the context of conceptualism, as we have seen, this idea took the form of treating sensations as though they were absolutely specific, and infinitely complicated, *thoughts*. And it is essential to an understanding of the empiricist tradition to realize that whereas the contemporary problem of universals primarily concerns the status of repeatable *determinate* features of particular situations, and the contemporary problem of abstract ideas is at least as much the problem of what it is to be aware of determinate repeatables as of what it is to be aware of determinable repeatables, Locke, Berkeley and, for that matter, Hume saw the problem of abstract ideas as the problem of what it is to be aware of *determinable* repeatables.[1] Thus, an examination of Locke's *Essay* makes it clear that he is thinking of

---

[1] For a systematic elaboration and defence of the following interpretation of Locke, Berkeley, and Hume, the reader should consult 'Berkeley's Critique of Abstract Ideas', a Ph.D. thesis by John Linnell, submitted to the Graduate Faculty of the University of Minnesota, June, 1954.

a sensation of white as the sort of thing that can become an abstract idea (occurrent) of White—a thought of White 'in the Understanding' —merely by virtue of being separated from the context of other sensations (and images) which accompany it on a particular occasion. In other words, for Locke an abstract (occurrent) idea of the determinate repeatable Whiteness is nothing more than an isolated *image of white*, which, in turn, differs from a *sensation of white* only (to use a modern turn of phrase) by being 'centrally aroused'.

In short, for Locke, the problem of how we come to be aware of *determinate* sense repeatables is no problem at all. Merely by virtue of having sensations and images we have this awareness. *His* problem of abstract ideas is the problem of how we come to be able to think of generic properties. And, as is clear from the *Essay*, he approaches *this* problem in terms of what might be called an 'adjunctive theory of specification', that is, the view that (if we represent the idea of a determinable as *the idea of being A*) the idea of a determinate form of A can be represented as *the idea of being A and B*. It is, of course, notorious that this won't account for the relation of *the idea of being red* to *the idea of being crimson*. By thinking of *conjunction* as the fundamental logical relation involved in building up complex ideas from simple ones, and as the principle of the difference between determinable and determinate ideas, Locke precluded himself from giving even a plausible account of the relation between ideas of determinables and ideas of determinates. It is interesting to speculate what turn his thought might have taken had he admitted *disjunctive* as well as *conjunctive* complex ideas, *the idea of being A or B* alongside *the idea of being A and B*.

27. But my purpose here is not to develop a commentary on the shortcomings of Locke's treatment of abstract ideas, but to emphasize that something which is a problem for us was not a problem for him. And it is therefore important to note that the same is true of Berkeley. His problem was not, as it is often construed, 'How do we go from the awareness of *particulars* to ideas of *repeatables*?' but rather, 'Granted that in immediate experience we are aware of absolutely *specific* sense qualities, how do we come to be conscious of genera pertaining to them, and in what does this consciousness consist?' (This is not the only dimension of 'abstraction' that concerned him, but it is the one that is central to our purpose.) And, contrary to the usual interpretation, the essential difference between his account and Locke's consists in the fact that whereas Locke was on the whole[1] committed to the view that there can be an idea which.

---

[1] I say that Locke was 'on the whole' committed to the view that there can be an idea which is *of* the genus without being *of* any of its species, because while he saw that it could not be *of* any one of the species to the exclusion of the others,

is *of* the genus without bein₃ ⸗f any of its species, Berkeley insists that we can have an idea *of* ⸗ genus only by having an idea *of* the genus *as*, to borrow a useful Scotist term, *'contracted' into one of its species.*

Roughly, Berkeley's contention is that if *being A* entails *being B*, then there can be no such thing as an idea which is *of A* without being *of B*. He infers that since *being triangular* entails *having some determinately triangular shape*, there cannot be an idea which is *of triangle* without being *of some determinately triangular shape.* We can be aware of generic triangularity only by having an idea which is of triangularity as 'contracted' into one of the specific forms of triangularity. Any of the latter will do; they are all 'of the same sort'.

28. Now, a careful study of the *Treatise* makes it clear that Hume is in the same boat as Berkeley and Locke, sharing with them the presupposition that we have an unacquired ability to be aware of determinate repeatables. It is often said that whereas he begins the *Treatise* by characterizing 'ideas' in terms which do not distinguish between *images* and *thoughts*, he corrects this deficiency in Book I, Part I, Section vii. What these students of Hume tend to overlook is that what Hume does in this later section is give an account *not* of what it is to think of *repeatables* whether determinable or determinate, but of what it is to think of *determinables*, thus of colour as contrasted with particular shades of colour. And his account of the consciousness of determinables takes for granted that we have a primordial ability to take account of *determinate* repeatables. Thus, his later account is simply built on, and in no sense a revision of, the account of ideas with which he opens the *Treatise*.

---

and saw no way of avoiding this except by making it *of none* of the species, he was greatly puzzled by this, for he saw that in some sense the idea *of the genus* must be *of all the species.* We have already noted that if he had admitted disjunction as a principle of compounding ideas, he could have said that the idea *of the genus* is the idea *of the disjunction of all its species,* that the idea of *being triangular* is the idea of *being scalene or isosceles.* As it was, he thought that to be of all the species it would have to be the idea of *being scalene and isosceles,* which is, of course, the idea of an impossibility.

It is interesting to note that if Berkeley had faced up to the implications of the criterion we shall find him to have adopted, this disjunctive conception of the generic idea is the one he would have been led to adopt. For since *being G*—where 'G' stands for a generic character—entails being S_1 or S_2 or S_3 . . . or S_n—where 'S_1' stands for a specific character falling under G—Berkeley should have taken as the unit of ideas concerning triangles, the idea of the genus Triangle as differentiated into the set of specific forms of triangularity. But, needless, to say, if Berkeley *had* taken this step, he could not have thought of a sensation of crimson as a determinate *thought.*

How, then, does he differ from Berkeley and Locke? The latter two had supposed that there must be such a thing as an *occurrent* thought of a determinable, however much they differed in their account of such thoughts. Hume, on the other hand, assuming that there are occurrent thoughts of *determinate* repeatables, *denies* that there are occurrent thoughts of *determinables*. I shall spare the reader the familiar details of Hume's attempt to give a constructive account of our consciousness of determinables, nor shall I criticize it. For my point is that however much Locke, Berkeley, and Hume differ on the problem of abstract ideas, they all take for granted that the human mind has an innate ability to be aware of certain determinate sorts— *indeed, that we are aware of them simply by virtue of having sensations and images.*

29. Now, it takes but a small twist of Hume's position to get a radically different view. For suppose that instead of characterizing the initial elements of experience as impressions *of*, e.g. *red*, Hume had characterized them as *red particulars* (and I would be the last to deny that not only Hume, but perhaps Berkeley and Locke as well, often treat impressions or ideas *of red* as though they were *red particulars*) then Hume's view, expanded to take into account determinates as well as determinables, would become the view that all consciousness of sorts or repeatables rests on an association of *words* (e.g. 'red') with classes of resembling particulars.

It clearly makes all the difference in the world how this association is conceived. For if the formation of the association involves not only the occurrence of resembling particulars, but also the occurrence of the awareness *that they are resembling particulars*, then the givenness of determinate kinds or repeatables, say crimson, is merely being replaced by the givenness of *facts* of the form *x resembles y*, and we are back with an unacquired ability to be aware of repeatables, in this case the repeatable *resemblance*. Even more obviously, if the formation of the association involves not only the occurrence of red particulars, but the awareness *that they are red*, then the conceptualistic form of the myth has merely been replaced by a realistic version, as in the classical sense-datum theory.

If, however, the association is not mediated by the awareness of facts either of the form *x resembles y*, or of the form *x is* ϕ, then we have a view of the general type which I will call *psychological nominalism*, according to which *all* awareness of *sorts, resemblances, facts*, etc., in short, all awareness of abstract entities—indeed, all awareness even of particulars—is a linguistic affair. According to it, not even the awareness of such sorts, resemblances, and facts as pertain to so-called immediate experience is presupposed by the process of acquiring the use of a language.

Two remarks are immediately relevant: (1) Although the form of psychological nominalism which one gets by modifying Hume's view along the above lines has the essential merit that it avoids the mistake of supposing that there are pure episodes of being aware of sensory repeatables or sensory facts, and is committed to the view that any event which can be referred to in these terms must be, to use Ryle's expression, a mongrel categorical-hypothetical, in particular, a verbal episode *as being the manifestation of associative connections of the word-object and word-word types*, it nevertheless is impossibly crude and inadequate as an account of the simplest concept. (2) Once sensations and images have been purged of epistemic aboutness, the primary reason for supposing that the fundamental associative tie between language and the world must be between words and 'immediate experiences' has disappeared, and the way is clear to recognizing that basic word–world associations hold, for example, between 'red' and red *physical objects*, rather than between 'red' and a supposed class of private red particulars.

The second remark, it should be emphasized, does not imply that private sensations or impressions may not be essential to the formation of these associative connections. For one can certainly admit that the tie between 'red' and red physical objects—which tie makes it possible for 'red' to mean the quality red—is *causally* mediated by sensations of red without being committed to the mistaken idea that it is 'really' sensations of red, rather than red physical objects, which are the primary denotation of the word 'red'.

VII. THE LOGIC OF 'MEANS'

30. There is a source of the Myth of the Given to which even philosophers who are suspicious of the whole idea of *inner episodes* can fall prey. This is the fact that when we picture a child—or a carrier of slabs—learning his *first* language, *we*, of course, locate the language learner in a structured logical space in which *we* are at home. Thus, we conceive of him as a person (or, at least, a potential person) in a world of physical objects, coloured, producing sounds, existing in Space and Time. But though it is *we* who are familiar with this logical space, we run the danger, if we are not careful, of picturing the language learner as having *ab initio* some degree of awareness—'pre-analytic', limited and fragmentary though it may be—of this same logical space. We picture his state as though it were rather like our own when placed in a strange forest on a dark night. In other words, unless we are careful, we can easily take for granted that the process of teaching a child to use a language is that of teaching it to discriminate elements

within a logical space of particulars, universals, facts, etc., of which it is already undiscriminatingly aware, and to associate these discriminated elements with verbal symbols. And this mistake is in principle the same whether the logical space of which the child is supposed to have this undiscriminating awareness is conceived by *us* to be that of physical objects or of private sense contents.

The real test of a theory of language lies not in its account of what has been called (by H. H. Price) 'thinking in absence', but in its account of 'thinking in presence'—that is to say, its account of those occasions on which the fundamental connection of language with non-linguistic fact is exhibited. And many theories which look like psychological nominalism when one views their account of thinking in absence, turn out to be quite 'Augustinian' when the scalpel is turned to their account of thinking in presence.

31. Now, the friendly use I have been making of the phrase 'psychological nominalism' may suggest that I am about to *equate* concepts with words, and thinking, in so far as it is episodic, with verbal episodes. I must now hasten to say that I shall do nothing of the sort, or, at least, that if I *do* do *something* of the sort, the view I shall shortly be developing is only in a relatively Pickwickian sense an equation of thinking with the use of language. I wish to emphasize, therefore, that as I am using the term, the primary connotation of 'psychological nominalism' is the denial that there is any awareness of logical space prior to, or independent of, the acquisition of a language.

However, although I shall later be distinguishing between *thoughts* and their verbal *expression*, there is a point of fundamental importance which is best made before more subtle distinctions are drawn. To begin with, it is perfectly clear that the word 'red' would not be a *predicate* if it did not have the logical syntax characteristic of predicates. Nor would it be the predicate it is, unless, in certain frames of mind, at least, we tended to respond to red objects in standard circumstances with something having the force of 'This is red'. And once we have abandoned the idea that learning to use the word 'red' involves antecedent episodes of the *awareness of redness*—not to be confused, of course, with *sensations of red*—there is a temptation to suppose that the word 'red' means the quality *red* by virtue of these two facts: briefly, the fact that it has the *syntax* of a predicate, and the fact that it is a *response* (in certain circumstances) to red objects.

But this account of the meaningfulness of 'red', which Price has correctly stigmatized as the 'thermometer view', would have little plausibility if it were not reinforced by another line of thought which takes its point of departure from the superficial resemblance of

>   (In German) *'rot'* means *red*

to such relational statements as

>   Cowley adjoins Oxford.

For once one assimilates the form

>   '. . .' means - - -

to the form

>   x R y

and thus takes it for granted that meaning is a relation between a word and a nonverbal entity, it is tempting to suppose that the relation in question is that of association.

The truth of the matter, of course, is that statements of the form '". . ." means - - -' are *not* relational statements, and that while it is indeed the case that the word *'rot'* could not mean the quality *red* unless it were associated with red things, it would be misleading to say that the semantical statement '*"Rot"* means *red*' says of *'rot'* that it associated with red things. For this would suggest that the semantical statement is, so to speak, definitional shorthand for a longer statement about the associative connections of *'rot'*, which is not the case. The rubric '". . ." means - - -' is a linguistic device for conveying the information that a *mentioned* word, in this case *'rot'*, plays the same role in a certain linguistic economy, in this case the linguistic economy of German-speaking peoples, as does the word 'red', which is not *mentioned* but *used*—used in a unique way; *exhibited*, so to speak—and which occurs 'on the right-hand side' of the semantical statement.

We see, therefore, how the two statements

>   *'Und* means *and*

and

>   *'Rot'* means *red*

can tell us quite different things about *'und'* and *'rot'*, for the first conveys the information that *'und'* plays the purely formal role of a certain logical connective, the second that *'rot'* plays in German the role of the observation word 'red'—in spite of the fact that *means* has the same sense in each statement, and without having to say that the first says of *'und'* that it stands in 'the meaning relation 'to Conjunction, or the second that *'rot'* stands in 'the meaning relation' to Redness.[1]

---

[1] For an analysis of the problem of abstract entities built on this interpretation of semantical statements, see my 'Empiricism and Abstract Entities' in Paul A. Schlipp (ed.), *The Philosophy of Rudolph Carnap*. Wilmette (Ill.), 1963; also 'Abstract Entities', *The Review of Metaphysics*, June, 1963.

These considerations make it clear that nothing whatever can be inferred about the complexity of the role played by the word 'red' or about the exact way in which the word 'red' is related to red things, from the truth of the semantical statement ' "red" means the quality *red*'. And no consideration arising from the 'Fido'-Fido aspect of the grammar of 'means' precludes one from claiming that the role of the word 'red' by virtue of which it can correctly be said to have the meaning it does is a complicated one indeed, and that one cannot understand the meaning of the word 'red'—'know what redness is'—unless one has a great deal of knowledge which classical empiricism would have held to have a purely contingent relationship with the possession of fundamental empirical concepts.

VIII. DOES EMPIRICAL KNOWLEDGE HAVE A FOUNDATION?

32. One of the forms taken by the Myth of the Given is the idea that there is, indeed *must be*, a structure of particular matter of fact such that (*a*) each fact can not only be non-inferentially known to be the case, but presupposes no other knowledge either of particular matter of fact, or of general truths; and (*b*) such that the noninferential knowledge of facts belonging to this structure constitutes the ultimate court of appeals for all factual claims—particular and general—about the world. It is important to note that I characterized the knowledge of fact belonging to this stratum as not only noninferential, but as presupposing no knowledge of other matter of fact, whether particular or general. It might be thought that this is a redundancy, that knowledge (not belief or conviction, but knowledge) which logically presupposes knowledge of other facts *must* be inferential. This, however, as I hope to show, is itself an episode in the Myth.

Now, the idea of such a privileged stratum of fact is a familiar one, though not without its difficulties. Knowledge pertaining to this level is *noninferential*, yet it is, after all, *knowledge*. It is *ultimate*, yet it has *authority*. The attempt to make a consistent picture of these two requirements has traditionally taken the following form:

Statements pertaining to this level, in order to 'express knowledge' must not only be made, but, so to speak, must be worthy of being made, *credible*, that is, in the sense of worthy of credence. Furthermore, and this is a crucial point, they must be made in a way which *involves* this credibility. For where there is no connection between the making of a statement and its authority, the assertion may express *conviction*, but it can scarcely be said to express knowledge.

The authority—the credibility—of statements pertaining to this level cannot exhaustively consist in the fact that they are supported by *other* statements, for in that case all *knowledge* pertaining to this level would have to be inferential, which not only contradicts the hypothesis, but flies

164

in the face of good sense. The conclusion seems inevitable that if some statements pertaining to this level are to express *noninferential* knowledge, they must have a credibility which is not a matter of being supported by other statements. Now there does seem to be a class of statements which fill at least part of this bill, namely such statements as would be said to *report observations*, thus, 'This is red.' These statements, candidly made, have authority. Yet they are not expressions of inference. How, then, is this authority to be understood?

Clearly, the argument contiñues, it springs from the fact that they are made in just the circumstances in which they are made, as is indicated by the fact that they characteristically, though not necessarily or without exception, involve those so-called token-reflexive expressions which, in addition to the tenses of verbs, serve to connect the circumstances in which a statement is made with its sense. (At this point it will be helpful to begin putting the line of thought I am developing in terms of the *fact-stating* and *observation-reporting* roles of certain sentences.) Roughly, two verbal performances which are tokens of a non-token-reflexive sentence can occur in widely different circumstances and yet make the same statement; whereas two tokens of a token-reflexive sentence can make the same statement only if they are uttered in the same circumstances (according to a relevant criterion of sameness). And two tokens of a sentence, whether it contains a token-reflexive expression —over and above a tensed verb—or not, can make the same *report* only if, made in all candour, they express the *presence*—in *some* sense of 'presence'—of the state of affairs that is being reported; if, that is, they stand in that relation to the state of affairs, whatever the relation may be, by virtue of which they can be said to formulate observations of it.

It would appear, then, that there are two ways in which a sentence token can have credibility: (1) The authority may accrue to it, so to speak, from above, that is, as being a token of a sentence type *all* the token of which, in a certain use, have credibility, e.g. '2+2=4'. In this case, let us say that token credibility is inherited from type authority. (2) The credibility may accrue to it from the fact that it came to exist in a certain way in a certain set of circumstances, e.g. 'This is red.' Here token credibility is not derived from type credibility.

Now, the credibility of *some* sentence types appears to be *intrinsic*—at least in the limited sense that it is *not* derived from other sentences, type or token. This is, or seems to be, the case with certain sentences used to make analytic statements. The credibility of *some* sentence types accrues to them by virtue of their logical relations to other sentence types, thus by virtue of the fact that they are logical consequences of more basic sentences. It would seem obvious, however, that the credibility of empirical sentence types cannot be traced without remainder to the credibility of other sentence types. And since no empirical sentence type appears to have *intrinsic* credibility, 'his means that credibility must accrue to *some* empirical sentence types by virtue of their logical relations to certain sentence tokens, and, indeed, to sentence tokens the authority of which is not derived, in its turn, from the authority of sentence types.

The picture we get is that of their being two *ultimate* modes of credibility: (1) The intrinsic credibility of analytic sentences, which accrues to tokens as being tokens of such a type; (2) the credibility of such tokens as 'express observations', a credibility which flows from tokens to types.

33. Let us explore this picture, which is common to all traditional empiricisms, a bit further. How is the authority of such sentence tokens as 'express observational knowledge' to be understood? It has been tempting to suppose that in spite of the obvious differences which exist between 'observation reports' and 'analytic statements', there is an essential similarity between the ways in which they come by their authority. Thus, it has been claimed, not without plausibility, that whereas *ordinary* empirical statements can be *correctly* made without being *true*, observation reports resemble analytic statements in that being correctly made is a sufficient as well as necessary condition of their truth. And it has been inferred from this—somewhat hastily, I believe—that 'correctly making' the report 'This is green' is a matter of 'following the rules for the use of "this", "is", and "green".'

Three comments are immediately necessary:

(1) First a brief remark about the term 'report'. In ordinary usage a report is a report made *by* someone *to* someone. To make a report is to *do* something. In the literature of epistemology, however, the word 'report' or '*Konstatierung*' has acquired a technical use in which a sentence token can play a reporting role (*a*) without being an *overt* verbal performance, and (*b*) without having the character of being 'by someone to someone'—even oneself. There is, of course, such a thing as 'talking to oneself'—*in foro interno*—but, as I shall be emphasizing in the closing stages of my argument, it is important not to suppose that all 'covert' verbal episodes are of this kind.

(2) My second comment is that while *we* shall not assume that because 'reports' *in the ordinary sense* are actions, 'reports' in the sense of *Konstatierungen* are also actions, the line of thought we are considering treats them as such. In other words, it interprets the correctness of *Konstatierungen* as analogous to the rightness of actions. Let me emphasize, however, that not all *ought* is *ought to do*, nor all correctness the correctness of *actions*.

(3) My third comment is that if the expression 'following a rule' is taken seriously, and is not weakened beyond all recognition into the bare notion of exhibiting a uniformity—in which case the lightning–thunder sequence would 'follow a rule'—then it is the knowledge or belief that the circumstances are of a certain kind, and not the mere fact that they *are* of this kind, which contributes to bringing about the action.

34. In the light of these remarks it is clear that *if* observation reports are construed as *actions*, *if* their correctness is interpreted as the correctness of an *action*, and *if* the authority of an observation report is construed as the fact that making it is 'following a rule' in the proper sense of this phrase, *then* we are face to face with givenness in its most straightforward form. For these stipulations commit one to the idea that the authority of *Konstatierungen* rests on nonverbal episodes of awareness—awareness *that* something is the case, e.g. *that this is green*—which nonverbal episodes have an intrinsic authority (they are, so to speak, 'self-authenticating') which the *verbal* performances (the *Konstatierungen*) properly performed 'express'. One is committed to a stratum of authoritative nonverbal episodes ('awarenesses'), the authority of which accrues to a superstructure of *verbal actions*, provided that the expressions occurring in these actions are properly *used*. These self-authenticating episodes would constitute the tortoise on which stands the elephant on which rests the edifice of empirical knowledge. The essence of the view is the same whether these intrinsically authoritative episodes are such items as the awareness that a certain sense content is green or such items as the awareness that a certain physical object looks to oneself to be green.

35. But what is the alternative? We might begin by trying something like the following: An overt or covert token of 'This is green' in the presence of a green item is a *Konstatierung* and expresses observational knowledge if and only if it is a manifestation of a tendency to produce overt or covert tokens of 'This is green'—given a certain set—if and only if a green object is being looked at in standard conditions. Clearly on this interpretation the occurrence of such tokens of 'This is green' would be 'following a rule' only in the sense that they are instances of a uniformity, a uniformity differing from the lightning–thunder case in that it is an acquired causal characteristic of the language user. Clearly the above suggestion, which corresponds to the 'thermometer view' criticized by Professor Price, and which we have already rejected, won't do as it stands. Let us see, however, if it cannot be revised to fit the criteria I have been using for 'expressing observational knowledge'.

The first hurdle to be jumped concerns the *authority* which, as I have emphasized, a sentence token must have in order that it may be said to express knowledge. Clearly, on this account the only thing that can remotely be supposed to constitute such authority is the fact that one can infer the presence of a green object from the fact that someone makes this report. As we have already noticed, the correctness of a report does not have to be construed as the rightness of an *action*. A report can be correct as being an instance of a general mode

167

of behaviour which, in a given linguistic community, it is reasonable to sanction and support.

The second hurdle is, however, the decisive one. For we have seen that to be the expression of knowledge, a report must not only *have* authority, this authority must *in some sense* be recognized by the person whose report it is. And this is a steep hurdle indeed. For if the authority of the report 'This is green' lies in the fact that the existence of green items appropriately related to the perceiver can be inferred from the occurrence of such reports, it follows that only a person who is able to draw this inference, and therefore who has not only the concept *green*, but also the concept of uttering 'This is green'— indeed, the concept of certain conditions of perception, those which would correctly be called 'standard conditions'—could be in a position to token 'This is green' in recognition of its authority. In other words, for a *Konstatierung* 'This is green' to 'express observational knowledge', not only must it be a *symptom* or *sign* of the presence of a green object in standard conditions, but the perceiver must know that tokens of 'This is green' *are* symptoms of the presence of green objects in conditions which are standard for visual perception.

36. Now it might be thought that there is something obviously absurd in the idea that before a token uttered by, say, Jones could be the expression of observational knowledge, Jones would have to know that overt verbal episodes of this kind are reliable indicators of the existence, suitably related to the speaker, of green objects. I do not think that it is. Indeed, I think that something very like it is true. The point I wish to make now, however, is that if it *is* true, then it follows, as a matter of simple logic, that one could not have observational knowledge of *any* fact unless one knew many *other* things as well. And let me emphasize that the point is not taken care of by distinguishing between *knowing how* and *knowing that*, and admitting that observational knowledge requires a lot of 'know how'. For the point is specifically that observational knowledge of any particular fact, e.g. that this is green, presupposes that one knows general facts of the form *X is a reliable symptom of Y*. And to admit this requires an abandonment of the traditional empiricist idea that observational knowledge 'stands on its own feet'. Indeed, the suggestion would be anathema to traditional empiricists for the obvious reason that by making observational knowledge *presuppose* knowledge of general facts of the form *X is a reliable symptom of Y*, it runs counter to the idea that we come to know general facts of this form only *after* we have come to know by observation a number of particular facts which support the hypothesis that X is a symptom of Y.

And it might be thought that there is an obvious regress in the view we are examining. Does it not tell us that observational knowledge at time t presupposes knowledge of the form *X is a reliable symptom of Y*, which presupposes *prior* observational knowledge, which presupposes *other* knowledge of the form *X is a reliable symptom of Y*, which presupposes still other, and *prior*, observational knowledge, and so on? This charge, however, rests on too simple, indeed a radically mistaken, conception of what one is saying of Jones when one says that he *knows* that-p. It is not just that the objection supposes that knowing is an *episode*; for clearly there are episodes which we can correctly characterize as knowings, in particular, *observings*. The essential point is that in characterizing an episode or a state as that of *knowing*, we are not giving an empirical description of that episode or state; we are placing it in the logical space of reasons, of justifying and being able to justify what one says.

37. Thus, all that the view I am defending requires is that no tokening by S *now* of 'This is green' is to count as 'expressing observational knowledge' unless it is also correct to say of S that he *now* knows the appropriate fact of the form *X is a reliable symptom of Y*, namely that (and again I oversimplify) utterances of 'This is green' are reliable indicators of the presence of green objects in standard conditions of perception. And while the correctness of this statement about Jones requires that Jones could *now* cite prior particular facts as evidence for the idea that these utterances *are* reliable indicators, it requires only that it is correct to say that Jones *now* knows, thus remembers,[1] that these particular facts *did* obtain. It does not require that it be correct to say that at the time these facts did obtain he *then* knew them to obtain. And the regress disappears.

Thus, while Jones's ability to give inductive reasons *today* is built on a long history of acquiring and manifesting verbal habits in perceptual situations, and, in particular, the occurrence of verbal episodes, e.g. 'This is green', which is superficially like those which are later properly said to express observational knowledge, it does not require that any episode in this prior time be characterizeable as expressing knowledge. (At this point, the reader should reread Section 19 above.)

38. The idea that observation 'strictly and properly so-called' is constituted by certain self-authenticating nonverbal episodes, the authority of which is transmitted to verbal and quasi-verbal performances when these performances are made 'in conformity with the semantical rules of the language', is, of course, the heart of the Myth of the Given. For the *given*, in epistemological tradition, is what is *taken* by these self-authenticating episodes. These 'takings' are, so to speak, the unmoved movers of empirical knowledge, the

[1] (Added 1963) My thought was that one can have direct (non-inferential) knowledge of a past fact which one did not or even (as in the case envisaged) *could* not conceptualize at the time it was present.

'knowings in presence' which are presupposed by all other knowledge, both the knowledge of general truths and the knowledge 'in
absence' of other particular matters of fact. Such is the framework in
which traditional empiricism makes its characteristic claim that the
perceptually given is the foundation of empirical knowledge.

Let me make it clear, however, that if I reject this framework, it is
not because I should deny that observings are *inner* episodes, nor that
strictly speaking they are *nonverbal* episodes. It will be my contention,
however, that the sense in which they are nonverbal—which is also
the sense in which thought episodes are nonverbal—is one which
gives no aid or comfort to epistemological givenness. In the concluding sections of this paper I shall attempt to explicate the logic of
inner episodes, and show that we can distinguish between observations and thoughts, on the one hand, and their verbal expression on
the other, without making the mistakes of traditional dualism. I shall
also attempt to explicate the logical status of *impressions* or *immediate
experiences*, and thus bring to a successful conclusion the quest with
which my argument began.

One final remark before I begin this task. If I reject the framework
of traditional empiricism, it is not because I want to say that empirical
knowledge has *no* foundation. For to put it this way is to suggest that
it is really 'empirical knowledge so-called', and to put it in a box with
rumours and hoaxes. There is clearly *some* point to the picture of
human knowledge as resting on a level of propositions—observation
reports—which do not rest on other propositions in the same way as
other propositions rest on them. On the other hand, I do wish to
insist that the metaphor of 'foundation' is misleading in that it keeps
us from seeing that if there is a logical dimension in which other
empirical propositions rest on observation reports, there is another
logical dimension in which the latter rest on the former.

Above all, the picture is misleading because of its static character.
One seems forced to choose between the picture of an elephant which
rests on a tortoise (What supports the tortoise?) and the picture of a
great Hegelian serpent of knowledge with its tail in its mouth (Where
does it begin?). Neither will do. For empirical knowledge, like its
sophisticated extension, science, is rational, not because it has a
foundation but because it is a self-correcting enterprise which can put
any claim in jeopardy, though not *all* at once.

IX. SCIENCE AND ORDINARY USAGE

39. There are many strange and exotic specimens in the gardens of
philosophy: Epistemology, Ontology, Cosmology, to name but a few.
And clearly there is much good sense—not only rhyme but reason—

to these labels. It is not my purpose, however, to animadvert on the botanizing of philosophies and things philosophical, other than to call attention to a recent addition to the list of philosophical flora and fauna, the Philosophy of Science. Nor shall I attempt to locate this new speciality in a classificatory system. The point I wish to make, however, can be introduced by calling to mind the fact that classificatory schemes, however theoretical their purpose, have practical consequences: nominal causes, so to speak, have real effects. As long as there was no such subject as 'philosophy of science', all students of philosophy felt obligated to keep at least one eye part of the time on both the methodological and the substantive aspects of the scientific enterprise. And if the result was often a confusion of the task of philosophy with the task of science, and almost equally often a projection of the framework of the latest scientific speculations into the common sense picture of the world (witness the almost unquestioned assumption, today, that the common sense world of physical objects in Space and Time must be *analysable* into spatially and temporally, or even spatiotemporally, related *events*), at least it had the merit of ensuring that reflection on the nature and implications of scientific discourse was an integral and vital part of philosophical thinking generally. But now that philosophy of science has nominal as well as real existence, there has arisen the temptation to leave it to the specialists, and to confuse the sound idea that philosophy is not science with the mistaken idea that philosophy is independent of science.

40. As long as discourse was viewed as a map, subdivided into a side-by-side of sub-maps, each representing a sub-region in a side-by-side of regions making up the total subject-matter of discourse, and as long as the task of the philosopher was conceived to be the piecemeal one of analysis in the sense of *definition*—the task, so to speak, of 'making little ones out of big ones'—one could view with equanimity the existence of philosophical specialists—specialists in formal and mathematical logic, in perception, in moral philosophy, etc. For if discourse were as represented above, where would be the harm of each man fencing himself off in his own garden? In spite, however, of the persistence of the slogan 'philosophy is analysis', we now realize that the atomistic conception of philosophy is a snare and a delusion. For 'analysis' no longer connotes the definition of terms, but rather the clarification of the logical structure—in the broadest sense—of discourse, and discourse no longer appears as one plane parallel to another, but as a tangle of intersecting dimensions whose relations with one another and with extra-linguistic fact conform to no single or simple pattern. No longer can the philosopher interested in perception say, 'Let him who is interested in prescriptive discourse

171

analyse its concepts and leave me in peace.' Most if not all philosophically interesting concepts are caught up in more than one dimension of discourse, and while the atomism of early analysis has a healthy successor in the contemporary stress on journeyman tactics, the grand strategy of the philosophical enterprise is once again directed towards that articulated and integrated vision of man-in-the-universe—or, shall I say, discourse-about-man-in-all-discourse—which has traditionally been its goal.

But the moral I wish specifically to draw is that no longer can one smugly say, 'Let the person who is interested in scientific discourse analyse scientific discourse and let the person who is interested in ordinary discourse analyse ordinary discourse.' Let me not be misunderstood. I am not saying that in order to discern the logic—the polydimensional logic—of ordinary discourse, it is necessary to make use of the results or the methods of the sciences. Nor even that, within limits, such a division of labour is not a sound corollary of the journeyman's approach. My point is rather that what we call the scientific enterprise is the flowering of a dimension of discourse which already exists in what historians call the 'prescientific stage', and that failure to understand this type of discourse 'writ large'—in science—may lead, indeed, has often led to a failure to appreciate its role in 'ordinary usage', and, as a result, to a failure to understand the full logic of even the most fundamental, the 'simplest' empirical terms.

41. Another point of equal importance. The procedures of philosophical analysis as such may make no use of the methods or results of the sciences. But familiarity with the trend of scientific thought is essential to the *appraisal* of the framework categories of the common sense picture of the world. For if the line of thought embodied in the preceding paragraphs is sound, if, that is to say, scientific discourse is but a continuation of a dimension of discourse which has been present in human discourse from the very beginning, then one would expect there to be a sense in which the scientific picture of the world *replaces* the common sense picture; a sense in which the scientific account of 'what there is' *supersedes* the descriptive ontology of everyday life.

Here one must be cautious. For there is a right way and a wrong way to make this point. Many years ago it used to be confidently said that science has shown, for example, that physical objects are not really coloured. Later it was pointed out that if this is interpreted as the claim that the sentence 'Physical objects have colours' expresses an empirical proposition which, though widely believed by common sense, has been shown by science to be false, then, of course, this claim is absurd. The idea that physical objects are not coloured can make sense only as the (misleading) expression of one aspect of a philosophical critique of the very framework of physical objects located in Space and enduring through Time. In short, 'Physical objects are not really coloured' makes sense only as a clumsy expression of the idea that there are no such things as the coloured physical objects of the common sense world, where this is interpreted, not as an empirical proposition—like 'There are no nonhuman featherless bipeds'—*within* the common sense frame, but as the expression of a rejection (in *some* sense) of this very framework itself, in favour of another built around different, if not unrelated, categories. This rejection need not, of course, be a *practical* rejection. It need not, that is, carry with it a proposal to brain-wash existing populations and train them to speak differently. And, of course, as long as the existing framework is used, it will be *incorrect* to say—otherwise than to make a philosophical point *about the framework*—that no object is really coloured, or is located in Space, or endures through Time. But, *speaking as a philosopher*, I am quite prepared to say that the common sense world of physical objects in Space and Time is unreal —that is, that there are no such things. Or, to put it less paradoxically, that in the dimension of describing and explaining the world, science is the measure of all things, of what is that it is, and of what is not that it is not.

43. There is a widespread impression that reflection on how we learn the language in which, in everyday life, we describe the world, leads to the conclusion that the categories of the common sense picture of the world have, so to speak, an unchallengeable authenticity. There are, of course, different conceptions of just what this fundamental categorial framework is. For some it is sense contents and phenomenal relations between them; for others physical objects, persons, and processes in Space and Time. But whatever their points of difference, the philosophers I have in mind are united in the conviction that what is called the 'ostensive tie' between our fundamental descriptive vocabulary and the world rules out of court as utterly absurd any notion that there are no such things as this framework talks about.

An integral part of this conviction is what I shall call (in an extended sense) the *positivistic conception of science*, the idea that the framework of theoretical objects (molecules, electro-magnetic fields, etc.) and their relationships is, to to speak, an *auxiliary* framework. In its most explicit form, it is the idea that theoretical objects and propositions concerning them are 'calculational devices', the value and status of which consist in their systematizing and heuristic role with respect to confirmable generalizations formulated in the framework of terms which enjoy a direct ostensive link with the world. One is tempted to put this by saying that according to these philosophers, the objects of ostensively linked discourse behave *as if* and *only as if* they were bound up with or consisted of scientific entities. But, of course, these philosophers would hasten to point out (and rightly so) that

X behaves as if it consisted of Y's

makes sense only by contrast with

X behaves as it does because it *does* consist of Y's

whereas their contention is exactly that where the Y's are *scientific* objects, no such contrast makes sense.

The point I am making is that as long as one thinks that there is a framework, whether of physical objects or of sense contents, the absolute authenticity of which is guaranteed by the fact that the learning of this framework involves an 'ostensive step', so long one will be tempted to think of the authority of theoretical discourse as entirely derivative, that of a calculational auxiliary, an effective heuristic device. It is one of my prime purposes, in the following sections, to convince the reader that this interpretation of the status of the scientific picture of the world rests on two mistakes: (1) a misunderstanding (which I have already exposed) of the ostensive element in the learning and use of a language—the Myth of the Given; (2) a reification of the *methodological* distinction between theoretical and non-theoretical discourse into a *substantive* distinction between theoretical and non-theoretical existence.

44. One way of summing up what I have been saying above is by saying that there is a widespread impression abroad, aided and abetted by a naïve interpretation of conecpt formation, that philosophers of science deal with a mode of discourse which is, so to speak, a peninsular offshoot from the mainland of ordinary discourse. The study of scientific discourse is conceived to be a worthy employment for those who have the background and motivation to keep track of it, but an employment which is fundamentally a hobby divorced from the perplexities of the mainland. But, of course, this summing up won't quite do. For all philosophers would agree that no philosophy would be complete unless it resolved the perplexities which arise when one attempts to think through the relationship of the framework of modern science to ordinary discourse. My point, however, is not that anyone would reject the idea that this is a proper task for philosophy, but that, by approaching the language in which the plain man describes and explains empirical fact with the presuppositions of *givenness*, they are led to a 'resolution' of these perplexities along the lines of what I have called the positivistic or peninsular conception of scientific discourse—a 'resolution' which, I believe, is not only superficial, but positively mistaken.

X. PRIVATE EPISODES: THE PROBLEM

45. Let us now return, after a long absence, to the problem of how the similarity among the experiences of *seeing that an object over there is red, its looking to one that an object over there is red* (when in point of fact it is *not* red) and *its looking to one as though there were a red object over there* (when in fact there is *nothing* over there at all) is to be understood. Part of this similarity, we saw, consists in the fact that they all involve the idea—the proposition, if you please—that the object over there is red. But over and above this there is, of course, the aspect which many philosophers have attempted to clarify by the notion of *impressions* or *immediate experience*.

It was pointed out in Sections 21 ff. above that there are prima facie two ways in which facts of the form *x merely looks red* might be explained, in addition to the kind of explanation which is based on empirical generalizations relating the colour of objects, the circumstances in which they are seen, and the colours they look to have. These two ways are (*a*) the introduction of impressions or immediate experiences as theoretical entities; and (*b*) the *discovery*, on scrutinizing these situations, that they contain impressions or immediate experiences as components. I called attention to the paradoxical character of the first of these alternatives, and refused, at that time, to take it seriously. But in the meantime the second alternative, involving as it does the Myth of the Given, has turned out to be no more satisfactory.

For, in the first place, how are these impressions to be described, if not by using such words as 'red' and 'triangular'. Yet, if my argument, to date, is sound, physical objects alone can be literally red and triangular. Thus, in the cases I am considering there is nothing to be red and triangular. It would seem to follow that 'impression of a red triangle' could mean nothing more than 'impression of *the sort which* is common to those experiences in which we either see that something is red and triangular, or something merely looks red and triangular or there merely looks to be a red and triangular object over there'. And if we can never characterize 'impressions' intrinsically, but only by what is logically a definite description, i.e. as *the kind of entity which* is common to such situations, then we would scarcely seem to be any better off than if we maintained that talk about 'impressions' is a notational convenience, a code, for the language in which we speak of how things look and what there looks to be.

And this line of thought is reinforced by the consideration that once we give up the idea that we begin our sojourn in this world with any—even a vague, fragmentary, and undiscriminating—awareness of the logical space of particulars, kinds, facts, and resemblances, and recognize that even such 'simple' concepts as those of colours are the fruit of a long process of publicly reinforced responses to public objects (including verbal performances) in public situations, we may well be puzzled as to how even if there are such things as impressions or sensations, we could come to know that there are, and to know what sort of thing they are. *For we now recognize that instead of coming to have a concept of something because we have noticed that sort of thing, to have the ability to notice a sort of thing is already to have the concept of that sort of thing, and cannot account for it.*

Indeed, once we think this line of reasoning through, we are struck by the fact that if it is sound, we are faced not only with the question, 'How could we come to have the idea of an "impression" or "sensation"?' but by the question, 'How could we come to have the idea of something's looking red to us, or', to get to the crux of the matter, 'of seeing that something is red?' In short, we are brought face to face with the general problem of understanding how there can be *inner episodes*—episodes, that is, which somehow combine *privacy*, in that each of us has privileged access to his own, with *intersubjectivity*, in that each of us can, in principle, know about the other's. We might try to put this more linguistically as the problem of how there can be a sentence (e.g. 'S has a toothache') of which it is *logically* true that whereas *anybody* can use it to state a fact, only *one* person, namely S himself, can use it to make a report. But while this is a useful formulation, it does not do justice to the supposedly *episodic* character of the items in question. And that this is the heart of the puzzle is shown by the fact that many philosophers who would not deny that there are short-term hypothetical and mongrel hypothetical–categorical facts about behaviour which others can ascribe to us on behavioural evidence, but which only *we* can *report*, have found it to be logical nonsense to speak of non-behavioural *episodes* of which this is true. Thus, it has been claimed by Ryle[1] that the very idea that there are such episodes is a category mistake, while others have argued that though there are such episodes, they cannot be characterized in intersubjective discourse, learned as it is in a context of public objects and in the 'academy' of one's linguistic peers. It is my purpose to argue that both these contentions are quite mistaken, and that not only are inner episodes *not* category mistakes, they are quite 'effable' in intersubjective discourse. And it is my purpose to show, positively, *how* this can be the case. I am particularly concerned to make this point in connection with such inner episodes as sensations and feelings, in short, with what has—unfortunately, I think—been called 'immediate experience'. For such an account is necessary to round off this

[1] Ryle, Gilbert, *The Concept of Mind.* London: Hutchinson's University Library, 1949.

examination of the Myth of the Given. But before I can come to grips
with these topics, the way must be prepared by a discussion of inner
episodes of quite another kind, namely *thoughts*.

XI. THOUGHTS: THE CLASSICAL VIEW

46. Recent empiricism has been of two minds about the status of
thoughts. On the one hand, it has resonated to the idea that in so far
as there are *episodes* which are thoughts, they are *verbal* or *linguistic*
episodes. Clearly, however, even if candid overt verbal behaviours by
people who had learned a language *were* thoughts, there are not
nearly enough of them to account for all the cases in which it would
be argued that a person was thinking. Nor can we plausibly suppose
that the remainder is accounted for by those inner episodes which are
often very clumsily lumped together under the heading 'verbal
imagery'.

On the other hand, they have been tempted to suppose that the
episodes which are referred to by verbs pertaining to thinking include
all forms of 'intelligent behaviour', verbal as well as nonverbal, and
that the 'thought episodes' which are supposed to be manifested by
these behaviours are not really episodes at all, but rather hypothetical
and mongrel hypothetical–categorical facts about these and still other
behaviours. This, however, runs into the difficulty that whenever we
try to explain what we mean by calling a piece of *nonhabitual* behaviour intelligent, we seem to find it necessary to do so in terms of
thinking. The uncomfortable feeling will not be downed that the
dispositional account of thoughts in terms of intelligent behaviour is
covertly circular.

47. Now the classical tradition claimed that there is a family of
episodes, neither overt verbal behaviour nor verbal imagery, which
are *thoughts*, and that both overt verbal behaviour and verbal imagery
owe their meaningfulness to the fact that they stand to these *thoughts*
in the unique relation of 'expressing' them. These episodes are introspectable. Indeed, it was usually believed that they could not occur
without being known to occur. But this can be traced to a number
of confusions, perhaps the most important of which was the idea that
thoughts belong in the same general category as sensations, images,
tickles, itches, etc. This mis-assimilation of thoughts to sensations and
feelings was equally, as we saw in Sections 26ff. above, a mis-
assimilation of sensations and feelings to thoughts, and a falsification
of both. The assumption that if there are thought episodes, they must
be immediate experiences is common both to those who propounded
the classical view and to those who reject it, saying that they 'find
no such experiences'. If we purge the classical tradition of these

confusions, it becomes the idea that to each of us belongs a stream of episodes, not themselves immediate experiences, to which we have privileged, but by no means either invariable or infallible, access. These episodes can occur without being 'expressed' by overt verbal behaviour, though verbal behaviour is—in an important sense—their natural fruition. Again, we can 'hear ourselves think', but the verbal imagery which enables us to do this is no more the thinking itself than is the overt verbal behaviour by which it is expressed and communicated to others. It is a mistake to suppose that we must be having verbal imagery—indeed, any imagery—when we 'know what we are thinking'—in short, to suppose that 'privileged access' must be construed on a perceptual or quasi-perceptual model.

Now, it is my purpose to defend such a revised classical analysis of our common sense conception of thoughts, and in the course of doing so I shall develop distinctions which will later contribute to a resolution, in principle, of the puzzle of *immediate experience*. But before I continue, let me hasten to add that it will turn out that the view I am about to expound could, with equal appropriateness, be represented as a modified form of the view that thoughts are *linguistic* episodes.

XII. OUR RYLEAN ANCESTORS

48. But, the reader may well ask, in what sense can these episodes be 'inner' if they are not immediate experiences? and in what sense can they be 'linguistic' if they are neither overt linguistic performances, nor verbal imagery '*in foro interno*'? I am going to answer these and the other questions I have been raising by making a myth of my own, or, to give it an air of up-to-date respectability, by writing a piece of science fiction—anthropological science fiction. Imagine a stage in prehistory in which humans are limited to what I shall call a Rylean language, a language of which the fundamental descriptive vocabulary speaks of public properties of public objects located in Space and enduring through Time. Let me hasten to add that it is also Rylean in that although its basic resources are limited (how limited I shall be discussing in a moment), its total expressive power is very great. For it makes subtle use not only of the elementary logical operations of conjunction, disjunction, negation, and quantification, but especially of the subjunctive conditional. Furthermore, I shall suppose it to be characterized by the presence of the looser logical relations typical of ordinary discourse which are referred to by philosophers under the headings 'vagueness' and 'open texture'.

I am beginning my myth *in medias res* with humans who have already mastered a Rylean language, because the philosophical situation it is designed to clarify is one in which we are not puzzled by how people acquire a language for referring to public properties of public objects, but are very puzzled indeed about how we learn to speak of inner episodes and immediate experiences.

There are, I suppose, still some philosophers who are inclined to think that by allowing these mythical ancestors of ours the use *ad libitum* of subjunctive conditionals, we have, in effect, enabled them to say anything that *we* can say when we speak of *thoughts, experiences* (seeing, hearing, etc.), and *immediate experiences*. I doubt that there are many. In any case, the story I am telling is designed to show exactly *how* the idea that an intersubjective language *must* be Rylean rests on too simple a picture of the relation of intersubjective discourse to public objects.

49. The questions I am, in effect, raising are, 'What resources would have to be added to the Rylean language of these talking animals in order that they might come to recognize each other and themselves as animals that *think, observe*, and have *feelings* and *sensations*, as we use these terms?' and, 'How could the addition of these resources be construed as reasonable?' In the first place, the language would have to be enriched with the fundamental resources of semantical discourse—that is to say, the resources necessary for making such characteristically semantical statements as ' "*Rot*" means red', and ' "*Der Mond ist rund*" is true if and only if the moon is round.' It is sometimes said, e.g. by Carnap,[1] that these resources can be constructed out of the vocabulary of formal logic, and that they would therefore already be contained, in principal, in our Rylean language. I have criticized this idea in another place[2] and shall not discuss it here. In any event, a decision on this point is not essential to the argument.

Let it be granted, then, that these mythical ancestors of ours are able to characterize each other's verbal behaviour in semantical terms; that, in other words, they not only can talk about each other's predictions as causes and effects, and as indicators (with greater or less reliability) of other verbal and nonverbal states of affairs, but can also say of these verbal productions that they *mean* thus and so, that they say *that* such and such, that they are true, false, etc. And let me emphasize, as was pointed out in Section 31 above, that to make a semantical statement about a verbal event is not a shorthand way of talking about its causes and effects, although there is a sense of 'imply' in which semantical statements about verbal productions do *imply* information about the causes and effects of these productions.

---

[1] Carnap, Rudolph, *Introduction to Semantics*. Chicago: University of Chicago Press, 1942.

[2] See Chapter 6, p. 200 ff.; also 'Empiricism and Abstract Entities' in Paul A. Schilpp (ed.) *The Philosophy of Rudolph Carnap*. Wilmette (Ill.), 1963.

Thus, when I say ' "*Es regnet*" means it is raining', my statement 'implies' that the causes and effects of utterances of '*Es regnet*' beyond the Rhine parallel the causes and effects of utterances of 'It is raining' by myself and other members of the English-speaking community. And if it did not imply this, it could not perform its role. But this is not to say that semantical statements are definitional shorthand for statements about the causes and effects of verbal performances.

50. With the resources of semantical discourse, the language of our fictional ancestors has acquired a dimension which gives considerably more plausibility to the claim that they are in a position to talk about *thoughts* just as we are. For characteristic of thoughts is their *intentionality, reference*, or *aboutness*, and it is clear that semantical talk about the meaning or reference of verbal expressions has the same structure as mentalistic discourse concerning what thoughts are about. It is therefore all the more tempting to suppose that the intentionality of *thoughts* can be traced to the application of semantical categories to overt verbal performances, and to suggest a modified Rylean account according to which talk about so-called 'thoughts' is shorthand for hypothetical and mongrel categorical–hypothetical statements about overt verbal and nonverbal behaviour, *and* that talk about the *intentionality* of these 'episodes' is correspondingly reducible to semantical talk about the verbal components.

What is the alternative? Classically it has been the idea that not only are there overt verbal episodes which can be characterized in semantical terms, but, *over and above these*, there are certain inner episodes which are properly characterized by the traditional vocabulary of *intentionality*. And, of course, the classical scheme includes the idea that semantical discourse about overt verbal performances is to be analysed in terms of talk about the intentionality of the mental episodes which are 'expressed' by these overt performances. My immediate problem is to see if I can reconcile the classical idea of thoughts as inner episodes which are neither overt behaviour nor verbal imagery and which are properly referred to in terms of the vocabulary of intentionality, with the idea that the categories of intentionality are, at bottom, semantical categories pertaining to overt verbal performances.[1]

---

[1] An earlier attempt of mine along these lines is to be found in 'Mind, Meaning and Behaviour' in *Philosophical Studies*, 3, pp. 83–94 (1952), and 'A Semantical Solution of the Mind–Body Problem' in *Methodos*, 5, pp. 45–84 (1953).

XIII. THEORIES AND MODELS

51. But what might these episodes be? And, in terms of our science fiction, how might our ancestors have come to recognize their existence? The answer to these questions is surprisingly straightforward, once the logical space of our discussion is enlarged to include a distinction, central to the philosophy of science, between the language of *theory* and the language of *observation*. Although this distinction is a familiar one, I shall take a few paragraphs to highlight those aspects of the distinction which are of greatest relevance to our problem.

Informally, to construct a theory is, in its most developed or sophisticated form, to postulate a domain of entities which behave in certain ways set down by the fundamental principles of the theory, and to correlate—perhaps, in a certain sense to identify—complexes of these theoretical entities with certain non-theoretical objects or situations; that is to say, with objects or situations which are either matters of observable fact or, in principle at least, describable in observational terms. This 'correlation' or 'identification' of theoretical with observational states of affairs is a tentative one 'until further notice', and amounts, so to speak, to erecting temporary bridges which permit the passage from sentences in observational discourse to sentences in the theory, and vice versa. Thus, for example, in the kinetic theory of gases, empirical statements of the form 'Gas g at such and such a place and time has such and such a volume, pressure, and temperature' are correlated with theoretical statements specifying certain statistical measures of populations of molecules. These temporary bridges are so set up that inductively established laws pertaining to gases, formulated in the language of observable fact, are correlated with derived propositions or theorems in the language of the theory, and that no proposition in the theory is correlated with a falsified empirical generalization. Thus, a good theory (at least of the type we are considering) 'explains' established empirical laws by deriving theoretical counterparts of these laws from a small set of postulates relating to unobserved entities.

These remarks, of course, barely scratch the surface of the problem of the status of theories in scientific discourse. And no sooner have I made them, than I must hasten to qualify them—almost beyond recognition. For while this by now classical account of the nature of theories (one of the earlier formulations of which is due to Norman Campbell,[1] and which is to be bound more recently in the writings

[1] Cambell, Norman, *Physics: The Elements*. Cambridge: Cambridge University Press, 1920.

of Carnap,[1] Reichenbach,[2] Hempel,[3] and Braithwaite[4]) does throw light on the logical status of theories, it emphasizes certain features at the expense of others. By speaking of the construction of a theory as the elaboration of a postulate system which is tentatively correlated with observational discourse, it gives a highly artificial and unrealistic picture of what scientists have actually done in the process of constructing theories. I do not wish to deny that logically sophisticated scientists today *might* and perhaps, on occasion, *do* proceed in true logistical style. I do, however, wish to emphasize two points:

(1) The first is that the fundamental assumptions of a theory are usually developed not by constructing uninterpreted calculi which might correlate in the desired manner with observational discourse, but rather by attempting to find a *model*, i.e. to describe a domain of familiar objects behaving in familiar ways such that we can see how the phenomena to be explained would arise if they consisted of this sort of thing. The essential thing about a model is that it is accompanied, so to speak, by a commentary which *qualifies* or *limits*—but not precisely nor in all respects—the analogy between the familiar objects and the entities which are being introduced by the theory. It is the descriptions of the fundamental ways in which the objects in the model domain, thus qualified, behave, which, transferred to the theoretical entities, correspond to the postulates of the logistical picture of theory construction.

(2) But even more important for our purposes is the fact that the logistical picture of theory construction obscures the most important thing of all, namely that the process of devising 'theoretical' explanations of observable phenomena did not spring full-blown from the head of modern science. In particular, it obscures the fact that not all common sense inductive inferences are of the form

All observed A's have been B, *therefore* (*probably*) all A's are B,

or its statistical counterparts, and leads one mistakenly to suppose that so-called 'hypothetic-deductive' explanation is limited to the sophisticated stages of science. The truth of the matter, as I shall shortly be illustrating, is that science is continuous with common

[1] Carnap, Rudolph, 'The Interpretation of Physics' in H. Feigl and M. Brodbeck (eds.), *Readings in the Philosophy of Science*, pp. 309–18. New York: Appleton-Century-Crofts, 1953. This selection consists of pp. 59–69 of his *Foundations of Logic and Mathematics*. Chicago: University of Chicago Press, 1939.

[2] Reichenbach, H., *Philosophie der Raum-Zeit-Lehre*. Berlin: de Gruyter, 1928, and *Experience and Prediction*. Chicago: University of Chicago Press, 1938.

[3] Hempel, C. G., *Fundamentals of Concept Formation in Empirical Science*. Chicago: University of Chicago Press, 1952.

[4] Braithwaite, R. B., *Scientific Explanation*. Cambridge: Cambridge University Press, 1920.

sense, and the ways in which the scientist seeks to explain empirical phenomena are refinements of the ways in which plain men, however crudely and schematically, have attempted to understand their environment and their fellow men since the dawn of intelligence. It is this point which I wish to stress at the present time, for I am going to argue that the distinction between theoretical and observational discourse is involved in the logic of concepts pertaining to inner episodes. I say 'involved in' for it would be paradoxical and, indeed, incorrect, to say that these concepts *are* theoretical concepts.

52. Now I think it fair to say that some light has already been thrown on the expression 'inner episodes'; for while it would indeed be a category mistake to suppose that the inflammability of a piece of wood is, so to speak, a hidden burning which becomes overt or manifest when the wood is placed on the fire, not all the unobservable episodes we suppose to go on in the world are the offspring of category mistakes. Clearly it is by no means an illegitimate use of 'in' —though it is a use which has its own logical grammar—to say, for example, that 'in' the air around us there are innumerable molecules which, in spite of the observable stodginess of the air, are participating in a veritable turmoil of episodes. Clearly, the sense in which these episodes are 'in' the air is to be explicated in terms of the sense in which the air 'is' a population of molecules, and this, in turn, in terms of the logic of the relation between theoretical and observational discourse.

I shall have more to say on this topic in a moment. In the meantime, let us return to our mythical ancestors. It will not surprise my readers to learn that the second stage in the enrichment of their Rylean language is the addition of theoretical discourse. Thus we may suppose these language-using animals to elaborate, without methodological sophistication, crude, sketchy, and vague theories to explain why things which are similar in their observable properties differ in their causal properties, and things which are similar in their causal properties differ in their observable properties.

XIV. METHODOLOGICAL VERSUS PHILOSOPHICAL BEHAVIOURISM

53. But we are approaching the time for the central episode in our myth. I want you to suppose that in this Neo-Rylean culture there now appears a genius—let us call him Jones—who is an unsung forerunner of the movement in psychology, once revolutionary, now commonplace, known as Behaviourism. Let me emphasize that what I have in mind is Behaviourism as a methodological thesis, which I shall be concerned to formulate. For the central and guiding theme

in the historical complex known by this term has been a certain conception, or family of conceptions, of how to go about building a science of psychology.

Philosophers have sometimes supposed that Behaviourists are, as such, committed to the idea that our ordinary mentalistic concepts are *analysable* in terms of overt behaviour. But although behaviourism has often been characterized by a certain metaphysical bias, it is not a thesis about the *analysis* of *existing* psychological concepts, but one which concerns the construction of new concepts. As a methodological thesis, it involves no commitment whatever concerning the logical analysis of common sense mentalistic discourse, nor does it involve a denial that each of us has a privileged access to our state of mind, nor that these states of mind can properly be described in terms of such common sense concepts as believing, wondering, doubting, intending, wishing, inferring, etc. If we permit ourselves to speak of this privileged access to our states of mind as 'introspection', avoiding the implication that there is a 'means' whereby we 'see' what is going on 'inside', as we see external circumstances by the eye, then we can say that Behaviourism, as I shall use the term, does not deny that there is such a thing as introspection, nor that it is, on some topics, at least, quite reliable. The essential point about 'introspection' from the standpoint of Behaviourism is that *we introspect in terms of common sense mentalistic concepts.* And while the Behaviourist admits, as anyone must, that much knowledge is embodied in common sense mentalistic discourse, and that still more can be gained in the future by formulating and testing hypotheses in terms of them, and while he admits that it is perfectly legitimate to call such a psychology 'scientific', he proposes, for his own part, to make no more than a heuristic use of mentalistic discourse, and to construct his concepts 'from scratch' in the course of developing his own scientific account of the observable behaviour of human organisms.

54. But while it is quite clear that scientific Behaviourism is *not* the thesis that common sense psychological concepts are *analysable* into concepts pertaining to overt behaviour—a thesis which has been maintained by some philosophers and which may be called 'analytical' or 'philosophical' Behaviourism—it is often thought that Behaviourism is committed to the idea that the concepts of a behaviouristic psychology must be so analysable, or, to put things right side up, that properly introduced behaviouristic concepts must be built by explicit definition—in the broadest sense—from a basic vocabulary pertaining to overt behaviour. The Behaviourist would thus be saying, 'Whether or not the mentalistic concepts of everyday life are definable in terms of overt behaviour, I shall ensure that this is true of the concepts that I shall employ.' And it must be confessed that many

behaviouristically oriented psychologists have believed themselves committed to this austere programme of concept formation.

Now I think it reasonable to say that, *thus conceived*, the behaviouristic programme would be unduly restrictive. Certainly, nothing in the nature of sound scientific procedure requires this self-denial. Physics, the methodological sophistication of which has so impressed —indeed, overly impressed—the other sciences, does not lay down a corresponding restriction on its concepts, nor has chemistry been built in terms of concepts explicitly definable in terms of the observable properties and behaviour of chemical substances. The point I am making should now be clear. The behaviouristic requirement that all concepts should be *introduced* in terms of a basic vocabulary pertaining to overt behaviour is compatible with the idea that some behaviouristic concepts are to be introduced as *theoretical* concepts.

55. It is essential to note that the theoretical terms of a behaviouristic psychology are not only *not* defined in terms of overt behaviour, they are also *not* defined in terms of nerves, synapses, neural impulses, etc. etc. A behaviouristic theory of behaviour is not, as such, a physiological explanation of behaviour. The ability of a framework of theoretical concepts and propositions successfully to explain behavioural phenomena is logically independent of the identification of these theoretical concepts with concepts of neurophysiology. What *is* true—and this is a logical point—is that each special science dealing with some aspect of the human organism operates within the frame of a certain regulative ideal, the ideal of a coherent system in which the achievements of each have an intelligible place. Thus, it is part of the Behaviourist's business to keep an eye on the total picture of the human organism which is beginning to emerge. And if the tendency to premature identification is held in check, there may be considerable heuristic value in speculative attempts at integration; though, until recently, at least, neurophysiological speculations in behaviour theory have not been particularly fruitful. And while it is, I suppose, noncontroversial that when the total scientific picture of man and his behaviour is in, it will involve *some* identification of concepts in behaviour theory with concepts pertaining to the functioning of anatomical structures, it should not be assumed that behaviour theory is committed *ab initio* to a physiological identification of *all* its concepts—that its concepts are, so to speak, physiological from the start.

We have, in effect, been distinguishing between two dimensions of the logic (or 'methodologic') of theoretical terms: (*a*) their role in explaining the selected phenomena of which the theory is the theory; (*b*) their role as candidates for integration in what we have called the 'total picture'. These roles are equally part of the logic, and hence the

N 185

'meaning', of theoretical terms. Thus, at any one time the terms in a theory will carry with them as part of their logical force that which it is reasonable to envisage—whether schematically or determinately —as the manner of their integration. However, for the purposes of my argument, it will be useful to refer to these two roles as though it were a matter of a distinction between what I shall call *pure theoretical concepts*, and hypotheses concerning the relation of these concepts to concepts in other specialities. What we *can* say is that the less a scientist is in a position to conjecture about the way in which a certain theory can be expected to integrate with other specialities, the more the concepts of his theory approximate to the status of pure theoretical concepts. To illustrate: we can imagine that Chemistry developed a sophisticated and successful theory to explain chemical phenomena before either electrical or magnetic phenomena were noticed; and that chemists developed as pure theoretical concepts, certain concepts which it later became reasonable to identify with concepts belonging to the framework of electro-magnetic theory.

XV. THE LOGIC OF PRIVATE EPISODES: THOUGHTS

56. With these all too sketchy remarks on Methodological Behaviourism under our belts, let us return once again to our fictional ancestors. We are now in a position to characterize the original Rylean language in which they described themselves and their fellows as not only a *behaviouristic* language, but a behaviouristic language which is restricted to the *non-theoretical* vocabulary of a behaviouristic psychology. Suppose, now, that in the attempt to account for the fact that his fellow men behave intelligently not only when their conduct is threaded on a string of overt verbal episodes—that is to say, as *we* would put it, when they 'think out loud'—but also when no detectable verbal output is present, Jones develops a *theory* according to which overt utterances are but the culmination of a process which begins with certain inner episodes. *And let us suppose that his model for these episodes* which initiate the events which culminate in overt verbal behaviour *is that of overt verbal behaviour itself. In other words, using the language of the model, the theory is to the effect that overt verbal behaviour is the culmination of a process which begins with 'inner speech'.*

It is essential to bear in mind that what Jones means by 'inner speech' is not to be confused with *verbal imagery*. As a matter of fact, Jones, like his fellows, does not as yet even have the concept of an image.

It is easy to see the general lines a Jonesean theory will take. According to it the true cause of intelligent nonhabitual behaviour is 'inner speech'. Thus, even when a hungry person overtly says, 'Here is an edible object', and proceeds to eat it, the true—theoretical—cause of his eating, given his hunger, is not the overt utterance, but the 'inner utterance of this sentence'.

57. The first thing to note about the Jonesean theory is that, as built on the model of speech episodes, *it carries over to these inner episodes the applicability of semantical categories*. Thus, just as Jones has, like his fellows, been speaking of overt utterances as *meaning* this or that, or being *about* this or that, so he now speaks of these inner episodes as *meaning* this or that, or being *about* this or that.

The second point to remember is that although Jones's theory involves a *model*, it is not identical with it. Like all theories formulated in terms of a model, it also includes a *commentary* on the model; a commentary which places more or less sharply drawn restrictions on the analogy between the theoretical entities and the entities of the model. Thus, while his theory talks of 'inner speech', the commentary hastens to add that, of course, the episodes in question are not the wagging of a hidden tongue, nor are any sounds produced by this 'inner speech'.

58. The general drift of my story should now be clear. I shall therefore proceed to make the essential points quite briefly:

(1) What we must suppose Jones to have developed is the germ of a theory which permits many different developments. We must not pin it down to any of the more sophisticated forms it takes in the hands of classical philosophers. Thus, the theory need not be given a Socratic or Cartesian form, according to which this 'inner speech' is a function of a separate substance; though primitive peoples may have had good reason to suppose that humans consist of two separate things.

(2) Let us suppose Jones to have called these discursive entities *thoughts*. We can admit at once that the framework of thoughts he has introduced is a framework of 'unobserved', 'nonempirical', 'inner' episodes. For we can point out immediately that in these respects they are no worse off than the particles and episodes of physical theory. For these episodes are 'in' language-using animals as molecular impacts are 'in' gases, not as 'ghosts' are in 'machines'. They are 'nonempirical' in the simple sense that they are *theoretical*—not definable in observational terms. Nor does the fact that they are, *as introduced*, unobserved entities imply that Jones could not have good reason for supposing them to exist. Their 'purity' is not a *metaphysical* purity, but, so to speak, a *methodological* purity. As we have seen, the fact that they are not introduced as physiological entities does not preclude the possibility that at a later methodological stage they may, so to speak, 'turn out' to be such. Thus, there are many

who would say that it is already reasonable to suppose that these *thoughts* are to be 'identified' with complex events in the cerebral cortex functioning along the lines of a calculating machine. Jones, of course, has no such idea.

(3) Although the theory postulates that overt discourse is the culmination of a process which begins with 'inner discourse', this should not be taken to mean that overt discourse stands to 'inner discourse' *as voluntary movements stand to intentions and motives.* True, overt linguistic events *can* be produced as means to ends. But serious errors creep into the interpretation of both language and thought if one interprets the idea that overt linguistic episodes *express* thoughts, on the model of the use of an instrument. Thus, it should be noted that Jones's theory, as I have sketched it, is perfectly compatible with the idea that the ability to have thoughts is acquired in the process of acquiring overt speech and that only after overt speech is well established, can 'inner speech' occur without its overt culmination.

(4) Although the occurrence of overt speech episodes which are characterizable in semantical terms is explained by the theory in terms of *thoughts* which are *also* characterized in semantical terms, this does not mean that the idea that overt speech 'has meaning' is being *analysed* in terms of the intentionality of thoughts. It must not be forgotten that *the semantical characterization of overt verbal episodes is the primary use of semantical terms, and that overt linguistic events as semantically characterized are the model for the inner episodes introduced by the theory.*

(5) One final point before we come to the denouement of the first episode in the saga of Jones. It cannot be emphasized too much that although these theoretical discursive episodes or *thoughts* are introduced as *inner* episodes—which is merely to repeat that they are introduced as *theoretical* episodes—they are *not* introduced as *immediate experiences.* Let me remind the reader that Jones, like his Neo-Rylean contemporaries, does not as yet have this concept. And even when he, and they, acquire it, by a process which will be the second episode in my myth, it will only be the philosophers among them who will suppose that the inner episodes introduced for one theoretical purpose—thoughts—must be a subset of immediate experiences, inner episodes introduced for another theoretical purpose.

59. Here, then, is the denouement. I have suggested a number of times that although it would be most misleading to say that concepts pertaining to thinking are theoretical concepts, yet their status might be illuminated by means of the contrast between theoretical and non-theoretical discourse. We are now in a position to see exactly why this is so. For once our fictitious ancestor, Jones, has developed the theory that overt verbal behaviour is the expression of thoughts, and

taught his compatriots to make use of the theory in interpreting each other's behaviour, it is but a short step to the use of this language in self-description. Thus, when Tom, watching Dick, has behavioural evidence whch warrants the use of the sentence (in the language of the theory) 'Dick is thinking "p" ' (or 'Dick is thinking that p'), Dick, using the same behavioural evidence, can say, in the language of the theory, 'I am thinking "p" ' (or 'I am thinking that p'). And it now turns out—need it have?—that Dick can be trained to give reasonably reliable self-descriptions, using the language of the theory, without having to observe his overt behaviour. Jones brings this about, roughly, by applauding utterances by Dick of 'I am thinking that p' when the behavioural evidence strongly supports the theoretical statement 'Dick is thinking that p'; and by frowning on utterances of 'I am thinking that p', when the evidence does not support this theoretical statement. Our ancestors begin to speak of the privileged access each of us has to his own thoughts. *What began as a language with a purely theoretical use has gained a reporting role.*

As I see it, this story helps us understand that concepts pertaining to such inner episodes as thoughts are primarily and essentially *inter-subjective*, as inter-subjective as the concept of a positron, and that the reporting role of these concepts—the fact that each of us has a privileged access to his thoughts—constitutes a dimension of the use of these concepts which is *built on* and *presupposes* this inter-subjective status. My myth has shown that the fact that language is essentially an *inter-subjective* achievement, and is learned in inter-subjective contexts—a fact rightly stressed in modern psychologies of language, thus by B. F. Skinner[1] and by certain philosophers, e.g. Carnap,[2] Wittgenstein[3]—is compatible with the 'privacy' of 'inner episodes'. It also makes clear that this privacy is not an 'absolute privacy'. For if it recognizes that these concepts have a reporting use in which one is not drawing inferences from behavioural evidence, it nevertheless insists that the fact that overt behaviour *is* evidence for these episodes *is built into the very logic of these concepts,* just as the fact that the observable behaviour of gases is evidence for molecular episodes is built into the very logic of molecule talk.

[1] Skinner, B. F., 'The Operational Analysis of Psychological Terms' in Volume LII of the *Psychological Review*, pp. 270–7 (1945). Reprinted in H. Feigl and Brodbeck (eds.), *Readings in the Philosophy of Science*, pp. 585–94. New York: Appleton-Century-Crofts, 1953.

[2] Carnap, Rudolph, *Psychologie in Physicalischer Sprache'*, *Erkentniss*, 3, pp. 107–42 (1933).

[3] Wittgenstein, Ludwig, *Philosophical Investigations*. London: Macmillan, 1953.

XVI. THE LOGIC OF PRIVATE EPISODES: IMPRESSIONS

60. We are now ready for the problem of the status of concepts pertaining to immediate experience. The first step is to remind ourselves that among the inner episodes which belong to the framework of *thoughts* will be perceptions, that is to say, *seeing that the table is brown, hearing that the piano is out of tune,* etc. Until Jones introduced this framework, the only concepts our fictitious ancestors had of perceptual *episodes* were those of overt verbal *reports,* made, for example, in the context of looking at an object in standard conditions. *Seeing that something is the case* is an inner episode in the Jonesean theory which has as its model *reporting on looking that something is the case.* It will be remembered from an earlier section that just as when I say that Dick *reported* that the table is green, I commit myself to the truth of what he reported, so to say of Dick that he *saw* that the table is green is, in part, to ascribe to Dick the idea '*this* table is green' and to endorse this idea. The reader might refer back to Sections 16ff. for an elaboration of this point.

With the enrichment of the originally Rylean framework to include inner perceptual episodes, I have established contact with my original formulation of the problem of inner experience (Sections 22ff.). For I can readily reconstruct in this framework my earlier account of the *language of appearing,* both *qualitative* and *existential.* Let us turn, therefore, to the final chapter of our historical novel. By now our ancestors speak a quite un-Rylean language. But it still contains no reference to such things as impressions, sensations, or feelings—in short, to the items which philosophers lump together under the heading 'immediate experiences'. It will be remembered that we had reached a point at which, as far as we could see, the phrase 'impression of a red triangle' could only mean something like 'that state of a perceiver—over and above the idea that there is a red and triangular physical object over there—which is common to those situations in which

   (*a*) he sees that the object over there is red and triangular;
   (*b*) the object over there looks to him to be red and triangular;
   (*c*) there looks to him to be a red triangular physical object over there'.

Our problem was that, on the one hand, it seemed absurd to say that impressions, for example, are theoretical entities, while, on the other, the interpretation of impressions as theoretical entities seemed to provide the only hope of accounting for the positive content and explanatory power that the idea that there are such entities appears to have, and of enabling us to understand how we could have arrived at this idea. The account I have just been giving of *thoughts* suggests how this apparent dilemma can be resolved.

For we continue the myth by supposing that Jones develops, in crude and sketchy form, of course, a theory of sense perception. Jones's theory does not have to be either well articulated or precise in order to be the first effective step in the development of a mode of discourse which today, in the case of some sense-modalities at least, is extraordinarily subtle and complex. We need, therefore, attribute to this mythical theory only those minimal features which enable it to throw light on the logic of our ordinary language about immediate experiences. From this standpoint it is sufficient to suppose that the hero of my myth postulates a class of inner—theoretical—episodes which he calls, say, *impressions*, and which are the end results of the impingement of physical objects and processes on various parts of the body, and, in particular, to follow up the specific form in which I have posed our problem, the eye.

61. A number of points can be made right away:

(1) The entities introduced by the theory are *states* of the perceiving subject, *not a class of particulars*. It cannot be emphasized too strongly that the particulars of the common sense world are such things as books, pages, turnips, dogs, persons, noises, flashes, etc., and the Space and Time—Kant's *Undinge*—in which they come to be. What is likely to make us suppose that *impressions* are introduced as particulars is that, as in the case of thoughts, this ur-theory is formulated in terms of a *model*. This time the model is the idea of a domain of 'inner replicas' which, when brought about in standard conditions, share the perceptible characteristics of their physical source. It is important to see that the model is the occurrence 'in' perceivers of *replicas*, not of *perceivings of replicas*. Thus, the model for an impression of a red triangle is a *red and triangular replica*, not a *seeing of a red and triangular replica*. The latter alternative would have the merit of recognizing that impressions are not particulars. But, by misunderstanding the role of models in the formulation of a theory, it mistakenly assumes that if the entities of the model are particulars, the theoretical entities which are introduced by means of the model must themselves be particulars—thus overlooking the role of the commentary. And by taking the model to be *seeing a red and triangular replica*, it smuggles into the language of impressions the logic of the language of thoughts. For seeing is a *cognitive* episode which involves the framework of thoughts, and to take it as the model is to give aid and comfort to the assimilation of impressions to thoughts, and thoughts to impressions which, as I have already pointed out, is responsible for many of the confusions of the classical account of both thoughts and impressions.

191

(2) The fact that *impressions* are theoretical entities enables us to understand how they can be *intrinsically* characterized—that is to say, characterized by something more than a *definite description*, such as 'entity of *the kind which* has as its standard cause looking at a red and triangular physical object in such and such circumstances' or 'entity of *the kind which* is common to the situations in which there looks to be a red and triangular physical object'. For although the predicates of a theory owe their meaningfulness to the fact that they are logically related to predicates which apply to the observable phenomena which the theory explains, the predicates of a theory are not shorthand for definite descriptions of properties in terms of these observation predicates. When the kinetic theory of gases speaks of molecules as having *mass*, the term 'mass' is not the abbreviation of a definite description of the form 'the property which . . .'. Thus, 'impression of a red triangle' does not simply mean 'impression such as is caused by red and triangular physical objects in standard conditions', though it is true—*logically* true—of impressions of red triangles that they are of that sort which *is* caused by red and triangular objects in standard conditions.

(3) If the theory of impressions were developed in true logistical style, we could say that the intrinsic properties of impressions are 'implicitly defined' by the postulates of the theory, as we can say that the intrinsic properties of sub-atomic particles are 'implicitly defined' by the fundamental principles of sub-atomic theory. For this would be just another way of saying that one knows the meaning of a theoretical term when one knows (*a*) how it is related to other theoretical terms, and (*b*) how the theoretical system as a whole is tied to the observation language. But, as I have pointed out, our ur-behaviourist does not formulate his theory in textbook style. He formulates it in terms of a model.

Now the model entities are entities which *do* have intrinsic properties. They are, for example, red and triangular wafers. It might therefore seem that the theory specifies the intrinsic characteristics of impressions to be the familiar perceptible qualities of physical objects and processes. If this were so, of course, the theory would be ultimately incoherent, for it would attribute to impressions—which are clearly not physical objects—characteristics which, if our argument to date is sound, only physical objects can have. Fortunately, this line of thought overlooks what we have called the commentary on the model, which qualifies, restricts, and interprets the analogy between the familiar entities of the model and the theoretical entities which are being introduced. Thus, it would be a mistake to suppose that since the *model* for the impression of a red triangle is a red and triangular wafer, the impression itself is a red and triangular wafer.

What can be said is that the impression of a red triangle is *analogous*, to an extent which is by no means neatly and tidily specified, to a red and triangular wafer. The *essential* feature of the analogy is that visual impressions stand to one another in a system of ways of resembling and differing which is structurally similar to the ways in which the colours and shapes of visible objects resemble and differ.

(4) It might be concluded from this last point that the concept of the impression of a red triangle is a 'purely formal' concept, the concept of a 'logical form' which can acquire a 'content' only by means of 'ostensive definition'. One can see why a philosopher might want to say this, and why he might conclude that in so far as concepts pertaining to immediate experiences are *intersubjective*, they are 'purely structural', the 'content' of immediate experience being incommunicable. Yet this line of thought is but another expression of the Myth of the Given. For the theoretical concept of the impression of a red triangle would be no more and no less 'without content' than *any* theoretical concept. And while, like these, it must belong to a framework which is logically connected with the language of observable fact, the logical relation between a theoretical language and the language of observable fact has nothing to do with the epistemological fiction of an 'ostensive definition'.

(5) The impressions of Jones's theory are, as was pointed out above, states of the perceiver, rather than particulars. If we remind ourselves that these states are not introduced as physiological states (see Section 55), a number of interesting questions arise which tie in with the reflections on the status of the scientific picture of the world (Sections 39–44 above) but which, unfortunately, there is space only to adumbrate. Thus, some philosophers have thought it obvious that we can expect that in the development of science it will become reasonable to identify *all* the concepts of behaviour theory with definable terms in neurophysiological theory, and these, in turn, with definable terms in theoretical physics. It is important to realize that the second step of this prediction, at least, is either a *truism* or a *mistake*. It is a truism if it involves a tacit redefinition of 'physical theory' to mean 'theory adequate to account for the observable behaviour of any object (including animals and persons) which has physical properties'. While if 'physical theory' is taken in its ordinary sense of 'theory adequate to explain the observable behaviour of physical objects' it is, I believe, mistaken.

To ask how *impressions* fit together with *electro-magnetic fields*, for example, is to ask a mistaken question. It is to mix the framework of *molar* behaviour theory with the framework of the *micro*-theory of physical objects. The proper question is, rather, 'What would correspond in a *micro*-theory of sentient organisms to *molar* concepts pertaining to impressions?' And it is, I believe, in answer to this question that one would come upon the *particulars* which sense-datum theorists profess to find (by analysis) in the common sense universe of discourse (cf. Section 23). Furthermore, I believe that in characterizing these particulars, the micro-behaviourist would be led to say something like the following: 'It is such particulars which (from the standpoint of the theory) are being responded to by the organism when it looks to a *person* as though there were a red and triangular physical object over there.' It would, of course, be incorrect to say that, in the ordinary sense, such a particular is red or triangular. What *could* be said,[1] however, is that whereas in the common sense picture physical objects are red and triangular but the impression 'of' a red triangle is neither red nor triangular, in the framework of this micro-theory, the theoretical counterparts of sentient organisms are Space-Time worms characterized by two kinds of variables: (*a*) variables which also characterize the theoretical counterparts of *merely* material objects; (*b*) variables peculiar to sentient things; and that these latter variables are the counterparts in this new framework of the perceptible qualities of the physical objects of the common sense framework. It is statements such as these which would be the cash value of the idea that 'physical objects aren't really coloured; colours exist only in the perceiver', and that 'to see that the facing surface of a physical object is red and triangular is to *mistake* a red and triangular sense content for a physical object with a red and triangular facing side'. Both these ideas clearly treat what is really a speculative philosophical critique (see Section 41) of the common sense framework of physical objects and the perception of physical objects in the light of an envisaged ideal scientific framework, as though it were a matter of distinctions which can be drawn *within* the common sense framework itself.

62. This brings me to the final chapter of my story. Let us suppose that as his final service to mankind before he vanishes without a trace, Jones teaches his theory of perception to his fellows. As before in the case of *thoughts*, they begin by using the language of impressions to draw theoretical conclusions from appropriate premises. (Notice that the evidence for theoretical statements in the language of impressions will include such introspectible inner episodes as *its looking to one as though there were a red and triangular physical object over there*, as well as overt behaviour.) Finally he succeeds in training them to make a *reporting* use of this language. He trains them, that is, to say 'I have

[1] For a discussion of some logical points pertaining to this framework the reader should consult the essay, 'The Concept of Emergence', by Paul E. Meehl and Wilfrid Sellars, on pp. 239–52 of Volume I of the *Minnesota Studies in the Philosophy of Science*, edited by Herbert Feigl and Michael Scriven and published by the University of Minnesota Press (Minneapolis: 1956).

the impression of a red triangle' when, and only when, according to the theory, they are indeed having the impression of a red triangle.

Once again the myth helps us to understand that concepts pertaining to certain inner episodes—in this case *impressions*—can be primarily and essentially *inter-subjective*, without being resolvable into overt behavioural symptoms, and that the reporting role of these concepts, their role in introspection, the fact that each of us has a privileged access to his impressions, constitutes a dimension of these concepts which is *built on* and *presupposes* their role in intersubjective discourse. It also makes clear why the 'privacy' of these episodes is not the 'absolute privacy' of the traditional puzzles. For, as in the case of thoughts, the fact that overt behaviour is evidence for these episodes is built into the very logic of these concepts as the fact that the observable behaviour of gases is evidence for molecular episodes is built into the very logic of molecule talk.

Notice that what our 'ancestors' have acquired under the guidance of Jones is not 'just another language'—a 'notational convenience' or 'code'—which merely enables them to say what they can already say in the language of qualitative and existential looking. They have acquired another language, indeed, but it is one which, though it rests on a framework of discourse about public objects in Space and Time, has an autonomous logical structure, and contains an *explanation of*, not just a *code for*, such facts as that *there looks to me to be a red and triangular physical object over there*. And notice that while our 'ancestors' came to notice impressions, and the language of impressions embodies a 'discovery' that there are such things, the language of impressions was no more tailored to fit *antecedent* noticings of these entities than the language of molecules was tailored to fit antecedent noticings of molecules.

And the spirit of Jones is not yet dead. For it is the particulars of the micro-theory discussed in Section 61 (5) which are the solid core of the sense contents and sense fields of the sense-datum theorist. Envisaging the general lines of that framework, even sketching some of its regions, he has taught himself to play with it (in his study) as a report language. Unfortunately he mislocates the truth of these conceptions, and, with a modesty forgivable in any but a philosopher, confuses his own creative enrichment of the framework of empirical knowledge, with an analysis of knowledge as it was. He construes as *data* the particulars and arrays of particulars which he has come to be able to observe, and believes them to be antecedent objects of knowledge which have somehow been in the framework from the beginning. It is in the very act of *taking* that he speaks of the *given*.

63. I have used a myth to kill a myth—the Myth of the Given. But

is my myth really a myth? Or does the reader not recognize Jones as Man himself in the middle of his journey from the grunts and groans of the cave to the subtle and polydimensional discourse of the drawing room, the laboratory, and the study, the language of Henry and William James, of Einstein and of the philosophers who, in their efforts to break out of discourse to an *arché* beyond discourse, have provided the most curious dimension of all.

6

TRUTH AND 'CORRESPONDENCE'

THE purpose of this chapter is to explore the cluster of ideas which made up the traditional 'correspondence theory of truth', with a view to determining what, if anything, of importance it contains in addition to that aspect which has recently been crystallized in the so-called 'semantic definition of truth'. I say 'explore', for I mean just that. The topic is a vast one, and the following line of argument is a rough-hewn path through the jungle, which may or may not reveal important geographical features.

It would seem clear that unless there is more to the 'correspondence' insisted on by classical correspondence theories of truth than is captured by the formulations of current semantic theory and unless this more can be shown to be an essential property of truth (or, at least, of a significant variety of truths), then the battle over correspondence, instead of being *won* by correspondence theorists, has shown itself to be a *Scheinstreit*. For, as has often been noted, the formula

'Snow is white' (in our language) is true≡Snow is white

is viewed with the greatest equanimity by pragmatist and coherentist alike. If the 'correspondence' of the correspondence theorist amounts to nothing more than is illustrated by such equivalences, then, while pragmatist and coherentist may hope to make important points, respectively, about 'truth and action' and 'truth and coherence', nothing further would remain to be said about 'truth and correspondence'.

Needless to say, the pragmatist and the coherentist have had to pay a price for this seeming trivialization of their once worthy opponent. For they can no longer claim, if they ever did, that 'truth' *means* successful working or that 'truth' *means* coherence. Yet they may well feel that it was worth this price to clear the way for an un-encumbered demonstration of the uniquely important connection between 'truth' and the concept of their choice. But what comfort can the correspondence theorist take in a victory which, to all appearances, reduces his claim to a formula which—whatever problems it poses to the specialist—has, according to his erstwhile antagonists, nothing to do with the philosophical problem of truth? Or has the semantical refinement of correspondence theories left untouched a *second* mode of 'correspondence' that might be essential to the understanding of truth? Is there a place for a correspondence theory of truth (*some* truth, at least) in addition to the semantical account? Or, at least, for a theory that finds a nontrivial job for a 'correspondence' other than that correspondence which finds its expression in the familiar equivalences of semantic theory? With the apparent achievement of a semantic *definition* of truth, 'pragmatic success', 'coherence', and (if there is a place for it) 'correspondence' in this putative second sense no longer appear as mutually exclusive claimants to be the essence of truth. They might well, however, be compatible *properties* of truth or essential features of different varieties of truths. And there is still plenty of room for controversy concerning the existence and, if existence, the respective roles and relative importance of connections between truth, on the one hand, and consequences, coherence, and, it may be, correspondence, on the other.

Now I shall take it as obvious that the most likely domain for a correspondence theory of truth bringing in such a second dimension of correspondence is the domain of empirical or matter-of-factual truth. And it is to this domain that I shall, in general, limit my attention. My topic, therefore, can be given a provisional formulation as follows: Is there a sense of 'correspond', other than that explicated by semantic theory, in which empirical truths correspond to objects or events in the world? I emphasize that this is a provisional formulation, because the terms in which it is put are at least as troublesome as the explicandum they attempt to locate. It is a question schema rather than a question, and *which* question is being asked depends on the philosophical treatment to which the other terms are submitted. Thus one can imagine a Thomist asking, 'Is there a correspondence between the intellect in act and the natural order other than the so-called correspondence of semantic theory?'

But to imagine any such question being asked is to presuppose (in imagination) that the questioner is happy about what semantic theory has to tell us about the correspondence it claims to have isolated and defined. And this makes it clear that, before we can ask about a correspondence other than the semantic, we must examine the claim of semantics to have shown that there is something significantly *semantical*, roughly *linguistic*, about truth.

Semantic theory purports to be a theory of the truth of such linguistic expressions as can be said to 'express propositions'. What it means to say of a linguistic expression that it expresses a proposition is, of course, a central issue in the philosophy of language, about which I shall have something to say. But part of its force is that to 'express a proposition' is to be either true or false. And this brings to mind one of the standard objections to the semantical account of truth—that 'true' and 'false' are predicates only *derivatively* applicable to linguistic expressions. It is objected that they apply *primarily* to *thoughts*, i.e. to such thoughts as are either true or false.

And, indeed, to be philosophically illuminating, a semantic theory of truth must take into account the distinction between linguistic utterances and the thoughts they express. But this way of putting it runs afoul of the notorious ambiguity of the word 'thought' and of the phrase 'express a thought'. Thus it might seem that the distinction between a linguistic utterance and the *thought* it expresses coincides with the distinction previously drawn between a form of words and the *proposition* it expresses. But while these distinctions are closely related, the ambiguities to which I have referred prevent any simple identification. Thus, 'thought' can refer to an *act* of thinking or to that which is thought by such an act. To say of a form of words that it expresses a thought in the latter sense is essentially the same as to say that it expresses a proposition, provided that the thought is such as to be either true or false. On the other hand, to say of a verbal utterance that it expresses an act of thinking is to characterize it as the culmination of a process of which the act of thinking is the initial stage. 'Expression' in *this* sense is a relation between particular existences or matters of fact—between two items in what would traditionally have been called the 'natural order'. When, on the other hand, a verbal utterance is said to express a proposition, e.g. the proposition that 2 plus 2 equals 4 or the proposition that Chicago is large, the relation, if such it can be called, is between a particular existent and something having quite a different status, something belonging to what might appropriately be called the 'logical order'.

In my opinion, the distinction between verbal utterances and the acts of thinking they express is genuine and irreducible. It is also my opinion, however, that the notion of an act of thinking is the notion of something analogous, in certain respects, to a verbal utterance, that the relation of an *act* of thinking to *what is thought* is to be construed by analogy with the relation between an utterance and the proposition it expresses, and that truth as it pertains to acts of thought is to be understood in terms of truth as it pertains to overt

199

discourse. I shall therefore direct my attention to truth as it pertains to such linguistic expressions as 'express propositions' and as it pertains to the propositions they 'express', in the conviction that any conclusion I may reach can be extended to truth as it pertains to *acts* of thought and as it pertains to thoughts in the sense of what is thought by these acts.

I

Assuming, therefore, with Plato, that thinking is a 'dialogue in the soul', let us take a closer look at the semantic theory as it pertains to overt discourse. And let us begin with the question: Does truth pertain primarily to forms of words such as would correctly be said to express propositions or to the propositions they would be said to express?

The contention is the familiar one that, since no form of words can properly be said to be true or false unless it expresses a proposition and since one and the same proposition can be expressed by using different sentences in different languages, any theory of the truth of forms of words must presuppose a prior theory of the truth of propositions. The conclusion is drawn that, if a 'semantic' theory of truth is a theory that claims that truth in a *primary* sense pertains to forms of words, then all 'semantic' theories are based on a mistake.

Now I share the conviction that there is an important sense in which the truth of propositions is prior to the truth of forms of words, i.e. in which statements of the form

That-p is true

are prior to statements of the form

S (in L) is true.

But if so, what are we to make of the fact that the by now classic formulations of the semantic theory of truth simply do not use either such propositional expressions as 'that-p' or statements of the form 'that-p is true'.

The key to the understanding of this fact is the peculiar character, as Max Black has emphasized, of Carnap's explication of statements of the form

Expression E (in L) means x.

According to this explication,

Word W (in German) means x

has the force of

> either $W=$'und' and $x=$and
> or $W=$'weiss' and $x=$white
> or $W=$'oder' and $x=$or
> or $W=$'New York' and $x=$New York

. . . .

It is surely obvious, however, that while for certain purposes it may be fruitful to stipulate that the former locution (under the guise of 'Word W (in German) *designates x*') is to have the sense of the latter, it does not actually have this sense. There is, indeed, no general formula that will tell us what German word has what meaning. A listing cannot be avoided. But the listing construed as a disjunction of conjunctions of identities is not an *explication* of 'Word W (in German) means x' as it occurs in ordinary usage, and, needless to say, it is the ordinary sense of 'means' that is bound up with the ordinary sense of 'true', which it is the task of philosophy to explicate.

What is the significance of this point? Note that, as long as one operates with what might be called the 'disjunctive' (or telephone-directory) counterpart of meaning, it is quite proper (suppressing some anxiety about putting the identity sign between expressions other than singular terms) to think of the expression 'Chicago is large' as it occurs in

> S (in L) means Chicago is large

as having the ordinary sense of 'Chicago is large'. Thus in

> S (in L) means Chicago is large *and* Chicago is large

both occurrences of the sentence in question would have the same sense. And, indeed, in Carnap's definition of 'true (in L)', which he develops on pp. 49 ff. of his *Introduction to Semantics*: roughly,

> S_i is true (in L)$=_{\text{Df}} (\exists p) (S_i \text{ Des } p \text{ (in L)} \cdot p)$

the two occurrences of the variable 'p' have, given the stipulations he has made, the same sense. There is no equivocation, and they both fall properly within the scope of the same quantifier.

But, in actual usage,

> Word W (in German) means x

no more has the sense of the disjunctive listing than

> x is a subscriber to the telephone company

has the sense of

> $x=$Jones or $x=$Smith or $x=$Taylor or $\cdots$

o

and, when we take this fact into account, we find that expressions
that occur as substituends for '*x*' in

Word *W* (in German) means *x*

as it is actually used do *not* have their ordinary sense. If this is so—
and I hope to convince you that it is—then Carnap's formula cannot
be regarded as an explication of 'true' as this term is ordinarily used.
(Let me hasten to add that this is not to say that the concepts he
defines are not coherent, legitimate, and illuminating.)

Now from the standpoint of a metaphysician in the tradition of
logical atomism, the virtue of the disjunctive treatment of meaning
statements is that it enables one to say of expressions of the form

W (in L) means *x*

that they assert a relationship between a *linguistic* and a *nonlinguistic*
item, but simultaneously to insist that this relationship is purely
logical in the narrowest sense, for it is definable in terms of disjunction, conjunction, and identity. *What* means *what*, in the case of
historical languages, must be determined by empirical investigation,
but *meaning itself* is a logical relationship definable in terms of the
conceptual apparatus of an extensional logic. The philosophical
interest of this thesis lies in the fact that, if the meaning *relationship*
is thus definable, then, in the context

S (in L) means *p*,

'*p*' is occurring in a context constructed out of the resources of an
extensional or truth-functional logic. And this would contribute to
the preservation of the central thesis of logical atomism, namely that
statements occur in statements only truth-functionally.

A further consequence would be that the truth of a statement,
though a 'relational property' of the statement, would be a relational
property only in an attenuated sense, for the relation in question, the
so-called relation of 'correspondence' would be the purely logical
relation characterized above. To put it bluntly, meaning would not
be a *real* relation, nor truth a *real* property.

Now I want to argue that the ordinary sense of

S (in L) means Chicago is large

is far more complicated, and that 'Chicago is large' occurs in it only
indirectly. That which occurs in it directly or primarily is ' "Chicago
is large" ', i.e. the *name* of a certain English expression. *As a first
approximation* we can say that it has the form

S (in L) means 'Chicago is large'.

202

But two comments are immediately in order: (1) This claim obviously won't do as it stands. To put quotation marks around the sentence 'Chicago is large' changes the sense of the original meaning statement. To keep the force of the latter as intact as we can, we must make compensating changes and, in the first place, substitute another expression for 'means'. Let me use, for the moment, the neutral term 'corresponds'. This gives us,

S (in L) corresponds to 'Chicago is large'.

(2) The moment we replace 'Chicago is large' by the name of an expression, the question arises concerning the language to which this expression belongs. And the answer is, obviously, *our* language, or, more precisely, the language we are speaking at the time we make the meaning statement. Thus our provisional interpretation of the meaning statement is

S (in L) corresponds to 'Chicago is large' in the language we are speaking.

Unfortunately, to say that one expression, in L, 'corresponds' to another in the language we are speaking is not to say very much. And to say *anything* more we must say a great deal. My treatment will necessarily be schematic, but the essential points are the following:

1. The 'correspondence' is a correspondence of *use*, or, as I prefer to say, role. Linguistic roles and role aspects differ in kind and complexity. Rarely does an expression in one language play exactly the same role as an expression in another. The closest approximation to identity of role is found in connection with logical and mathematical words. There are degrees of likeness of meaning, and meaning statements are to be construed as having a tacit rider to the effect that the correspondence is in a relevant respect and obtains to a relevant degree.

2. Not all roles are conceptual roles, i.e. roles that contribute to the conceptual character of a linguistic expression. Thus, 'Hélas!' and 'Ach weh!' play much the same role in French and German, respectively, as 'alas!' in English, but we should scarcely say that 'Ach weh! expresses a concept. It seems to me that the distinguishing feature of conceptual roles is their relation to inference. This feature has found a diversity of expressions in recent and contemporary philosophy, perhaps the most familiar of which is Carnap's attempt to explicate all concepts pertaining to logical syntax in terms of the relation of 'direct consequence'. But that a conceptual item is the conceptual item it is by virtue of the difference it makes to at least some inferences in which it occurs is a familiar theme in contemporary philosophy.

203

3. In accordance with the operative assumption of this paper that concepts pertaining to thinking are to be understood by analogy with concepts pertaining to overt discourse, principles of inference pertaining to reasonings are the counterparts of principles pertaining to verbal moves from statement to statement; and the intellectual commitment of the mind to a principle of inference is the counterpart of a person's commitment as a language user to principles pertaining to these verbal moves. The latter find their overt expression in the syntactical metalanguage of the language in question.

4. Other important role dimensions are those which concern sequences not, as in inference, from one form of words to another, but from an extra-linguistic situation to a linguistic one (thus, from the presence of a red object in standard conditions to the utterance 'Red here now') or from a linguistic to an extra-linguistic situation (thus, from 'I shall now raise my hand' to the raising of the hand). But of this more later.

With these qualifications and promissory notes in hand, let us reformulate the above explication of the rubric

E (in L) means ——

to read

E (in L) plays the role played in our language by ——

Thus, to give two examples,

'Rouge' (in French) means red

would have the same force as

'Rouge' (in French) plays the role of 'red' in our language

while

'Chicago est grande' (in French) means Chicago is large

would have the same force as

'Chicago est grande' (in French) plays the role of 'Chicago is large' in our language.

As I see it, abstract singular terms such as 'redness', 'triangularity' and 'that Chicago is large' are to be construed, in first approximation, as singular terms for players of linguistic roles, as 'the pawn', 'the bishop' etc. are singular terms for players of chess roles. Corresponding to the common nouns 'pawn', 'bishop' etc. would be the common nouns ' "red" ',' ' "triangular" ',' and ' "Chicago is large" '. (Cf. 'There are fifteen 'and's on this page.) A closer approximation is obtained if we form these common nouns by the use of special quotes and

204

stipulate that they are to expressions of whatever language which play the role played by the designs enclosed between the quotes in our language. Let us speak of the ˙red˙ (= redness), the ˙triangular˙ (= triangularity) and the ˙Chicago is large˙ (= that Chicago is large) as *senses*, so that to express in some language or other the sense triangularity is to be a ˙triangular˙. From this point of view the statements at the end of the preceding paragraph have the force, respectively, of

'Rouge' (in French) expresses the sense redness

and

'Chicago est grande' (in French) expresses the sense that Chicago is large.

or, since senses can be divided into predicative senses (Frege's concepts), propositions, logical connectives etc.,

'Rouge' (in French) expresses the concept redness

and

'Chicago est grande' (in French) expresses the proposition that Chicago is large.[1]

Now if the above remarks are on the right track and not totally misguided, they have interesting and important consequences for the theory of truth. Let us take another look at the Carnapian formula. The first thing we note is that, if we attempt to use it with the above theory of meaning, we can no longer begin the definiens with quantification over a variable that takes sentences as its substituends. In effect we must write

($\exists$ that-p) (S (in L) expresses the proposition that-p)

and, if this is the case, we can no longer simply add, as in Carnap's formula, the conjunct 'p'. For our quantifier covers only variables of the form 'that-p', and a conjunction sign requires to be followed by a sentence or sentence variable, not by something of the form 'that-p'.

Having made this beginning, the only thing to do is to add the conjunct 'that-p is true', or 'that-p is the case'. And if so, this accounts for the widespread conviction that the truth of a form of words, such as 'Chicago est grande' (in French), is derivative from that of propositions, in accordance with the formula

$$\text{'Chicago est grande' (in French) is true} \equiv (\exists \text{ that-p)('Chicago est grande' (in French) expresses the proposition that-}p \cdot \textit{that-p is true}).$$

[1] This paragraph was substituted in proof for the original to bring the argument in line with the interpretation of abstract singular terms developed in a paper on 'Abstract Entities' in the June, 1963 issue of *The Review of Metaphysics*.

Thus, the approach we have taken does, indeed, reduce the question: What does it mean to say of 'Chicago est grande' (in French) that it is true? to the question: What is meant by statements of the form

That-*p* is true?

It is in this sense that the truth of *forms of words* is derivative from the truth of *propositions*. And this enables us to see exactly where the necessary equivalences highlighted by the semantic theory come in. They now appear, however, in the form

That snow is white is true ≡ Snow is white.

Furthermore, the equivalence sign is misleading, for we have here a logical equivalence, or, more accurately, a reciprocal entailment. We might put it as follows:

'That snow is white is true' entails and is entailed by 'Snow is white'.

But by the time we have specified that the expressions in question belong to the English language and that the entailment does its job for *our* use of 'true' only because English is *our* language, we see that what we have here is the principle of inference:

That that snow is white is true entails and is entailed by that snow is white

which governs such inferences as

That snow is white is true.
So, Snow is white.

But if the word 'true' gets its sense from this type of inference, we must say that, instead of standing for a relation or relational property of statements (or, for that matter, of thoughts), 'true' is a sign *that something is to be done*—for inferring is a doing.[1]

Furthermore, if the above argument is correct, we can understand how statements can occur in meaning statements—thus 'Chicago is large' in 'S (in L) means Chicago is large'—although the latter are not extensional or truth-functional contexts. They occur as statements *to be made* (on a certain hypothesis). Thus, in the above context, 'Chicago is large' has the force of 'that Chicago is large', and this is governed by the inference patterns:

That Chicago is large is true.   and   Chicago is large.
So, Chicago is large.   So, that Chicago is large is true.

Now the points I have been making are general in scope in that they apply *mutatis mutandis* to all truths, whether empirical or

[1] See note at end of this chapter.

mathematical or metaphysical or moral. It has served, at best, to set the stage for the topic I proposed to discuss. It will be remembered, I hope, that this topic is: Is there a sense of 'correspond' other than that explicated by semantic theory, in which empirical truths correspond to objects or events in the world? To this I now turn.

II

I shall introduce my discussion by examining Wittgenstein's contention in the *Tractatus* that statements are 'logical pictures' (4.03) of facts in the light of the distinctions sketched above.

It is often thought, not without reason, that Wittgenstein's conception of statements as logical pictures of facts, to the extent that it is not hopelessly confused, is essentially a sophisticated version of the correspondence theory and that, however subtle and important the distinctions he draws (or, better, hints at) between statements proper and various kinds of quasi-statements, his conception of statements proper as 'pictures' contains no insights over and above those which came to fruition in the semantic theory of truth. And it must, I think, be granted that *part* of what Wittgenstein had in mind when he spoke of statements proper as logical pictures of facts has been clarified by semantic theory—if, that is to say, the latter is interpreted along the lines of the previous section. I also think, however, that he obviously had something else in mind, inadequately distinguished, which is of vital importance for understanding the truth of empirical statements.

Let me begin by summarizing certain doctrines the presence of which in the *Tractatus* is relatively noncontroversial. Of these, the most important is the thesis that all statements proper, or statements in a technical sense of this term, are truth functions of elementary statements. Two comments are immediately in place: (1) Wittgenstein so uses 'statement' that unless a verbal performance says that something *is* the case (as opposed to 'ought to be the case' or 'shall be the case' or 'might be the case'), it is not a statement, though it may well be significant or meaningful; and (2) he draws a sharp distinction between truth functions and what he calls 'material functions' (5.44). 'Not', for example, neither is the *name* of an object, nor does it stand for a property of a proposition or state of affairs. Logical constants are not predicates. Thus 'not p' is not analogous to 'Red(x)'. Wittgenstein speaks of 'truth operations', which turn statements into other statements that are truth functions of them (5.3), and writes, 'My fundamental thought is that the logical constants do not represent' (4.0312).

Now the thesis that all statements are truth functions of atomic statements, taken in deadly earnest, has troublesome consequences

207

when combined with another central thesis of the *Tractatus*. I refer to the thesis that the world consists of atomic facts and that elementary statements are 'logical pictures' of these facts. For, if we attempt to combine these theses, we are faced, it would seem, by the paradox that to say of a certain atomic fact that it is 'pictured' by a certain elementary statement, we must use a statement *in which the elementary statement occurs, but in which it does not occur truth-functionally.* We must say something like

(1) *S* (in L) pictures *aRb*.

And the puzzle arises that we are somehow able to recognize a picturing relation between statements and extra-linguistic matters of fact, which relation cannot be expressed by a statement. When we remember that, for Wittgenstein, *thinking* that something is the case, although distinguishable from *saying* that something is the case, is analogous to the latter in all respects pertaining to the theories of the *Tractatus*, we have the paradox that we are able to recognize a relationship that we can neither state, think, nor, to use Ramsey's turn of phrase, whistle.

Now it is reasonable to demand of a philosophy that it be self-referentially consistent; i.e. that its claims be consistent with its own meaningfulness, let alone truth. The question, therefore, arises: Is there any way out of the above paradox consistent with the fundamental theses of the *Tractatus*? There are two possible avenues of escape. The first is to deny that the statement *'aRb'* occurs in (1). The other is to grant that it does occur but to deny that (1) itself is a statement in the technical sense to which the thesis of truth-functionality applies. Either of these approaches, if successful, would avoid a clash with the principle that statements proper occur in a statement proper only truth-functionally.

If we interpret (1) as having the sense of

(1') *S* (in L) *means aRb*

as we have explicated this form, we can make consistent sense of the *three* ideas: (*a*) that elementary statements picture facts; (*b*) that *'aRb'* does *not* occur in the 'ladder language' formula

(1) *S* (in L) pictures *aRb*

(or, rather, occurs in a peculiar way); and (*c*) that 'ladder language' statements are 'statements' only in that broad sense in which statements can contain such words as 'shall' or 'ought' or 'correct'. That what Wittgenstein *says* must be interpreted along these lines if his position is to be self-referentially consistent emerges when we notice that *picturing* is a relation one term of which is a *statement*. For what,

208

then, is the other *relatum*? Whatever it is, '*aRb*' is standing for it. Clearly, to stand for a *relatum*, '*aRb*' must be standing for a term, an *object*, in a suitably broad sense.

It might be thought that '*aRb*' is standing for the objects *a* and *b*. In this event, (1) would have the form

(1″) *S* (in L) pictures *a* and *b*.

But while this suggestion contains an important idea which will be the key to that aspect of Wittgenstein's thought which is not captured by the semantic theory of truth, it does not explain the formula with which we are now concerned. For, according to this formula, what is pictured is not *a* and *b* but a *fact about a* and *b*, the *fact* that *aRb*. Thus (1) has the form

(1‴) *S* (in L) pictures the fact that *aRb*.

This requires, of course, that the fact that *aRb* be in some sense an *object*. But if so, it is a peculiar kind of object, for objects proper are *named*, rather than stated, whereas facts—even though they may in some sense be named, in any case referred to—are essentially the sort of thing that is *stated*.

Now to say that facts are quasi-objects is, surely, in the context of the *Tractatus*, to say that they are linguistic. The only objects that are *in* the world are *objects proper*. And if one is tempted to reply that, if the world consists of *facts* and if facts are quasi-objects, then quasi-objects must be 'in' the world, the reply is that the sense in which facts are 'in the world' is as different from that in which objects proper are in the world as the sense in which facts are objects is different from that in which objects proper are objects.

But this merely postpones the moment of truth. For if facts belong to the linguistic order, then 'picturing' is a relation between statement and statement. And the attempt to understand picturing would appear to confront us with a thorough-going linguistic idealism. If facts belong to the linguistic order and the world consists of facts, must not the world belong to the linguistic order? And is not this a miserable absurdity?

If, however, we take the ladder-language formula

S (in L) pictures the fact that *aRb*

to have the force of

S (in L) means *aRb*, and that *aRb* is a fact

we can apply to this conception of 'picturing' the distinctions we drew in our discussion of the semantic theory of truth.

But it springs to the eyes that Wittgenstein must have had something more than this in mind when he spoke of statements as 'logical pictures' of facts. For, as I have already emphasized, it is notorious that the semantic theory of truth applies to statements that are neither elementary matter-of-factual statements nor truth functions of them. Wittgenstein himself emphasized, in his recently published notebook, that it is as proper to say

'2 plus 2=4' is true if and only if 2 plus 2=4

as to say

'aRb' is true if and only if aRb.

And, of course, it is familiar fact that Wittgenstein restricts his conception of picturing to matter-of-factual statements in the narrow sense.

In a number of passages Wittgenstein sketches a theory of elementary statements and their meaning, and these passages may, perhaps, contain a clue to the second dimension of 'correspondence' for which we are looking. The central theme is that elementary statements are configurations of names and that these configurations of names picture configurations of objects. Part of what he has in mind is that statements are not *lists* of words. This, however, is a general point which applies not only to statements proper but to statements in that extended sense which reaches to the boundaries of meaningfulness. More specifically, he has in mind that in those statements which use *names* to refer to one or more objects and use *predicates* to characterize them, the *non-names*, i.e. the predicates, are playing so radically different a role that they could be dispensed with altogether, provided that we write the *names* in a variety of configurations corresponding to the variety of predicates to be replaced. Thus, instead of using a variety of two-place predicates to say that pairs of objects are related in various ways, we can simply write the names of these pairs of objects in various dyadic relationships to one another.

Now this, I believe, is an important and illuminating point. But from the standpoint of our problem are we any better off than before? Suppose that in a certain perspicuous language, L, the fact that object a is larger than object b is expressed by writing the name of a above the name of b. Then we can say

That N_1 is above N_2 (in L) pictures that a is larger than b.

And if this language, L, were incorporated into English and if we had the two ways of saying that a was larger than b: '$\frac{a}{b}$' and 'a is larger than *b*', then we could say in our semantical metalanguage, indifferently,

That '*a*' is written above '*b*' (in our language) says that $\frac{a}{b}$

or

That '*a*' is written above '*b*' (in our language) says that *a* is larger than *b*.

But on examination, this turns out to be a logical point *about subjects and predicates generally* and one, therefore, which cannot explain the relationship between the linguistic and the nonlinguistic orders. For exactly the same points can be made about the statement

Triangularity is more complex than linearity.

It amounts to nothing more than the thesis that any statement consisting of one or more *referring* expressions and a *characterizing* expression can be translated into a (contrived) perspicuous language that contains referring expressions to translate the referring expressions but contains no characterizing expressions, using rather a manner of writing the referring expressions to translate the characterizing expression. Once again the essential core of 'picturing' has turned out to be *translation*.

III

Is there no relation of picturing which relates the linguistic and the nonlinguistic orders and which is essential to meaning and truth?

In the passages with which we have been concerned, Wittgenstein has been characterizing picturing as a relation between statements *considered as facts* and another set of *facts* which he calls the world. Roughly, he has been conceiving of picturing as a relation between facts about linguistic expressions, on the one hand, and facts about nonlinguistic objects, on the other.

If we speak of a fact about nonlinguistic objects as a nonlinguistic fact, we are thereby tempted to think of facts about nonlinguistic objects as nonlinguistic entities of a peculiar kind: nonlinguistic pseudo-entities. We have seen, however, that 'nonlinguistic facts' in the sense of facts about nonlinguistic entities are *in another sense* themselves *linguistic* entities and that their connection with the nonlinguistic order is something done or to be done rather than a relation. It is the inferring from 'that-*p* is true' to '*p*'. And as long as picturing is construed as a relationship between *facts* about linguistic objects and *facts* about nonlinguistic objects, nothing more can be said.

But what if, instead of construing 'picturing' as a relationship between *facts*, we construe it as a relationship between linguistic and nonlinguistic *objects*? The very formulation brings a sense of relief, for in everyday life we speak of pictures of things or persons, not of facts. Roughly, one *object* or *group of objects* is a picture of another *object* or *group of objects*. Yet since objects can picture objects only by virtue of facts about them (i.e. only by virtue of having qualities and standing in relations), it may seem a quibble to insist that it is objects and not facts that stand in the picturing relation. It is not, however, a quibble, but the heart of the matter.

Two preliminary remarks are in order before we develop this suggestion:

1. If picturing is to be a relation between objects in the natural order, this means that the linguistic objects in question must belong to the natural order. And this means that we must be considering them in terms of empirical properties and matter-of-factual relations, though these may, indeed must, be very complex, involving all kinds of constant conjunctions or uniformities pertaining to the language user and his environment. Specifically, although we may, indeed must, know that these linguistic objects are subject to rules and principles—are fraught with 'ought'—we abstract from this knowledge in considering them as objects in the natural order. Let me introduce the term 'natural-linguistic object' to refer to linguistic objects thus considered.

2. We must be careful *not* to follow Wittgenstein's identification of complex objects with facts. The point is a simple, but, for our purposes, a vital one. There is obviously *some* connection between complex objects and facts. Thus, if C consists of O_1 and O_2 in a certain relation, then if O_1 and O_2 were not thus related, there would be nothing for 'C' to refer to. But even if we construe the relation between the referring expression 'C' and the fact that O_1 and O_2 are related in a certain way as tightly as possible, by assuming that the fact that O_1RO_2 is involved in the very sense of the referring expression, it nevertheless remains logical nonsense to say that the complex C *is* the fact that O_1RO_2. The most one is entitled to say is that statements containing the referring expression 'C' are, in principle, unpackable into statements about O_1 and O_2 *and that among these statements will be the statement 'O_1RO_2'*. It is, however, the *statement* 'O_1RO_2' that occurs in the expansion, not the *fact-expression* 'that O_1RO_2'. For there are two senses in which a statement can be said to be 'about a fact', and these two senses must not be confused: (*a*) The statement contains a *statement* which expresses a true proposition. In this sense any truth function of a true statement is 'about a fact.' (*b*) It contains a fact-expression, i.e. the name of a fact, rather

212

than a statement. Thus, 'That Chicago is large is the case' contains the fact expression 'that Chicago is large' and is 'about a fact' in that radical sense which gives it a metalinguistic character.

This point is important, for if statements about complex objects were 'about facts' in the sense of containing fact expressions, then, granting the metalinguistic status of facts, the statement

$$C \text{ pictures } y$$

where C is a complex natural-linguistic object, would have the form

$$\text{That-}p \text{ pictures } y.$$

Thus, while ostensibly referring to a complex natural-linguistic object, 'C' would actually refer to the statement which describes its complexity, and statements ostensibly to the effect that certain natural-linguistic objects are pictures of other objects in nature would only ostensibly be about *natural-linguistic* objects in the sense we have defined and would actually be about statements in the full sense which involves the conception of norms and standards.

That if complex objects were facts, only simple nonlinguistic objects could be pictured is a further consequence, which would lead to the familiar antinomy of absolute simples that must be there and taken account of if language is to picture the world, but of which no examples are forthcoming when a user of the language is pressed to point one out. Both of these difficulties are short-circuited by the recognition that complexes are not facts.

But we have at best taken the first step on a road which may lead nowhere. For granted that there are complex natural-linguistic *objects* to do the picturing, what do they picture, and how do they do it?

Let me begin by commenting on a feature of Wittgenstein's treatment of picturing which, as I see it, contains the key to the answer, but which he put to the wrong use by tying it too closely to the

$$\text{fact pictures fact}$$

model. For, although this model enables him to make a sound point about the logical form of elementary statements, it loses the specific thrust of the idea that whatever else language does, its central and essential function, the *sine qua non* of all others, is to enable us to *picture* the world in which we live. It was, indeed, a significant achievement to show that it is n-adic configurations of referring expressions that represent n-adic states of affairs. But of itself this thesis throws no light on the crucial question: What is there about *this specific n*-adic configuration of referring expressions that makes the configuration say that the items referred to are related in *that specific n*-adic way? One is tempted to say that the connection between linguistic configurations and nonlinguistic configurations (i.e. between predicates and properties) is simply conventional, and let it go at that.

From this standpoint, the difference between a *map* and a verbal description in terms of elementary statements is the difference between a convention that represents *n*-adic relationships of size and location by *n*-adic spatial configurations of referring expressions and one that represents these *n*-adic relationships by *n*-adic configurations of referring expressions without requiring that they be *n*-adic *spatial* configurations. And, indeed, when Wittgenstein contrasts maps as pictures that are *both spatial* and *logical* pictures with statements which are *logical* pictures but not spatial pictures, he appears to be committing himself to the view that the only *essential* feature of the picturing he has in mind is that *n*-adic atomic facts be pictures by *n*-adic configurations of names.

I hope to show, on the other hand, that the analogy between statements and cartographical facts, instead of being contracted along the above lines, requires to be expanded. The first point I want to make, however, may seem to strike at the very heart of the map analogy. For it is that what we *ordinarily* call maps are logical pictures only in a parasitical way. Wittgenstein himself emphasizes that a logical picture is such only by virtue of its existence in the space of truth operations. Thus, the fact that a certain dot (representing Chicago) is between two other dots (representing, respectively, Los Angeles and New York) can say that Chicago is between Los Angeles and New York only because it is connected, by virtue of certain general and specific conventions, with the statement 'Chicago is between Los Angeles and New York'. For only with respect to statements such as the latter do we actually carry on such logical operations as negation, alternation, conjunction, and quantification. The cartographically relevant fact that the one dot is between the other two is the counterpart of the statement viewed as a triadic configuration of names. It is, however, only on the latter configuration that we perform the logical operations which are as essential to its being a statement as the fact that it is a configuration. Furthermore, even if we did perform truth operations directly on cartographical configurations, a map language for spatial relationships could exist only as a small part of a more inclusive universe of discourse, and the problem recurs: Is there anything in common between what *all* elementary statements do and the sort of thing that map configurations do, over and above the feature summed up in the slogan that an *n*-adic configuration of names pictures an *n*-adic configuration of objects?

Needless to say, my answer is in the affirmative. And if, as I have suggested, the key to the answer lies in the substitution of the schema

[natural-linguistic objects] $O_1', O_2', \ldots, O_n'$ make up a picture of [objects] $O_1, O_2, \ldots, O_n$ by virtue of such and such facts about $O_1', O_2', \ldots, O_n$

for the Tractarian schema

Linguistic fact pictures nonlinguistic fact

the account I am going to sketch nevertheless preserves in a modified way the Wittgensteinian theme that it is configurations of names that picture configurations of objects. For, to anticipate, the natural-linguistic objects which, by virtue of standing in certain matter-of-factual relationships to one another and to these nonlinguistic objects, constitute a picture of them in the desired sense, are the linguistic counterparts of nonlinguistic *objects* (*not facts*), and it is not too misleading to speak of them as 'names'. To add that it is a system of elementary *statements* (*qua* natural-linguistic objects) that is the picture, is to draw upon Wittgenstein's insight that the occurrence of an elementary statement is to be construed as the occurrence *in a certain manner* of the names of the objects referred to.

Let me emphasize, however, that, in my account, the *manner* in which the 'names' occur in the 'picture' is not a conventional symbol for the *manner* in which the objects occur in the world, limited only by the abstract condition that the picture of an n-adic fact be itself an n-adic fact. Rather, as I see it, the manner in which the names occur in the picture is a projection, in accordance with a fantastically complex system of rules of projection, of the manner in which the objects occur in the world. I hasten to add, however, that in my opinion the germs of the account I am about to offer are present in the *Tractatus*, that jewel box of insights, though submerged by the translation themes I have attempted to disentangle in the previous sections.

In the following argument I shall draw heavily on a principle which I shall simply formulate and apply without giving it the defence it requires, relying, instead, on its intuitive merits. Before I state it, let me emphasize that my argument involves neither a naturalistic reduction of 'ought' to 'is' nor an emotivist denial of the conceptual character of the meaning of normative terms. It will also be remembered that, although I am making my points in connection with overt discourse, I believe that they can be extended by analogy to thoughts (in the sense of acts of thought).

The principle is as follows: Although to say of something that it *ought* to be done (or *ought not* to be done) in a certain kind of circumstance is not to say that *whenever* the circumstance occurs it *is*

215

done (or *is not* done), the statement that a person or group of people think of something as something that ought (or ought not) to be done in a certain kind of circumstance entails that *ceteris paribus* they actually *do* (or refrain from doing) the act in question whenever the circumstance occurs. I shall leave the phrase 'ceteris paribus' without unpacking it, and I shall put the principle briefly as follows: Espousal of principles is reflected in uniformities of performance. I shall not attempt to analyse what it is to espouse a principle, nor shall I attempt to explicate the meaning of normative terms. I am not claiming that to *follow* a principle, i.e. act on principle, is identical with exhibiting a uniformity of performance that accords with the principle. I think that any such idea is radically mistaken. I am merely saying that the espousal of a principle or standard, *whatever else it involves*, is characterized by a uniformity of performance. And let it be emphasized that this uniformity, though not the principle of which it is the manifestation, is describable in matter-of-factual terms.

The importance of this principle for my purposes may perhaps be appreciated if one reviews the variety of respects in which linguistic performances can be said to be 'correct' or 'incorrect'. Obviously many of these respects are irrelevant to our problem. The correctnesses and incorrectnesses with which we are concerned are those which pertain to the logical syntax of basic statements and to what I shall call 'observation contexts'. In what follows, I shall assume that elementary propositions and only elementary propositions are always spontaneously thought *out loud*. This, of course, leaves a great deal of thinking to be done 'in the head'. My problem is to see whether, on certain idealized assumptions, a mode of picturing can be defined with respect to overt discourse that might then be extended to acts of thought in their character as analogous to statements in overt discourse.

The uniformities to which I am calling particular attention fall into two categories:

1. Statement-statement. These are uniformities that correspond at the overt level to espoused principles of inference. To characterize these uniformities presupposes, of course, that they involve verbal patterns that conform to the 'formation rules' of the language.

2. Situation-statement. These are uniformities of the kind illustrated by a person who, in the presence of a green object in standard conditions, thinks, roughly, 'Green here now' and, hence, on our assumption, makes spontaneously, the corresponding statement.

Important distinctions are to be drawn within both kinds of uniformity. Furthermore, a more elaborate discussion, pointed in the direction of a theory of the mutual involvement of thought and action, would require mention of a third category of uniformities, involving a transition from statement to situation, as when a person says 'I shall take a step to the right' and proceeds to do so. This would require a discussion of the force of the word 'shall' and of the sense in which 'I shall do *A* here and now' includes the statement 'I am about to do *A* here and now'. I have touched on these topics elsewhere.[1] For my present purposes, however, I can safely assume that the 'volitions' that culminate in overt action, whether verbal or non-verbal, do not themselves find overt expression.

Now it is familiar fact that Hume was wobbly about the distinction between mental episodes that are thoughts that-*p* and images. It is, perhaps, equally familiar that he could do this without obvious absurdity because he simultaneously treated impressions as though they were *knowings*, e.g. *seeings that-p*. To have the impression of a red object is to see *that* a red item is in a certain place in the visual field. By contrast, to have an 'idea' of a red item is to *think*, rather than to *see*, while to have a 'vivid idea' is to *believe in*, rather than to *merely think of*, a certain state of affairs.

Thus, Hume's terminology does enable him to do a measure of justice to important distinctions. And, by reminding you of certain characteristic doctrines, I may, perhaps, be able to lay the foundation for the view I wish to propose. The Hume I want you to consider, however, is the Hume who believes that our 'perceptions' are 'likenesses' of states of affairs in a public spatiotemporal world. Thus, an 'impression' of lightning is a 'likeness' of the occurrence of a flash of lightning, and an 'impression' of thunder a likeness of the occurrence of a clap of thunder. Of course, for Hume the likeness in question is a conflation of the 'likeness' (however it is to be construed) that a sensation has to its external cause and the 'likeness' we are seeking to explicate, between an elementary *act of thought*, or, in terms of the device we shall use, an elementary linguistic inscription, and an event in nature.

Now Hume lays great stress on the theme that *uniformities* relating perceptible events in nature tend to be reflected in *uniformities* in our 'ideas' of the lightning-thunder sequence, for instance, in an idea-of-lightning–idea-of-thunder sequence. And, of course, he speaks of a case of the latter sequence in which the prior 'perception' of lightning is an 'impression' or 'vivid idea' as an inference

---

[1] For a systematic discussion of the interconnections among situation-statement, statement-statement, and statement-situation uniformities as they pertain to object languages and metalanguages, see Chapter 11.

culminating in a belief about thunder. That Hume's account of inference is as confused and inadequate as his account of impressions and ideas is a point on which I shall not dwell. My concern is rather with the fact that by concentrating his attention on the case where the inference is, in effect, of the form

> Lightning now.
> So, Thunder shortly.

he obscures the distinction between the dates of the acts of thought and the dates of the lightning and thunder that the thoughts are about. This is not unrelated, of course, to the fact that Hume finds it difficult to account for the reference of a present idea to a prior event.

But, whatever the flaws in his argument, Hume put his finger on an essential truth, which, glimpsed now and then by his successors, was invariably overwhelmed by the other ingredients of the classical correspondence theory of truth. What Hume saw, put in a terminology reasonably close to his own, was that 'natural inference' supplements 'recall' and 'observation' to generate a growing system of 'vivid ideas', which constitutes a 'likeness' (sketchy though it may be) of the world in which we live.

On the other hand, by failing to do justice to the propositional form of what he calls 'ideas' and by failing to take into explicit account the fact that the 'subjects' of these propositional ideas are individuated by virtue of the spatiotemporal relationships in which they stand, he cut himself off, as we have seen, from giving an explicit account of the difference between the inferences:

> Lightning now.   Lightning yesterday at 10 a.m.
>   and
> So, Thunder shortly.   So, Thunder yesterday at 10:01.

Hume's blurring of the distinction between thoughts and images permits him to assume that natural inference not only is successive *as inference*, but must concern events that are successive. This rules out the inferences:

> Smoke here yesterday at 10 a.m.
> So, Fire here yesterday at 10 a.m.

and, of course,

> Thunder now.
> So, Lightning a moment ago.

Obviously, Hume's theory of natural inference must be extended to cover these cases.

Again, in developing his form of the classical doctrine that the mind knows the world by virtue of containing a 'likeness' of it, Hume assumes, without careful explication, that the 'perception' of a configuration of objects is a configuration of 'perceptions'. This principle, though sound at the core, involves difficulties enough when 'perception' is taken in the sense of 'sensation or image'. It poses even greater problems when 'perception' is taken in the radically different sense of *propositional act of thought*. Yet it is central to Hume's conception of the mind as building, through observation, recall, and natural inference, a system of 'vivid ideas' which pictures (schematically) its world (including itself). For this system, as it exists at any one time, represents events by 'ideas' which are 'like' them and matter-of-fact relationships between events by 'like' matter-of-fact relationships between the corresponding 'ideas'.

Our problem, of course, is how this 'likeness' is to be construed, if the propositional character of the 'idea' is taken seriously; that is to say, if we are to preserve the essence of Hume's contention, while avoiding his mistake of thinking of 'ideas' as likenesses in the sense of duplicates. This essence is the contention that the 'likeness' between elementary thoughts and the objects they picture is definable in matter-of-factual terms as a likeness or correspondence or isomorphism between two systems of objects, each of which belongs in the natural order.

What matter-of-factual relationships has our previous discussion made available? In the first place there are the uniformities or constant conjunctions involved in the connection of language with environment in the observational situations. Here it is essential to think of these uniformities as a matter of responding to objects with *statements* rather than by referring expressions, thus to a green object with 'This here now is green'. This point remains, even though, from a more penetrating point of view, this statement is a referring expression.[1]

Let us suppose, therefore, that observation reports have the forms illustrated by

> This here now is green
> This is one step to the right of that
> This is one heartbeat after that

and let us imagine a super-inscriber who 'speaks' by inscribing statements in wax and is capable of inscribing inscriptions at an

---

[1] The temptation to think of the report in question as a configuration of the referring expressions 'this' and 'green' leads to an oversimplified conception of the way in which objects in the world are pictured by statements as complex natural-linguistic objects. This oversimplified conception (cf. Bergmann) is tied to a Platonic realism with respect to universals. For an elaboration of this point, see Chapter 7.

incredible rate, indefinitely many 'at once'. It must not be forgotten, however, that he is a thinker as well as an inscriber, and thinks far more thoughts than he expresses by inscriptions.

Now, whenever the inscriber sees that a certain object in front of him is green, or one step to the right of (or to the left of) another, or experiences that one happening is a heartbeat later than another, he makes the corresponding inscription. We must also imagine, as we have in effect done already, that the inscriber has a system of co-ordinates metrically organized in terms of steps and heartbeats and that he knows how to measure and count. And we shall suppose that he uses a 'co-ordinate language' in which names are ordered sets of numerals, three for space, one for time, which are assigned to events on the basis of measurement. Let us further suppose that the inscriber continuously inscribes statements of the form

$$1 = now$$
$$2 = now$$
$$3 = now$$
$$........$$

in the proper order one heartbeat apart, and continually inscribes statements of the form

$$/x,y,z/ = here$$

where the value of 'x' or 'y' or 'z' changes in a way illustrated by the sequence

$$/2,5,9/ = here \quad \text{Step taken in direction } z_+$$
$$/2,5,10/ = here.$$

These inscriptions, which give expression to the inscriber's awareness of where is here and when is now, are involved in uniformities of the following kind. The inscriber observes a green object immediately in front of him. He inscribes,

This here now is green $\quad /2,5,9/ = here \quad 4 = now$

and proceeds to inscribe

... $/2,5,9;4/$ is green $\quad /2,5,9/ = here \quad 5 = now.$

Roughly, he goes from a 'this here now statement' to a statement in which the event in question is referred to by a co-ordinate name.

Let us now suppose that whenever a 'this here now' statement has been thus transformed, the inscriber keeps on inscribing the result at all subsequent moments. His inscriptions are cumulative.

Another supposition: The inscriber writes his inscriptions in an order that corresponds to an ordering of the names that appear in them according to the values of the numerals of which they are composed. To simplify, let us suppose that his space has only one dimension, so that names have the form '$/s;t/$', and that the principle of order is that of inscribing all sentences involving a given value of 't' in the order of the values of 's', thus:

$\ldots /9,t/$ is green $/10,t/$ is blue

and only after all inscriptions involving that value of 't' have been inscribed does the inscription continue with inscriptions involving the next value of 't', thus:

$\ldots /101,10/$ is red $/9,11/$ is blue.

If we add that the inscriber writes numerals without the use of definitional abbreviations, so that the names have the form,

$/0'''', 0'''\ldots'/$

we see that the inscriptions will reflect, in their multiplicity, the multiplicities of *heartbeats* and *steps* that separate the events which, speaking from without, we know to be referred to by the inscriptions.

We have taken into account, so far, some, at least, of the uniformities that reflect the conceptual processes involved in the observation and retention of matters of fact. The next step is to take into account the fact that our inscriber is, in the full sense, a rational being. For, in the rich inner life we have given him and which is only partially expressed by the inscriptions he makes, there is a substantial body of inductive knowledge. And without this inductive knowledge there can be no rational extension of one's picture of the world beyond what has been observed and retained. Let us imagine that, whatever the form of the reasoning by which one infers from the occurrence of an observed event of one kind to the occurrence of an unobserved event of another, by means of an inductive generalization, it finds its expression at the inscriptional level in a sequence of two inscriptions, the former of which describes the observed event, while the latter describes the inferred event. And, as in the case of observation, let us suppose that once the latter inscription is inscribed, it continues to be inscribed.

Before attempting to draw any morals from this story of an industrious super-inscriber, let me remind you that inscriptions of the form

$/x,y,z;t/$ is green

must not be construed as involving two names, '$/x,y,z;t/$' and 'green'. The whole inscription '$/x,y,z;t/$ is green' *is to be construed as a way* of writing the *one* name '$/x,y,z;t/$'. Again, more intuitively, given the above account of the arranging and rearranging of the elementary

221

inscriptions, two names, by virtue of occurring in a certain order, constitute a dyadic relational statement to the effect that the objects named stand in a certain spatio-temporal relationship to one another.

But, whatever subtleties might have to be added to the above to make it do its work, an objection can be raised to the whole enterprise. For, it might be argued, even if it were made to work, it could not do what I want it to do. For, surely, I have at best indicated how a structure of natural-linguistic objects might correspond, by virtue of certain 'rules of projection' to a structure of nonlinguistic objects. But to say that a manifold of linguistic objects *correctly* pictures a manifold of nonlinguistic objects is no longer to consider them as mere 'natural-linguistic objects'—to use your term—but to consider them as linguistic objects proper, and to say that they are *true*. Thus, instead of finding a mode of 'correspondence' *other than truth* that accompanies truth in the case of empirical statements, your 'correspondence' is simply truth all over again.

So the objection. I reply that to say that a linguistic object *correctly* pictures a nonlinguistic object in the manner described above is not to say that the linguistic object is *true*, save in that metaphorical sense of 'true' in which one geometrical figure can be said to be a 'true' projection of another if it is drawn by correctly following the appropriate method of projection.

If it is objected that to speak of a linguistic structure as a *correct* projection is to use normative language and, therefore, to violate the terms of the problem, which was to define 'picturing' as a relation *in rerum natura*, the answer is that, while to say of a projection that it is *correct* is, indeed, to use normative language, the principle which, it will be remembered, I am taking as axiomatic assures us that corresponding to every espoused principle of correctness there is a matter-of-factual uniformity in performance. And it is such uniformities, which link natural-linguistic objects with one another and with the objects of which they are the linguistic projections, that constitute picturing as a relation of matter of fact between objects in the natural order.

And, indeed, it seems to me that, given the assumptions we have been making, the matter-of-factual uniformities exhibited by our ideal inscriber are the counterpart of 'rules of projection' in terms of which an inscription string can be regarded as a projection of the spatiotemporal region in which the inscriber has been moving around, observing and inferring. I say this in the full realization that the preceding remarks are at best a groping indication of a line of attack, rather than a 'clear and distinct' or 'adequate' solution of the problem of empirical truth. To bring this exploration to an end, the following remarks may serve to highlight the larger-scale structure of the argument:

1. The correspondence for which we have been looking is limited to elementary statements, or, more accurately, to the elementary thoughts which are expressed by elementary statements and which we conceive of by analogy with elementary statements.

2. The foregoing can be construed as an attempt to explain the fundamental kind of role played by matter-of-factual statements (or acts of thought). We were led to the notion of the role played by a form of words that is used to make an empirical statement, by reflecting on what it means to say of a form of words that it is true. We were led to the equivalence

| 'Chicago est grande' (in French) is true | $=$ Df | (∃ that-p) 'Chicago est grande' (in French) expresses the sense that-p *and* that-p is true. |

where

'Chicago est grande' (in French) expresses the sense that Chicago is large

was interpreted as saying that in French instances of a certain design, by virtue of playing a certain (complex) role, are ˙Chicago is large˙s, as in chess objects of a familiar shape, by virtue of playing a certain (complex) role, are pawns.[1]

3. We saw that, while *all* true statements of whatever kind are true in the same sense of 'true', the roles of different kinds of statement are different; thus the role of '2 plus 2 equals 4' is different from that of 'This is red'. My argument is that, in the case of matter-of-factual statements (and, in the last analysis, the acts of thought to which they give expression), this role is that of constituting a projection in language users of the world in which they live.

Thus, while to say

That /9,7/ is green is true

is not to *say* that tokens of '/9,7/ is green/' as natural-linguistic objects correspond in ways defined by certain rules of projection to the object /9,7/, but is, in an appropriate sense, its picture, yet it *implies* that it so corresponds. For to commit oneself to

That /9,7/ is green is true

is to commit oneself to

/9,7/ is green

---

[1] This sentence was substituted in proof to bring the formulation in line with the interpretation of abstract singular terms in 'Abstract Entities', *The Review of Metaphysics*, June, 1963.

and if to understand a language involves knowing (though not at the level of philosophical reflection) that uniformities such as were described in the myth of the perfect inscriber are involved in the use of language and if, therefore, I recognize (though not at the level of philosophical reflection) that, to the extent to which roles are executed and rules conformed to, statements are complex objects in a system that is a picture of natural events, surely I must recognize in my statement '/9,7/ is green' the projection of the object /9,7/.

That the projection exists in any completeness at the level of *acts of thought* rather than statements is a theme the exploration of which would require a complete philosophy of mind.

Note: I now (1963) think that the matter is even more straightforward, for the 'premise' of this inference can be reconstructed—in first approximation—as "The 'Snow is white' is assertable" and stands to the 'conclusion' as authorization to performance. If so, then the entailment 'That that snow is white is true entails that snow is white' is derivative from this performance authorizing force of truth statements. The same can be shown, by a somewhat more complicated argument, to be true of the converse entailment.

Again, when statements seem to occur in non-truth-functional contexts, the verbal patterns which would ordinarily be these statements occur in a name-forming capacity. They form illustrating common nouns for the linguistic performables in any language which are subject to rules analogous to those which govern these patterns in our language. Thus 'S (in L) means snow is white' contains the pattern 'snow is white' not as a statement, but as a picture of a statement *to be made*—in appropriate circumstances. For an elaboration of these points see 'Abstract Entities,' *The Review of Metaphysics*, June, 1963.

7

NAMING AND SAYING

This chapter adopts the Tractarian view that configurations of objects are expressed by configurations of names. Two alternatives are considered: The objects in atomic facts are (1) without exception *particulars*; (2) one or more particulars plus a *universal* (Gustav Bergmann). On (1) a mode of configuration is always an empirical relation: on (2) it is the logical nexus of 'exemplification'. It is argued that (1) is both Wittgenstein's view in the *Tractatus* and correct. It is also argued that exemplification is a 'quasi-semantical' relation, and that it (and universals) are 'in the world' only in that broad sense in which the 'world' includes linguistic norms and roles viewed (thus in translating) from the standpoint of a fellow participant.

THE topics I am about to discuss have their roots in Wittgenstein's *Tractatus*. My point of departure will be Professor Irving Copi's paper on 'Objects, Properties and Relations in the *Tractatus*'[1] in which, after a decisive critique of certain misinterpretations of Wittgenstein's so-called picture theory of meaning with particular reference to relational statements, he proceeds to attribute to Wittgenstein, on the basis of a by no means implausible interpretation of certain texts, a puzzling construction of Wittgenstein's objects as 'bare particulars'.[2]

I shall not waste time by formulating the misinterpretations in question and summarizing Copi's admirably lucid critique. For my concern is with the theory of relational statements as pictures which, in my opinion, he correctly attributes to Wittgenstein, and, specifically, with the power of this theory to illuminate traditional philosophical puzzles concerning predication generally.

The crucial passage, of course, is 3.1432, 'We must not say: "The complex sign 'aRb' says '*a* stands in the relation R to *b*'"; but we must say, "*That* 'a' stands in a certain relation to 'b' says *that* aRb."' Part of Wittgenstein's point is that though names and statements are both complex in their empirical character as instances of sign designs,

[1] *Mind*, 67, 1958.   [2] Ibid.,·p. 163.

and hence, from his point of view, are equally *facts*, the fact that a name consists (in various ways) of related parts is not relevant to its character as name in the way in which the division of such a statement as (schematically)

aRb

into just the parts 'a', 'R', and 'b' is to its character as making the statement it does. The latter parts are themselves functioning (though not in the same way) as signs, whereas no part of a name is functioning as a sign. But the crucial point that Wittgenstein is making emerges when we ask, 'What are the parts of the statement in question the relation of which to one another is essential to its character as statement?' For in spite of the fact that the obvious answer would seem to be 'the *three* expressions "a", "R", and "b"', this answer is incorrect. 'R' is, indeed, functioning in a broad sense as a sign, and is certainly involved in the statement's saying what it does, but it is involved, according to Wittgenstein, in quite a different way than the signs 'a' and 'b'. To say that 'R' is functioning as a predicate, whereas 'a' and 'b' are functioning as names, is to *locate* the difference, but to remain open to perplexity. What Wittgenstein tells us is that while superficially regarded the statement is a concatenation of the three parts 'a', 'R', and 'b', viewed more profoundly it is a two-termed fact, with 'R' coming in to the statement as bringing it about that the expressions 'a' and 'b' are dyadically related in a certain way, i.e. as bringing it about that the expressions 'a' and 'b' are related as having an 'R' between them. And he is making the point that what is essential to any statement which will say that aRb is not that the names 'a' and 'b' have a relation word between them (or before them or in any other relation to them), but that these names be related (dyadically) *in some way or other* whether or not this involves the use of a third sign design. Indeed, he is telling us that it is philosophically clarifying to recognize that instead of expressing the proposition that a is next to b by writing 'is next to' between 'a' and 'b', we could write 'a' in some relation to 'b' using only these signs. In a perspicuous language this is what we would do. Suppose that the Jumblies have such a language. It contains no relation words, but has the same name expressions as our tidied up English. Then we could translate Jumblese into English by making such statements as

$$\begin{array}{l} \text{'a'} \\ \text{b} \end{array}$$ (in Jumblese) means *a is next to b*

and be on our way to philosophical clarification. Of particular interest in this connection would be the Jumblese translation of *Appearance and Reality*.

226

It will be noticed that I have correlated the fact that in 'aRb' the 'R' plays the predicate role with the fact that in Jumblese the proposition expressed by 'aRb' would be expressed by relating the two names without the use of a predicate expression. Now in Frege's system, 'R' would be said to stand for (*bedeuten*) a concept, whereas 'a' and 'b' stand for objects. Thus what Wittgenstein puts by saying that configurations of objects are represented by configurations of names (3.21)—so that Jumblese $\frac{a}{b}$ and PMese 'aRb' are equally configurations of two names, though the latter is not perspicuously so—could also be put by saying that to represent that certain objects satisfy an n-adic concept, one makes their names satisfy an n-adic concept.[1] Roughly, Wittgenstein's configurations are the counterparts of a subset of Frege's concepts, and Wittgenstein is taking issue with Frege by insisting that a perspicuous language would contain no concept words functioning predicatively, that is to say, as 'R' functions when we say that aRb. How a perspicuous language would do the job done by concept words in their non-predicative use is something on which Wittgenstein throws less light, though his sketchy treatment of the parallel problem of how a perspicuous language would handle belief statements in which, according to Frege, the *Bedeutung* of the subordinate clause is what would ordinarily be its sense, gives some clue to the answer.

Now the above remarks adumbrate many topics of importance for ontology and the philosophy of logic. Some of them I shall pick up at a later stage in the argument. For the moment, however, I shall concentrate on the question, 'What sort of thing are Wittgenstein's objects?' And the first thing I shall say is that in my opinion Copi is undoubtedly right in insisting that Wittgenstein's objects are particulars. To put the same point in a somewhat different way, Wittgenstein's names are names of particulars. This is not to say, of course, that expressions which function in unperspicuous languages in a superficially name-like way, but do not name particulars, are meaningless. It is simply to say that they would not translate into the names of a perspicuous language. Roughly, unperspicuous name-like expressions fall into two categories for Wittgenstein: (1) Those which would translate into a perspicuous language as, on Russell's theory of descriptions, statements involving descriptive phrases translate into unique existentials (compare Wittgenstein's treatment of complexes in 3.24); (2)—which is more interesting—those which would not translate at all into that part of a perspicuous language which is used to make statements about what is or is not the case in the world.

---

[1] *Which* n-adic concept the names are made to satisfy is, of course, as philosophers use the term, a matter of convention.

It is the latter which are in a special sense without meaning, though not in any ordinary sense meaningless. The 'objects' or 'individuals' or 'logical subjects' they mention are pseudo-objects in that to 'mention them' is to call attention to those features of discourse about what is or is not the case in the world which 'show themselves', i.e. are present in a perspicuous language not as words, but in the manner in which words are combined.[1] Thus it is perfectly legitimate to say that there are 'objects' other than particulars, and to make statements about them. These objects (complexes aside) are not in the world, however, nor do statements about them tell us how things stand in the world. In Wittgenstein's terminology no statements about such objects are 'pictures', and, therefore, in the sense in which 'pictures' have sense they are without sense.

Now one can conceive of a philosopher who agrees with Wittgenstein that in a perspicuous language the fact that two objects stand in a dyadic relation would be represented by making their names stand in a dyadic relation, but who rejects the idea that the only objects or individuals *in the world* are particulars. Such a philosopher might distinguish, for example, within the fact that a certain sense-datum (supposing there to be such entities) is green, between two objects, a *particular* of which the name might be 'a', and an item which, though equally an *object* or *individual*, is not a *particular*. Let us suppose that the name of this object is 'green'.[2] Let us say that green is a universal rather than a particular, and that among universals it is a quality rather than a relation. According to this philosopher,[3] the perspicuous way of saying that *a* is green (abstracting from problems pertaining to temporal reference) is by putting the two names 'a' and 'green' in some relation, the same relation in which we would put 'b' and 'red' if we wished to say that b is red. Let us suppose that we write 'Green a'.

Our previous discussion suggests the question: What would be the *unperspicuous* way of saying what is said by 'Green a', i.e. which would stand to 'Green a' as, on Wittgenstein's view 'aRb' stands to, say, $\frac{a}{b}$? The philosopher I have in mind proposes the following answer:

a exemplifies green.

[1] One is reminded of the peculiar objects which, according to Frege, one talks about when one attempts to talk about concepts.

[2] I shall subsequently discuss the dangers involved in the use of colour examples with particular reference to the interpretation of colour words as names.

[3] The philosopher I have in mind is Professor Gustav Bergmann and the views I am discussing are those to be found, I believe, in certain passages of his interesting paper on 'Ineffability, Ontology and Method' which appeared in the January, 1960, number of the *Philosophical Review*.

And this is not unexpected, for where, as in this case, two objects are involved, what is needed for the purpose of *un*perspicuity is a two place predicate which is appropriately concatinated with the name of a particular on one side and the name of a universal on the other, and this is one of the jobs we philosophers pay 'exemplifies' to do. Thus this philosopher would be saying that as on Wittgenstein's view the perspicuous way of saying that a is next to b is by writing 'a' in some relation to 'b', so the perspicuous way of saying that a exemplifies green is by writing 'a' in some relation to 'green'. Having thus made use of Wittgenstein's ladder, he would climb off on to his own pinnacle. For he must claim that Wittgenstein made a profound point with the wrong examples. He must, in short, deny that the perspicuous way of saying that a is next to b is by writing 'a' in some relation to 'b'. That this is so is readily seen from the following considerations.

Exemplification is not the sort of thing that philosophers would ordinarily call an empirical relation. This title is usually reserved for such relations as spatial juxtaposition and temporal succession. Yet exemplification might well be an—or perhaps *the*—empirical relation[1] in a more profound sense than is usually recognized, as would be the case if the simplest atomic facts in the world were of the kind *perspicuously* represented by 'Green a' and *unperspicuously* represented by 'a exemplifies green'.

For let us see what happens to what we ordinarily refer to as empirical relations if relational statements are approached in a manner consistent with the above treatment of 'a is green'. According to the latter, the fact that a is green is perspicuously represented by the juxtaposition of two names, 'a' and 'green', and unperspicuously represented by a sentence which contains three expressions, two of which are names, while the third, which might be taken by unperceptive philosophers to be a third *name*, actually serves the purpose of bringing it about that a distinctive dyadic relation obtains between the names. It is clear, then, that the parallel treatment of 'a is below b' would claim that it is perspicuously represented by a suitable juxtaposition of *three* names, 'a', 'b', and 'below', thus,

Below a b

and unperspicuously represented by a sentence which uses *four* expressions, thus, perhaps

Exempl[2] a b below.

---

[1] Cf. Bergmann, op. cit., p. 23, n. 2.

[2] I use this way of putting the matter to make the point with minimum fuss and feathers. It is worth reflecting, however, that the grammatical parallel to 'a exemplifies green' would be either 'a exemplifies being below b' or 'a and b jointly exemplify below-ness (the relation of one thing being below another)'.

I will comment later on the interpretation of 'below' as a name, and on the fact that it is prima facie less plausible than the similar move with respect to 'green'. I should, however, preface the following remarks by saying that I share with Professor Bergmann the sentiment which might be expressed by saying that ordinary grammar is the paper money of wise men but the gold of fools. For my immediate purpose is to contrast the Tractarian theory of predication with that of Professor Bergmann, who, though he decidedly prefers Saul to Paul, is by no means an orthodox exponent of the Old Testament; and I regard the point as of great philosophical significance.

According to the Tractatus, then, the fact that *a* is below *b* is *perspicuously* represented by an expression consisting of *two* names dyadically related, and *unperspicuously* represented by an expression containing, in addition to these two names, a two-place predicate expression. According to Professor Bergmann, if I understand him correctly, such facts as that *a* is below *b* are perspicuously represented by expressions consisting of *three* names triadically related, and unperspicuously represented by an expression containing, in addition to these three names (suitably punctuated) an expression having the force of 'exemplifies'. What exactly does this difference amount to? And which view is closer to the truth?

To take up the first question first, the difference can be reformulated in such a way as to bring out its kinship with the old issue between realists and nominalists. Wittgenstein is telling us that the only objects in the world are particulars, Bergmann is telling us that the world includes as objects both particulars and universals. Bergmann, of course, has his own razor and in his own way gives the world a close shave, but not quite as close as does Wittgenstein. Another way of putting the difference is by saying that whereas for Wittgenstein (Saul) it is *empirical* relations in the world that are perspicuously expressed by relating the names of their relata, for Bergmann empirical relations appear in discourse about the world as *nominata*, and it is *exemplification* and *only* exemplification which is perspicuously expressed by relating the names of its relata.

To clarify the latter way of putting the matter, some terminological remarks are in order. If we so use the term 'relation' that to say of something that it is a relation is to say that it is perspicuously represented in discourse by a configuration of expressions rather than by the use of a separate expression, then for Bergmann there is, refinements aside, only *one* relation, i.e. exemplification,[1] and what are ordinarily said to be relations, for example *below*, would occur in the world as *relata*. Thus if we were to continue to use the term 'relation'

---

[1] Strictly speaking, there would be a relation of exemplification for each order of fact, and, on non-elementaristic views, a family of such relations for each type.

in such a way that *below* would be a relation, then exemplification, as construed by Bergmann, would not be a relation. For although, as he sees it, both *below* and exemplification are in the world, the former appears in discourse as a nominatum, whereas exemplification does not, indeed *can* not.

To keep matters straight, it will be useful to introduce the term 'nexus' in such a way that to say of something that it is a nexus is to say that it is perspicuously represented in discourse by a configuration of expressions rather than by a separate expression. If we do this, we can contrast Bergmann and Wittgenstein as follows:

> *Wittgenstein:* There are many *nexūs* in the world. Simple relations of matter of fact are *nexūs*. All objects or individuals which form a nexus are particulars, i.e. individuals of type 0. There is no relation or nexus of exemplification in the world.

> *Bergmann:* There is only one[1] nexus, exemplification. Every atomic state of affairs contains at least one (and, if the thesis of elementarism be true, at most one) individual which is not a particular.

If one so uses the term 'ineffable' that to eff something is to signify it by using a name, then Wittgenstein's view would be that what are ordinarily called relations are ineffable, for they are nexūs and are expressed (whether perspicuously or not) by configurations of names. For Bergmann, on the other hand, what are ordinarily called relations are effed; it is exemplification which is ineffable.

Before attempting to evaluate these contrasting positions, let us beat about the neighbouring bushes. And for a start, let us notice that Wittgenstein tells us that atomic facts are configurations of objects, thus

2.0272 The configuration of the objects forms the atomic fact.

The question I wish to raise is how strictly we are to interpret the plural of the word 'object' in this context. Specifically, could there be a configuration of one object? It must be granted that an affirmative answer would sound odd. But, then, it sounds odd to speak of drawing a conclusion from a null class of premises. Philosophers of a 'reconstructionist' bent have often found it clarifying to treat one thing as a 'limiting case' of another; and if Russell, for one, was willing to speak of a quality as a monadic relation, there is no great initial improbability to the idea that Wittgenstein might be willing to speak of a monadic configuration.

Would he be willing to do so? The question is an important one, and calls for a careful examination of the text. I do not think that

[1] See fn. 9.

2.0272, taken by itself, throws much light on the matter. Yet when it is taken together with such passages as

> 2.031 In the atomic fact the objects are combined in a definite way.

> 2.03 In the atomic fact objects hang in one another like the members of a chain.

which are accompanied by no hint that there might be monadic 'combinations' or, so to speak, chains with a single link, the cumulative effect is to buttress the thesis that there is no provision in the *Tractatus* for monadic atomic facts.

Yet at first sight, at least, this would not seem to be inevitable. After all, one who says that the fact that *a* is below *b* would be perspicuously represented by an expression in which the name 'a' stands in a dyadic relation (to 'b') might be expected to say that the fact that *a* is green would be perspicuously represented by an expression in which the name 'a' stands in a monadic relation, i.e. in a more usual way of speaking, is of a certain quality. Thus one can imagine a philosopher who says that in a perspicuous language, monadic atomic facts would be represented by writing the name of the single object they contain in various colours or in various styles of type. The idea is a familiar one. Is there any reason to suppose that it was not available to Wittgenstein?

One line of thought might be that in such a symbolism we could not distinguish between a name and a statement. After all, a name has to be written in some style or other, and, if so, would not every occurrence of a name, in this hypothetical symbolism, have by virtue of its style the force of a statement, and therefore not be a name at all? This objection, however, overestimates the extent to which empirical similarities between expressions imply similarity of linguistic role. Obviously, writing 'a' alongside 'b' might be saying that *a* temporally precedes *b*, whereas an 'a' below a 'b' might have no meaning at all. Thus, to write 'a' in boldface might be to say that *a* is green, whereas an 'a' in ordinary type might function merely as a name. How this might be so will be discussed later on. My present point is simply that to understand expressions is to know which of the many facts about them (shape, size, colour, etc.) are relevant (and in what way) to their meaning. It could surely be the case that in a perspicuous language the fact that a heap of ink was a token of a certain name was a matter of its being an instance of a certain letter of the alphabet written in one or another of a certain number of manners. But one or more of these manners might be, so to speak, 'neutral' in that to write the name in such a manner would not be to make an assertion, but simply to write the name, whereas to write the name in other manners would be to make various assertions. Only, then, in the case of the non-'neutral' manners would the writing of the name be the assertion of a monadic fact.

Another line of thought would be to the effect that in a language in which monadic atomic facts (if such there be) were expressed by writing single names in various manners, there would be a difficulty about variables—not about variables ranging over particulars, for here the device of having special letters for variables could be used, but about variables such as would be the counterparts of the monadic predicate variables of *Principia* notation. Thus we could represent the sentential function 'x is green' by using the variable 'x' and writing it in boldface, thus

$$\mathbf{x}$$

But how would one say of *a* that it was of some quality or other? What would correspond to 'a is f' and '(Ef) a is f' as 'x' to 'x is green' and '(Ex) **x**' to '(Ex) x is green'? Would we not have to introduce an expression to be the variable—after all, one cannot write a manner by itself—and if one has separate variables to make possible the expression of what would be expressed in PMese by

$$(Ef) \; fa, \; (g) \; gb, \; etc.$$

i.e. variables ther than those which range over *particulars*, would this not be, in effect, to treat the atomic propositions which are supposedly represented perspicuously by, for example,

$$\mathbf{a}$$

as involving two *constants*, and hence two *names*? Must not its truly perspicuous representation be rather

$$Green \; a$$

as Bergmann claims?

Consider the following schema for translation from PMese into Jumblese:

PMese	*Jumblese*
I. *Names of particulars*	
a, b, c, ...	The same letters written in a variety of neutral styles, the variety being a matter of height, the neutrality a matter of the use of the ordinary font:
	a, b, c, ...; a, b, c, ...; a, b, c, ...

II. *Statements* (not including relational statements, which will be discussed shortly)

    Green a, red a, ...   **a**, *a*, ...

III. *Statement functions*

    (1) *Predicate constant, individual variable;*

    Green x, red y, ...   **x**, *y*, ...

    (2) *Predicate variable, individual constant;*

    fa, gb, ...   Names in neutral styles (see I):

                    a, ...; a, ...; a, ...

    (3) *Predicate variable, individual variable;*

    fx, gy, ...   Name variables in neutral styles:

                    x, y, z, ...; **x, y, z**, ...; **X, y, Z**, ...

IV. *Quantification*

    (Ex) green x   (Ex) **x**

    (Ef) fa, (Eg) ga, ...   (E() a, (E() a, ...

    (Ef) (Ex) fx, (Eg) (Ex) gx, ... (E() (Ex) x, (E() (Ex) x, ...

Notice that in the final samples of Jumblese, the (-shaped symbols serve to represent a neutral style; *which* depends on its size.

It is to be noted that in this form of Jumblese, the neutral styles by virtue of which an expression functions as a name without making a statement is also the neutral style which is illustrated by the expressions serving as the counterparts of the predicate variables of PMese. It is therefore an interesting feature of this form of Jumblese that expressions which function as names but not as statements *have the form of a statement*. It is often said with reference to PMese that the form of a predicate is, for example,

Red x.

It is less frequently said that the form of a name is, for example,

f a.

In the variety of Jumblese sketched above, the latter would be as true as the former. (Cf. *Tractatus* 3.311.) This point clearly should be expanded to take account of the forms of relational statements, but I shall not attempt to do this, save by implication, on the present occasion.

Now the difficulty, if there is one, pertaining to predicate variables

234

is not limited to predicate variables pertaining to these putative monadic atomic statements. If there were a point to be made along the above line, it would pertain as well to dyadic and polyadic statements as Wittgenstein interprets them. Thus, to continue with our translation schema, we have

PMese	Jumblese
Larger (ab), Redder (ab)	^a_b, ^a_b
R(ab), S(ab), T(ab), ...	ab, a b, a b, ...
Larger (xy), Redder (xy), ...	^x_y, ^x_y, ...
R(xy), S(xy), ...	xy, x y, x y, ...
(Ex) (Ey) Larger (xy)	(Ex) (Ey) ^x_y
(ER) R(ab), (ES) S(ab), ...	(E ..) ab, (E . .) a b, ...
(ER) (Ex) (Ey) R(xy)	(E ..) (Ex) (Ey) xy

Here again we find the introduction of symbols to be the counterparts of the relation variables of PMese, i.e. symbols to illustrate the neutral manners which in

$$ab, a\ b, a\ \ b, a\ \ \ b, etc.$$

express what is expressed in PMese by the statement functions

$$R(ab), S(ab), T(ab), etc.$$

Thus, in addition to the variables '(', '(', '(', ... which correspond to the one place predicate variables of *Principia*, we have the variables '..', '. .', '. .', ... to correspond to the dyadic predicate variables of *Principia*.

The topic of perspicuousness with respect to variables and quantification is an interesting and important one in its own right, and the above remarks have barely scratched the surface. The only point I have wanted to make is that if considerations pertaining to quantification or to distinguishing between names and statements support the idea that the atomic statements of a perspicuous language must contain at least two names, these considerations would do so *not* by supporting the idea that a minimal atomic statement would contain the names of two *particulars*, but by supporting the idea that it would contain the name of a universal. In other words, they would point to Bergmann's form of logical atomism as contrasted with that of Wittgenstein.

Now I side with Wittgenstein on this matter, that is to say I would argue that the atomic descriptive statements of an ideal language would contain names of particulars only. As I see it, therefore, it is of crucial importance to ontology not to confuse the contrast between *constant* and *variable* with that between *name* and *variable*. For to confuse these two contrasts is to move from the correct idea that

Green a

can be viewed against the doubly quantified statement

(Ef) (Ex) fx

to the incorrect idea that

Green a

is the juxtaposition of two *names*, and says perspicuously what would be unperspicuously said by

a exemplifies green.

To view the Jumblese statement

a

against the doubly quantified statement

(E()) (x) x

is, indeed, to highlight two facts about the expression '**a**', the fact by virtue of which it is a writing in some style or other of a certain name, and the fact by virtue of which, to speak metaphorically, green comes into the picture. But I see no reason to infer that because the expression's being a case of a certain name, and the expression's pertaining to green are each bound up with a monadic (though not, of course, atomic) fact about the expression, that both its being about *a* and its being about green come into the picture in the same way, i.e. that they are both *named*.[1]

For the being about *a* and the being about green could each be true of the expression by virtue of monadic facts about it, and still not pertain to its meaning *in the same way* in any more important sense. The crucial thing about an expression is the role it plays in the language, and the fact that a certain expression is an '**a**' in some style or other, and the fact that it is in boldface, may both be monadic facts and yet play different roles in the language. In which connection it is relevant to note that the monadic fact about the expression by virtue of which it pertains to green is not the monadic fact that it is thick, but the monadic fact that it is a thick instance of a name or name variable.

[1] For an earlier exploration of this point see my contribution to a symposium with P. F. Strawson on 'Logical Subjects and Physical Objects' in *Philosophy and Phenomenological Research*, 17, 1957.

Before continuing with the substantive argument of this paper, I shall say something more to the historical question as to whether Wittgenstein himself 'countenanced' monadic atomic facts. I have argued that the passages in which he speaks of atomic facts as configurations of objects (in the plural) are not decisive, by pointing out that Russell might have spoken of atomic facts as related objects, but have so used the term 'relation' that one could speak of monadic relations. It seems to me that similar considerations prevent such passages as

2.15 That the elements of the picture are combined with one another in a definite way represents that the things are so combined with one another.

3.21 To the configuration of the single signs in the propositional sign corresponds the configuration of the objects in the state of affairs.

from deciding the issue against the idea that an atomic proposition might contain only one name.

On one occasion Wittgenstein seems to me to come as close to saying that there are monadic atomic propositions as he could have come without saying it in so many words. Thus consider

4.24 The names are the simple symbols. I indicate them by single letters ('x', 'y', 'z').

The elementary proposition I write as function of the names, in the form 'fx', '$\phi(x,y)$', etc.

This passage is the more striking in that it occurs very shortly after

4.22 The elementary proposition consists of names. It is a connection, a concatenation of names.

Now to interpret 4.24 it is important to note that although Wittgenstein tells us that atomic facts to the effect that two objects are dyadically related would be perspicuously represented by placing the names of these objects in dyadic relation without the use of any relation word, the *Tractatus* contains no *use* but only *mentions* (and indirect ones at that) of such perspicuous representations. Thus Wittgenstein does not *use* Jumblese, but always PMese, in illustrating the form of atomic propositions, thus always 'aRb' (cf. the '$\phi(x,y)$' of 4.24). What he does do is tell us that the symbol 'R' serves not as a name, but as a means of bringing it about that the names 'a' and 'b' are dyadically related.

This being so, Wittgenstein is telling us in 4.24 that when he uses an expression of the form 'fx' to write an elementary proposition, the function *word* represented by the 'f' is occurring not as a name, but as

237

bringing it about that the name represented by 'x' occurs in a certain manner, i.e. that the name as occurring in a certain monadic configuration is a proposition.

Now if a philosopher combines the two theses, (1) there are no atomic facts involving only one particular, (2) all objects are particulars, it would be reasonable to say that he is committed to a doctrine of bare particulars. For, speaking informally, he holds that though objects stand in empirical relations, they have no qualities. Notice that this would not be true of Bergmann's position, for while he holds that there are no atomic facts containing only one *object*, he insists that there are atomic facts which contain only one *particular*. Thus he can deny that there are bare particulars by insisting that every object exemplifies a quality.

Now in my opinion Copi is correct in attributing to Wittgenstein the second of the above two theses (all objects are particulars). If, therefore, he were correct in attributing to Wittgenstein the first thesis, his claim that Wittgenstein is committed to a doctrine of bare particulars would be sound. Conversely, if Wittgenstein did hold a doctrine of bare particulars, then he was committed to the thesis that there are no monadic atomic facts. It is not surprising, therefore, to find Copi arguing that his contention that Wittgenstein rejects monadic atomic facts is supported by what he (somewhat reluctantly) takes to be an affirmation of the doctrine of bare particulars. Thus after confessing that, 'It must be admitted that several of Wittgenstein's remarks suggest that objects have "external" properties as well as "internal" ones (2.01231, 2.0233, 4.023),' he writes (p. 163):

> Despite the difficulty of dealing with such passages, there seems to me to be overwhelming evidence that he regarded objects as bare particulars, having no material properties whatever.
>
> In the first place, Wittgenstein explicitly denies that objects can have properties. His assertion that 'objects are colourless' (2.0232) must be understood as synechdochical, for the context makes it clear that he is not interested in denying colour qualities only, but all qualities of 'material properties' (the term first appears in the immediately preceding paragraph (2.0232)).

Now I think that this is simply a misunderstanding. The correct interpretation of the passage in question requires only a careful reading of the context. What Wittgenstein says is, 'Roughly speaking (*Beilauefig gesprochen*): objects are colourless', and this remark occurs as a comment on

> 2.0231 The substance of the world *can* only determine a form and not any material properties. For these are first presented by the propositions —first formed by the configuration of the objects.

What Wittgenstein is telling us here is that *objects* do not determine *facts*: thus even if a is green, the fact that a is green is not determined by a. It is interesting, in this connection, to reflect on

2.014 Objects contain the possibility of all states of affairs.

Thus, while a does not determine the fact that it is green, it does determine the range of possible facts of which the fact that it is green is but one.

Names exist in a logical space which includes the predicates which combine with it to make statements. (*In a perspicuous language—Jumblese—the predicate words, as has been pointed out, would appear as manners of being names, as, in a literal sense, internal features of the names.*) And no atomic statement is analytic, hence,

2.0132 In order to know an object, I must know not its external but its internal properties.

When Wittgenstein says that

2.0123 If I know an object, then I also know all the possibilities of its occurrence in atomic facts.

this is as much as to say that if I understand a name, then I also know all the possibilities of its occurrence in atomic statements. When he says

2.013 Everything is, as it were, in a space of possible atomic facts.

this is as much as to say that every name is, as it were, in a space of possible atomic statements.[1] And when he says

2.0131 ... A speck in a visual field need not be red, but it must have a colour.

he is making the point that objects are internally related to sets of 'external' properties, but not to any *one* 'external' property, i.e. that names are internally related to sets of primitive predicates[2] (configurations; cf. Jumblese).

Thus it is not surprising to us (though disturbing to Copi) to find Wittgenstein saying in the passage following that in which he says that (roughly speaking) objects are colourless,

2.0233 Two objects of the same logical form are—apart from their external properties—only differentiated from one another in that they are different.

---

[1] When he adds that 'I can think of this space as empty, but not of the thing without the space', he suggests the intriguing possibility that we can make sense of the idea that the language we use might have had no application.

[2] Whether these sets constitute embracing sets of primitive predicates of different orders, or whether they fall into subsets (families of determinates) is a topic for separate investigation.

For this means *not*, as it might seem, that objects are *bare*, but simply that two objects of the same logical form[1] determine the same range of possible facts, i.e. two names of the same logical form belong to the same range of configurations.

As far as I can see, Copi's second argument to show that Wittgenstein's objects are bare particulars is also a misunderstanding. He begins by correctly pointing out that according to Wittgenstein objects are named, whereas states of affairs are 'described'—the word is Wittgenstein's. He then writes (p. 164):

> . . . if an object *had* a property, that would be a fact whose assertion would constitute a *description* of that object. But objects can not be so described, whence it follows that objects have no properties.

This argument overlooks the fact that Wittgenstein, under the influence of logistical jargon, uses the term 'describe' where one would expect 'assert' (cf. 3.221). Thus he is simply telling us that objects cannot be 'described', i.e. *asserted*; from which it by no means follows that they cannot be described in the ordinary sense. Indeed, in 4.023, Wittgenstein writes, 'As the description of an object describes it by its external properties, so propositions describe reality by its internal properties.'

The third argument has the form '. . . if an object had a material property, *that* it had the property would be a fact involving only one particular, hence no object can have any material property, and all particulars are bare' (p. 164). The hypothetical is sound. The evidence adduced for denying the consequent is 4.032 which is interpreted as saying that all propositional signs are composite, and must consequently contain at least two elements, that is, at least two names. But 4.032 does not say that all propositional signs are *composite*, but that they are all 'logically articulate', and I have attempted to explain how a propositional sign can consist of *one logically articulated name*. I grant that in a parenthetical remark which immediately follows Wittgenstein writes, '(Even the proposition "ambulo" is composite for its stem gives a different sense with another termination, or its termination with another stem),' but I do not believe that this remark, which correctly points out that ordinary Latin is not perspicuous with respect to logical articulation, is decisive. (I am happy to acknowledge that my interpretation, like Copi's, has its difficulties.)

Copi's concluding argument is to the effect that Wittgenstein tells us in the *Investigations* that the objects of the *Tractatus* were primary

---

[1] I find here the implication that primitive one-place predicates (configurations) —if not all primitive predicates—come in families (determinates) and that objects are of different logical form if, for example, one exists in the logical space of colour, the other in the logical space of sound.

elements like those described in the *Theaetetus* (21e). This would be cogent if we were given a reason for supposing either that the elements of *Theaetetus* 21e were bare particulars, or that Wittgenstein thought they were. I see no reason to think that either is the case.

The most telling argument in Copi's paper against the idea that the *Tractatus* countenanced monadic atomic facts is not used by Copi directly to this end, but as part of his brief for the sound thesis that Wittgenstein's objects are not properties. Slightly redirected, it is to the effect that if there are any monadic atomic facts, surely they include such facts as that a certain point in a visual field is red. But, the argument proceeds, if 'a is red' is an elementary proposition, then 'a is blue' cannot contradict it. But, as is well known, Wittgenstein tells us (6.3751) that 'For two colours, e.g. to be at one place in the visual field, is impossible, logically impossible, for it is excluded by the logical structure of colour. . . . (It is clear that the logical product of two elementary propositions can neither be a tautology nor a contradiction.)' Copi draws the conclusion (p. 162) that 'colour predications are *not* elementary predications'.

Now, two points require to be made in this connection. The first is that one might be convinced that there *could* be monadic atomic facts (in that peculiar sense in which, for any n there could be n-adic atomic facts) without being able to give any examples. It is worth noting, in this connection, that in *Some Main Problems of Philosophy*, Moore, in effect, wonders whether there are any qualities (as opposed to relational properties), and specifically explores the logical space of colours to see if it provides us with examples of qualities. Moore was prepared to find that there are no qualities, i.e. that the simplest facts are already relational. True, Moore's qualitative facts would be Bergmanian rather than Wittgensteinian, that is, would each be a nexus of a particular *and a universal*, but the fact that Moore was prepared to suspend judgement with respect to the question 'Are there qualities?' combined with the fact that he found the logical structure of colour to be very complex indeed, suggests that Wittgenstein might well have taken a similar attitude. After all, as Anscombe points out, Wittgenstein regards it as in some sense a matter of fact that the most complex *atomic* fact is n-adic rather than m-adic ($m > n$) —cf. 4.2211. Could it not be in the same sense a matter of fact that the least complex is, say, dyadic rather than monadic?

Thus, *perhaps* the correct answer to the historical question is that Wittgenstein would have regarded the question 'Are particulars bare?' as, in a deep sense, a factual one, a question to which he did not claim to have the answer, and to which, as logician, he was not required to have the answer. I regard this as most unlikely.

The second remark is that Wittgenstein may well have thought that there are monadic atomic facts, indeed that their existence is obvious, but that no statement in ordinary usage represented such a fact, so that no example could be given in the sense of written down. Although he thought that ordinary language contained elementary propositions, he emphasizes that they are contained in a way which is not perspicuous. There is no presupposition that any ordinary sentence as ordinarily used in the context of everyday life ever expresses an atomic proposition. Indeed, the presupposition is to the contrary.

III

It has been said by Broad, among others, that philosophers have been led into error in perception theory by concentrating their attention on visual examples. In my opinion they have been at least as frequently led into error in logical theory by a similar concentration on colour. The danger arises from the fact that such a word as 'red', for example, is really three words, an adjective, a common noun, and a proper name, rolled into one. Thus we can say, with equal propriety,

> The book is red
> Scarlet is a colour
> Red is a colour.

A moment ago I urged the importance of the distinction between descriptive *constants* and *names*. I suggested that while it would be correct to say that the statement

$$\text{Green a}$$

consists of two *constants*, as is brought out by viewing it against the three quantified statements,

$$(Ex) \text{ Green x}$$
$$(Ef) \text{ fa}$$
$$(Ef) (Ex) \text{ fx}$$

it is most misleading to say that it consists of two names. And the reason, by now, should be clear. For if one does view the sentence 'Green a' as a juxtaposition of *names*, one will be bound, particularly if one has read the *Tractatus*, to think that by juxtaposing the names 'Green' and 'a' it affirms that the two objects or individuals or logical subjects *green* and *a* are 'united' or 'hang in each other' or are bound together by a 'characterizing tie' or whatever.

Now what makes this move all the more plausible is that there *is* an 'object' *green* and that there *is* a 'relation' which is often called exempli-

242

fication such that if a is green *then it is also true that a exemplifies green.* Thus it is tempting indeed to say that

a exemplifies green

is simply an unperspicuous way of saying what is said perspicuously by

Green a.

And the fascinating thing about it is that this claim would be absolutely correct *provided that 'green a' was not taken to say what is ordinarily said by 'a is green'.*

The point stands out like a sore thumb if one leave colours aside and uses a geometrical example. Thus consider the statement

a is triangular

or, for our purposes,

Triangular a.

It would clearly be odd to say

a exemplifies triangular

although it is not odd to say

a exemplifies green.

The reason is that 'triangular' unlike 'green' does not function in ordinary usage as both an adjective and a singular term. What we must say is

a exemplifies triangularity.

Now in a perspicuous language, i.e. a language which had a built-in protection against Bradley's puzzle we might say *that a exemplifies triangularity* by concatenating 'a' and 'triangularity' or *that Socrates exemplifies Wisdom* by writing

Socrates: Wisdom.

Our language is not such a perspicuous one, and to bring this out in this connection, we might write,

We must not say, 'The complex sign "a exemplifies triangularity" says "a stands in the exemplification relation to triangularity",' but we must say "*that* 'a' stands in a certain relation to 'triangularity' says that a exemplifies triangularity."

Thus it is correct to say that

Green a

says perspicuously what is said by

a exemplifies green

243

only if 'green' is used in the sense of the singular term 'greenness'. And when it is used in this sense, the statement

Green a

does not have the sense of the ordinary statement

a is green,

though it is logically equivalent to it.

Professor Bergmann thinks that

Green a

consists of two names, 'a', the name of a particular, and 'green', the name of a universal, and, by being their juxtaposition, asserts that the one exemplifies the other. On his view, philosophers who insist that 'a is green' says that a exemplifies green but do not realize that 'a exemplifies green' is simply an unperspicuous way of juxtaposing 'a' with 'green' are attempting to eff the ineffable. He thinks, to use the terminology I proposed earlier, that exemplification is the nexus, the mode of configuration of objects which can only be expressed by a configuration of names. Professor Bergmann sees configurations of particulars and universals where Wittgenstein saw only configurations of particulars.

But what does

a exemplifies triangularity

say if it is not an unperspicuous way of saying

Triangular a.

Instead of giving an answer (as I have attempted to do on other occasions) I shall attempt an analogy, and then claim that it is more than a mere analogy. It seems to me that the necessary equivalence but non-synonymy of

a exemplifies triangularity

with

a is triangular

is analogous to the necessary equivalence but non-synonymy of

That a is triangular is true

with

a is triangular.

That the analogy is more than a mere analogy is suggested by the fact that instead of saying that a exemplifies triangularity, we might with equal propriety say that triangularity is true of a, or holds of a.

Now if

> a exemplifies triangularity
> triangularity is true of a
> triangularity holds of a

are to be elucidated in terms of

> That a is triangular is true

then exemplification is no more present in the world of fact in that narrow sense which tractarians like Professor Bergmann and myself find illuminating, than is meaning, or truth, *and for the same reason.*

The crucial ineffability in the *Tractatus* concerns the relation between statements and facts. Is there such a relation? And is it ineffable? The answer seems to me to be the following. There is a meaning relation between statements and *facts*, but both terms are in the linguistic order. To say that a statement means a fact is to say, for example,

> 'Gruen a' (in German) means *Green a*, and it is a fact that Green a.

The first conjunct appears to assert a relation between a linguistic and a nonlinguistic item, between a statement and an item in the real order. And the second conjunct to say of this item that it is a fact. As I see it, the first conjunct does assert a relation, but the relation obtains between a German expression and an English expression *as being an expression in our language.* It has the force of

> 'Gruen a' (in German) corresponds to 'Green a' in our language.

We could also put this by saying

> 'Gruen a' (in German) means *that green a*

for to put 'that' before a sentence has the force of quoting it with the implication that the sentence is in our language, and is being considered as such.[1] The reason why we find it counter-intuitive to put it in this way is that since 'means' is the translation rubric, this would conflict with the usage according to which we say

> 'Dass gruen a' (in German) means *that green a.*

Suppose it is granted that meaning is the translatability relation between an expression which may or may not be in our language and

---

[1] It is to form the name of the sense expressed in our language by the design which follows it. See Chapter 6 above, pp. 204–5.

one which is, and is being considered as such. What, then, does it mean to say

That green a is a fact.

Clearly this is equivalent to saying

That green a is true

which calls to mind the equivalence

That green a is true≡green a.

This, however, is not the most perspicuous way to represent matters, for while the equivalence obtains, indeed necessarily obtains, its truth depends on the principle of inference—and this is the crux—

From 'that green a is true' (in our language) to infer 'green a' (in our language).

And it is by virtue of the fact that we *draw* such inferences that meaning and truth talk gets its connection with the world. In this sense, the connection is *done* rather than *talked about*.

Viewed from this perspective, Wittgenstein's later conception of a language as a form of life is already foreshadowed by the ineffability thesis of the *Tractatus*. But to see this is to see that *no* ineffability is involved. For while to infer is neither to refer to that which can be referred to, nor to assert that which can be asserted, this does not mean that it is to fail to eff something which is, therefore, ineffable.

8

GRAMMAR AND EXISTENCE:
A PREFACE TO ONTOLOGY

MY purpose in this chapter is to examine the current dogma that to sanction the move from

(1) S is white

to

(2) (Ef) S is f

or from

(3) S is a man

to

(4) (EK) S is a K

or from

(5) Tom is clever or Tom is tall

to

(6) (Ep) p or Tom is tall

is to sanction the move from empirical statements to statements asserting the existence of *entities* of a higher order than perceptible individuals. I shall begin by assuming that if these moves, each of which is a form of what is called 'existential quantification', do involve a commitment to such entities, the entities in question are such straightforward abstract entities as Triangularity, Mankind, and the proposition *that* Tom is clever. I shall subsequently turn my attention to the idea, recently elaborated by Peter Geach, but which stems from the work of Gottlob Frege, that what one is committed to by these moves, or their ordinary language counterparts, is not *abstract*

247

individuals, entities which ape the individuality of perceptible things, but rather what, for the moment, I shall simply refer to as *non-individual entities*, entities which have no *names*, but are, somehow, *stood for* by parts of speech other than names.

I shall begin by exploring the move from (1) to (2), taking as my point of departure the fact that the latter is often 'informally' rendered by

(2¹) There is an f such that S is f.

For, I believe, a careful examination of this 'reading' will enable us to put our finger on the source of the dogma in its first or orthodox form.

Now a first glance at (2¹) may well lead one to think that the expression 'an f' in 'There is an f . . .' has the form of the particle 'an' followed by a variable which takes common nouns, or expressions having the force of common nouns, as its values. Another glance, however, raises the question, 'If the first "f" is a common noun variable, must not the same be true of the second?' One sees immediately, however, that if the *second* 'f' were a common noun variable, the 'white' from which the quantification began would have to be a common noun. We should accordingly expect (1) to read,

(1¹) S is *a* white

and even if we hastily transform (1¹) into

(1²) S is a white thing

we are startled to think that 'quantification over predicate variables' involves the questionable idea that 'S is white' has the form 'S is a white thing', or must be transformed into the latter as a condition of the quantification. We also notice that this line of thought carries with it the implication that (2¹) should read

(2²) There is an f such that S is *an* f.

Now it is perfectly clear that something has gone wrong; a conviction which is conclusively reinforced by the reflection that if we 'read'

(7) (Ex) x is white

as

(7¹) There is an x such that x is white

parity of reasoning would require us to interpret the second 'x' as a common noun variable, which it simply cannot be.

What, then, are we to make of the expressions 'an x' in (7¹) and 'an f' in (2¹)? Since we cannot dodge the fact that in their ordinary use the context 'a(n)—' calls for a common noun to fill the gap, is there any other way than the above in which these expressions can be construed in terms of common nouns? The answer, of course, is obvious to one who knows the literature of the problem, for one immediately thinks of those curious common nouns 'individual' and 'quality', and of the locutions, 'There is an individual . . .' and 'There is a quality . . .'. Surely, then, it is the *category* words, 'individual' and 'quality', which belong after the 'There is a . . .' in the 'informal readings' of (2) and (7).

If we follow up this line of thought, we end up with *something* like

(2³) There is a quality, f, such that S is f,

and

(7²) There is an individual, x, such that x is white

and with the idea that the 'f' which occurs in the context 'an f' of the original 'informal reading' is playing a dual role: (*a*) the role of the category word (*constant*) 'quality'; (*b*) the role of a *variable* which reappears at the end of the sentence. But is (2³) a well-formed sentence? Here is the rub; for notice that 'There is a quality, f, . . .' commits us to the form

(8) f is a quality

and, if 'white' is to be a value of 'f', to

(9) White is a quality.

But if so, this means that just as 'quality' plays in (9) a role analogous to that of 'man' in 'Tom is a man', so 'white' is playing a role analogous to that of 'Tom'. We have, it appears, avoided the Scylla of turning 'white' into a *common noun*, only to whirl into the Charybdis of the idea that 'quantification over a predicate variable' involves turning it into a *proper name*, with a consequent commitment to Platonism. And this fact stands out even more clearly if we replace our original sentence (1) by

(10) S is triangular.

For whereas 'white' can play both the adjective and noun roles, so that (9) is a proper English sentence, we must actually transform 'triangular' into 'triangularity' to get the statement which corresponds to (9), namely

(11) Triangularity is a quality.

R   249

II

I asked a moment ago if (2^3) is a well-formed sentence, and we now have serious grounds for doubt. For while, as we have just seen, the first 'f' in (2^3) must be a variable which takes such *singular terms* as 'white(ness)' and 'triangularity' for its values, the *second* 'f' is required by *its* context, namely 'S is—', to take *adjectives*. If, therefore, 'f' is to be the same variable throughout the sentence, the concluding context must be reformulated to admit of a variable which also takes singular terms. How this might be done is no mystery. We simply construct our variable with the aid of the most convenient of the suffixes which are used to form abstract nouns from adjectives, thus 'f-ness', and rewrite (2^3) to read

(2^4) There is a quality, f-ness, such that S has f-ness

and discover that what our 'informal reading' of (2) has given us is an existential statement which stands to

(1^1) S has whiteness

as 'There is a man, x, such that S loves x' stands to 'S loves Socrates'.

Well, then, to go from (1) to a quantified statement in which 'the predicate is quantified', must we first, in effect, transform it into (1^1) —in which, after all, the predicate is no longer '(is) white' but 'exemplifies whiteness'? Does all quantification presuppose a point of departure in which the constants to be replaced by variables are *singular terms*? The answer, surely, is a categorical No. The contrary supposition is generated *not* by reflecting on the logic of quantification as such, but by reflecting, as we have been doing, on an '*informal reading*' of quantified statements, a reading which may have much to recommend it in the way of making certain logical relationships intuitive, but is far from giving us the *ordinary language equivalent* of these quantified statements. The 'informal reading' is a *contrived* reading which generates puzzles as soon as its auxiliary role is overlooked, and it is made the focal-point of philosophical reflection on quantification and existence.

III

But what, then, it may well be asked, *is* the correct reading of (2), if it is neither 'There is an f such that S is f' (2^1) nor 'There is a quality, f-ness, such that S has f-ness' (2^4)? In other words, how *would* we ordinarily say what the logistician says by means of (2)? Now it is easy enough, if I may be permitted a paradox, to *invent* an 'ordinary language equivalent' of (2). One simply begins by noting that the force in the case of quantification over variables of type 0, the force of '(Ex) x is white' (7) is captured by

(7^3) *Something* is white

and proceeds to represent (2) by

(2^5) S is *something*.

The latter both preserves the form '. . . is . . .' (as contrasted with '. . . has (or exemplifies) . . .') and, by avoiding the reading 'There is an f . . .' by-passes the stream of thought explored in sections I and II above.

Now, if we could convince ourselves that (2^5) would be a *reasonable* invention—or, better, that it is not *really* an invention at all—we would have gained an important vantage-point in the battle over abstract entities. The above suggestion, however, in the absence of an elaborate interpretation and defence, is scarcely more than a promissory note. And there is no dodging the fact that most if not all of the general statements we make which correspond to logistically formulated statements in which there is quantification over variables which take adjectives, common nouns, verbs, and sentences for their values, do involve the use of category words. And since the use of category words involves a prima facie commitment to abstract singular terms such as 'Triangularity'—and others which we shall be exploring in a moment—the question naturally arises, 'Does the use of these singular terms involve a commitment to Platonism?'

But before we begin to explore the significance of the fact that we do make use of category words and abstract singular terms, it is important to dwell for a moment on the claim which is implicit in the argument up to this point. This claim—which it is my purpose to defend—can be summed up by saying that one no more has to construe '(Ef) S is f' (2) as saying 'There is a quality, f-ness, such that S has f-ness' (2^4) than we have to construe 'S is white' (1) as *really* saying 'S has whiteness' (1^1).[1]

---

[1] It might be thought illuminating to replace the original statement, (1), by

(1^2) S: Whiteness

and the statement

(9) White is a quality

by

(9^1) Whiteness: Qualitykind

and to say that in (1^2) 'Whiteness' is the 'predicate', whereas in (9^1) it is the 'subject'. It must be pointed out, however, that one has not shown that (1^2) is not simply a *rewriting* of the *categorial counterpart* of (1), namely

(1^1) S has whiteness

[that 'whiteness' is juxtaposed to 'S' says that S has whiteness] or, indeed, a rewriting of (1) itself [that 'whiteness' is juxtaposed to 'S' says that S is white]—in

251

Another way of making this claim is by saying that the widespread view that the introduction of predicate variables carries with it the use of such category words as 'quality', 'attribute', or 'property' is simply a mistake.

Indeed, from this point of view, not only is the 'introduction of the category word "quality"' a distinct step in 'committing oneself to a framework of qualities', this 'commitment' involves the introduction of a *new* set of variables ('f-ness' as opposed to 'f') and a set of singular terms (e.g. 'whiteness', 'triangularity') to be their values. According to this claim, it is a mistake to suppose that a *predicate* variable belongs in the context '. . . is a C' where 'C' is a category word. Thus 'f is a quality' (8) would be ill formed, the proper expression being

(12) f-ness is a quality.

For while the singular term 'Socrates' belongs in both the ordinary context 'Socrates is a man' and the categorizing context

(13) Socrates is a particular

and the singular term variable 'x' belongs in both the context '— is white' and the context '— is an individual', 'triangular' must be turned into 'triangularity' and 'f' to 'f-ness' as one moves from 'S is —' to '— is a quality'. The reason, of course, is that 'Socrates' is a singular term, and 'x' a singular term variable to begin with, while 'triangular' and 'f' are not. (It should not be assumed that 'Socrates' is unambiguously the same singular term in both cases.)

IV

Before taking the next step in the argument, it will be useful to develop the parallel claim—which I also wish to defend—in connection with the move from 'S is a man' (3) to '(EK) S is a K' (4). To read (4) as

(4¹) There is a K such that S is a K

and to take the context 'There is a K . . .' seriously leads one to

---

which case the singular term 'whiteness' would be a sham—unless one sketches the *modus operandi* of a new form of language which breaks away from our ordinary categories of 'singular term', 'common noun', 'adjective', etc., and which cannot in any straightforward sense be translated into the language we actually use. That (1¹)—or (1)—could be *rewritten* as (1²), and that (9) could be *rewritten* as (9¹) has not the slightest tendency to show that they have a common logical form to be represented by '— : . . .'. Compare Peter Strawson's contribution to the symposium on 'Logical Subjects and Physical Objects' in Volume XVII of the *Philosophy and Phenomenological Research* (1957), and my criticisms thereof.

(4^2) There is a class,[1] K-kind, such that S *is a member of* K-kind just as 'There is an f such that S is f' (2^1) led us to 'There is a quality, f-ness, such that S *has* f-ness' (2^4). Furthermore, just as 'S has whiteness' (1^1) is the *categorial counterpart* of (1), so

(3^1) S *is a member of* mankind

is the categorical counterpart of (3). And, it seems to me, 'man' is no more functioning as the *name* of a *class* in (3) than 'white' is functioning as the *name* of a *quality* in (1). Furthermore, just as the 'is' in the latter is not 'has' or 'exemplifies' in disguise, so the 'is a' in the former is not 'is a member of' in disguise. It is surely as incorrect to regard 'S is a man' as a class-membership statement, as it is to regard 'S is triangular' as a quality-exemplification statement.

The 'introduction of classes' *as extensional entities* takes its point of departure from common nouns (and expressions having the force of common nouns) which are applied to a certain domain of logical subjects—where a logical subject is, roughly, an item referred to by a singular term.[2] If we limit our attention to classes pertaining to physical things, the point I wish to make can best be put by saying that once one has made the move from statements of the forms

(14) S is a K

and

(15) S is an f-thing[3]

to their categorial counterparts

---

[1] By no means all common nouns and common noun expressions stand for *kinds* of thing. Kinds are a distinctive subset of *classes*, and we speak of the *instances* rather than the *members of kinds*. Since I am not concerned in this paper with the distinctive character of kinds, I shall refer to kinds simply as classes and speak of their members rather than their instances.

[2] The term 'individual' is often used in the sense of 'logical subject' as characterized above. In this broad use, 'individual' is to be contrasted with 'particular', for particulars are, *roughly*, those individuals which are referred to by the singular terms which occur in observation statements.

[3] It is important to note that while we can form the expression 'white-thing' from the adjective 'white' and the category word 'thing' in accordance with the formula

(16) S is a white-thing $=_{\mathrm{Df}}$ S is a thing . S is white

it would be a serious mistake to suppose that all common nouns pertaining to physical objects are built from adjectives and the category word 'thing' in accordance with the formula

(17) S is an N $=_{\mathrm{Df}}$ (S is a thing) and S is $A_1 \ldots A_n$

(where 'N' is a common noun and the 'A_1's adjectives). To suppose that 'thing' is the sole *primitive* common name is (*a*) to overlook the fact that the category word 'thing' has a use only because there are statements of the form 'S is an N'; (*b*) to expose oneself to all the classical puzzles about *substrata*. (This point is

(14¹) S *is a member of* K-kind

and

(15¹) S *is a member of* the class of f-things

it is an *additional* step to introduce *classes* as extensional entities in terms of co-extensive classes. For it is simply not true that in non-technical contexts classes are identical if their memberships coincide.

To resume, just as the transition from (1) to (2) does not involve treating 'f' as a variable for which *singular terms* ('names of properties') are values, so, I wish to argue, the transition from 'S is a man' (3) to '(EK) S is a K' (4) and from 'S is a white-thing' (1²) to

(18) (E f-thing) S is an f-thing

do not involve treating 'K' or 'f-thing' as variables for which *singular terms* ('names of kinds') are values.

Again, just as it is, I believe, clarifying to read '(Ex) x is white' as '*Something* is white', rather than 'There is an individual, x, such that x is white', and '(Ef) S is f' as 'S is something' rather than 'There is a property, f-ness, such that S has f-ness', so I believe it to be clarifying to read '(EK) S is a K' (4) as

(4³) S is a *something*

rather than as 'There is a class, K-kind, such that S is a member of K-kind' (4²).

Finally, to mobilize the force of these considerations, note that the statement

(19) (EK) : : (Ex)(Ey) x is a K · y is a K · x≠y · (z)
z is a K ⊃ : z=x $\lor$ z=y

does not *say* 'There is a class . . .', though what it *does* say can be put categorizingly by saying 'There is a *class* which has a *member* and another *member*, and all its *members* are identical with either of these'.

V

Similar considerations apply, *mutatis mutandis*, to the move from 'Tom is clever or Tom is tall' (5) to '(Ep) p or Tom is tall' (6). The variable 'p' is no more to be construed as taking singular terms for its values, than is 'f' or 'K'. On the other hand, the statement

---

elaborated in my 'Substance and Form in Aristotle: an Exploration' in *The Journal of Philosophy*, 54 (1957), pp. 688–99.) Reflection on the first of these points makes it clear, incidentally, that it is a mistake to view the category of substance or thinghood as a *summum genus*.

(5^1) (The proposition) *that* Tom is clever is a disjunct of (the proposition) *that* Tom is tall

is the categorial counterpart of (5) just as 'S has (the quality) whiteness' is the categorial counterpart of (1) 'S is white'. It will be convenient to use the expression 'that-p' as the variable which corresponds to 'p' as 'f-ness' to 'f', and 'K-kind' to 'K'. And to conclude the drawing of parallels, I believe it to be clarifying to read '(Ep) p or Tom is tall' (6) as

(6^1) *Something* or Tom is tall.

Note, by the way, that if, as it seems reasonable to suppose, 'that it is raining' is functioning as a singular term in

(20) Jones believes *that* it is raining,

the quantified statement corresponding to (20) as (6) corresponds to (5) would be *not*

(21) (Ep) Jones believes p

but rather

(21^1) (E that-p) Jones believes (the proposition) that-p.

But we shall have something more to say on this topic in our concluding remarks.

VI

Let us suppose, for the moment, that the above line of thought can be carried through and defended. And let us ask what light it throws on the idea that the 'existentially quantified' formulae of the logistician are the counterparts of the statements in everyday discourse in which, to use Quine's phrase, we make ontological commitments, i.e. say that there are objects or entities of such and such kinds? Just this, that they are *not* the counterparts. Or, more precisely, that there is no *general* correspondence between *existentially quantified formulae* and *existence statements*. Only in those cases where the variable which is quantified is a variable of which the values are singular terms will a quantified formula be the counterpart of an existence statement. Nor is this all; not even all (so-called) existential quantification over singular term variables has the force of an existence statement. For the latter involve common nouns or expressions having the force of common nouns. Thus,

(22) There are tame tigers

involves the context

(23) x is a tame tiger.

255

Failure to see that common nouns or expressions having the force of common nouns are essentially involved in existence statements is due, in part, to the mistaken idea that such a statement as 'S is white' (1), in which occurs the adjective 'white', differs only, so to speak, graphologically from 'S is a white thing' (1^2), in which occurs the common noun expression 'white-thing'. For if this were so, then 'Something is white' would differ only graphologically from 'Something is a white thing' and we could use indifferently the formulae '(Ex) x is white' (7) and '(Ex) x is a white thing' (7^4). It is important to see that it is just as incorrect to read '(Ex) x is white' as 'There is a thing which . . .' as to read '(Ef) S is f' as 'There is a property . . .'. For unless one sees that not even quantification over singular term variables of type 0 makes, *as such*, an existence commitment involving an ontological category, i.e. *says* 'There are particulars', one is likely to think that 'There are particulars' is unavoidable in a way in which 'There are qualities' *might* not be. For while we can scarcely hope to dispense with quantification over variables of type 0, able philosophers have found it possible to hope that quantification over variables of higher types can (in principle) be dispensed with, or at least reduced to the status of a bookkeeping device for dealing with cash in which it does not appear.

We have already had something to say about the force of 'thing' in the noun expression 'white thing', and we shall have more to say about the category words 'individual' and 'particular' at the end of the argument. The point I am concerned to press at the moment, however, is that among the forms by the use of which one most clearly and explicitly asserts the existence of objects of a certain sort —I am not concerned with singular existence statements, which raise their own problems—are the forms 'There is an N', 'Something is an N' and 'There are Ns', and that the logistical counterpart of these forms is

(24) (Ei) i is an N

where 'i' is a variable taking singular terms of a given type as its values, and 'N' is an appropriate common noun.

We can sum this up by saying that only where the so-called 'existential quantification' is a quantification over a context of the form 'i is an N' is a quantified statement the counterpart of a statement asserting the existence of objects of a certain sort—and this, after all, is analytic.[1]

Put this positively, the thesis seems to ring true. If, however, we

---

[1] It follows that the phrase 'existential quantification' should be dropped and replaced by (rather than abbreviated into) one of its logistical equivalents, e.g. Σ-quantification.

make the same point negatively, by saying that to quantify over an adjective-, common noun-, or sentence variable is not to make the PMese equivalent of a statement asserting the existence of attributes, kinds, or propositions, it becomes clear that we have much more work to do. For, to take but the case of quantification over an adjective variable, our claim that it is illuminating to parallel the reading of '(Ex) x is white' (7) as '*Something* is white' (7^3), by a reading of '(Ef) S is f' (2) as 'S is *something*' (2^5) stand in urgent need of expansion and clarification.

Perhaps the best way of accomplishing this is by examining the constructive views advanced in Peter Geach's contribution to the Aristotelian Society symposium[1] on 'What there is' which takes its point of departure from Quine's provoking essay of this name. Geach sees that Quine's account won't do. He sees, to put the matter in terms of our examples, that the statement 'S is white' (1) entails the general statement

(2^6) There is something which S *is*

(i.e. white) and insists, correctly, that the latter is not to be confused with

(2^7) There is something which S *has*

(i.e. whiteness). To take another example, he sees that

(25) Jack and Jill are both tall

entails the general statement

(26) There is something which Jack and Jill both *are*

and that the latter statement is not to be confused with

(26^1) There is something which Jack and Jill *have in common*.

It would be incorrect to attach the rider 'i.e. tallness' to the former. The proper rider would be 'i.e. tall', thus

(26^2) There is something (i.e. tall) which Jack and Jill both *are*.

Now Geach's '*There is something* which S *is*' corresponds to our 'S is *something*'. And his insistence that the something which S *is* is *white* and not *whiteness* corresponds to our distinction between 'S is something' and 'S has (i.e. exemplifies) something'. Thus, in the terms of our analysis, Geach's 'There is something which S *is*' (2^6) is the counterpart of '(Ef) S is f' (2) and he has correctly seen that the latter does not involve a commitment to the use of such abstract singular terms as 'whiteness' or 'tallness'.

[1] Supplementary Volume XXV (1951).

But while he is on the right track up to this point, he builds the above insight into a larger mistake. For he is misled by his own formulation into supposing that

(26²) *There is something* (i.e. tall) which both Jack and Jill are

although it does not commit us to the 'abstract or universal entity' *tallness*, does commit us to the 'property' *tall*. Thus he tells us that while the predicate 'red' is not to be construed as a *name*, it does 'stand for' something, and he proposes 'property' as a 'general term for what predicates stand for'. He continues, 'This way of speaking [saying that what a predicate stands for is a property] has its dangers, but can be given a harmless interpretation; "property" may here be taken to be just short for "something that an object is or is not".'[1] Now Geach's *properties* are essentially the same sort of thing as Frege's *concepts*. Indeed, it is clear from other statements of his that Geach would have used Frege's term were it not for its conceptualistic connotations. I shall shortly be discussing a difficulty which is present in Frege's account of concepts. It will, however, be convenient to lay the groundwork by exploring what Geach has to say about properties.

Now it is important to realize that Geach gives *two* accounts of the term 'property'; one of which, though cautious, is based on a simple grammatical mistake, while the other is derived from Frege's account, and is more difficult to expose. The cautious account is contained in the passage quoted above, in which he stipulates that 'property' is to be equivalent to 'something that an object is or is not'. The Fregean account is the one in which properties are introduced as *what predicates stand for*. We shall return at a later stage in the argument to the dangers involved in the idea that predicates stand for properties. Our present concern is with the force of the statement 'There is something which Jack and Jill both *are*' (26).

Let me begin by noting that in our illustration, 'There is something which Jack and Jill both *are*' (26), was a generalization from 'Jack and Jill are both tall' (25). Now to move from the latter to

(27) Jack and Jill are both *something*[2]

is to avoid at least the appearance of an existence statement. For the hypothesis with which we are working is that only those 'something-' statements which are of the form 'Something is an N', where 'N' is

---

[1] op.cit., p. 133.
[2] Clearly the reading of '(Ef) S is f' as 'S is something' would require the use of indices to draw distinctions which become relevant when it is a question of reading such statements as (27). For if Jack were tall and Jill were short, it would follow that Jack and Jill were both *something*, though they would not be 'the *same* something'.

a common noun, have the force of existence statements—thus of the statement 'There are Ns'. But Geach's formulation, beginning, as it does, with 'There is . . .', though it is equally legitimate and equally involves no commitment to abstract singular terms, has the prima facie appearance of an existence statement. And, I am sorry to say, Geach has been taken in by it. And if the entities he introduces are what things *are* rather than what they *exemplify*, they are abstract entities, none the less, as Quine has noted in his reply,[1] and Geach's denial that these entities are *individually* referred to by such *singular terms* as 'Tallness 'is open, as we shall see, to the reply that he has avoided the abstract individual *tallness* only at the expense of treating the adjective 'tall' as a peculiar kind of singular term, and hence introducing the abstract individual *tall*.

The key point to notice is that unlike existence statements proper, the statement

(26) *There is something* which Jack and Jill both *are*

begins not with 'There is *a* . . .', not with 'There is *a something* . . .', but simply with 'There is something . . .'. If it began with 'There is a something . . .', thus using 'something' as a common noun, one might well look for a common noun, such as 'property', to pinpoint just what *sort* of 'something' 'there is' which Jack and Jill both are. We could then have

(26³) There is a property which Jack and Jill both *are*.

But all this, as by now should be obvious, is logical nonsense. 'Something' is *not* a common noun, and it is incorrect, therefore, to introduce 'property' as equivalent to 'something which an object is or is not'. The term 'property' has, as a common noun, the form '— is a property' whereas, *unless 'something' is to be construed as a common noun*, the supposed equivalent has the form '— is something which an object is or is not', thus

(28) Tall is something which an object is or is not

and *not* '— is *a* something which an object is or is not'. Only if the expression 'something which an object is or is not' were a common noun expression (which it is not) would it be correct to introduce the common noun 'property' as its stipulated equivalent. In short, *this* way of introducing the term 'property' is simply a mistake.

[1] op.cit., pp. 149ff.

It is important to remember that I have not criticized Geach's claim that there is something which Jack and Jill both *are*. It is to what he proceeds to *make* of this claim that I took exception. I want now to examine this claim in closer detail, for I think that once we get the hang of Geach's formulation we will be less tempted to make his mistake.

Suppose we had begun with an example which involved the common noun 'man', instead of the adjective 'tall', say

(29) Tom is a man.

The corresponding generalization, as we have represented it, would be,

(30) Tom is a *something*

where the fact that the 'something' comes after the indefinite article makes it clear that 'something' is, so to speak, quantifying over a common noun variable.

How would we express this generalization in the manner of Geach? Certainly we can say

(30¹) There is something which Tom is.

But this does not distinguish the result of generalizing from (29) on the one hand, and from

(31) Tom is tall

on the other. While to say 'There is *a* something which Tom is' is to court disaster. The answer suggests itself when we note that the 'There is something which . . .' manner of expressing quantification rests on a rhetorical device which I shall call 'question-echoing counterparts'. The point is simply that such a statement as

(10) S is triangular

can serve as the answer to either of the following questions,

(32) *What* is triangular?

and

(33) S is *what*?

Now to the original statement there correspond the following pair of question-echoing counterparts,

(10¹) *S* is what is triangular: *Triangular* is what S is.

It is important to note that although the adjective 'triangular' is serving as the *grammatical* subject of the second of these statements the 'role' it is playing is a unique one, and is, indeed, *rhetorical* in character. It would surely be a howler to suppose that because it is functioning in this context as a grammatical subject, it is in any more profound sense functioning as a subject. *Its role is rhetorically derivative from its adjectival role in the original, or non-question-echoing statement.* Other examples of question-echoing counterparts would be '*Tom* is who is a man': '*A man* is what Tom is' and '*Tall* is what Jack and Jill both are': 'It is *Jack and Jill* who are both tall.'

Now the question-word 'what?' plays a number of roles in English which might well be split up among a number of interrogatives. In particular, we might introduce the interrogative 'quale?' to indicate that the answer is to be in terms of an adjective, and the interrogative 'quid?' to indicate that the answer is to be in terms of a common noun. Then we would have the question-echoing counterparts

(31¹) *Tall* is *quale* Tom is: *Tom* is *who* is tall,
(29²) *A man* is *quid* Tom is: *Tom* is *who* is a man.

To the first of each of these pairs there would correspond a general statement which would bear the mark of its origin, thus,

(34) *There is something* which is *quale* Tom is (i.e. tall).
(35) *There is something* which is *quid* Tom is (i.e. a man)

or, more concisely,

(34¹) *There is somequale* which Tom is (i.e. tall).
(35¹) *There is somequid* which Tom is (i.e. a man).

VIII

I pointed out above that Geach gives *two* accounts of how the general term 'property' might be introduced. Of these two accounts we have so far considered only one—the 'cautious' one, we have called it—and found it to be a mistake. The second account, as we noted, derives from Frege, and our discussion of it will be usefully prepared by a theme from Frege's 'On Concept and Object'.[1]

It will be remembered that Frege distinguishes between *concepts* and *objects* and is faced by the problem: 'How can one say of anything that it is a concept?' For the term 'concept' being,

[1] First published in Volume XVI of the *Vierteljahrschrift fuer Wissenschaftliche Philosophie* (1892), pp. 192–205; translated by Peter Geach and published in *Translations from the Philosophical Writings of Gottlob Frege* by Peter Geach and Max Black (New York, Philosophical Library, 1952).

presumably, a common noun, we should be able to make statements of the form

(36) — is a concept.

Frege, however, proceeds to rule out such statements as

(37) The concept *square root of four* is a concept

on the ground that the expression 'the concept *square root of four*', being a singular term, refers to an *object* rather than a concept. The same objection would, presumably, hold against

(38) The concept *man* is a concept

and

(39) The concept *triangular* is a concept

and, even more obviously, against

(38¹) Man-kind is a concept

and

(39¹) Triangularity is a concept.

Since, presumably, *something* can fill the blank in '— is a concept', we seem to be left with

(38²) *Man* is a concept

and

(39²) *Triangular* is a concept.

These sentences, however, are puzzling, to say the least, for it is difficult to repress the feeling that since 'concept' is a common noun, the context '— is a concept' requires a singular term rather than an adjective or a common noun to complete it.

Now our discussion of Geach has made it clear that we *can* form sentences in which something other than a singular term is the grammatical subject. Consider, for example,

(40) *Triangular* is what (quale) the table is

and

(41) *Men* is what (quid) Tom and Dick are.

Or, as we can also put it,

(40¹) *Triangular* is something which the table is.
(41¹) *Men* is something which Tom and Dick are.

262

But, as we emphasized at that time, there is nothing in these contexts which authorizes the introduction of a common noun, whether 'concept' or 'property'. There is, however, another context which tempts one to introduce such a common noun, namely,

(42) — is what 'triangular' stands for.
(43) — is what 'man' stands for.

For, one is tempted to expostulate with Geach, surely adjectives and common nouns *stand for something*—though, of course, they are not *names*. Surely we can say

(44) 'Triangular' stands for something

or

(44¹) There is something which 'triangular' stands for.

And can we not therefore legitimately introduce the common noun 'concept' as having the force of 'something which a predicate stands for'? The answer is, as before, No; not, however, because it is incorrect to say that there is something which 'triangular' stands for (or *bedeutet*), but because the expression 'something which a predicate stands for' like the expression 'something which an object is or is not' does not play the sort of role which would make it proper to introduce a common noun as its stipulated equivalent. This time, however, the matter is not quite so simple, for there is a related line of thought which does seem to authorize without grammatical absurdity the introduction of a common noun having the force of Frege's 'concept' or Geach's 'property'. This line of thought rests on the idea that 'means'[1]—which I shall now use in place of 'stands for' because its simpler grammatical form will make the point more intuitive—has at least the appearance of being a *transitive verb*. That this appearance is misleading will be the burden of a subsequent stage in my argument. But accepting, for the moment, this appearance at its

---

[1] There is a family of semantical concepts each of which might be (and has been) conceived of as a 'mode of meaning'. Thus we might say that in our language 'triangular' *connotes* triangularity, *denotes*$_1$ triangular things, and *denotes*$_2$ the class of triangular things. Each of these is a legitimate concept and a proper subject for logical investigation. But none of them, obviously, is what Geach has in mind when he speaks of 'triangular' as *standing for* something. The sense of 'meaning' which I have in mind is that in which it is an *informative* statement for us to say that 'dreieckig' (in German) means *triangular*, whereas '"triangular"' (in our language) means *triangular*' is as 'trifling' as 'White horses are white'. That the *design* 'triangular' (in our language) means *triangular* is, of course, a contingent fact.

263

face value, and taking as our starting-point, without comment, the sentence

(45) 'Triangular' means triangular,

the following moves all seem in good order; first to

(45¹) Triangular is meant by 'triangular'

then, on the analogy of the move from 'x is victimized by y' to 'x is the victim of y', to

(45²) Triangular *is the meaning of* 'triangular',

which involves the common noun 'meaning'. It is then a simple step to stipulate that 'concept', 'property', 'nature', and 'form' are to be general terms for the meanings of adjectives and common nouns.

I shall be subjecting this line of thought to a severe critique in a moment. For the time being, however, I shall simply postulate that this mode of introducing such sentences as 'Triangular is a meaning', 'Triangular is a concept', and 'Triangular is a property' is in some sense misguided. For I want to go on to the question, Would this mean that Frege's notion of a concept is misguided? The answer is No rather than Yes. Frege did have something important in mind which he builds into his notion of a concept, and which does not require the use of adjectives, common nouns, or verbs as the grammatical subjects of sentences. For the significant core of Frege's doctrine is compatible with the idea that the common noun context '— is a concept' requires *something like* a singular term for its subject, and hence with the rejection of a simple concept–object dichotomy. The clue to the correct formulation of this core theme is found in his characterization of concepts as 'unsaturated' (*ungesaettigte*). For, in effect, this means that we may be able to get somewhere with 'unsaturated' singular terms—if we can find such—as the subject of statements of the form '— is a concept'. And once we have hit upon this suggestion, the next move follows of itself. For among the singular terms available to us from the previous discussion are singular terms of the form 'that-p', and we know what an 'unsaturated' singular term of this form would look like. In short, we hit upon, for example,

(39³) *That x is triangular* is a concept.

On this analysis, concepts would be 'unsaturated' propositions. And if, as Frege seems to do, we use the term 'object' in such a manner that anything referred to by a singular term is an object, we would have to say that concepts differ from objects not by being *non*-objects, but by being 'unsaturated' or 'incomplete' objects. Thus,

264

when Frege says that to 'assert something about a concept . . . it must first be converted into an object, or, speaking more precisely, represented by an object' (p. 46), his thought was undoubtedly guided by the fact that (39^3) comes as close as it does to having the *adjective* 'triangular' as its subject, by having the *unsaturated* singular *term* 'that x is *triangular*' as its subject instead.

Now if the above line of thought is sound, we would no longer be precluded from saying that triangularity is a concept (39^1) by the fact that 'triangularity' is a singular term. The fundamental difference between 'triangularity' and '*that* x is triangular' would be that the latter makes explicit a *gappiness* or *incompleteness* which is perhaps implicit in the former. Indeed, it is tempting to suppose that the abstract singular term 'triangularity' simply has the force of the unsaturated singular term 'that x is triangular'. We shall subsequently see that this is not the case, but if we permit ourselves this supposition for the moment, then we would interpret the statement 'Triangularity is a quality' (11) as, so to speak, a rewriting of

(11^1) *That x is triangular* is a quality

and, consequently, regard a *quality* as a specific form of *concept*, the latter being a more inclusive notion, including as it does *multiply* as well as *singly* unsaturated propositions, and a variety of each.

Now it must be admitted that the idea that there are abstract entities such as triangularity, mankind, etc., takes a most interesting, if disturbing, turn if these entities are to be equated with gappy or unsaturated propositions. The notion of a *gappy* entity is a puzzling one, even if it is softened into the idea of an *incomplete* entity. On the other hand, it appears to illuminate contrasting historical positions. For if one accepts the idea that 'Triangularity' is simply, so to speak, a rewriting of 'That x is triangular', one is tempted to say that the difference between the Platonic and the Aristotelian conceptions of universals is that Plato takes the abstract singular term 'triangularity' to be a name which conceals no gaps, whereas Aristotle, by denying the apartness of the universal, is, in effect, recognizing the unsaturated, incomplete, or gappy status which is made explicit by the unsaturated abstract singular term 'that x is triangular'. There is, I believe, some truth to this suggestion—though I do not think that it does justice to the radical character of Aristotle's rejection of Plato's Ideas. But that is a story for another occasion.

IX

Let us suppose, for the time being, then, that the abstract singular term 'triangularity' simply has the force of 'that x is triangular'. Then in addition to its intrinsic interest, the above discussion has shown us a way of saying something about triangularity without using the singular term 'triangularity'. Thus, instead of saying

(46) Triangularity implies having three sides

we can say

(46¹) *That* anything is triangular implies *that* it has three sides.

The latter preserves—indeed, highlights—the adjectival role of 'triangular'.

No sooner have we said this, however, than we see how little we have said, if our aim is to avoid Platonistic anxieties. For if we put aside the complications introduced by the *generality* of (46¹) and turn our attention, instead, to

(47) *That S is triangular* implies *that S has three sides*

it becomes manifest that we have avoided the singular term 'triangularity' only to embrace the singular term 'that S is triangular', and that we have escaped *universals* only to accept *propositions*.

Actually, however, this new turn of events has brought us to the very heart of the matter. Statement (47) is, indeed, of the form

(48) *that-p* implies *that-q*

and does involve two singular terms. *But not all logical connectives play a predicate role*, and while those which *do* connect *singular terms* of the form 'that-p', those which do *not* connect *statements* and statement expressions, and statements are *not* singular terms, having, as they do, the form 'p' rather than 'that-p'. Both predicative and non-predicative connectives have their legitimate place in the grammar of our language, but unless these places are carefully distinguished and correctly understood, philosophical perplexities of the most pervasive sort will be endemic.

The story is, in essence, a familiar one. Truth-functional connectives do not require that the connected expressions function as singular terms. Thus, as we saw above, while 'Tom is clever or Tom is tall' (5) and '(Ep) p or Tom is tall' (6) have *categorial counterparts* which *are* built around the singular terms 'that Tom is clever', 'that Tom is tall', and the singular term variable 'that-p', neither (5) nor (6) itself contains any other singular term than 'Tom'.

Can we, then, say what is said by '*That* S is triangular implies *that* S has three sides' (47) and '*That* anything is triangular implies *that* it has three sides' (46¹) without committing ourselves to singular terms formed from statements? Surely it will be said, all we need to do is to make use of the familiar symbol '⊃' which was specifically designed to be the *non-predicative core* of the predicative term 'implies'. We would then have

(47¹) S is triangular $\supset$ S has three sides

and

(46²) (x) x is triangular $\supset$ x has three sides

and if this move is successful, we should have freed ourselves (temporarily, at least) not only from expressions of the form 'that-p', but also, unless we find other reasons for reintroducing them, from unsaturated singular terms of the forms 'that x is f' and 'that x is a K'; and hence from 'f-ness' and 'K-kind'. We would indeed have extricated ourselves from Plato's beard.

X

It is well to pause for a moment to let the fact sink in that our argument has brought the problem of abstract entities face to face with the problem of *necessary connection*; and to note that it is but a short step to the problem of 'causal connection' or 'natural implication', and to the realization that 'causally implies' like 'logically implies' is a *predicative* connective and requires the use of abstract singular terms as in

(49) *That* it has just lightninged (causally) implies *that* it will shortly thunder

and

(50) *That* x is released (causally) implies *that* x will fall.

XI

Even if we could take it as established that to quantify over adjective-common noun- and statement-variables is not to assert the existence of qualities, kinds, or propositions, we would sooner or later have to face the fact that ordinary language does involve the use of the singular terms and the common nouns which raise the spectre of Platonism —and, indeed, that we do make the existence statements which the Platonist hails as the substance of his position. For we do make such statements as 'There is a quality (thus triangularity) which . . .', 'There is a class (thus, dog-kind—or the class of white things) which . . .', and 'There is a proposition (thus, *that* Caesar crossed the Rubicon) which . . .'. These statements, genuinely existential in character, make forthright ontological commitments. Or are these commitments, perhaps, less forthright than they seem? Can they, perhaps, be 'reduced' to statements which make no reference, explicit or implicit, to ontological categories?

We asked above 'Is there any way of saying something about triangularity without actually using the abstract singular term "triangularity"?' This question led us first to the idea of the *predicative* implication-statement 'That anything is triangular implies that it has three sides', which avoids 'triangularity' but at the expense of using the unsaturated abstract singular term 'that x is triangular'. The effort to avoid even these abstract singular terms led us then to the notion of a general truth-functional statement to be represented as

(46²) (x) x is triangular ⊃ x has three sides.

Without questioning the soundness of this notion, I shall now ask instead, 'Is there any statement of which the subject is "f-ness" which *cannot* be reformulated as a statement in which "f-ness" is replaced by the sentential function "x is f" (N.B.: *not* "that x is f")?' To this question correspond a number of others of which two are more directly germane to our argument, namely, 'Is there any statement of which the subject is "K-kind" which *cannot* be reformulated as a statement in which "K-kind" is replaced by "x is a K" (not "that x is a K")?' and 'Is there any statement of which the subject is "*that*-p" which cannot be reformulated as a statement in which "*that*-p" is replaced by "p"?' And to these questions the direct and simple answer is Yes. For neither

(51) f-ness is a quality

nor

(52) K-kind is a class

nor

(53) *That* p is a proposition

can be so reformulated.

But if these contexts (which we have called categorizing contexts) do not admit of the desired reformulation, and consequently revive our Platonistic anxieties, it is equally true that these anxieties can be at least temporarily stilled by a relatively simple and straightforward therapy. This relief is provided by pointing out that whereas the truth or falsity of statements to the effect that a physical object belongs to an empirical kind is ascertained by observing or inferring that it satisfies certain empirical criteria, the truth or falsity of such categorizing statements as

(11) Triangularity is a quality,
(54) Dog-kind is a class,
(55) *That* Chicago is large is a proposition,

268

is ascertained *not* by 'examining' triangularity, betweenness, dog-kind, or *that* Chicago is large, but by reflecting on the role in discourse of the corresponding expressions. This is the insight contained in Carnap's contention (in *The Logical Syntax of Language*) that the above statements are in the 'material mode of speech' and are the 'quasi-syntactical' counterparts (roughly—for I am following the general spirit, rather than the letter of Carnap's account) of

(11²) 'Triangular' (N.B.: *not* 'triangularity') is an adjective (in English),[1]

(54¹) 'Dog' (N.B.: *not* 'dog-kind') is a common noun (in English),

(55¹) 'Chicago is large' (N.B.: *not* 'that Chicago is large') is a sentence (in English).

But surely, it will be said, the word 'triangular' is just as abstract an entity as triangularity. Where is the 'nominalistic' gain? Is not the term ' "triangular" ' as much a singular term as 'triangularity', and 'adjective' as much a common noun as 'quality'? The answer is simple and straightforward. ' "Triangular" ' is not a singular term, but a common noun, and the gain arises in that we can hope to equate (11³) with *something* like

(11³) (x) x is a 'triangular' $\supset$ x is an adjective

where ' "triangular" ' is a common noun referring to items playing a certain *linguistic role*, as 'bishop' is a common noun referring to items playing a certain *chess* role. 'A "triangular" is an adjective' would be the counterpart of 'A bishop is a diagonal-mover'.[2]

Unfortunately, no sooner is one relaxed by this therapy, and considering the possibility of extending it to some other contexts in which 'abstract entities are acknowledged', than a number of more serious objections arise which threaten a relapse.

The first of these objections grants that *if* the only contexts involving such expressions as 'triangularity', 'betweenness', 'dog-kind', and '*that* Chicago is large' which could not be reformulated in the object

---

[1] This Carnapian interpretation of categorizing statements would carry with it a reinterpretation of the categorial counterparts of such statements as (1). Thus, 'S exemplifies f-ness' would be the equivalent in the material mode, a *quasi-semantical* equivalent of ' "f" is *true of* S'. The relation of the latter to ' "S is f" is true' would remain to be explored. Again, 'S is a member of K-kind' would be the quasi-semantical equivalent of ' "K" is *true of* S'. The latter, however, would seem to be as closely related to 'S satisfies the criteria of "K" ' as to ' "S is a K" is true'.

[2] For an interpretation of 'triangularity' as a singular term related to a common noun for linguistic role players as 'the pawn' is related to 'pawn' see Chapter 6 above; also 'Abstract Entities', *The Review of Metaphysics*, June, 1963.

language without the use of abstract singular terms were *categorizing statements* such as (11), (54), and (55) above, or such other statements as might be capable of straightforward treatment under the more general notion of 'quasi-syntactical statements in the material mode of speech', *then* the Carnapian therapy—vintage 1932—would be successful. After granting this, however, it proceeds to argue that there are contexts in which abstract singular terms occur, which neither can be reformulated in the object language, to avoid them, nor respond to this syntactical treatment. Consequently, it continues, there are reasons which cannot be dispelled by any therapy yet mentioned for thinking that we are committed to the straightforward existence of qualities, relations, kinds, propositions, etc. And if, it concludes, by way of counter-attack, there *are* such entities, then even the idea that such a categorizing statement as

(11) Triangularity is a quality

is *really* about the adjective 'triangular' instead of, as it purports to be, about triangularity, must be simply a mistake.

XII

Now the task of examining all contexts in which abstract singular terms occur to see if they admit of an interpretation free of Platonistic implications, is an intricate and demanding one which, even if I were prepared to undertake it, would require a larger canvas than is at hand. I shall therefore limit myself to a few manageable points which, as I see it, lay the groundwork for a successful use of a therapy essentially the same as the one proposed by Carnap (but which, of course, has a much longer—and indeed, venerable—history).

The first point I wish to make arises from the fact that if we press the above critic to specify the contexts he has in mind, the chances are that he will come up with examples from discourse in which we are either explaining what a word means or characterizing the thoughts and beliefs of intelligent beings.

It goes without saying that one of the oldest and strongest roots of conceptual realism is the conviction that we cannot make sense of thinking in its various modes unless we interpret it as involving something like an 'intellectual perception' of abstract entities. Thus the road we are travelling leads sooner or later to the problem of problems, the Mind–Body problem, the Gordian knot which has been cut so often, but never untied. I do not propose to untie it on this occasion. I shall therefore turn my attention to discourse about the meanings of words to see if it involves a commitment to abstract entities.

Let us consider, therefore, such a context as the following:

(56) 'Dreieckig' (in German) means. . . .

And let us ask what we should place at the end of this context to make a well-formed sentence. A number of answers suggest them-selves, of which the first, and most obviously *un*satisfactory, is that what we should place there is the quoted expression ' "triangular" '. This clearly won't do, at least as it stands, for the simple reason that if we were looking for the *beginning* of a sentence which has as its ending

(57) . . . (in German) means 'triangular'

we would find the answer—assuming that Germans form the names of expressions, as we do, by means of the quoting device—in

(58) ' "Triangular" ' (in German) means 'triangular'.

Now we might try to put this informally by saying that the German word 'dreieckig' means a *quality* and not a *word*, and that if any German expression means the *word* 'triangular' it is the German expression ' "triangular" '. But so to put the matter raises more puzzles than it resolves, for when we say that the German word 'dreieckig' means a *quality*, we imply that the proper way to complete the original context (56), is by the use of the abstract singular term 'triangularity', which would give us

(59) 'Dreieckig' (in German) means (the quality) triangularity,

and a moment's reflection tells us that this won't do at all. For surely the German word which means triangularity is 'Dreieckigkeit' and *not* 'dreieckig', thus

(60) 'Dreieckigkeit' (in German) means triangularity.[1]

Now the source of our trouble is that we have been taking for granted that what belongs in the place of the dots in (56) is a singular term. But, then, it will be said, is not 'means' a transitive verb? And does it not, therefore, require to be followed by an expression which refers to an *object*, as do the concluding expressions in

(61) Tom hit *Harry*,
(62) Tom hit *a man*,
(63) Tom hit *the man next door*.

It is this reasoning which confronts us with our dilemma, for if the context takes a singular term, and if, as we have seen, it does not take

[1] See footnote 1, p. 263.

'triangularity', what else is there for it to take but ' "triangular" '. We must apparently choose between

(64) 'Dreieckig' (in German) means 'triangular'

which is false, and,

(65) 'Dreieckig' (in German) means triangular

which because it uses the adjective 'triangular' rather than a singular term is, apparently, ill-formed.

Now the way out of this labyrinth consists in recognizing that it is incorrect to say that 'dreieckig' means a *word*, and equally incorrect to say that it means a *non-word*, for the simple reason that 'means' is not a *transitive* verb. Not that it is an *intransitive* verb, for it is neither, and the attempt to fit it under one or the other of these headings, on the supposition that they are not only mutually exclusive but jointly exhaustive, is the cause of the puzzle.

Once this point has been made, however, it can be granted that even though

(64) 'Dreieckig' (in German) means 'triangular'

is false, there is a sense in which the *true* statement

(65) 'Dreieckig' (in German) means *triangular*

is about the English word 'triangular'. For by making statements of this form we bring people to understand the German word 'dreieckig', for example, by leading them to reflect on their use of its English counterpart. It is because the understanding of (53) involves an imaginative rehearsal of the *use* of 'triangular' that (53) differs from a simple statement to the effect that 'dreieckig' is the German counterpart of the English word 'triangular'. The latter statement could be *fully* understood, as the former could not, by someone who did not have the English word 'triangular' in his active vocabulary.

Now the prime result of all this logic chopping is that the context

(66) '—' (in L) means . . .

does *not* require a singular term to fill the right-hand blank. Thus, to use other relevant examples,

(67) 'Homme' (in French) means *man* [not *mankind*]

and

(68) 'Paris est belle' (in French) means *Paris is beautiful* [not *that Paris is beautiful*].

272

It follows that the existentially quantified counterparts of (65), (67), and (68) are

(69) (Ef) 'dreieckig' (in German) means f,
(70) (EK) 'Homme' (in French) means K,
(71) (Ep) 'Paris est belle' (in French) means p,

and that it would be as incorrect to read these as 'There is a quality . . .', 'There is a class . . .', and 'There is a property . . .', as we found it to be to make the corresponding readings in the case of (2), (4), and (6).

We are now in a position to grant that we do speak of the 'meaning' of a word while insisting that the common noun 'meaning' (or its sophisticated counterparts, 'concept' (Frege) and 'property' (Geach)) —far from embodying a fundamental logical category—arises from contexts of the form ' "—" means . . .' (66), by treating 'means' as of a piece with ordinary transitive verbs. Thus, by analogy we have

(65¹) *Triangular* is meant (in German) by 'dreieckig',

(65²) *Triangular* is what 'dreieckig' (in German) means,

(69¹) There is something (i.e. *triangular*) which 'dreieckig' (in German) means

and while none of these involves a commitment to a common noun expression having the force of 'meaning' the fact that one of the principles of linguistic development is *analogy*, easily generates the common noun 'meaning' and permits us to say

(65³) *Triangular* is *the meaning of* 'dreieckig' (in German)

and to make the statement properly existential in form,

(69²) There is *a* meaning which 'dreieckig' (in German) means

or, with Geach,

(69³) There is a *property* which 'dreieckig' (in German) *stands for*.

In other words, while it would be incorrect simply to say that there are no such things as meanings, or Frege's concepts, or Geach's properties, to trace the common noun 'meaning' to its source in the translation rubric ' "—" (in L) means . . .' (66) is to make what amounts to this point in a less misleading and dogmatic way.

The upshot of the foregoing discussion of meaning with respect to the primary theme of this article can be summed up by saying that the translation context (66) does not properly take a singular term on the right-hand side unless the expression of L which is placed in the single quotes of the left-hand side is itself a singular term. In

273

other words, this context does not of itself *originate* a commitment to abstract entities.

This point might be obscured by a failure, where the quoted expression of L is a sentence, to distinguish between the context

(72) '—' (in L) means p

and the context

(73) X—by uttering '. . .' (in L)—asserts *that*-p

where X is a person. The former context abstracts from the many specific ways in which the English sentence represented by 'p' and the corresponding sentence of L function in discourse. That the context

(74) X asserts that-p

unlike context (72) above does involve the use of the abstract singular term 'that-p' is a point to which we shall return at the close of the argument.

XIII

Perhaps the most interesting consequence of the above analysis is the fact that it frees the 'semantical definition of truth' from the commitment to propositions which it has often been taken to involve. Thus, the definiens of Carnap's definition of 'true sentence of L' developed on pages 49ff. of his *Introduction to Semantics*, namely,

(75) S is a true sentence of $L=_{Df}(Ep)$ S designates p (in L) $\cdot$ p

is incorrectly read as 'there is a proposition, p, such that S designates p (in L) and p'. It can readily be seen that this reading exhibits inconsistencies which are the counterpart of those explored in the opening section of this chapter in connection with the 'informal reading' of '(Ef) S is f' as 'there is an f such that S is f'. Thus, whereas 'S designates p' requires that 'p' be a sentential variable and not a singular term variable, the context 'there is a proposition, p, . . .' requires that 'p' be a singular term variable of the form 'that-p'. And if we revise the definition to avoid the inconsistency by taking 'S' to be the name of a that-clause (in L) rather than the name of a sentence, thus obtaining

(76) S is a true that-clause (in $L)=_{Df}$. There is a proposition, that-p, such that S designates *that-p* (in L) and that-p

we see at once that we have an ill-formed expression on our hands, for the concluding conjunct 'p' of the original definiens has been turned into the *singular term* variable 'that-p', and to patch *this* up

274

we must turn 'and that-p' into 'and that-p *is the case*', where 'that-p is the case' is the categorized counterpart of 'p', as 'S has f-ness' is of 'S is f'.

The 'propositional' reading of Carnap's definition becomes, under the pressure of the demand for consistency,

(77) T is a true that-clause (in L)$=_{Df}$ there is a proposition, that-p, such that T designates *that-p* (in L) and that-p is the case,

and while I do not wish to impugn the consistency of the notion, thus introduced, of the truth of a that-clause, I do wish to insist that this notion is philosophically unsound in so far as it *rests on* the mistaken idea that the truth must be defined in terms of propositions, and *leads to* the mistaken idea that the truth of *statements* is derivative from that of *that-clauses*.[1]

XIV

Our success in showing that the context ' "—" (in L) means . . .' does not *originate* a commitment to the use of abstract singular terms (though it accepts them with grace if they are already in use) raises the hope that *all* other uses of abstract singular terms stem from their use in 'quasi-syntactical statements in the material mode of speech'. In other words, the hope is revived that what we have called the syntactical therapy will work. If, however, as a result of this optimism we take a closer look at this therapy, we find that it is not without its own difficulties. Indeed, it is apparently open to a simple and devastating objection. How can 'Triangularity is a quality' (11) have something like the force of ' "Triangular" (in English) is an adjective' (11²) in view of the fact that (11) *makes no reference to the English language*? The objection is no mere question begging, for it presents an argument to prove that (11) makes no reference to the English language in general nor to the English word 'triangular' in particular. It points out that the German translation of (11) is

(11g) Dreieckigkeit ist eine qualitaet

and argues that there is just as much reason to say that (11g) is about the German word 'dreieckig' as to say that (11) is about the English word 'triangular'. Since (11g) presumably makes the same statement as its English counterpart (11), the objection concludes that neither of these statements is about either word.

---

[1] To point out that Carnay's definition of 'true sentence of L' does not have these consequences is not to endorse his definition as an *explication* of the concept of truth. See Chapter 6 above.

Again, how can the truth of (11) be ascertained by reflecting on the use of the word 'triangular' if, were a German to say

(78) Dreieckigkeit ist eine qualitaet, aber es gibt keine Englische Sprache,

his colleagues would recognize that his statement was only contingently false? For if his statement is only contingently false, it might have been true, and if it had been true, he could have made a true statement, namely (11g) above even though there was no English language in general, nor, in particular, such an English word as 'triangular'. And if there is only a contingent connection between the truth of (11g) and the existence of the English language, how *could* we English users ascertain the truth of (11) simply by reflecting on the syntax of the English word 'triangular'?

The answer to this puzzle involves two steps, the first of which we have already taken, for it consists in reminding ourselves that

(79) 'Dreieckigkeit ist eine qualitaet' (in German) means *triangularity is a quality*

does not involve the singular term '*that* triangularity is a quality'. Consequently, the fact that (11g) 'has the meaning it does' does not commit us to the existence of a nonlinguistic abstract entity (a proposition) of which (11g) is the German name; nor, *a fortiori*, does the fact that (11) and (11g) 'have the same meaning' commit us to the existence of a nonlinguistic abstract entity which stands over and against both languages and has a name in each. That there is a *linguistic* abstract entity, of which 'that triangularity is a quality' is the English name, is indeed the case. But, as has been pointed out, 'that triangularity is a quality' stands to all vocables, English or German, which play a certain (complex) linguistic role as 'the pawn' stands to pawns of whatever shape, size, or colour. It has been pointed out above, that statements involving abstract singular terms are reducible to statements involving no abstract singular terms.

Now if we take seriously the fact that the *inter-translatability* of (11) and (11g), their existence as *counterparts* of one another in the two languages, does not involve the existence of a proposition which they both name, we are in a position to approach the question 'By virtue of what are these two sentences counterparts?' without being tangled *ab initio* in a commitment to Platonic entities. In other words, we can look for a role which (11) might play in English and for a role which (11g) might play in German which would make (11) and (11g) *counterparts* and appropriately *inter-translatable*, unhampered by the mistaken idea that two inter-translatable expressions must be different names of one entity.

And once we undertake this unhampered search, the result is surely a foregone conclusion. Thus the second step consists in noting that while

(80) Triangularity is a quality, but 'triangular' is not an adjective in the language I speak

is not in any simple sense self-contradictory, as is shown by the fact that *one* of its German counterparts,

(80g) Dreieckigkeit ist eine qualitaet aber 'triangular' ist nicht ein Adjectiv in seine (Sellars) Sprache

is only contingently false, it is nevertheless 'logically odd' in a way which requires its falsity. Notice that not only (83g) but both

(80^1) Triangularity is a quality, but 'triangular' was not an adjective in the language I spoke yesterday

and

(80^2) Triangularity is a quality, but 'triangular' will not be an adjective in the language I will speak tomorrow

are *contingently* false. The logical oddity of (80) consequently hinges on the fact that I cannot—and *this* is a matter of strict logic—simultaneously make understanding use of 'triangularity is a quality' while understandingly denying that 'triangular' is an adjective. And the reason for this is simply that to know how to use singular terms ending in '-ity' is to know that they are formed from adjectives; while to know how to use the common noun 'quality' is (roughly) to know that its well formed singular sentences are of the form '— is a quality' where the blank is appropriately filled by an abstract noun. (That the parallel points about '-keit' and 'qualitaet' in German are genuine parallels is clear.) Thus a more penetrating examination (80) shows it to be self-contradictory in spite of the fact that *one* of its German counterparts is not.

Thus, while my ability to use 'triangular' understandingly involves an ability to use sentences of the form '— is triangular' in reporting and describing matters of physical, extralinguistic fact, my ability to use 'triangularity' understandingly involves no new dimension of the reporting and describing of extralinguistic fact—no scrutiny of abstract entities—but constitutes, rather, my grasp of the adjectival role of 'triangular'.

Is this all there is to it? Is the story really so simple? Of course not. Philosophy moves along asymptotes, and to move along one, it must move along many. Progress is dialectical, and comes from raising and answering objections. This time the objection is that the above account makes unintelligible the plain fact that we have the *two* sentences 'Triangularity is a *quality*' (11) and '"Triangular" (in English) is an *adjective*' (11²). Why should our 'grasp of the adjectival role of "triangular"' be embodied in the former, when the latter does exactly this job in such a straightforward and successful way?

The answer to this question is best approached by noting an important difference between the two abstract singular-term expressions 'triangularity' and 'that x is triangular', which we have hitherto taken to have the same force. The existence of such a difference is made clear by the fact that there is something odd about the statement '*That x is triangular* is a quality' (11¹) and even odder about

(81) *That Socrates is a K* is a particular.

To begin with, it is, surely, *triangularity* which is the quality just as it is *Socrates* which is the particular. If so, a distinction is called for between 'Triangularity is a quality' (11) and what we might represent as

(82) *That x is triangular* is a particular–gappy proposition

and, correspondingly, between

(83) Socrates is a particular

and

(84) *That Socrates is a K* is a kind–gappy proposition.

Thus, if we assume for the moment that *ontological* categories are the material mode of speech for *syntactical* categories, then the syntactical counterpart of 'Triangularity is a quality' (11) would not be

(11⁴) 'x is triangular' is a singular-term gappy attributive sentence

but simply '"Triangular" (in English) is an adjective' (11²) and the syntactical counterpart of 'Socrates is a particular' (83) not

(84¹) 'Socrates is a K' is a common-noun gappy classifying sentence

but simply

(83¹) 'Socrates' is a singular term (of type 0).

The non-self-sufficiency, then, of universals and individuals is not a matter of gappiness, but rather a reflection of the fact that adjectives, common nouns, and singular terms alike are what they are because of their different contribution to the statement-making role performed by the *sentence*.

It is often said that 'one place predicate' is a more penetrating syntactical concept than that of an adjective—even when the latter is expanded to include adjectival expressions as well as simple adjectives. And there is certainly an element of truth in this contention which we might try to put by saying that 'one place predicate' makes explicit reference to the way in which adjectives are incomplete. But once we try to spell this out, we see that the point is not that 'adjective' obscures the fact that adjectives are incomplete—for it does not—but rather that it does not give us, so to speak, an intuitive picture of this incompleteness. Indeed, we are only half-way to this intuitive picture if we replace (11²) by

(11⁵) 'Triangular' (in English) is a one place predicate.

To get it we must say

(11⁶) '— is triangular' (in English) is a singular-term-gappy-attributive sentence.

Consider, now, the statement

(82¹) *That — is triangular* is a particular-gappy state of affairs

(which is a candid reading of what might also be rendered by

(82²) *That x is triangular* is a propositional (*N.B.*: *not* sentential) function).

What can we make of it? Are we not tempted to think that (82¹) is simply a rewriting of (11⁶)? For, we might argue, how *could* (82¹) be true if it were *not* a rewriting of (11⁶)? Can it be a complete sentence if it *contains* a gap instead of *mentioning* it? And where can an appropriate gap be found if not in the gappy sentence '— is triangular'?

Why, then, would we hesitate? What is there about the 'feel' of (82¹) which militates against the idea that it could be a rewriting of (11⁶)? I think I can put my finger on it by calling attention to the fact that a foreigner who was learning English and had made substantial progress, but had not yet added the word 'triangular' to his vocabulary, could fully understand (11⁶), whereas (82¹) cannot be fully understood unless one not only knows that 'triangular' is an English word, but actually has it in one's active vocabulary.

But if this is the source of our hesitation, we are in a position to answer our original question. For we have now located a difference between the 'material' and the 'formal' modes of speech which enables us to see how they can 'have the same force' without one being a simple *rewriting* of the other. For while it would be incorrect to say that '*That — is triangular* is a particular-gappy state of affairs' (82¹) is a *mere* rewriting of '"— is triangular" (in English) is a

279

singular-term-gappy attributive sentence' (11⁶), it is at least a reasonable next step in the direction of the truth to interpret it as a rewriting which presupposes that 'writer' and 'reader' are able to *use* as well as *mention* sentences of the form '— is triangular'.

It should be noted, in this connection, that a similar point can be made about the difference between ' "Dreieckig" (in German) means *triangular*' (65) and

(65⁴) 'Dreieckig' (in German) is the counterpart of the English word 'triangular'.

For the former presupposes, as the latter does not, that the English-speaking person to whom it is addressed not only recognizes that 'triangular' is an English word, but enjoys its presence in his active vocabulary. It is, as we have seen, by leading those to whom it is addressed to rehearse in imagination the role of 'triangular' that (65) is an explanation of the German word 'dreieckig'. Thus (65) has essentially the force of ' "dreieckig" (in German), plays the same role as "triangular" in *our* language'.

And this is the place to pick up a topic which was raised towards the end of our first bout with the rubric ' "—" means . . .' only to be dropped like the hot potato it is. I there pointed out that the context ' "—" (in L) means *p*' (72), where '—' is a *sentence* of L, must not be confused with 'X, by uttering "—" (in L), asserts *that-p*' (73). The latter *does*, whereas the former does not, involve the use of the singular term 'that-p'. What then are we to do about *this* apparent commitment to Platonic entities? The clue is contained in (73) itself. I am not, however, suggesting that 'X asserts that-p' (74) is a simple *rewriting of*

(85) X utters '—' (in L)

which won't do at all for the obvious reason that one can assert, for example, that it is raining without using any given language, L. Shall we, then, accept the equation.

(86) X asserted that-p $=_{Df}$. There is a language, L, and a sentence S, such that S is a sentence of L *and* S (in L) means *p and* X, speaking L, uttered S?

This might be the *beginning* of an analysis, for our discussion of the material mode of speech has shown us that 'X asserts that-p' (74) might *mention* a sentence (in this case a sentence in an unspecified language), even though it does not appear to do so, and that 'that-p' can be construed as the name of a role which is played in different languages by different vocables and in the unspecified language by unspecified vocables. On the other hand, that 86 cannot be the *end* of the analysis is clear.

XV

I began by arguing that 'existential quantification over predicate or sentential variables' does not assert the existence of abstract entities. I then suggested that if the only contexts involving abstract singular terms of the forms 'f-ness', 'K-kind', and 'that-p' which could not be reformulated in terms of expressions of the forms 'x is f', 'x is a K', and 'p' were categorizing statements such as 'f-ness is a quality', 'K-kind is a class', 'that p is a proposition', then we might well hope to relieve Platonistic anxieties by the use of syntactical therapy. I then examined a context which has been thought to correlate words with extralinguistic abstract entities, namely the context ' "—" (in L) means . . .', and found that it does not do so. Encouraged by this, I proceeded to examine the distinction between the material and the formal modes of speech to see if the idea that such categorizing statements as 'Triangularity is a quality' have the force of syntactical statements such as ' "triangular" is an adjective' can run the gauntlet of familiar objections, with what I believe to be hopeful results.

Yet if I stand off and scrutinize the argument, my enthusiasm cannot but be sobered by a consciousness of how much remains to be done before something like a nominalistic position is secure. For I cannot overlook the fact that two of the most puzzling contexts in which abstract singular terms occur have been noted only to be passed over in search of simpler game. I refer, of course, in the first place to *mentalistic* contexts such as

(87) Jones inferred *that* S is f

and, in the second, to such 'nomological' contexts as

(88) *That* it has just lightninged implies *that* it will shortly thunder.

Then there are such evaluative contexts as

(89) *That* he was late is better than *that* he not have come at all.

The task of clarifying the force of contexts such as these is as large as philosophy itself. And to this task the foregoing is but a prolegomenon.

9

PARTICULARS

THERE are two obvious ways in which a philosopher can attack a theory which he believes to be mistaken. He can seek to reduce it to absurdity by developing its implications and showing them to be either mutually inconsistent or incompatible with the incontrovertible. Or he can attempt to trace the error back to its roots, and show why those who defend it have been led to speak as they do. Of these two methods, it is clear that only the latter is capable of definitive results. A mistaken theory can be compared to a symptom of a disease. By the use of inadequate medicaments one can often 'cure' the symptoms while leaving the disease untouched. And by exposing the absurdity of a theory, one can often prevent philosophers from espousing it, at least overtly, though only too often they react to a proof that their theory conflicts with 'obvious common sense' by piling a Pelion of paradox on the original Ossa. Even should the theory be abandoned, at least as an overt article of faith, the root confusion is left untouched by this method, and, like many a versatile disease, finds other ways of making its presence felt. Indeed, to change our metaphor, philosophers can often be observed to leap from the frying-pan of one absurdity into the fire of another, and from there into the well of a third, and *da capo* as long as a fundamental confusion remains uncovered.

My purpose in rehashing this familiar theme has been to provide a text for the argument to follow. Thus, the point of departure of the present chapter is one more flogging of the absurd notion that this colourful universe of ours contains such queer entities as featureless substrata or bare particulars. That this notion is indeed absurd, few, if any, contemporary philosophers would deny. In short, the first method of attack has achieved a full measure of success.[1] Bare parti-

---

[1] Perhaps the neatest way in which to expose the absurdity of the notion of bare particulars is to show that the sentence, 'Universals are exemplified by bare particulars,' is a self-contradiction. As a matter of fact, the self-contradictory character

282

culars and featureless substrata have been driven into the philosophical underground, and remain unacknowledged even by those who are committed to them. But what of the second method? Has its goal, too, been reached? Does no confusion remain, to manifest itself, perhaps, in the invention of still other absurdities to which philosophers might cling in terror of falling back into the quicksand of bare particulars? What of Lord Russell's dogged attempts to conceive of particulars as complexes of universals? Has he not repeatedly assured us[1] that only in this way can we lay the spectre of bare particulars? And what of those philosophers who persist in accounting for the sense of universal words in terms of resembling particulars—are they not motivated, at least in part, by the conviction that to 'accept universals' is to commit oneself either to bare particulars, or to Russell's expedient, which, as they see it, is, if anything, even more absurd? I shall contend that the fundamental confusion underlying the notion of bare particulars remains indeed to plague us, in spite of the moribund character of the doctrine itself, and that bare particulars, particulars as complexes of universals and universals as sets of resembling particulars can be taken, respectively, as the frying-pan, the fire, and the well of the metaphor at the end of the preceding paragraph.

Yet it is not for want of attempts to expose and sterilize the source of the notion of bare particulars that these confusions persist. Many such attempts have been made, often, it has seemed, with complete success. Indeed, it must be admitted that certain confusions which lead to the postulation of substratum particulars have been clarified and removed from the stream of progressive philosophical thought. Thus, one traditional line of argument in support of substratum particulars, that, namely, which moves from the sameness of a thing throughout its successive states to the positing of a substratum entity which 'has' these states, has been undercut by pointing out that the elements in a pattern (e.g. the notes in a melody), 'belong to the same thing' without requiring the existence of an additional particular which 'has' them. It was a signal merit of the doctrine of logical constructions to have freed us once and for all from the tendency to look for a substratum particular behind every patterned object. On the other hand, it is just not true, as many seem to have thought, that it was the confusion thus exposed which was responsible for *bare* particulars. Consider the following argument: Pierre and François

[1] Most recently in *Human Knowledge, its Scope and Limits*, pp. 292ff.

of this sentence becomes evident the moment we translate it into the symbolism of *Principia Mathematica*. It becomes, '$(x) \cdot (\exists\phi)\phi x \supset -(\exists\phi)\phi x$' or, in other words, 'If a particular exemplifies a universal, then there is no universal which it exemplifies.'

are citizens of the same state, therefore there must surely be a particular which is the same state to which both Pierre and François stand
in the relation *being a citizen of*. Clearly, what is being posited here is
not a *bare* particular, but rather a particular which is a state. Or take
the case of a melody. The parallel argument would be: The first and
third notes whistled by Jones belong to the same performance of the
tune *Lillibulero*, therefore there must be a particular which is the same
melody-performance to which these notes belong. What is posited
here is obviously not a *bare* particular, but rather a particular which
is a melody-performance as contrasted with the note-performances
which belong to it. In short, this confusion interprets the identity of
a pattern of particulars in terms of an additional particular which
exemplifies a Gestalt universal, and to which the original particulars
belong in an appropriate mode of this relation. These surplus particulars, which are the 'whole' as opposed to the 'parts' (and might
therefore appropriately be called *holoi*), are not introduced as bare
particulars, then, but as melody-performances, states, etc. The business of the *holoi* with which this confusion populates the world is to
be instances of irreducible *Gestalt* universals, as it is the business of
ordinary particulars to be instances of ordinary universals, and there
is no more reason to describe *holoi* as bare particulars than to describe
any other particulars.

The argument from the identity of a changing thing through the
successive events in which it is said to participate is particularly
instructive. Consider, for example, the career of an oaktree. By itself,
the confusion we have been discussing would merely result in the
postulation of a *holon* which was the oaktree in contrast to the
successive states which would be chronicled in giving its history. This
time the surplus particular would be an instance of Oaktree, misconceived to be an irreductible *Gestalt* universal of the type which
finds its instances in a special set of *holoi*, namely continuants. How,
then, does the temptation to think of changing things as built on an
abiding bare substratum arise? Actually, there are at least two confusions which yield this result without any assistance from the confusion
we have been examining, though historically all these distinguishable
confusions have been confused together. One of these, the mare's nest
concealed in Aristotle's distinction between form and matter, is
irrelevant to the argument of this chapter, and I shall do no more
than refer the reader to the analysis which I have given of it in another
place.[1] The other leads directly to our central theme. Thus, suppose
the philosopher who is worried about the sameness of a thing

[1] 'Aristotelian Philosophies of Mind' in *Philosophy for the Future*, a collection
of essays edited by R. W. Sellars, M. Farber, and V. J. McGill, and published by
the Macmillan Co., 1949.

throughout change is already committed to the view that an object's having a character is to be understood in terms of a relation between a bare particular and a universal. Then, of course, he will be tempted to hold that the oaktree's continuance through change consists in the relation of its substratum to different sets of universals at different times. But even should he be led, by reflection on time and temporal relations, to recognize events as particulars, and hence to postulate a separate bare particular for each successive state of the object, he will also be led to postulate an additional abiding or continuant bare particular should he be guilty of the *Gestalt* confusion. For, in accordance with the above commitment, he will think of the *holon* which he introduces to be the identity of the oaktree in contrast to the multiplicity of its successive states as being a bare particular which participates in the *Gestalt* universal Oaktree.

Now, the contention that the notion of bare particulars has its primary source in confusions relating to the exemplification of universals by particulars is by no means a novel one, and if it had been the sole function of the preceding paragraphs to usher in this claim, they need not have been written. However, besides introducing the main theme of this chapter, they have not only made the worthwhile if negative point that bare particulars were not sired by the *Gestalt* confusion, but also, by focusing attention on the concept of logical construction, mobilized for subsequent use the most powerful tool of modern philosophical analysis. The key role played by the concept of logical construction in the clarification of puzzles relating to universals and particulars will emerge in the course of the next few pages.

II

I shall begin the constructive argument of this chapter by constructing a universe of discourse in which the temptation to speak of bare particulars has been reduced to a minimum, yet which recognizes the distinction between universals and particulars to be ultimate. I shall then show how, by making one apparently innocuous change in this framework, one is put in the position of being able to avoid bare particulars only at the cost of embracing one or other of the equally absurd expedients for dodging them which misguided philosophical ingenuity has invented. In short, I shall recommend the conceptual frame I am about to sketch on the ground that by adopting it, and only by adopting it, can we avoid the merry-go-round of confusions on which so much time and energy has been wasted. Not on this negative ground only, however, is it to be recommended, for though when first encountered this frame inevitably wears an air of paradox, a closer acquaintance reveals it to be a source of positive clarification

285

and insight, with decisive implications for other problems in this neighbourhood.

Let us consider a domain of particulars each of which is an instance of one and only one simple non-relational universal.[1] Furthermore, it is not to be as a mere matter of fact that this is so, as though these particulars *could* exemplify more than one, but do not happen to do so. It is to be a defining characteristic of the conceptual frame we are elaborating that no particular belonging to it *can* exemplify more than one simple non-relational universal. Let us call these particulars *basic particulars*, and the simple non-relational universals they exemplify, *qualia*. Now the first step in removing the air of complete unreality which surrounds the above stipulation is to point out that even though the basic particulars of this universe each exemplify one and only one *quale*, it is nevertheless possible for this universe to contain complex objects exemplifying complex properties. To say this, of course, is not to assert that *over and above* basic particulars exemplifying *qualia*, the universe under consideration might contain additional particulars and universals, only this time, complex ones. For sentences attributing complex properties to complex particulars are logical shorthand for conjunctions of sentences each of which attributes a *quale* to a basic particular, or a simple dyadic (or triadic) relation to a pair (or trio) of basic particulars. In short, the fundamental principle of this conceptual frame is that what is ostensibly a single particular exemplifying a number of universals, is actually a number of particulars exemplifying simple universals.

We shall shortly be concerned to explore some of the implications of this framework for the tangle of puzzles described in our opening remarks. First, however, we must dispose of an immediate challenge which, if left unanswered, would make further elaboration pointless. The objection takes its point of departure in the fact that the proposed framework, whatever its peculiarities, involves an ultimate dualism of universals and particulars. It runs as follows: 'Any dualism of universals and particulars amounts to a distinction within things between a factor responsible for the particularity of the thing and a factor responsible for its character; in brief, a *this*-factor and a *such*-factor. But surely this is exactly the doctrine of bare particulars!' Now this argument has a venerable history, but it is beyond question as unsound as an argument can be. Its plausibility rests on a confusion between *particulars* and *facts*. Suppose that a certain particular *a* exemplifies ϕ. Then *a* is an instance of ϕ, but ϕ is not a component of *a*. On the other hand, ϕ is a component of the fact that *a* is ϕ. But

[1] To which should be added that each pair of these particulars is an instance of at most one simple dyadic relation, and similarly in the case of simple triadic relations should these be needed or granted.

the fact that a is ϕ is not itself an instance of ϕ. Thus, the notion of a thing which (1) has ϕ for a component, and yet (2) is an instance of ϕ, is a confusion which blends a and the fact that a is ϕ into a philosophical monstrosity. We can, indeed, say that the fact that a is ϕ consists of a '*this*-factor' and a '*such*-factor', but the '*this*-factor', instead of being a bare particular, is nothing more nor less than an instance of ϕ, and the 'thing' which consists of these factors is so far from exemplifying ϕ that it cannot be meaningfully said to do so. To say that a blue particular consists of Blue and a particular is indeed to talk nonsense; but it is nonsense which arises not out of a dualism of particulars and universals, but out of a confusion between particulars and facts.

At this point the reader may be moved to exclaim, 'Yes, the source of bare particulars does indeed lie in the confusion of facts with particulars. But is not this the end of the story? You didn't need your rigmarole of particulars instancing only one *quale* in order to make this point. Why complicate your presentation with an unnecessary assumption? After all, is it not perfectly clear that one and the same particular *can* exemplify more than one *quale*?' The reply to this challenge takes us to the heart of the chapter. But before going one step further, let me remind the reader that of course I admit that one and the same 'particular' can have more than one quality. I insist only that such 'particulars' are actually logical constructions out of particulars proper. Stripped of this possible source of misunderstanding, the above challenge reads, 'Why did you introduce the assumption that basic particulars can exemplify only one *quale*,[1] since you did not need it to expose the confusion between particulars and facts which is the true source of bare particulars?' *My answer will consist in the attempt to show that it is only possible to think of a basic particular as exemplifying two or more simple non-relational universals if one is guilty of exactly this same confusion!*

Let us return to the discussion of the basic particular a which we supposed to be an instance of ϕ. To make our example more intuitive,[2] however, let us substitute for 'ϕ' the expression 'Greem', which we shall suppose to designate a simple non-relational universal capable of being exemplified by basis particulars, that is, a *quale*. In a, then, we have a particular which is greem. If we were to be aware of a we should be aware of something greem. Neither Greemness, nor the

[1] Notice that, for reasons which will come out shortly, I have avoided referring to the simple non-relational universals exemplified by basic particulars as *qualities*.

[2] The primary purpose of using 'greem' and, later, 'kleem' rather than 'ϕ' and 'ψ' is to bring into play the subtleties of the logical grammar of the English language. I do not wish to be taken as hinting that the colour predicate mimicked by 'greem' stands for a universal whose instances are basic particulars; though I am taking advantage of the fact that this is often thought to be the case.

fact that *a* is greem, is greem. It is *a* that is greem. When we say that *a* is greem, we imply no internal complexity in *a*. Greemness is not an element of *a*, though it is of the fact that *a* is greem. Consider now the class of basic particulars which are instances of Greemness. Suppose that the class is designated by 'Grom', and that a member of the class is said to be a *grum*. Then *a* is a grum; and its being a grum involves no internal complexity.

In these terms our problem is the following: Is it possible for a basic particular, a particular which is not itself a structure of particulars, to be an instance of Greemness and also of another *quale*, say, Kleemness? Is it possible for *a*, *without internal complexity*, to be both greem and kleem, to be both a grum and a klum? The phrase 'without any internal complexity' is, of course, the heart of the matter. For if it is said that *a* must be complex to be both greem and kleem, then either the elements of the complex are particulars, in which case my principle has been granted, or else the elements of the complex are universals. In the latter case we have the old mistake of supposing that Greemness is an element in an item which is greem.[1] Now it is obvious that should we be guilty of this mistake, and think of the instancing relation as a relation which binds *a* and Greemness to constitute a greem item, then we should find no immediate absurdity in the claim that a basic particular can be an instance of both Greemness and Kleemness, for this would amount to the claim that one and the same basic particular can stand in the same relation to two universals, and surely one item can stand in the same relation to two other items. Roger is brother to Robert and also to John. Why could not one and the same basic particular *a* co-operate with Greemness to form a greem item, and with Kleemness to form a kleem item? To conceive of instancing in this way, however, is an obvious howler. Indeed, it is a self-contradictory mistake, since to say that *a* is an instance of Greemness is exactly to say that *a* is greem, whereas the theory says that not *a* but the complex *a-instancing-Greemness* is greem. In short, the price we would be paying for thinking of *a* as 'instancing' both Greemness and Kleemness would be the prohibitive one of making it an instance of neither, but rather a bare particular.

On the other hand, once the confusion between particulars and facts is completely avoided, the notion that a basic particular can be an instance of two *qualia* not only loses all plausibility, but is seen to

[1] It must be borne in mind that the argument of the chapter moves within the framework of the assumption that the distinction between universals and particulars is ultimate and irreducible, and that the contention that particulars are 'complexes of universals' is as unsound as the notion of bare particulars. For an incisive critique of the doctrine that particulars are reducible to universals see Gustav Bergmann's 'Russell on Particulars', *Philosophical Review* (1948); also J. R. Jones, 'Simple Particulars', *Philosophical Studies* (1950).

be absurd. A basic particular which is an instance of Greemness is not a bare particular standing in a relation to Greemness, it is a grum. A basic particular which is an instance of Kleemness is not a bare particular standing in a relation to Kleemness, it is a klum. Surely, however intimately related a grum and a klum may be, they cannot be identical![1]

It is only 'complex particulars', then, which can be both greem and kleem. To say this, of course, is to say that a sentence attributing these qualities to a complex particular is logical shorthand for a conjunction of sentences to the effect that certain basic particulars are greem, others are kleem, while the set of basic particulars as a whole is an instance of such and such a pattern or structure. Why we dignify this rather than that type of structure with such logical shorthand is a matter for study in the philosophy of science, in what, but for the unfortunate phenomenalistic connotations Carnap has given the term, might be called *Konstitutionstheorie*. But that we must use what, from the standpoint of logical theory, would be the highly derived superstructure of an ideal language is, of course, a matter of practical necessity. The subject-predicate form of ordinary language can only be understood in this setting. The objects designated by the subject term in singular sentences of this form are, without exception, complex particulars, *and the logical structures which find expression in the subject–predicate form of ordinary language are, strictly speaking, as many as there are types and levels of logical construction.* Thus, it is only scratching the surface to say, as we must, that the verb 'to be' has a different logical grammar when used in sentences attributing a *quality* to a complex particular, from that which it has in sentences to the effect that a basic particular is an instance of a *quale*.

We are now in a position to point out that if we were to use the same words 'greem' and 'kleem' in both of the latter types of sentence, they would nevertheless have a different logical grammar in the two usages. Thus, where S is a complex particular, not only is the 'is' of 'S is greem' different from the 'is' of 'a is greem' (where *a* is a basic particular as before), so also is the 'greem' a different, though related,

---

[1] (Added 1963) This argument is not convincing. It tacitly treats 'greem' and 'kleem' as common nouns indistinguishable from 'grum' and 'klum'. Common nouns pertaining to basic particulars are tacitly assumed to be primitive, for if

Grum = $_{Df}$ greem-item

and

Klum = $_{Df}$ kleem-item

the argument fails. A more penetrating argument for the idea that the basic particulars of a perspicuous world would satisfy the principle in question is advanced in 'The Logic of Complex Particulars', *Mind*, 58, 1949.

'greem'. In other words, Greemness as a quality of complex particulars must not be confused with Greemness as a *quale*, even though saying of a complex particular that it has the former entails that some basic particulars are instances of the latter. It is a mistake to speak of basic particulars as instances of qualities, and it was for this reason that we introduced the term 'quale' to designate the simple non-relational universals of which basic particulars are instances.[1] It is even more obviously a mistake to speak of basic particulars themselves as qualities, and proclaim that the qualities of things are as particular as the things themselves. For while it is true that to say of a thing that it is greem is, in effect, to say that it consists, *inter alia*, of grums, it is a sheer mistake in logical grammar to speak of grums as qualities. It is a type confusion, a mixing of levels of discourse.

Let me conclude this section of the chapter by recognizing that in view of the fact that the reader rightly suspects my use of 'greem' to be a thinly disguised appeal to our intuitions concerning the colour green, it is incumbent on me to make some sort of reply to the challenge: 'How, on your position, can "x is green" entail (as it obviously does) "x is extended"? Green is surely a *quale*, and your argument, therefore, implies that "x is green" and "x is extended" can't both be true.' My answer is, of course, that the predicate 'green' of ordinary usage has a complex logical structure. It designates a quality rather than a *quale*, and the particulars to which it applies are complex particulars. It applies, indeed, to *continua*, the elements of which have the logical properties of points. It is these points which are the basic particulars, and the *quale* which they exemplify has no designation in ordinary usage. We might well introduce the word 'greem' for this purpose. It is a *synthetic* necessary truth that the instances of *greem* are points in a *continuum*. On the other hand, 'x is *green*'='x is a *continuum* of which the elements are *greem*'; so that 'x is *green*' analytically entails 'x is extended'.

III

In the concluding paragraphs of this chapter, I want to explore a traditional puzzle which, though of ancient vintage, has achieved a noticeable degree of clarification only in the last half-century. It

---

[1] It is essential to note that the distinction between a *quale* and a quality by no means coincides with that between a simple and a complex quality. Simple and complex qualities alike are logical constructions out of *qualia*, the distinction being (roughly) that a simple quality is a logical construction out of a single *quale*, whereas a complex quality is a logical construction out of several *qualia*. More accurately, to predicate a simple quality of a complex particular is to say that some of its constituent basic particulars are instances of one certain *quale*, whereas to predicate a complex quality of it is to assert that it includes instances of several specified *qualia*.

runs as follows: Granted that the distinction between particulars and *some* type of abstract entity[1] is ultimate and irreducible, must we accept *both* universals and classes as equally ultimate, or can entities of one of these types be defined in terms of entities of the other? And if so, which? Fortunately, there is little to be gained from a survey of recent discussions of this topic, since the instruments we have forged enable us to penetrate beneath their common presuppositions to a foundation on which can be built a simple and straightforward solution.

Consider a model universe the basic particulars of which are instances of the *qualia* A, B, C. . . .[2] Suppose that A is instanced by basic particulars $x_1, \ldots x_m$ while B is instanced by $x_n, \ldots x_w$. Let us pose the following question which will take us directly to the heart of the matter. Can we identify the class whose members are $x_1, \ldots x_m$ with the universal A; the class α with the *quale* A? In short, can we claim that at the level of basic particulars no distinction can be drawn between a *quale* and the class of its instances? Can we, to take an earlier example, identify Greemness with the class of grums? Is 'x is greem' just another way of writing 'x is a member of Grom'? 'A(x)' of writing 'x ϵ α'? In favour of this claim is the fact that no basic particular can be an instance of two *qualia*. This entails that if x is an instance of both F and G, then F and G must be identical. In short, two *qualia* with the same instances must, it would seem, be the same *quale*. Here we would have an identify condition which parallels the familiar identify condition for classes, for two classes are notoriously the same class if they have the same members.

Unfortunately, the matter is not quite so simple, and we should not be warranted in jumping to the conclusion that a *quale* is identical with the class of its instances. Thus, suppose that F and G are two *qualia* which *might* have been instanced in our model universe, but which in point of fact do not happen to have been so. (That this is a perfectly sensible assumption is made clear by the following 'ideal experiment'. Suppose that colours are *qualia* which depend for their exemplification on the excitation of nervous systems, and that our

---

[1] The use of this expression must not be taken to imply acceptance of a Platonistic ontology. The present paper has nothing to say on the interesting question, 'Are there abstract entities?' agitated of late by Quine, Carnap, and Ryle. The substantive contentions of my argument belong to logic rather than to the philosophy or epistemology of logic, and if, particularly in the following paragraphs, I have given them, on occasion, an overly 'ontological' formulation, I have done so solely for the sake of simplicity and convenience.

[2] Ordered couples of these basic particulars will be instances of simple dyadic relations, etc. It is important to note that the account of the ultimate identity of universals and classes which is developed in the text for the case of *qualia* applies also to relations. The reader will have noticed that the distinction we have drawn between *qualia* and simple qualities should also be drawn in the case of relations.

universe happened never to develop the necessary conditions for the emergence of life.) On this assumption, the classes corresponding to F and G would both be null classes, and hence the same class—whereas *ex hypothesi* F and G are different *qualia*. It is clear, then, that the framework we have so far developed can at best take us part of the way towards the identification at the level of basic particulars of universals with classes. Of course, if one were prepared to argue that it is logical nonsense to speak of a simple universal which has no instances, then the identification of *qualia* with the classes of their instances could be made without further ado. That to speak this *is* logical nonsense has indeed been argued. Formulated in traditional terms, the argument appeals to a supposedly evident principle of acquaintance to the effect that a term cannot designate a simple universal unless those who use this term intelligently have been acquainted with instances of the universal in question, from which it would follow that if 'A' designates a *quale*, the *quale* A must have had instances. I have explored elsewhere[1] the confusions which under-lie the 'Principle of Acquaintance' and the related concept of 'Ostensive Definition'. I shall therefore move directly to a brief exposition of what I take to be the correct account of the identity of *qualia* with the classes of their instances.

To sketch the background of this new picture, we need a broader canvas. Its fundamental theme can be put by saying first that the meaning of a term lies in the rules of its usage, and then adding that the rules in question are rules of inference.[2] Rules of inference, in turn, are of two types: *formal* and *material*. This classification corresponds to Carnap's distinction, in his *Logical Syntax of Language*,[3] between two types of 'transformation rule' (Carnap's term for rule of inference): (1) Logical or L-rules, which validate inferences in which the factual predicates, to use Quine's happy phrase, occur vacuously —that is, could be systematically replaced by any others of the same type and degree without destroying the validity of the argument; (2) Physical or P-rules, which validate inferences in which the factual

---

[1] Chapters 5, 10, and 11. For an earlier attempt, see my essay, 'Language, Rules and Behaviour' in *John Dewey: Philosopher of Science and Freedom*, edited by Sidney Hook, and published in 1950 by the Dial Press, New York.

[2] For an elaboration and defence of this conception, see the essay referred to in the previous footnote. I there distinguish between the rule-governed aspects of a language, and the causal tie between linguistic and nonlinguistic events which constitutes its application. The latter is not a matter of *rules*, though it is, of course, a matter of *uniformities*. The notion that in addition to syntactical rules there are 'semantical rules' co-ordinating language and world is shown to be a mistake.

[3] Rudolf Carnap, *The Logical Syntax of Language* (London, Kegan, Paul, Trench, Truebner & Co. Ltd., 1937), pp. 180ff.

predicates have an essential rather than vacuous occurrence. My only quarrel with Carnap is that he commits himself to the thesis that P-rules are a luxury which a language with factual predicates can take or leave alone. I have argued in a number of papers, as I am now arguing, that P-rules, or material rules of inference or, as I have also called them, *conformation* rules (by analogy with *formation* and *transformation* rules of inference—to express the *coherence* they give to the expressions of a language) are as essential to a language as L-rules or formal rules of inference.

To illustrate these distinctions, that 'ϕx' is inferrable from '$\phi x \cdot \Psi x$'[1] is a matter of a formal rule of inference. On the other hand, if it is a law of nature that if anything were a case of ϕ it would be a case of Ψ, the inference from 'ϕx' to 'Ψx' is warranted by a material rule of inference; *indeed, these are but two ways of saying the same thing.* Notice that if 'Ψx' is thus inferrable from 'ϕx', the generalized material implication,

$$(x)\,\phi x \supset \Psi x,$$

can be asserted on the basis of a rule of the language. It can also be said to be true by virtue of the meanings of 'ϕ' and 'Ψ', for it was our contention above that the meaning of a term lies in the rules of inference, formal *and* material, by which it is governed.[2] I would certainly be willing to say that '$(x)\,\phi x \supset \Psi x$' is, in these circumstances, a synthetic *a priori* proposition. I see nothing horrendous in the notion that a language or conceptual framework brings with it a commitment to certain logically synthetic propositions, provided that it is recognized that there is more than one pebble on the beach, i.e. that there are many alternative frameworks, one of which the world *persuades* us to adopt (or, better, adumbrate), only to persuade us later to abandon it for another. This, I believe, is a pragmatic conception of the *a priori* akin to that developed under this heading

---

[1] It will be noticed that for the sake of simplicity, the illustrations in this paragraph are formulated in terms of complex particulars and their properties.

[2] If, as I am claiming, the sentences which formulate what we regard as the laws of the world in which we live are true *ex vi terminorum*, then how can it be rational to abandon such a sentence? What role could observational evidence play in the 'establishing' of sentences which are to be true *ex vi terminorum*?

The inductive establishing of laws is misconceived if it is regarded as a process of supplementing observation sentences formulated in a language whose basic conceptual meanings are plucked from 'data' and immune from revision ('Hume's Principle'). The rationality of 'induction' is, rather, the rationality of adopting that framework of material rules of inference (meanings—even for observation predicates) and, within this framework, those (sketchy) statements of unobserved matters of fact (world picture) which together give maximum probability to our observation utterances *interpreted as sentences in the system*. Only if we do this do we adopt (and this is, of course, an analytic proposition) that world picture which is 'most probable on the basis of our observations'.

by C. I. Lewis in his *Mind and the World Order*[1], though I should reject the phenomenalism in which he clothes his formulation. Notice also that where 'Ψx' is not inferrable from 'ϕx', we say that '$(x)\phi x \supset \Psi x$' if true, is so as a mere matter of fact.

Now, we are all familiar with the Leibnitzian manner of explicating the laws of logic in terms of possible worlds. Can this same device be used to clarify the difference between laws of logic and laws of nature? Not only can it be done, but it is extremely helpful to do so, particularly in dealing with the problem we have in mind. However, whereas Leibnitz, on the whole, limited himself to the contrast between truths which do, and truths which do not, hold of all possible worlds, we shall need a somewhat more complicated apparatus with which to do our job. We must interpose between the notion of a possible world, and that of the totality of all possible worlds, the notion of a *family* of possible worlds. Before turning to our task, let us drop the adjective 'possible' and speak of worlds instead of possible worlds. The point of this proposal will emerge at the end of the following paragraph.

A world, then, is a set of basic particulars which exemplify the *qualia* and simple relations which make up what we shall call a battery of simple universals. *It must constantly be borne in mind that these basic particulars are not bare particulars.* Thus, suppose that one of the *qualia* in question is Greemness, and that the world in question, let us call it W_1, includes the particular x_1, which is greem. Then, although 'x_1 is greem' is not an analytic proposition, nor 'x_1 is kleem' a contradiction, x_1 *is* a grum, and there is no such thing as a world in which x_1 is *not* grum. What might be confused with such a world is a *possible state of W_1*. Thus, although x_1 is a grum, the sentence 'x_1 is kleem' is a synthetic proposition, and can accordingly be said to express a possibility. A set of atomic sentences which constitutes a complete description of the particulars of W_1 and which includes the sentence 'x_1 is kleem'[2] can be said to describe a possible but not actual state of W_1. The 'possible worlds' of many neo-Leibnitzian treatments of logic are actually what we have called possible states of one and the same world. We have dropped the adjective 'possible' and speak in terms of worlds instead of possible worlds, since otherwise we should have to use, on occasion, the clumsy and confusing phrase, 'possible state of a possible world'.

---

[1] Clarence Irving Lewis, *Mind and the World Order* (New York, Scribners, 1928).

[2] It will be remembered that a basic particular cannot be an instance of more than one *quale*. Thus, at the level of basic particulars the form '$\phi x \cdot \psi x$' is logical nonsense. Thus, if the above set of sentences includes the sentences 'x_1 is greem', it cannot include the sentence 'x_1 is kleem'.

If the challenge were pressed, 'Why isn't what you are calling "a possible but not actual state of W_1", just another world, say W_2, so that whereas in W_1 x_1 is a grum, in W_2 x_1 is a klum?' the answer would lie in pointing out that this objection involves the mistake of bare particulars. To see this, we need only remind ourselves that x_1, a particular belonging to W_1 is *ex hypothesi* a grum. Now, to say that it is logically possible for x_1 (which is a grum) to be a klum, in short, to point out that 'x_1 is kleem' is not a contradiction, *does not in the slightest entail that* x_1 *is somehow neutral as between Greenness and Kleemness, i.e. is a bare particular.* Thus, while it is a possibility with respect to W_1 that x_1 be kleem, there can be nothing identical with x_1 which *is* a klum, and hence no world which includes x_1 as an instance of Kleemness. Each world, then, has its own set of particulars, there being no overlap between the particulars of one world and those of another.[1]

What, then, is a family of worlds? To construct this notion, conceive of a set of sentences with the following characteristics: (1) each sentence is a generalized material implication which is not logically true; (2) these sentences are certified by the material rules of inference of the language in which they are formulated, in the manner illustrated above; (3) the sentences are about basic particulars and the *qualia* and simple relations they exemplify; (4) no further sentence of this type could be added to the set without resulting in inconsistency. Now, one simple way of describing this set of sentences is to say that they constitute an implicit definition of the battery of predicates involved. Another way is to say that they formulate internal relations or real connections between the universals designated by these predicates. Still another way is to say that they state uniformities which hold in all systems of particulars which exemplify these *qualia* and relations. The last of these needs only minor rephrasing to be what we are looking for. The sentences give expression to a set of uniformities which hold in all worlds of the *family* associated with this battery of simple universals. Every basic particular belongs to a world; every world belongs to a family. Laws of logic are generalizations which hold of all worlds of all families;[2] laws of nature are generalizations

---

[1] I have gone into this point in some detail, because I have found, on the basis of responses to my paper, 'Concepts as Involving Laws and Inconceivable without them', *Philosophy of Science* (1948), that this difference between a possible state of a world, and another (possible) world is as difficult to grasp as it is essential to a correct formulation of the distinction between 'necessary' and 'contingent' truths in the neo-Leibnitzian manner.

[2] It is clear from this that Russell's worries about the need for an axiom of infinity stem from the fact that what he calls the domain of the logically possible is actually the domain of what we should call possible states of *this* world. Since there are, presumably, possible worlds which contain a finite number of basic

which hold of all worlds of a family. There are no *worlds* which violate the laws of nature. What might be mistaken for such a world is a logically possible state of a world, but we need scarcely emphasize again that a logically possible state of a world is not another world.

Now, all this jargon of worlds and families may strike the reader as an unusually complicated way of making points which might better have been left in the idiom of the distinction between the vacuous and essential occurrence of predicates in arguments warranted, respectively, by formal and material rules of inference. Let me emphasize once more that I am not disputing this. The fact remains, however, that the 'ontological' jargon of worlds and possibilities has long been used by philosophers and logicians in their attempts to understand the structure of conceptual systems. Indeed, it is by no means entirely foreign to common usage; it was not constructed out of whole cloth by minute philosophers. Most of the puzzles which are the inherited stock-in-trade of contemporary philosophy either belong in this frame, or else concern the very status of the frame itself. Even should this 'ontological' frame be but the shadow of rules of language, it by no means follows that there is no point in the effort to develop it more consistently and systematically than has been done in the past. Puzzles and antinomies within the frame (though not perplexities concerning the frame itself) *can* be resolved within the frame, even though the resulting clarification is but the shadow of an insight into linguistic usage which *might* have been obtained directly. The problems with which I am concerned in this chapter, problems relating to universals, classes and particulars, and their mutual connections, are part and parcel of this 'ontological' frame, and this is where I am proposing to resolve them,[1] leaving to others or to another day the attempt to translate the fruits into insights concerning linguistic usage. However, it would be disappointing, would it not, to discover that this translation was really the same thing all over again?

Revenons à nos moutons! The problem which led us to elaborate this framework of worlds and possibilities concerned the relation of *qualia* to the classes of their instances. We were on the point of asserting their identity when it occurred to us that it makes sense to say that the world might have contained no instances of two *qualia* F and G, even though in point of fact it does do so. F and G, then,

[1] For a resolution within this frame of the problem of negative facts, see the dialogue contained in my paper 'On the Logic of Complex Particulars', *Mind* (1949).

particulars, Russell is correct in claiming that it is not a truth of logic that the number of basic particulars in *this* world is infinite. He is wrong, however, in assuming that logic is concerned with *this* world to the exclusion of other (possible) worlds.

would both determine the null class of basic particulars. They could not, we concluded, be identical with the classes of their instances, for then they would be identical, whereas *ex hypothesi* they are distinct. Notice, however, that in the framework we have since developed, we no longer speak in terms of *the* world (that is, the world which includes *this*), but rather in terms of a set of worlds subdivided into families. Consequently, instead of speaking of the instances of F in *the* world, we must distinguish between the instances of F in a given world, and the instances of F in the totality of worlds with which the *quale* F is associated. While the classes of instances of F in some worlds of the family are null classes, this cannot be true of the classes of instances of F in all worlds of the family. For this would amount to saying that F was a *quale* which *could not have instances*, an obvious piece of logical nonsense. The way is therefore open to an identification of *qualia*, not with the classes of their instances in *a* world, let alone *the* world, but with the classes of their instances in *all* worlds of the family with which each is associated. Thus, Greemness would be identical with the class of all grums in the family of worlds with which is associated the battery of simple universals one of which is Greemness. The identity of *qualia* with these classes of their instances provides a basis for the analysis of the relations of universals and classes at the level of complex particulars. For every statement about the properties of complex particulars or the classes to which they belong, is, in principle, translatable into sentences mentioning only basic particulars and the *qualia* and simple relations they exemplify.[1] Indeed, it provides the basis for a completely extensional formulation of logical and semantical concepts. But that is a story for another occasion.

[1] See footnote p. 290 above.

IO

IS THERE A SYNTHETIC
A PRIORI?

1. *Introduction.* A survey of the literature on the problem of the synthetic *a priori* soon reveals that the term 'analytic' is used in a narrower and a broader sense. In the narrower sense, a proposition is analytic if it is either a *truth of logic* or is *logically true.* By saying of a proposition that it is logically true, I mean, roughly, and with an eye on the problem of the relation of logical categories to natural languages, that when defined terms are replaced by their definientia, it becomes a substitution instance of a truth of logic. And a truth of logic can be adequately characterized for present purposes as a proposition which occurs in the body of *Principia Mathematica,* or which would properly occur in a *vermehrte und verbesserte Auflage* of this already monumental work. If we now agree to extend the convenient phrase 'logically true' to cover truths of logic as well as propositions which are logically true in the sense just defined, we can say that an analytic proposition in the narrower sense is a proposition which is logically true.

On the other hand, we find many philosophers using the term 'analytic' in the sense of *true by virtue of the meanings of the terms involved.* These philosophers seem, for the most part, to be under the impression that this sense of 'analytic' coincides with that defined above. And if 'p is logically true' did entail and were entailed by 'p is true by virtue of its terms', little damage would result from this ambiguity. Unfortunately, this is not the case, as will be argued in a later section of this chapter. Indeed, the more interesting examples given by these philosophers of propositions which are analytic in their sense turn out on examination *not* to be logically true. From which it follows that unless they are mistaken in applying their own criteria, 'analytic' in their sense cannot be logically equivalent to 'analytic' in the sense defined above. That *true by virtue of the mean-*
298

ings of the terms involved is indeed a broader sense of 'analytic' than *logically true*—broader in that it has a greater denotation—will be a central theme of this chapter.

To avoid possible misunderstanding, let me make it clear that I shall use the term 'analytic' only in the first or narrower of the two senses distinguished above, and that where I want to refer to the views of philosophers who use the term in the broader sense, I shall make the appropriate translation of 'analytic' into 'true by virtue of the meanings involved'. Accordingly, 'synthetic' will be used to mean *neither logically true nor logically false*, and the question under discussion becomes: Are there propositions which are *a priori* yet not logically true?

To answer this question even provisionally, we must decide on a meaning for '*a priori*'. Here the going is more difficult, and we shall have to be content with a rather schematic discussion. By and large philosophers have given (or have believed themselves to give) four different but closely related senses to this phrase. In the first place we have Kant's joint criteria of universality and necessity. The propositions traditionally characterized as *a priori*, with the possible exception of the proposition 'God exists' (in the context of the ontological argument) have been universal propositions—*a priori* knowledge about individuals presupposing a minor premise of subsumption. Now when he explicates the criterion of universality, Kant makes it clear that it is intended to exclude such universal judgements as are true merely as a matter of fact, so that universality merges with the criterion of necessity. If our knowledge that all A is B is to be *a priori*, it must be correct to say 'All A *must* be B'.

But while we should all agree that a person cannot properly be said to know *a priori* that all A *is* B unless he can also be said to know that all A is *necessarily* B—so that knowing that all A is necessarily B is a *necessary condition* of knowing *a priori* that all A is B—it does not, at least at first sight, seem to be a sufficient condition. There is no immediate appearance of contradiction in the statement, 'It is highly probable that all A is necessarily B', so that there would seem to be no absurdity in speaking of knowing *a posteriori* that all A *must* be B, though just what account might be given of such knowledge is another, and extremely perplexing, matter to which we shall return at the conclusion of our argument.

This brings us to the second of the four interpretations of apriority. According to this approach, we have *a priori* knowledge that all A is B, when we *know for certain* that all A is B. If we ask what is meant by 'knowing for certain', we are told that this is not a mere matter of feeling confident that all A is B. It must be *reasonable* to assert 'All A is B' where this reasonableness is not grounded on knowledge that on such and such evidence *e* is probable that all A is B, nor on an argument of which one of the premises is of this form. Furthermore, not only must it be reasonable to assert 'All A is B' but it must in some sense be asserted *because* it is reasonable. In traditional terminology, *knowing for certain* is contrasted with both *probable opinion* and *taking for granted.*

This second approach leads smoothly and easily into the third and fourth explications of apriority. The third arises by scarcely more than a minor reformulation of what we have just said. For to say that the reasonableness of asserting 'All A is B' does not rest on knowledge of the form 'It is probable on *e* that all X is Y' is but a pedantic way of saying that the reasonableness of asserting 'All A is B' does not rest on, or is independent of, experience. And according to the third approach, our knowledge that all A is B is *a priori*, if it is *independent of experience.*

But if the reasonableness of asserting 'All A is B' does not rest on experience, on what does it rest? The answer to this question brings us to the fourth approach. This reasonableness, we are told, rests solely on a correct understanding of the meanings of the terms involved. In short, *a priori* truth is truth *ex vi terminorum.*

Now, in sketching these familiar explications of *a priori* knowledge —namely as knowledge of the necessary, as certain knowledge of universal truths, as knowledge independent of experience, and as knowledge *ex vi terminorum*—I have made it clear that to my way of thinking there is a general confluence of these four criteria, such that each, on reflection, leads to the others. Much more would have to be done before we could claim to have disentangled the various meanings which have traditionally been given to the term '*a priori*', and we shall have to return to this topic before this chapter is complete. But schematic though the above discussion may be, it provides a useful background for a provisional choice of a sense of this term for the interpretation of the question: Is there a synthetic *a priori*? Accordingly, I shall select the fourth of the above criteria as the defining property of the *a priori*. Our question thus becomes, 'Are there any universal propositions which, though they are not logically true, are true by virtue of the meanings of their terms?'

2. *A Divergent Usage; C. I. Lewis.* It will prove useful to contrast our provisional explication of the original question with what one gets if one adopts the conventions implicit in C. I. Lewis's use of the terms 'synthetic' and '*a priori*'. Since he appears to use 'analytic' as we are using '*a priori*' and '*a priori*' to mean *holding of all possible objects of experience*, in his hands the question 'Is there a synthetic *a priori*?' becomes 'Are there any universal propositions which, though they are not true by virtue of the meaning of their terms, hold

of all possible objects of experience?' To *this* question Lewis answers 'no'. That he is correct in doing so becomes clear once it is realized that Lewis picks his meanings for *both* 'analytic' and '*a priori*' from our list of four traditional criteria of *a priori* knowledge. In other words, if we are justified in speaking of a confluence of these criteria, and given Lewis's interpretation of the terms 'synthetic' and '*a priori*', he is on solid ground in claiming that it is *logically impossible* that there be any propositions which are both synthetic and *a priori*.

On the other hand, it can be argued that to *our* question Lewis gives an affirmative answer, since he can be shown to accept as analytic in his sense (true *ex vi terminorum*) certain propositions which do not seem to be logically true. I am not convinced, however, that Lewis intends to adopt this position.

3. *Linguistic Rules and Ordinary Usage.* I shall open the next stage of my argument by pointing out that the phrase 'true by virtue of the meaning of its terms' can reasonably be said to have the same sense as 'true by definition'.[1] This brings us face to face with a sticky issue. Human knowledge is presumably the sort of thing that finds its fitting expression in the *ordinary usage* of expressions in *natural languages*. Have we not therefore reached a point at which the horsehair couch is a more appropriate instrument of philosophical clarification than the neat dichotomies and tidy rule-books of the professional logicians? I do not think so. Not, however, because I frown on philosophical therapeutics (on the contrary!), but because it seems to me that the successes achieved in recent decades by putting ordinary language on the couch were made possible by the brilliant use of tools developed in *Principia Mathematica*; and I believe that recent logical theory has developed new tools which have not yet been put to adequate use in the exploration of philosophical perplexities.

Now I submit that the logician's concepts of *formation rule, transformation rule*, and *rule permitting the substitution of one expression for another*, have legitimate application to natural languages. By this I mean not that it is possible for the logician to construct such rules for natural languages, but rather that rules of these types are embedded in natural languages themselves without any help from the logician. That the vague, fluctuating, and ambiguous character of ordinary usage extends to these rules is, indeed, granted. But does not the same hold true with respect to the logician's concept of a sentence? Or of a predicate? Yet we do not hesitate to discuss natural languages in these terms. I see no reason in the Heracleitean character

---

[1] 'Definition' is here used in a deliberately broad sense so that later it can be construed to cover both 'explicit' and 'implicit' definition. It is, I take it, clear that not all analytic truths are true by explicit definition. It should be equally clear that not all statements which are true by implicit definition are synthetic.

of ordinary usage to reject what would seem to be the obvious implication of the fact that natural languages can be illuminated by confronting them with artificial languages obeying explicitly formulated rules of transformation and synonymity.

Indeed, can we make sense of critical appraisals of linguistic phenomena as *correct* or *incorrect* by persons uncorrupted by scrutiny of esoteric rule-books, without supposing that linguistic rules are embedded in ordinary usage? And the fact that rustics playing a game handed down for generations without benefit of Hoyle would be hard put to it to formulate a set of rules for the game, is surely not incompatible with the idea that when they play the game they do what they do *because of* the very rules they would find it so difficult to formulate! One wonders when philosophers will finally abandon the fiction that rules exist only in public utterance of phonemes or displays of printers' ink.

It is also worth noting that partisans of ordinary usage do not always make clear just what they intend as the opposite of ordinary usage. Sometimes it seems to be extra-ordinary usage; at other times the fictitious or imaginary usage of artificial languages invented by professors of logic. Extra-ordinary usage is, after all, actual usage, and is, presumably, in most respects, the same sort of thing as ordinary usage. And if it should be the usage of highly articulate and intelligent people, we might well expect to find it clarifying. On the other hand, it *is* reasonable to doubt the philosophical value of utterances made by fictitious users of unused calculi. Ordinary usage in the sense of *actual* usage contains the language of science. Even the logician cannot talk about artificial languages without actually using language, and if he can not only criticize his own usage, but formulate the very rules he has violated, we have an example of syntactical rules in *actual*, and therefore, in an important sense, *ordinary* usage.

4. *Explicit and Implicit Definition.* The purpose of the preceding section has been to restore some semblance of plausibility to the notion that the concepts *analytic* and *true by definition* can usefully be applied to natural languages. If we have succeeded, we have shown that in the sense in which ordinary usage contains predicates, it may also be said to contain propositions which are analytic and true *ex vi terminorum*, and which can therefore be said to formulate analytic *a priori* knowledge. But a synthetic *a priori* proposition, on our account, is one that is both synthetic and true *ex vi terminorum*. Can there be such a thing?

Now it is at once clear that the 'definition', if such it can be called, by virtue of which a synthetic *a priori* proposition would be true *ex vi terminorum* cannot be *explicit* definition; for the *a priori* truth to which these give rise is analytic. If anything that has been called

302

definition can serve this purpose, it is what, following Schlick, we shall call *implicit* definition—to an examination of which we now turn.

In rough-and-ready terms, a number of predicates without explicit definition are said to be implicitly defined if they appear in a set of logically synthetic general propositions which are specified as axioms or primitive sentences by the rules of the language to which they belong. To say that these propositions are axioms or primitive sentences is to say that they are specified to be *unconditionally assertable* by syntactical rules of the language. This account is deliberately skeletal, and is intended to gain flesh from the argument which follows shortly.

If we use the familiar illustration of a geometry, the following points may be noted: (1) Neither the axioms nor the theorems are logically analytic, though the implicative proposition whose antecedent is the conjunction of the axioms, and whose consequent is one of the theorems *is* logically analytic. (2) If the geometry should be of the Euclidean type, then the theorem 'The area of a triangle is $\frac{1}{2}$bh', which is logically synthetic, must not be confused with the proposition 'The area of a *Euclidean* triangle is $\frac{1}{2}$bh', which is indeed an analytic proposition, but one which presupposes both the theorem, and an explicit definition of 'Euclidean triangle' in terms which specify that an object does not belong to this category unless the axioms and therefore all their logical consequences hold of it.[1] Similarly, the axiom 'A straight line is the shortest distance between two points', which is logically synthetic, must not be confused with 'A *Euclidean* straight line is the shortest distance between two points', which, though analytic, depends on an explicit definition of 'Euclidean straight line'.

(3) The non-logical terms of an uninterpreted calculus should not be interpreted as variables. The interpretation of such a calculus by establishing translation rules correlating its non-logical terms with expressions in actual use must not be confused with the assigning of values to variables. (4) The postulates of a Euclidean geometry do not constitute an implicit definition of its non-logical terms unless they are specified as unconditionally assertable (and hence as more than generalized material implications, equivalences, etc.) by the syntactical rules of the calculus. (5) A deductive system can gain application

---

[1] Unless I am much mistaken, C. I. Lewis thinks of his 'categorial principles' as unquestionably analytic, because he thinks of them as analogous to 'The area of a *Euclidean* triangle is $\frac{1}{2}$ bh.' Now, if he intends this analogy, then his categorial principles are indeed logically true. But then, if the above discussion is sound, must there not be a corresponding set of propositions which are *not* logically true, and which contain a set of predicates which are not explicitly defined in terms of these propositions? predicates which correspond to 'triangle' as occurring in Euclidean axioms, rather than to 'Euclidean triangle'?

either by (*a*) translating its non-logical terms into express.ons in actual use, or (*b*) by building it on to language in actual use by establishing rules of inference to take one from sentences in the calculus to sentences in actual use (and vice versa); or by a combination of (*a*) and (*b*).

The most useful way of developing this skeletal account of implicit definition is to confront it with some frequently raised objections. Perhaps the most common complaint is that a set of terms may be 'implicitly defined' in the above manner and yet have no 'real' or extra-linguistic meaning.[1] 'Implicit definition', it is pointed out, is a purely syntactical affair, and to expect it to give rise to extra-linguistic meaning is as sensible as expecting a number of people to lift each other by their boot-straps.

That this objection calls attention to an essential feature of meaningful language, a feature which is not accounted for by implicit definition conceived as above, is doubtlessly true. But its force as an argument against the definitional character of implicit definition is somewhat less keenly felt when one realizes that when explicit definition is conceived in purely syntactical terms, exactly the same objection can be raised against it. Both explicit and implicit definition are matters of syntax. The difference is that whereas in the case of explicit definition the definiendum and the definientia are distinct, and the 'giving extra-linguistic meanings'—however this is done—to the definientia fixes the extra-linguistic meaning of the definiendum; in the case of implicit definition the extra-linguistic meaning must be 'given' to all the predicates 'simultaneously', as they are all both definienda and definientia rolled into one.

A second objection points out that a set of predicates may be implicitly defined in terms of one another, and yet admit a multiplicity of real meanings. But, as before, the same is true of an explicitly defined term and its definientia. To the set consisting of 'man', 'rational', and 'animal' could belong either the real meanings *man*, *rational*, and *animal*, or the real meanings *brother*, *male*, and *sibling*. It may be granted that to the extent that the definientia themselves are explicitly defined in terms of other predicates, and the definientia of these in turn, and so on, the alternative real meanings capable of belonging to the terms in the chain are increasingly

---

[1] Let me make it clear from the beginning that my willingness to use the phrase 'real or extra-linguistic meaning' in building up the dialectical structure of my argument does not reflect an acceptance on my part of a Platonic or Meinongian metaphysics of meaning. My purpose in this paper is to explore the controversy over the synthetic *a priori* sympathetically and from within, in the conviction that the truth of the matter lies separated from itself in the opposing camps. Some light will be thrown on the status of 'real meanings' by the discussion of ' "..." means - - -' in section 8 below.

restricted. But it is by no means obvious that the terms in however long a definition chain could not possess any one of a number of sets of real meanings. In any event, to the fact that the syntactical structure of a chain of explicit definitions limits the number of alternative real meanings which can be possessed by the predicates in the chain, corresponds the fact that the number of possible 'interpretations' of a set of implicitly defined terms can frequently be narrowed by adding a new axiom to the original set. In neither case would the utility of the definition seem to depend on its admitting only one set of real meanings. The purposes of unambiguous communication require only that where one and the same abstract syntactical structure is associated with two different sets of extra-linguistic meanings, this structure be embodied in two sets of visually and audibly different symbols—one for each 'interpretation'.

But the above is but prelude to the most searching of the objections to the notion of implicit definition. The objection is based on broad philosophical considerations, and takes us to the heart of our problem. Its point of departure is the above familiar distinction between the 'linguistic meanings' of an implicitly defined set of predicates, and the 'real meanings', the properties and relations, which are correlated with these predicates. As its first step it reminds us that what the implicit definition does is specify that certain sentences containing these predicates are unconditionally assertable. In other words, that we are authorized by the rules of the language to assert these sentences without either deriving them from other sentences, or establishing probability relations between them and observation sentences. But, the objection continues, even though the implicit definition may permit us unconditionally to assert certain sentences involving the predicates 'A', 'B', 'C', etc., the *truth* of what we assert depends solely on the relation of the *real* meanings of these predicates to the world. Thus, even should there be a syntactical rule (implicit definition) authorizing us to assert 'All A is B' unconditionally (and therefore to derive 'x is B' from 'x is A') might there not be an object which conforms to the real meaning of 'A' without conforming to the real meaning of 'B'? If this were the case, then as far as its real meaning was concerned, 'All A is B' would be false, even though the rules of the language blandly authorized us to assert it. There would be a tension between what was authorized by the *linguistic* meanings of 'A' and 'B', and what was appropriate to their *real* meanings. On the other hand, the objection continues, no such contretemps can arise in the case of explicit definition, for it is not logically possible that something conforms to the real meaning of 'C' and yet not to the real meaning of 'D' where 'C' is explicitly defined in terms of 'D'.

To this the objection adds that even though *as a matter of fact* all items which conform to the real meaning of 'A' did conform to the real meaning of 'B', we could nevertheless *conceive* of objects conforming to the real meaning of 'A' but not to that of 'B'. If, therefore, we were to adopt a syntactical rule authorizing us to derive 'x is B' from 'x is A', we should be tailoring the verbal clothing of our thought to be shorter than its reach.

The objector grants that it might, in some circumstances, be sensible or convenient to adopt a language in which 'x is B' is syntactically derivable from 'x is A', even though something might *conceivably* exemplify the real meaning of 'A' without exemplifying the real meaning of 'B', provided that one were extremely confident on inductive grounds in the truth of the generalization, 'If anything exemplifies the real meaning of "A" then it exemplifies the real meaning of "B".' But, he continues, it just would not do to say that 'All A is B' is true by virtue of the meaning of its terms. Implicit definition, he concludes, is a pale imitation of explicit definition, for it lacks the power to yield statements which are true by definition.

5. *Implicit Definition; A Traditional Defence.* Now the above is only one prong of the attack on implicit definition. But before we develop the other prong, we must take into account the classic counter to this first offensive. For the defenders are ready with an equally venerable reply.

It will have been noticed that lurking in the premises of the above critique was the idea that even should it be true that everything which exemplified the real meaning of 'A' also exemplified the real meaning of 'B', it would be so *as a matter of fact*. So that it would be *conceivable* that something might conform to that of 'A' without conforming to that of 'B'. If pressed, the critics would give the following reason for this supposition. After all, they would say, since the statement 'All A is B' is admittedly *synthetic*, it must be *logically possible* and hence *possible* and hence *conceivable* that something might exemplify the real meaning of 'A' without exemplifying that of 'B'.

It is here that the defence, clothed in the dignity of *philosophia perennis*, quietly adds that for 'All A is B' to be synthetic yet true *ex vi terminorum*, it is not sufficient that 'x is B' be syntactically derivable from 'x is A'; there must also be an *extra-linguistic* or *real connection* between the real meaning of 'A' and the real meaning of 'B'. In other words, given real meanings for 'A', 'B', 'C', etc., an implicit definition of these predicates in terms of one another will be adequate only if to the syntactical derivations authorized by the definition, there correspond *synthetic necessary connections* between the properties which are the real meanings of these predicates. Indeed, the defence continues, it will be appropriate to give an implicit definition of these terms only to the extent that one *apprehends* these necessary connec-

306

tions. For only to this extent could we exclude, merely on the basis of what we mean by, say 'A' and 'B', the possibility that something might conform to the real meaning of 'A' but not to that of 'B'.

6. *Implicit Definition: The Attack Continued.* The opposition to implicit definition now develops the second prong of its offensive, focusing attention on the notion of real or synthetic necessary connection. It reveals itself to be an 'empiricist' opposition, claiming that this notion is incompatible with the most elementary principles of the empiricist tradition.

Historically, the characteristic doctrines of empiricism have been grounded in a theory, or better a type of theory, of concept formation. Theories of this type form a spectrum which at one end touches and is easily confused with a radically different approach (to be developed at the close of our argument) which can also with some justice claim the title 'empiricism', though it is committed to few if any of the dogmas associated with this term. Let us begin by reflecting on the consequences for our problem of a characteristic (if somewhat over-simplified) formulation of what we shall call *concept-empiricism*. It goes as follows: Concepts of qualities and relations are formed from particulars. We can, indeed, have concepts of qualities and relations of which we have encountered no instances; but only if these concepts 'consist' of concepts which have been formed from instances.

Now, from this theory, together with certain appropriate assumptions concerning the composition of concepts, it follows that we can have no concepts of universals which are not satisfied by particulars. 'Satisfied by particulars' here means 'would be satisfied by particulars if satisfied at all'. In this sense the property Centaur is satisfied by particulars, even though it actually has no instances.

The implication of concept empiricism with respect to the concept of real connection is immediate and murderous. There is no such concept. Yet here we must be careful. It is sometimes thought that when Hume and his followers are criticizing rationalistic discourse about necessary connections, their application of concept empiricism consists in pointing out that *they* find no instances of necessary connection among sensibly experienced particulars, and predict that we shall find none. If this were the heart of the matter, the obvious comeback would be, 'You are either looking in the wrong place, or are necessary-connection-blind.' The truth, of course, is that if there is such a thing as necessary connection, it is a relation satisfied by *universals* (a relation whose terms are universals), and *not* by particulars. Thus, for the concept empiricist, our failure to have such a concept is not a mere matter of failing to find any particulars which exemplify it; we could not find particulars which exemplify it.

It should be noted that unqualified concept empiricism equally entails that we have no concept of *logical* necessity, not to mention conjunction, disjunction, negation, and class-membership, though concept empiricists have not been quite as assiduous in pointing this out as they have been in scoffing at real connection. And even should the concept empiricist seek to define logical necessity in psychological terms, or, perhaps, give an emotivist analysis of such terms as 'necessary' and 'must', denying them cognitive meaning, he can scarcely treat such useful terms as 'and', 'or', 'not', and 'is a member of' in either of these ways. Sooner or later he is led to distinguish between two types of cognitively meaningful expression: (1) those which stand for concepts, e.g. 'red', and 'centaur', and (2) those which, while they do not stand for concepts, have a legitimate (and indeed indispensable) syntactical function in language.

But more of this later. For the moment it is sufficient to note that whatever else he may be committed to, the concept empiricist can have no truck with a relation of real connection between extra-linguistic or real meanings. As a result, if he has any use at all for the phrase 'implicit definition', it can mean nothing more to him than the building of empirical generalizations of which we are highly confident into the very syntactical structure of our language. The concept empiricist is thus in a position to return to the first prong of the attack on the notion of implicit definition by insisting once again, this time on explicit empiricist grounds, that even should an 'implicit definition' authorize us to derive 'x is B' from 'x is A' at the linguistic level, it nevertheless cannot prevent us from conceiving of something which exemplifies the real meaning of 'A' without exemplifying that of 'B'.

7. *Concept Empiricism: The Conservative Approach.* The moral of the argument to date is that only if concept empiricism is rejected is it possible to hold that there are non-logically true propositions which are true *ex vi terminorum.*

There are many to whom this would be the end of the matter, as they find some version of concept empiricism to be beyond dispute. Indeed, there was a time, not too long ago, when I myself was a convinced concept empiricist—though I was not as aware of its implications and presuppositions as I should have been. For a number of years, however, I have been a renegade, and in the following pages I shall indicate some of the considerations which led me to abandon concept empiricism, as well as the resulting changes in my interpretation of the synthetic *a priori.*

In the preceding section it sufficed for our purposes to introduce concept empircism by means of a studiously vague formulation. We must now call attention to the fact that the phrase denotes two radically different lines of thought which agree, however, in concluding that the basic concepts in terms of which all genuine concepts are defined are concepts of qualities and relations exemplified by particulars in what is called 'the given' or 'immediate experience'.

In its more traditional and conservative form, concept empiricism distinguishes sharply between the intellectual awareness of qualities and relations, and the formulation of this awareness by the use of symbols. In short, it accepts without question a venerable but, at present, unfashionable distinction between thought and its expression in language (or, as it is sometimes put, between 'real thinking' and 'symbolic thinking'). Thus the concept empiricist of this brand conceives of such symbols as 'red' and 'between' as acquiring meaning by virtue of becoming associated with such abstract entities as redness and between-ness, the association being mediated by our awareness of these entities. His attention is thus focused on the question, 'How, and in what circumstances, do we become aware of abstract entities?'

Now it is characteristic of the concept empiricist to be convinced that an essential role in the process whereby we come to be aware of universals is played by particulars which exemplify these universals. In its more coherent form, the primary ground of this conviction seems to have been a metaphysical conviction to the effect that abstract entities exist only *in rebus*, that is, in particulars, so that only through particulars could mind enter into relations with them. This was usually coupled with the claim that our ability to be aware of even the most complex and recondite universal can be explained on the hypothesis that in the last analysis all awareness of universals is derived from the awareness of instances, together with a more or less crude attempt to fill in the psychological details.

In its classical form, concept empiricism can be dramatized as follows: A mind is about to learn the meaning of the word 'red'. The abstract entity in question is lurking in the manifold of sense. But so are many others. This one stands out clearly. Here! and here! No, that can't be it! Aha! a splendid specimen. By the methods of Mill! That must be what Mother calls 'red'!

No one, of course, would recognize a theory of his own in such an absurd picture. Empiricism is notoriously a tough-minded theory, whereas the above is soft-headed. Nevertheless, it is my conviction that although most philosophers who call themselves empiricists would reject it out of hand, they fail to appreciate the extent to which it is part and parcel of the empiricist inheritance, as well as the extent to which some of the most characteristic dogmas of empiricism are expressions of the hold it still has on the empiricist imagination.

This is not the occasion for a detailed discussion of this first main

309

type of concept empiricism. Our present concern is rather with its underlying presupposition of a distinction between the pure awareness of an abstract entity on the one hand, and the linguistic or, in general, symbolic expression of this pure awareness on the other. That I regard this distinction as a mistake will scarcely cause surprise. The proposal to abandon it has lost its revolutionary ring. Once a radical innovation, the notion that thought is a 'symbolic process' has become a commonplace, almost a truism. Unfortunately, as is the case with many contentions that have become truisms, its implications are no longer as passionately scrutinized as they were when it was new, and it is often combined with modes of theorizing with which it is radically incompatible. In view of the widespread acceptance of the thesis in question, there is little need to construct one more argument in its defence. Instead, I shall concern myself with certain of its implications which bear on the synthetic *a priori*.

Let us assume, then, that the situation which obtains when it is true to say that Jones is aware of a quality or relation or possibility or, even, a particular, can (in principle) be exhaustively described in terms of and dispositions relating to the use of linguistic symbols[1] (predicates, sentences, names, descriptions). Indeed, since the tidy, socially stabilized structures we call languages are continuous with more rudimentary conceptual mechanisms, let us assume that the above Jonesean situations can (in principle) be exhaustively described in terms of habits and dispositions relating to the use of symbols. Now, this assumption has an obvious implication of great importance for our problem. If what occurs when we are 'aware of a universal' is the use of a symbol, it follows that learning to use a symbol cannot be based on the awareness of universals. In other words, we are committed to the abandonment of what has happily been called the metaphor of the mental eye, which is so deeply rooted in the grand tradition of Western philosophy (and is one of the major points on which East Meets West) that its influence crops up where least expected.

If we put this implication in a slightly different way, we immediately establish contact with a characteristic contention of Professor Lewis. All classification of objects, however confident and preemptory, is a venture, a venture which at no point finds its justification in a pre-symbolic vision of generic and specific hearts on the sleeves of the objects of experience. Classification resembles the grasping tentacles of an octopus, now tentative, now confident, rather than a salesman's selection of a suit for a customer after a glance at

[1] It should not be assumed that in calling an event a *symbol* we are describing the event. We are rather serving notice that our discussion of the event will be in semantical terms.

310

his build. I am afraid, however, that our agreement with Lewis is more shadow than substance. For while he writes in this manner of the interpretation of the given by means of concepts whose implications transcend the given, he also holds that the sensible appearances of things *do* wear their hearts on their sleeves, and that we do have a cognitive vision of these hearts which is direct, unlearned, and incapable of error—though we may make a slip in the expressive language by which these insights are properly formulated. In other words, the assumption to which we are committed requires to extend to all classificatory consciousness whatever, the striking language in which Lewis describes our consciousness of objects.

8. *Concept Empiricism, Syntactics, Semantics, and Pragmatics.* We distinguished above between two radically different lines of thought which lead to the conclusions characteristic of concept empiricism. Of these we have taken a brief look at the first or mental eye variant. Before turning to the second, let me point out that although for analytical purposes we are drawing a sharp distinction between these two approaches, historically they have usually been blended into one confused argument.

The concept empiricism we are now defining arose *pari passu* with the development of association theories of learning in psychology, and has felt as much at home in more recent behaviouristic formulations as in the earlier (mentalistic) varieties of this psychological movement. In its traditional form, this second approach, although it agrees verbally with the more conservative form of concept empiricism that such words as 'red' acquire meaning by becoming associated with universals (though it tends to stress classes rather than qualities and relations), insists that this association develops by the joint occurrence in the mind of instances of the word and of the characteristic in question, in this case redness, unmediated by awareness of abstract entities. In other words, while it is redness that is associated with 'red', the mechanism whereby this association is created does not involve awareness of redness, but only the joint occurrence in experience of instances of redness with tokens of 'red'. In this respect it differs radically from the first approach, for which the formation of the association involves awareness of the universal. In short, the concept empiricism which develops in this context, if it does not entirely escape from the metaphor of the mental eye, at least does not include abstract entities within its visual field.

Now, if we do not limit ourselves to the account thus crudely sketched, but embrace in our view the more sophisticated theories of this general type, there is clearly *something* to them. A philosopher who rejects the mental eye approach and all its implications is indeed committed to the view that it is by the causal interplay of the individual and his physical and social environment, without benefit of a prehension of eternal objects, whether *in re* or *extra rem*, that concepts, meaningful symbols, arise. However, while there is indeed *something* to theories of the above type, they are guilty of a radical confusion, and are in large part responsible for the more implausible features of contemporary empiricism.

Our first comment on the theory sketched above is a restatement and pressing of a point made earlier in this paper. It is simply that unqualified concept empiricism is patently incapable of accounting for many of our most familiar concepts, among others those of logic and mathematics. To remedy this defect, the theory is usually modified by introducing a radical dualism into its account of concepts and concept formation. The theory now recognizes a second mode of concept formation, namely the learning to use symbols in accordance with rules of logical syntax. The concepts of logic and mathematics are held to be symbols which gain meaning in this second way, rather than by association with empirical phenomena.

It is even more important to note than even those terms, such as 'red', which are supposed by the theory to gain meaning by association, share in the second mode of concept formation, for only by being used in accordance with rules of logical syntax can they perform the functions by virtue of which a concept is a concept.

Clearly, then, the learning to use symbols in accordance with rules is a pervasive feature of concept formation. Up until now the rules we have considered in this chapter have been *syntactical* rules, rules according to which assertable expressions are put together, and properly derived from one another. However, some proponents of the second approach to concept empiricism have been so impressed with the philosophical power of the concept of rule, that they have applied it to the association of a term with an extra-linguistic class of objects, which association, as we have seen, is the core of their theory. Thus we find them characterizing the learning to use a language or system of concepts as the learning to use symbols in accordance with two types of rule: (*a*) rules of syntax, relating symbols to other symbols; (*b*) semantical rules, whereby basic factual terms acquire extra-linguistic meaning. It takes but a moment, however, to show that this widespread manner of speaking involves a radical mistake. A rule is always a rule for *doing* something in some circumstance. Obeying a rule entails recognizing that a circumstance is one to which the rule applies. If there *were* such a thing as a semantical rule by the adoption of which a descriptive term acquires meaning, it would presumably be of the form 'Red objects are to be designated by the word "red".' But to recognize the circumstances in which this rule has application, one must already have the concept of red! Those who speak in this sense[1] of semantical rules, therefore, are committed to the view that an awareness of abstract entities is a precondition of learning the intelligent use of symbols.

Now, once the concept empiricist acknowledges the force of these considerations, he is committed to a revision of his theory which, in effect, changes its whole spirit and orientation, and, indeed, deprives it of many of the philosophical implications which are so dear to traditional empiricism. But before developing this point let us briefly review the fundamentals of concept formation as they appear in this new perspective. The learning of a language or conceptual frame involves the following logically (but by no means chronologically) distinguishable phases:[2] (1) The acquisition of habits pertaining to the arranging of sounds and visible marks into patterns and sequences of patterns. The acquisition of these habits can be compared to the setting up that part of the wiring of a calculating machine which takes over once the 'problem' has been 'punched in'.[3] (2) The acquisition of thing–word connections. This can be compared to the setting up of that part of the wiring of a calculating machine which permits the 'punching in of information'. These connections are a matter of being *conditioned* to respond to kinds of situation with kinds of verbal pattern, e.g. to respond to the presentation of a green object with 'This is green'; it is *not* a matter of 'learning to say ". . ." when one observes that the situation is thus and so'. Observing that the situation is thus-and-so already involves the use of a conceptual frame.[4]

---

[1] I hasten to add that I am aiming this criticism at those uses of the phrase 'semantical rule' only which evoke this phrase, as above, to explain the acquisition of extra-linguistic meaning by linguistic expression. [Semantical rules as rules of *translation* into expression in our language which already have a use are not open to this criticism.]

[2] I leave out of account, as a topic too large to be introduced into this discussion, though of equal importance for the understanding of the nature of conceptual systems, the prescriptive or conduct guiding aspect of language. This topic will be discussed in Chapter 11.

[3] Note that while the activation of these habits results in verbal behaviour which *conforms to* syntactical rules, it cannot be the *obeying* of syntactical rules unless the subject has learned the prescriptive syntactical metalanguage which permits the formulation of these rules. For an elaboration of this point, see Chapter 11.

[4] Just as an intra-linguistic move is not in the full sense an *inference* unless the subject not only conforms to, but obeys, syntactical rules (though he may conceive them to be rules justifying the transition not from one *linguistic expression* to another, but from one *thought* to another); so a language entry transition is not in the full sense an *observation* unless the subject not only (in normal circumstances) tokens 'This object is green' if and only if a green object is present to his senses, but is able to infer (in a pragmatic metalanguage) from 'The thought *this object is green* occurred to Jones at time t in place s in circumstances c' to 'a green object was present to Jones's senses at t in s'.

Let us refer to these two dimensions of (descriptive) concept formation as the learning of *intra-linguistic moves* and *language entry transitions*.[1] Now, it might be thought that while a descriptive word like 'red' would not be a *word* unless it played the syntactical role of a predicate in intra-linguistic moves, its possession of empirical meaning, indeed the fact that it is the word it is, is constituted by its role as a conditioned response to red things. And, indeed, there is a certain plausibility to the idea that to say of the German word '*rot*', for example, that it means *red*, is to say that this vocable is associated (by Germans) with red things. Certainly, if they did not (tend to) respond to red things with '*rot*', it could not be true that this German word means *red*. But, as we shall see, to grant the latter point is by no means to concede the former.

Sentences of the form '"*Rot*" means *red*' have had no less a hypnotic and disastrous effect on empiricists engaged in formulating theories of concept formation, than on the most naïve mental oculists. Such sentences, which appear to present meaning as a tête-à-tête relation between a word and a universal, have been misinterpreted as entailing what might well be called a 'matrimonial' theory of the meaning of primitive or undefined descriptive predicates according to which the fact that these terms have meaning is constituted by the fact that they are associated with (married to) classes of objects. Yet that these sentences *entail* no such consequences becomes obvious once we reflect that it is just as legitimate and, indeed, true to say 'The German word "*und*" means *and*' as it is to say 'The German word "*rot*" means *red*'; where it is clear that '*und*' gains its meaning not by a process of association with Conjunction or a class of conjoined objects, but rather by coming to be used with other symbols in accordance with familiar syntactical rules.

Let us examine the force of the form '" . . ." means —'. Suppose Smith says, 'When Schmidt says "*und*" it means *and*.' This statement clearly conveys the information that Schmidt has habits with respect to '*und*' which parallel his own (Smith's) with respect to '*and*'. Yet it must not be assumed that if it is the business of a statement to convey information of a certain kind, this information must be asserted by the statement *in the sense that a definitional unpacking of the statement would reveal it*. 'Jones *ought to* do A' conveys the information that Jones *can* do A; yet it is a mistake to suppose that a definitional unpacking of the former would reveal a sentence asserting the latter. Thus, Smith is not mentioning his habits, or the habits of English-speaking people generally, with respect to 'and'. He mentions the

[1] That the acquisition of a conceptual frame also involves *language departure transitions*, and that this notion is the key to the status of prescriptive discourse is argued in Chapter 11.

German vocable '*und*' but *uses* the English vocable 'and'. He uses the latter, however, in a peculiar way, a way which is characteristic of *semantical* discourse. He presents us with an instance of the word itself, not a name of it, and, making use of the fact that we belong to the same language community, indicates to us that we have only to rehearse our use of 'and' to appreciate the role of 'und' on the other side of the Rhine.[1]

Now suppose Smith to say, 'When Schmidt says "*rot*" it means *red*.' Once again this statement conveys the information, i.e. in *some* sense implies, that Schmidt has habits with respect to a German word which parallel his own (Smith's) with respect to an English word. But whereas if one supposes that Smith's statement *mentions* habits, the fact that it mentions '*rot*' but uses 'red' is naturally taken to imply that the habits in question are of the word–thing variety, we now see that the statement has no such implication. Smith's statement conveys the information that Schmidt has word–thing habits with respect to '*rot*' only in the course of conveying the *global* information that in *all* relevant respects Schmidt's habits with respect to '*rot*' parallel his own (Smith's) with respect to 'red'.

Thus, instead of leading us to adopt a matrimonial theory of 'the meaning relation between "*rot*" and *red*', the explication of '"*rot*" means *red*' makes it clear that this sentence is not a relation-sentence at all, or, at least, that it is a relation-sentence only in a purely grammatical sense of this term. For its business is not to describe '*rot*' and *red* as standing in a relation, but rather to convey the information characterized above.[2]

---

[1] Descriptive discourse, prescriptive discourse, and semantical discourse are three different modes of speech. Nevertheless, by virtue of what is presupposed by their correct utterance, statements in one of these modes may convey information properly formulated in another mode.

[2] The fact that such a statement as ' "*rot*" means *red*' conveys descriptive information about '*rot*' but does not describe it, undercuts the traditional problem of universals (and abstract entities generally). If one misunderstands the function of such statements, and supposes that ' "*rot*" means *red*' describes '*rot*' as standing in a relation to *red*, then, if one is anti-Platonist, one will be reluctant to use the semantical mode of speech, and will be particularly unwilling to allow an inference from ' "*rot*" means *red*' to 'There is a quality which "*rot*" means'. Statements of the latter kind appear to make bold assertion of the *factual existence* of abstract entities which are suspected to infect the former. The truth of the matter is that the 'There is a quality (relation, possibility, particular . . .) . . .' of the latter is a purely logical device which has no connection with 'factual existence'. To say 'There is an obligation more stringent than promise keeping' is not to attribute 'factual existence' to obligations! For an elaboration of this and related points, see my essay 'Empiricism and Abstract Entities' in *The Philosophy of Rudolf Carnap*, edited by P. A. Schilpp, Library of Living Philosophers, Open Court Publishing Co., Wilmette, Illinois, 1963.

Now, the moral of all this is that we need no longer be hypnotized by the facile contrast between the 'linguistic meaning' and the 'real meaning' of a word. For to say that *'rot'* has real meaning, and, indeed, the real meaning *red*, is merely to convey the information that *'rot'* is the subject (beyond the Rhine) of a full-blooded set of habits sufficient to constitute it a word in actual use, and, indeed, a use which parallels our own use of 'red'. Consequently, to come to the point, if our use of 'red' involves extra-logical syntactical rules ('P-rules') as well as 'L-rules', it follows that *'rot'* could not have the 'real meaning' it does unless it, too, were subject to 'P-rules' and, indeed, 'P-rules' which parallel those obeyed by 'red'.

I shall suppose, then, that the conceptual status of descriptive predicates can correctly be attributed to the fact that they are governed by rules of usage. These rules of usage include extra-logical rules (about which we shall say more in a moment) as well as logical rules in the narrow sense (Carnap's L-rules). Those descriptive predicates which are conditioned responses to situations of the kind they are correctly said to mean, are called *observation predicates*. If a language did not contain observation predicates it would not be *applied*. Descriptive predicates other than observation predicates gain application through rules tying them to observation predicates. However, only if one supposes that for an undefined descriptive predicate to have descriptive meaning is for it to be associated with an extra-linguistic class of objects, is one forced to hold that all primitive descriptive predicates are observation predicates. One can, indeed, say that all the other descriptive predicates of a language must be 'defined' in terms of observation predicates; but it would be a mistake to suppose that in every case these definitions will be *explicit* definitions.

9. *Conceptual Status and Implicit Definition.* The above dialectical examination of concept empiricism has been so designed as to bring me to the position I wish to defend, a position which, as I see it, represents a meeting of extremes, a synthesis of insights belonging to the two major traditions of Western philosophy, 'Rationalism' and 'Empiricism'. Stated summarily, it claims that conceptual status, the conceptual status of descriptive as well as logical—not to mention prescriptive—predicates, is constituted, *completely* constituted, by syntactical rules. Notice that I am *not* saying that '"*rot*" means *red*' is true merely by virtue of the intra-linguistic moves proper to *'rot'* (in German). For '"*rot*" means *red*' can be true only if in addition to conforming to syntactical rules paralleling the syntax of 'red', it is *applied* by Germans to red objects; that is, if it has the same *application* as 'red'. Thus, the 'conceptual status' of a predicate does not exhaust its 'meaning'. The rules on which I wish to focus attention

are rules of inference.[1] Of these there are two kinds, *logical* and *extra-logical* (or 'material'). I can best indicate the difference between them by saying that a logical rule of inference is one which authorizes a logically valid argument, that is to say, an argument in which the set of descriptive terms involved occurs vacuously (to use Quine's happy phrase); in other words, can be replaced by any other set of descriptive terms of appropriate type to obtain another valid argument. On the other hand, descriptive terms occur essentially in valid arguments authorized by extra-logical rules.

Let me now put my thesis by saying that the conceptual meaning of a descriptive term is constituted by what can be inferred from it in accordance with the logical and extra-logical rules of inference of the language (conceptual frame) to which it belongs. (A technically more adequate formulation would put this in terms of the inferences that can be drawn from sentences in which the term appears.)

Finally, let me make the same claim in still another way by pointing out that where 'x is B' can be validly inferred from 'x is A', the proposition 'All A is B' is unconditionally assertable on the basis of the rules of the language. Our thesis, then, implies that every primitive descriptive predicate occurs in one or more logically synthetic propositions which are unconditionally assertable—in short, true *ex vi terminorum*; or, as it was put at the end of the preceding section, true by implicit definition. But a logically synthetic proposition which is true *ex vi terminorum* is, by the conventions adopted at the opening of the chapter, a synthetic *a priori* proposition.[2]

10. *The Synthetic* a priori: *A Terminological Decision.* If I had the courage of my definitions, then, it seems that I should proclaim myself a proponent of the synthetic *a priori*. Yet I feel uncomfortable. Is the synthetic *a priori* described above a *real* synthetic *a priori*? Would those who have fought and suffered for the cause of the synthetic *a priori* (and one has only to speak to a 'believer' to realize that it *is* a cause) welcome me to their ranks? I am afraid that the answer is No; that they would spurn my support and say that if this is all the synthetic *a priori* amounts to, it is not worth the name, and is probably a peculiar kind of *a posteriori*.

It does not take long to discover the reasons for their discontent, and the results throw new light on a venerable controversy. At the

---

[1] A more detailed statement and defence of my thesis will be found in 'Inference and Meaning', *Mind*, 1953.

[2] Note that, strictly speaking, one can only say that a sentence of L is true *ex vi terminorum*, as one can only say that a sentence of L is true *simpliciter*, if one's own language contains a translation of these sentences, which will not be the case if expressions occurring in these sentences conform to different P-rules from those obeyed by their closest counterparts in one's own language.

beginning of the chapter we considered four traditional criteria of *a priori* knowledge: (1) It is knowledge of *necessary* truth; (2) It is *certain* knowledge; (3) It is knowledge *independent of experience*; (4) It is knowledge of truth *ex vi terminorum*. We found it plausible to say that ultimately these four criteria coincide—after which we moved into the detail of our argument. I want now to bring out a certain ambiguity in the second and third of these criteria, and by so doing make clear that whether or not the position I have sketched is committed to a synthetic *a priori* is a matter for terminological decision.

Consider, to begin with, the third criterion, namely, *independent of experience*. Let us suppose that in our language 'All A is B' is one of the propositions which implicitly define the predicates 'A' and 'B' so that it is true *ex vi terminorum* that all A's are B. Using, as we do, this language or conceptual structure, we know that all A's *must* be B, that something which is not B cannot be A. This knowledge is independent of experience in the perfectly straightforward sense that it is a function of the very concepts with which we approach the world. As long as we continue to use these words in the same sense, continue, that is, to use the same concepts, we can never find an instance of A which fails to be B.

But though in this sense our knowledge that all A's are B is independent of experience, there is another sense in which it most certainly does depend on experience. After all, the learning of a conceptual frame, the learning to use symbols in accordance with certain logical and extra-logical rules is a psychological process essential elements of which are sensory stimuli, together with the rewards and punishments which the environment (including the social environment) brings to our motivations. The conceptual frame we have developed is only one of a vast number of alternative frames any one of which we might have been brought to adopt by a more or less radical shift in the course of our environment. The claim that our conceptual frame is only one among many possible conceptual frames, and that our adoption of it is to be explained in terms of learning theory rather than of insight into abstract entities, is what led our true blue proponent of the synthetic *a priori* to say that our synthetic *a priori* is a peculiar kind of *a posteriori*.

Next, a closely related remark on the second criterion, namely *certainty*. Let us suppose that a person has acquired a firmly embedded conceptual frame. In employing this frame, he will distinguish between those propositions which are *certain* and those which are *at best merely probable* on the evidence. The former will coincide with propositions which, in his frame, are true *ex vi terminorum*. Notice, however, that when the learning process begins to bring about a modification of his conceptual frame, he will admit to being 'uncertain' of even those propositions which, in that frame, are true *ex vi terminorum*. It is clear from this description that *we are dealing with two different senses of the contrast between certainty and uncertainty*. The first may be called the 'intra-conceptual', the second the 'extra-conceptual' sense. Thus, it makes good sense to say, 'I am uncertain about its being certain that all A's are B.' Uncertainty in this *second* sense is not something that can be remedied by 'paying closer attention to what we mean'. It can be overcome (should this be desirable) only by more firmly learning to apply the conceptual system in question to experience, without hesitation or uneasiness.

But is this the goal of wisdom? Not if we are correct in maintaining that to all conceptual structures there are alternatives; and that no conceptual frame carries the imprint 'sterling' certifying it to be *the* conceptual frame to which all others, to the extent that they are 'coherent', approximate. The essence of scientific wisdom consists in being uncertain$_2$ about what is certain$_1$, in a readiness to move from one conceptual frame to another.[1] For not only can we be *caused* to modify out linguistic frame, we can deliberately modify it—teach ourselves new habits—and give reasons for doing so. Now, the use of a conceptual frame is the awareness of a system of logical and extra-logical necessities. The essence of scientific wisdom, therefore, lies in being tentative about what one takes to be extra-logically necessary.

In conclusion, if one means by synthetic *a priori* knowledge, knowledge which is logically synthetic, yet true *ex vi terminorum*, then, indeed, there is synthetic *a priori* knowledge. If one means by it, synthetic knowledge to which there is no significant alternative, then synthetic *a priori* knowledge is a myth, a snare, and a delusion. The question 'Is there a synthetic *a priori*?' calls, therefore, for a decision, before it calls for an answer. What the decision should be, that is, which meaning (if any) should be attached to the term '*a priori*', it is by no means easy to say. Many factors are involved, by no means the least of which is a sense of belonging to one or other of the two major traditions of Western philosophy. If one's overall loyalty is to Sextus and to Hume, one will be moved to say 'There is no synthetic *a priori*' and, hence, to choose a sense of '*a priori*' which will make this statement true. If one's heart beats with the rationalists, one will long to say 'There is a synthetic *a priori*', and will make the

---

[1] For an account in the spirit of the above argument of the causal modalities and the nature and rationality of induction, see my essay on 'Counterfactuals, Dispositions and the Causal Modalities' in Volume II of *Minnesota Studies in the Philosophy of Science*, edited by Herbert Feigl and Michael Scriven, Minneapolis, 1957.

corresponding terminological decision. If one is tired of philosophical shibboleths, and finds important insights on both sides of the fence, one will content oneself with pointing out that while every conceptual frame involves propositions which, though synthetic, are true *ex vi terminorum*, every conceptual frame is also but one among many which compete for adoption in the market-place of experience.

II

SOME REFLECTIONS ON LANGUAGE GAMES

INTRODUCTORY

1. It seems plausible to say that a language is a system of expressions, the use of which is subject to certain rules. It would seem, thus, that learning to use a language is learning to obey the rules for the use of its expressions. However, taken as it stands, this thesis is subject to an obvious and devastating refutation. After formulating this refutation, I shall turn to the constructive task of attempting to restate the thesis in a way which avoids it. In doing so, I shall draw certain distinctions the theoretical elaboration of which will, I believe, yield new insight into the psychology of language and of what might be called 'norm conforming behaviour' generally. This chapter contains an initial attempt along these lines.

2. The refutation runs as follows:

Thesis. Learning to use a language (L) is learning to obey the rules of L.

But, a rule which enjoins the doing of an action (A) is a sentence in a language which contains an expression for A.

Hence, a rule which enjoins the using of a linguistic expression (E) is a sentence in a language which contains an expression for E—in other words, a sentence in a *meta*language.

Consequently, learning to obey the rules for L presupposes the ability to use the metalanguage (ML) in which the rules for L are formulated.

So that learning to use a language (L) presupposes having learned to use a metalanguage (ML). And by the same token, having learned to use ML presupposes having learned to use a *meta*-metalanguage (MML) and so on.

But this is impossible (a vicious regress).

Therefore, the thesis is absurd and must be rejected.

321

3. Now, at first sight there is a simple and straightforward way of preserving the essential claim of the thesis while freeing it from the refutation. It consists in substituting the phrase 'learning to *conform to* the rules . . .' for 'learning to obey the rules . . .' where 'conforming to a rule enjoining the doing of A in circumstances C' is to be equated simply with 'doing A when the circumstances are C'—regardless of how one comes to do it. (It is granted that 'conforming to' is often used in the sense of 'obeying' so that this distinction involves an element of stipulation.) A person who has the habit of doing A in C would then be conforming to the above rule even though the idea that he was to do A in C had never occurred to him, and even though he had no language for referring to either A or C.

4. The approach we are considering, after proposing the above definition of 'conforming to a rule', argues that whereas *obeying* rules involves using the language in which the rules are formulated, *conforming* to rules does not, so that whereas the thesis put in terms of *obeying* rules leads to a vicious regress, it ceases to do so once the above substitution is made. Learning to use a language (L) no longer entails having learned to use the metalanguage (ML) nor does learning ML entail having learned MML, and so on. Of course, once one has learned ML one may come to *obey* the rules for L to which one hitherto merely conformed, and similarly in the case of the rules for ML, and so on.

5. After all, it could be argued, there are many modes of human activity for which there are rules (let us stretch the word 'game' to cover them all) and yet in which people participate (play) without being able to formulate the rules to which they conform in so doing. Should we not conclude that playing these games is a matter of *doing A when the circumstances are C, doing A' when the circumstances are C'*, etc., and that the ability to formulate and obey the rules, although it may be a necessary condition of playing 'in a critical and self-conscious manner', cannot be essential to playing *tout court*. It would be granted, of course, that the formulation and promulgation of rules for a game are often indispensable factors in bringing it about that the game is played. What is denied is that playing a game *logically* involves obedience to the rules of the game, and hence the ability to use the language (play the language game) in which the rules are formulated. For it was this idea which led to the refutation of an otherwise convincing thesis with respect to the learning to use a language. One can suppose that the existence of canasta players can be traced to the fact that certain people formulated and promulgated the rules of this game. But one cannot suppose that the existence of language speakers can be traced to the fact that certain *Urmenschen* formulated and promulgated the rules of a language game.

6. What are we to make of this line of thought? The temptation is to say that while the proposed revision of the original thesis does, indeed, avoid the refutation, it does so at too great a cost. Is conforming to rules, in the sense defined, an adequate account of playing a game? Surely the rules of a game are not so 'externally related' to the game that it is logically possible to play the game without 'having the rules in mind'! Or, again, surely one is not making a move in a game (however uncritically and unselfconsciously) unless one is making it *as a move in the game*. And does this not involve that the game be somehow 'present to mind' in each move? And what is the game but the rules? So must not the rules be present to mind when we play the game? These questions are both searching and inevitable, and yet an affirmative answer would seem to put us back where we started.

7. It may prove helpful, in our extremity, to note what Metaphysicus has to say. As a matter of fact, he promises a way out of our difficulty which combines the claim that one is not playing a game —even a language game—unless his is *obeying* (not just *conforming to*) its rules, with the claim that one may obey a rule without being able to use the language—play the language game—in which its rules are formulated. To do this he distinguishes between the verbal formulation of a rule and the rule itself as the *meaning* of the verbal formula. He compares the relation of rules to rule sentences with that of propositions to factual sentences. Whether as Platonist he gives rules an 'objective' status, or as Conceptualist he makes their *esse* dependent on *concipi*, he argues that they are entities of which the mind can take account before it is able to give them a verbal clothing. Thus, Metaphysicus distinguishes between the rule sentences, 'Faites A en C!' 'Tu A in C!' (and 'Do A in C!'), and the common rule to which they give expression, *Do A in C!* (Strictly speaking, as we shall see, rules as indicative 'ought' sentences are to be distinguished from the imperatives—even the universal imperatives—the issuance of which would be justified with reference to them.) He continues by proposing to represent these rules by the form 'D (doing A in C)' where this indicates that the doing of A in C has the 'demanded' character which makes it a rule to do A in C.

8. Having developed this account of rules, Metaphysicus proceeds to argue that to learn a game is to become aware of a structure of *demands* (which may or may not have found expression in a language) and to become able to realize these demands and motivated to do so. With respect to the latter point, he argues that to play a game is to be moved to do what one does, at least in part, *to satisfy these demands*. A person whose motivation in 'playing a game' is merely to realize some purpose external to the game (as when one 'plays golf' with the company president) would correctly be said to be merely going

through the motions! Thus as Metaphysicus sees it, to learn to play a game involves:

(*a*) becoming aware of a set of demands and permissions, D (A in C), P (A′ in C′), etc.,

(*b*) acquiring the ability to do A in C, A′ in C′, etc.,

(*c*) becoming intrinsically motivated to do them *as demanded* (for the reason that they are demanded) by the rules of the game.

9. Without pausing to follow Metaphysicus in his elaboration of this scheme, let us turn directly to its application to the problem at hand. To learn to use a language—play a language game—is, on this account, to become aware of a set of demands concerning the manipulation of symbols, to acquire the ability to perform these manipulations, and to become motivated to do them as being demanded. Since, Metaphysicus insists, the awareness of these demands does not presuppose the use of verbal formulae, one can learn to obey the set of demands for a language L without having had to learn the metalanguage (ML) in which these demands would properly be formulated. Thus, he concludes, our problem has been solved.

10. Unfortunately, a closer examination of this 'solution' reveals it to be a sham. More precisely, it turns out, on analysis, to be in all respects identical with the original thesis, and to be subject to the same refutation. The issue turns on what is to be understood by the term 'awareness' in the phrase 'becoming *aware* of a set of demands and permissions'. It is clear that if Metaphysicus is to succeed, becoming aware of something cannot be to make a move in a game, for then learning a game would involve playing a game, and we are off on our regress. Yet when we reflect on the notion of being aware of propositions, properties, relations, demands, etc., it strikes us at once that these awarenesses are exactly *positions* in the 'game' of *reasoning*. It may be an over-simplification to identify reasoning, thinking, being aware of possibilities, connections, etc., with playing a *language* game (e.g. French, German), but that it is playing a game is indicated by the use of such terms as 'correct', 'mistake', etc., in commenting on them.

PATTERN GOVERNED AND RULE OBEYING BEHAVIOUR

11. But while the attempt of Metaphysicus to solve our problem has proved to be a blind alley, it nevertheless points the way to a solution. To appreciate this it is necessary only to ask 'What was it about the proposal of Metaphysicus which seemed to promise a solution?' and to answer in a way which separates the wheat from the chaff. Surely

the answer is that Metaphysicus sought to offer us an account in which learning a game involves learning to do what one does *because doing these things is making moves in the game* (let us abbreviate this to 'because of the moves [of the game]') where doing what one does *because of the moves* need not involve using language about the moves. Where he went astray was in holding that while doing what one does because of the moves need not involve using language about the moves it does involve *being aware* of the moves demanded and permitted by the game, for it was this which led to the regress.

12. But how could one come to make a series of moves *because* of the system of moves demanded and permitted by the rules of a game, unless by virtue of the fact that one made one's moves *in the light of* these demands and permissions, reasoned one's moves in terms of their place in the game as a whole? Is there then no way of denying that one is playing a game if one is merely conforming to its rules, of insisting that playing a game involves doing what one does because doing it is making a move in the game, which does not lead to paradox? Fortunately, no sooner is the matter thus bluntly put, than we begin to see what is wrong. For it becomes clear that we have tacitly accepted a dichotomy between

(*a*) *merely conforming to rules;* doing A in C, A' in C', etc., where these doings 'just happen' to contribute to the realization of a complex pattern;

(*b*) *obeying rules;* doing A in C, A' in C', etc., with the intention of fulfilling the demands of an envisaged system of rules.

But surely this is a false dichotomy! For it required us to suppose that the only way in which a complex system of activity can be involved in the explanation of the occurrence of a particular act, is by the agent envisaging the system and intending its realization. This is as much as to say that unless the agent conceives of the system, the conformity of his behaviour to the system must be 'accidental'. Of course, in *one* sense of the term it *would* be accidental, for on one usage 'accidental' *means* unintended. But in another sense 'accidental' is the opposite of 'necessary', and there can surely be an unintended relation of an act to a system of acts, which is nevertheless a necessary relation—a relation of such a kind that it is appropriate to say that the act occurred because of the place of that kind of act in the system.

13. Let me use a familiar analogy to make my point. In interpreting the phenomena of evolution, it is quite proper to say that the sequence of species living in the various environments on the earth's surface took the form it did because this sequence maintained and improved a biological *rapport* between species and environment. It

is quite clear, however, that saying this does not commit us to the idea that some mind or other envisaged this biological *rapport* and intended its realization. It is equally clear that to deny that the steps in the process were intended to maintain and improve a biological *rapport* is not to commit oneself to the rejection of the idea that these steps occurred because of the system of biological relations which they made possible. It would be improper to say that the steps 'just happened' to fit into a broad scheme of continuous adaptation to the environment. Given the occurrence of mutations and the facts of heredity, we can translate the statement that evolutionary phenomena occur because of the biological *rapport* they make possible—a statement which appears to attribute a causal force to an abstraction, and consequently tempts us to introduce a mind or minds to envisage the abstraction and be the vehicle of its causality—into a statement concerning the consequences to particular organisms and hence to their hereditary lines, of standing or not standing in relations of these kinds to their environments.

14. Let me give another example somewhat more closely related to our problem. What would it mean to say of a bee returning from a clover field that its turnings and wigglings occur *because* they are part of a complex dance? Would this commit us to the idea that the bee *envisages* the dance and acts as it does by virtue of intending to realize the dance? If we reject this idea, must we refuse to say that the dance pattern as a whole is involved in the occurrence of each wiggle and turn? Clearly not. It is open to us to give an evolutionary account of the phenomena of the dance, and hence to interpret the statement that *this* wiggle occurred because of the complex dance to which it belongs—which appears, as before, to attribute causal force to an abstraction, and hence tempts us to draw upon the mentalistic language of intention and purpose—in terms of the survival value to groups of bees of these forms of behaviour. In this interpretation, the dance pattern comes in not as an abstraction, but as exemplified by the behaviour of particular bees.

15. Roughly, the interpretation would contain such sentences as the following:

(*a*) The pattern (dance) is first exemplified by particular bees in a way which is *not* appropriately described by saying that the successive acts by which the pattern is realized occur *because of the pattern*.

(*b*) Having a 'wiring diagram' which expresses itself in this pattern has survival value.

(*c*) Through the mechanisms of heredity and natural selection it comes about that all bees have this 'wiring diagram'.

It is by a mention of these items that we would justify saying of the contemporary population of bees that each step in their dance behaviour occurs because of its role in the dance as a whole.

16. Now, the phenomena of learning present interesting analogies to the evolution of species. (Indeed, it might be interesting to use evolutionary theory as a *model*, by regarding a single organism as a series of organisms of shorter temporal span, each inheriting disposition to behave from its predecessor, with new behavioural tendencies playing the role of mutations, and the 'law of effect' the role of natural selection.) For our purposes it is sufficient to note that when the learning to use a language is viewed against the above background, we readily see the general lines of an account which permits us to say that learning to use a language is coming to do A in C, A' in C', etc., *because* of a system of 'moves' to which these acts belong, while yet denying that learning to use a language is coming to do A in C, A' in C', etc., *with the intention of realizing* a system of moves. In short, what we need is a distinction between 'pattern governed' and 'rule obeying' behaviour, the latter being a more complex phenomenon which involves, but is not to be identified with, the former. Rule obeying behaviour contains, in some sense, both a game and a metagame, the latter being the game in which belong the rules obeyed in playing the former game as a piece of rule obeying behaviour.

17. To learn pattern governed behaviour is to become conditioned to arrange perceptible elements into patterns and to form these, in turn, into more complex patterns and sequences of patterns. Presumably, such learning is capable of explanation in S-R-reinforcement terms, the organism coming to respond to patterns as wholes through being (among other things) rewarded when it completes gappy instances of these patterns. Pattern governed behaviour of the kind we should call 'linguistic' involves 'positions' and 'moves' of the sort that *would be* specified by 'formation' and 'transformation' rules in its metagame if it *were* rule obeying behaviour. Thus, learning to 'infer', where this is purely a pattern governed phenomenon, would be a matter of learning to respond to a pattern of one kind by forming another pattern related to it in one of the characteristic ways specified (at the level of the rule obeying use of language) by a 'transformation rule'—that is, a formally stated rule of inference.

POSITIONS AND MOVES: ENTRY AND DEPARTURE TRANSITIONS

18. It is not my aim, even if I were able, to present a detailed psychological account of how an organism might come to learn pattern

governed behaviour. I shall have achieved my present purpose if I have made plausible the idea that an organism might come to play a language game—that is, to move from position to position in a system of moves and positions, and to do it 'because of the system' without having to *obey rules*, and hence without having to be playing a *meta*language game (*and a meta-meta*language game, and so on).

19. I pointed out above that the moves in a language game as pattern governed behaviour are exactly the moves which, if the game were played in a rule obeying manner, would be made in the course of obeying formation and transformation rules formulated in a metalanguage game. If we now go on to ask 'under what circumstances does an organism which has learned a language game come to behave in a way which constitutes *being at a position* in the game?' the answer is clearly that there are *at least* two such circumstances. In the first place, one can obviously be at a position by virtue of having *moved* there from another position (inference). Yet not all cases of being at a position can arise out of moving there from a prior position. A glance at chess will be instructive. Here we notice that the game involves an *initial* position, a position which one can be at without having moved to it. Shall we say that language games involve such positions? Indeed, it occurs to us, are not 'observation sentences' exactly such positions? Surely they are positions in the language game which one occupies without having moved there from other positions *in the language*.

20. No sooner have we said this, however, than we note a significant difference between the observation sentences of a language and the initial position of chess. It does not belong to chess to specify the circumstances in which the initial position is to be 'set up'. On the other hand, it does seem to belong to English that one set up the position 'This is red' when one has a certain visual sensation (given that one believes that he is looking at the object in standard conditions, and is asking after its colour). In short, the transition from the sensation to being at the position 'This is red' seems to be a *part* of English in a sense in which *no* transition to the initial position of chess belongs to chess. For that matter, as we shall see, the transition from being at the position 'I shall do A' or 'I ought to do A' to my doing A (given that certain other conditions obtain which I shall not attempt to specify), seems to be a part of English in a sense in which *no* transition from the final or 'checkmate' position belongs to chess.

21. Reflection on these facts might tempt us to say that the transition from having a certain visual sensation to occupying the position 'This is red' is a *move* in English. Yet, no sooner do we try this than we see that it won't do. For while the transition docs indeed belong

to English, it would be a mistake to classify it with *moves in English* (and hence to classify the sensation itself as a *position in English*), without explicitly recognizing the significant respects in which they differ from the moves and position we have been considering under these names. To occupy a position in a language is to think, judge, assert *that so-and-so*; to make a move in a language is to infer *from so-and-so, that so-and-so*. And although sensations do have status in the English language game, their role in bringing about the occupation of an observation sentence position is not that of a thought serving as a premise in an inference.

22. Let us distinguish, therefore, between two kinds of learned transition which have status in a language game: (1) moves, (2) transitions involving a situation which is not a position in the game and a situation which is a position in the game. Moves are transitions (S-R connections) in which both the stimulus (S) and the response (R) are positions in the game functioning as such. Let us represent them by the schema '(S-R)^g'. The second category subdivides into two subcategories: (2.1) *language entry transitions*, as we shall call those learned transitions (S-R connections) in which one comes to occupy a position in the game (R is a position in the game functioning as such), but the *terminus a quo* of the transition is not (S is not a position in the game functioning as such). Let us represent these by the schema 'S-(R)^g'. The language entry transitions we have particularly in mind (observation sentences) are those which satisfy the additional requirement that S would be said to be 'meant by' R.

Example: When Jacques's retina is stimulated by light coming from an orange pencil, he says 'Ce crayon est orange'—from which he may *move* to 'Ce crayon a une couleur entre rouge et jaune'.

23. Turning now to the second subcategory (2.2), we shall call *language departure transitions* these learned transitions (S-R connections) in which from occupying a position in the game (S is a position in the game functioning as such) we come to behave in a way which is not a position in the game (R is not a position in the game functioning as such). Let us represent these by the schema '(S)^g-R'. The language departure transitions we have particularly in mind are those which involve the additional requirement that R would be said to be 'meant by' S.

Example: When Jacques says to himself 'Je dois lever la main' he raises his hand.

24. Notice that an item of kind K may function in one kind of context as a position in a game, and in another kind of context it may not. Thus, in the usual context the noise *red* may be responded to as the word 'red', but a singing instructor may respond to the same noise as a badly produced note. It may indeed function for him as

a language entry stimulus taking him to the position 'This is a flat note'. Thus we have

$$(\text{in } C_1) \ (K\text{-}R)^g$$
$$(\text{in } C_2) \ K\text{-}(R)^g$$

AUXILIARY POSITIONS: FORMAL AND MATERIAL PRINCIPLES OF INFERENCE

25. In 19 it was claimed that there are at least two ways of properly coming to be at a position in a language game. Two ways were thereupon discussed which can be indicated by the words 'observation' and 'inference'. There is, however, a third way of properly coming to be at a position. Here one comes to be at certain positions without having moved to them from other positions (in which position it resembles observation), and without having made a language entry transition (in which respect it resembles inference). The positions in question are 'free' positions which can properly be occupied at any time if there is any point to doing so. Obviously what I have in mind are the sentences the status of which, when used in a rule obeying manner, is specified as that of 'primitive sentence' (i.e. as unconditionally assertable) by a rule of the metalanguage. (Thus, 'All A is B' might be specified as a primitive sentence of language game L.) Are such sentences properly called *positions*? Their 'free' status and their 'catalytic' function make them a class apart, yet it is less misleading to call them positions than it would be to call sensations positions. Let us call them 'auxiliary positions'.

26. We now notice that a language game which contains the auxiliary position 'All A is B' make possible the syllogistic from 'This is A and All A is B' to 'It is B'. An alternative way of going from 'This is A' to 'It is B' would exist if the game included a direct move from positions of the form '. . . is A' to positions of the form '. . . is B'. We thus notice a certain equivalence between *auxiliary positions* and *moves*. We also notice that while it is conceivable that a language game might dispense with auxiliary positions altogether, though at the expense of multiplying moves, it is not conceivable that moves be completely dispensed with in favour of auxiliary positions. A game without moves is *Hamlet* without the Prince of Denmark indeed!

27. Now, if a language game contains the auxiliary position 'All A is B' we can imagine that the fact that this sentence is an auxiliary position might come to be signallized. Such a signal might be the pattern 'necessarily'; thus 'All A is (necessarily) B'. And we can imagine that the same signal might come to be used where a *sentence* corresponds to a *move* as 'All C is D' corresponds to the move from positions of the form '. . . is C' to positions of the form '. . . is D'.

Indeed, it is sufficient for my present purposes to suggest that these signals might develop into the pieces, positions, and moves characteristic of modal discourse, so that, in spite of the interesting relations which exist in sophisticated discourse between modal talk 'in the object language' and rule talk 'in the metalanguage', modal talk might well exist at the level of pattern governed (as contrasted with rule obeying) linguistic behaviour. Nevertheless, as we shall see, the full flavour of actual modal discourse involves the way in which sentences in the first-level language game containing modal words parallel sentences containing rule words ('may', 'ought', 'permitted', etc.) in the syntactical metalanguage. This parallelism is quite intelligible once one notes that the moves which are signallized in the object language by sentences containing modal words are *enjoined* (*permitted*, etc.) by sentences containing rule words in the syntactical metalanguage.

28. Now the moves (inferences) and the auxiliary positions (primitive sentences) of a language can be classified under two headings. They are either *analytic* or *synthetic*, or, as I prefer, in view of the ambiguity of these terms in contemporary philosophical discussion, either *formal* or *material*. This distinction is that which appears at the level of logical criticism as that between arguments and primitive sentences whose validity does not depend on the particular predicates they contain (thus, perhaps, 'This is red, therefore it is not non-red' and 'All men are men') on the one hand, and arguments and primitive sentences the validity of which does so depend (thus, perhaps, 'Here is smoke, therefore here is fire' and 'All colours are extended') on the other.

29. Now to say that it is a law of nature that all A is B is, in effect, to say that we may infer 'x is B' from 'x is A' (a *materially* valid inference which is not to be confused with the formally valid inference from 'All A is B *and* x is A' to 'x is B'). To this, however, we must at once add a most important qualification. Obviously, if I learn that in a certain language I may make a material move from 'x is C' to 'x is D', I do not properly conclude that all C is D. Clearly, the language in question must be the language I myself use, in order for me to assert 'All C is D'. But with this qualification we may say that it is by virtue of its *material* moves (or, which comes to the same thing, its *material* auxiliary positions) that a language embodies a consciousness of the lawfulness of things.[1]

---

[1] For a further discussion of the concept of a law of nature, with particular attention to the 'problem of induction', i.e. the problem of justifying the adoption of a material move or material auxiliary position into our language, see below, sections 75 ff.

SEMANTICAL RULES AND THE 'MEANING RELATION'

30. It is high time we paused to pay our respects to a question the raising of which even the most friendly of readers has undoubtedly felt to be long overdue. It is all very well, the question has it, to speak of a language as a game with pieces, positions, and moves; this is doubtless both true and fruitful as far as it goes. But must we not at some stage recognize that the 'positions' in a language *have meaning*, and differ in this key respect from positions we actually *call* games in a non-metaphorical sense? Was it not claimed (in 22) that to say of a position of the form 'Das ist rot' in the German language that it is an observation position is to say that a language entry transition has been made to it from a situation of the kind *meant by* 'rot'? Must we not admit, then, that in describing a language game, we must not only mention its elements, positions, and moves, but must also mention *what its expressions mean*?

31. It is, of course, quite correct to say of the German expression 'Es regnet' that it *means* it is raining. And it is quite true that in saying this of 'Es regnet', one is not saying that the pattern 'Es regnet' plays a certain role in the pattern governed behaviour to be found behind the Rhine. But it would be a mistake to infer from these facts that the semantical statement ' "es regnet" means *it is raining*' gives information about the German use of 'Es regnet' which would *supplement* a description of the role it plays in the German language game, making a *complete* description of what could otherwise be a partial account of the properties and relations of 'Es regnet' as a meaningful German word. To say that ' "*rot*" means *red*' is not to describe 'rot' as standing 'in the meaning relation' to an entity *red*; it is to use a recognized device (the semantical language game) for bringing home to a *user* of 'red' how Germans use 'rot'. It conveys no information which could not be formulated in terms of the pieces, positions, moves, and transitions (entry and departure) of the German language game.[1]

32. The fundamental danger of the form ' "..." means —' is that the unwary tend to conclude that the meaningfulness of the German word '*rot*' is a matter of a relation (mediated by the habits of German-speaking persons) between the vocable '*rot*' and *redness* or *the class of red things*. This picture, which was criticized in Chapter 10, seems to support a fundamental contention of classical empiricism; namely that 'simple concepts' are logically independent, or, to put the matter

---

[1] For an interpretation of mentalistic discourse based on these considerations pertaining to 'meaning', see my paper, 'A Semantical Solution of the Mind–Body Problem', *Methodos*, 1953.

in our frame of reference, that *material* moves or *material* auxiliary positions are dispensable features of a language or conceptual system. Thus, it is thought, the factual meaning of *'rot'* is a matter of its relation to redness or red things, and not at all a matter of material moves connecting it with other predicates in the language, though, of course, it must participate in *formal* moves to be a linguistic expression at all.

33. Many philosophers characterize the acquiring of a language or system of concepts as the learning to use symbols in accordance with two types of rule: (*a*) rules of syntax, relating symbols to other symbols; (*b*) semantical rules, whereby basic factual terms acquire 'extra-linguistic meaning'. And, at first sight, there might seem to be a close similarity between this account and the one we have been giving. For, as we have presented it, the learning of a language or conceptual frame involves the following logically (but not chronologically) distinguishable phases:

(*a*) the acquisition of S-R connections pertaining to the arranging of sounds and visual marks into patterns and sequences of patterns. (The acquisition of these 'habits' can be compared to the setting up of that part of the wiring of a calculating machine which takes over once the 'problem' and the relevant 'information' have been punched in.)

(*b*) The acquisition of thing–word connections. (This can be compared to the setting up of that part of the wiring of the machine which enables the punching in of 'information'.)

But, it will be remembered, we have emphasized that the latter connections are a matter of being *conditioned* to respond to kinds of situation with kinds of verbal pattern—e.g. to respond to the presentation of a green object (in standard conditions) with 'This is green' —and that it is *not* a matter of 'learning to say ". . ." *when one observes that* the situation is *thus and so*'. Observing that the situation is *thus and so* already involves the use of a conceptual frame.

34. Now it is obvious that acquiring the concept of red cannot be equated with coming to *obey* a semantical rule. To put the same point in more elementary terms, the application of the concept *red* to an object in the process of *observing* that something is red, cannot be construed as *obeying* a semantical rule, for a rule is always a rule for doing something in some circumstances, and *obeying* a rule presupposes the recognition that the circumstances are of a kind to which the rule applies. If there were a semantical rule by learning to *obey* which we would come to have the concept of red, it would presumably be of the form *Red objects are to be called 'red'*—a rule to which we could clearly give linguistic expression only *ex post facto.*

But, to recognize the circumstances to which the rule applies, one must already have the concept of red—not to mention all the other concepts constitutive of the rule. One would have to have the concept of red before having it, and to apply it before one could apply it.

35. 'But,' it might be said, 'why suppose that applying a concept like *red* is *obeying* a rule? Why not use your distinction between *obeying* and *merely conforming to* a rule, and say that to acquire a concept such as red is, in addition to acquiring certain syntactical abilities, to come to *conform to* a semantical rule. Surely,' the objection might continue, 'just as, on your account, one starts out by *conforming to* syntactical rules and then, by acquiring the syntactical rule metalanguage, comes to be able to *obey* these rules, so we start out by merely conforming to *semantical* rules, and end up by obeying them.' The imperceptiveness of this reply emerges when one realizes that, whereas the transition from 'All A is B' to 'Some A is B' can be the obeying of a syntactical rule, the *observational application* of a concept cannot be the obeying of a rule at all. It is *essentially* the actualization of a thing–word S-R connection.

36. It is indeed true that just as an intralinguistic move is not in the full sense an *inference* unless the subject not only conforms to but obeys syntactical rules (though he may conceive them to be rules justifying the transition from one *thought* to another, rather than from one linguistic expression to another), so that he is able to *criticize* verbal sentences; so a language entry transition is not in the full sense an *observation*, unless the subject has more than the bare ability to respond with tokens of 'This object is green'—in standard conditions, and given a certain mental set—if and only if a green object is present to his senses. But the *more* in the latter case is not a matter of obeying semantical rules, but rather of the ability to infer (in a pragmatic metalanguage) from 'The thought *this object is green* occurred to X at time t in place s in circumstances c' to 'In all probability a green object was present to X's senses at t in s.'

37. The idea that 'undefined descriptive predicates' (e.g. 'red') acquire meaning because we come to obey 'semantical rules' (e.g. *red objects are to be called 'red'*) clearly presupposes the existence of prelinguistic concepts. Now there appear to be two possible lines that can be taken with respect to such ur-concepts:

(1) They are interpreted as a structure of symbols and, hence, *in our broader sense*, as a *language*. In this case, it is as though when asked, 'How did German words come to be meaningful to Schmidt?' someone were to say, 'Well, before learning German he knew English —though not to speak out loud—and his compatriots, by a clever combination of gestures and the production of vocables in the

presence of objects, brought him to formulate to himself (in English) and obey such rules as "red objects are to be called *rot*".' Clearly, a regress is lurking which can be stopped only by admitting that the meaningfulness of at least one symbolic system is not clarified by the idea of obeying semantical rules.

(2) As a second alternative, the ur-concepts may be conceived as pre-symbolic abilities to recognize items as belonging to *kinds*, or, perhaps, to systems of resembling particulars. This, of course, puts one squarely in a classic 'mental eye' type of position according to which the human mind has an innate ability to be aware (given some contextual focusing) of abstract entities. And a mental eye is a mental eye even if its objects are such modest items as *that* one immediately experienced item is red, or *that* one such item resembles another.

38. Suppose it to be granted, then, that the observation role of such words as 'red' is not a matter of *rules* but of conditioned responses. The danger still exists, however, that the fact that the word 'red' means the quality *red* may be identified with the fact that 'red' is a conditioned response to red things. That is to say, it might be thought that while 'red' would not even be a word unless it played the syntactical role of a predicate in intralinguistic moves, its possession of empirical meaning—indeed, the fact that it is the word it is— is constituted by its role as conditioned response to red things. And, indeed, there is a certain plausibility to the idea that to say of the German word '*rot*' that it means *red* is to say that this vocable is associated (by Germans) with red things. And it is certainly true that if they did not (tend to) respond to red things in standard conditions with '*rot*'—when 'looking to see what colour it has'—it could not be true that the German word '*rot*' means *red*. But, as we have seen, to grant the latter point is by no means to grant the former.[1]

MEANING AND IMMEDIATE EXPERIENCE

39. Another source of the naïve realism—I use the term in its broad sense—which is characteristic of the standard empiricist picture of the relation of thought to experience is the confusion of the sense in which an 'immediate experience' or 'sensation' or 'impression' *of red* is 'of red'—a non-epistemic sense which is a matter of designating these items by their standard physical counterparts—with the sense in which a thought *of red* is 'of red'—an epistemic sense involving the *aboutness* which is clarified by assimilation to the *designates* or *means* of semantical discourse. This confusion has persuaded empiricists, and not only empiricists, that there is an immediate experience of facts, a knowing of facts—a limited domain of facts involving only

---

[1] Chapter 10, pp. 314 ff.

'sense qualities' to be sure, but facts none the less—which is anterior to the development of symbolic systems, and which, even when a symbolic system has been acquired, is what justifies or provides the authority for occupying a position in a language game. There is, of course, no such thing. A sensation of a red triangle is 'of a red triangle', but it is not the knowing that an item is red and triangular. Failure to distinguish the epistemic and non-epistemic senses of 'immediate experience'—roughly *sensation* and *inspection* respectively —carries with it a failure to appreciate that 'He noticed that something was red' is, so to speak, in indirect discourse, a cousin of 'He said that something was red'. There is no more such a thing as a non-symbolic noticing that something is red, than there is a non-symbolic saying that something is red.

40. Sensations are no more epistemic in character than are trees or tables, and are no more ineffable. They are private in the sense that only one person can notice them; but they are public in the sense that, in principle, I can state the same facts about your sensations that you can report, and can state the same facts about your sensations that I can report about my own. As a parallel, it might be pointed out that only our contemporaries can notice physical events now going on—*that* lightning flash, for example—whereas, in principle, our ancestors and descendants can state any facts we can report.[1]

41. The claim that observing *that-p* is, at bottom, responding to p with S, where S says that-p, is often met with the argument that to observe is to have an experience, or at least involves having an experience, whereas a responding, even of the above kind, need not be an experiencing. Now it is certainly true that the mechanism whereby human beings observe—i.e. see, hear, etc.—that something is the case, involves the occurrence of experiences in the non-epistemic sense. Indeed, it is analytic of these specific modes of observation that they involve experiences of these non-epistemic varieties. But we are working with an abstract notion of observing in which it is not analytic to say that observing involves having sensations or impressions. In the specific context of human observation, the statement 'Observation predicates mean *experienceable* qualities' is not the mere tautology 'Observation predicates mean *observable* qualities'. For red objects not only trigger off the reliable response 'This is red'; they do this in a way which involves an experience which we refer to as the experience *of red*. My purpose in

[1] See 'Realism and the New Way of Words' in *Readings in Philosophical Analysis*, edited by Herbert Feigl and Wilfrid Sellars, and published by Appleton-Century-Crofts (New York, 1949), especially pp. 437 and 445 ('No Predicaments'). See also Stuart Hampshire's 'The Analogy of Feeling', *Mind*, January, 1952.

these remarks has been to emphasize that the 'of red' at the end of the preceding sentence is a non-epistemic use of this phrase.

42. At the pre-theoretical level of discourse, 'immediate experience of red' means to me 'experience of the kind that is common to the following situations: (a) I see that something over there is red; (b) There merely looks to be something over there which is red' and has the corresponding meanings for you. Notice that 'x looks red to me now', though a report, is not a report of a minimal observation such that *being red* is definable in terms of *looking red*. In essence, 'x looks red' is what we learn to say when we wish to convey that, although our experience may be indistinguishable, as experience, from one which we would be willing to characterize as *seeing that x is red*, if we were willing to commit ourselves to the idea, which the experience involves, that x is red, we have reasons to doubt that x *is* red, or, at least, to refrain from endorsing this idea. Now, given the above account of 'immediate experience of red', it is clearly meaningful to ask 'Might not it be the case that when we both see that an object is red, my immediate experience differs from yours?' and even to suppose that my immediate experience on seeing that an object is red might be like your immediate experience on seeing that an object is green, and so on, systematically, complementary colour by complementary colour. Indeed, it is meaningful to suppose that this might be so even on the assumption that no *empirical* way, that is, no way not involving the use of *theoretical* entities, exists for determining that this is the case. Suppose that when I have an immediate experience of red, I feel elated, and when I have an immediate experience of green, I feel depressed; but you truthfully report the contrary. I might, at the empirical level, have no means of choosing between saying (a) our experiences on looking at similar objects are similar, but have opposite effects, and (b) our experiences are systematically different, but similar experiences have similar effects.

43. Suppose, now, that ϕ-state, ψ-state, etc., are the theoretical counterparts of immediate experiences in an ideal psychology of the other one, and that they are theoretical entities proper; that is to say, entities introduced by postulates in a system only partially co-ordinated with statements pertaining to observable behaviour. It might turn out that on the evidence we present, the theoretical counterpart of my 'immediate experience of red' is a ϕ-state, and of my 'immediate experience of green' a ψ-state, and that the same is true in your case. In other words, there may be theoretical reasons for deciding in favour of alternative (a) above. But it might turn out the other way; and, until the later stages of behavioural science, we might not be able to predict which way it would turn out. Now, to say that the theory is the 'ideal' theory implies that we could teach ourselves to

use the language of the theory as the language game in which we introspect our immediate experiences and describe those of others; and if we did so, then the impossibility of 'everything else being the same but your immediate experiences being systematically different from mine' would be ruled out by the very logic of the language used to describe and introspect immediate experiences. Thus, to recapitulate, it makes sense at the empirical level to wonder whether our sensations might not be systematically and undetectably different. When we move to the theoretical level, it makes sense to suppose that our sensations on looking at objects in standard conditions are systematically reversed, as long as we are in doubt about what form a completed theory of the causes and effects of immediate experience will take. But to have good reason for supposing that we have a completed theory of immediate experience is *eo ipso* to have good reason for ruling out as meaningless the idea that everything else might be the same, yet you and I have interchanged experiences.

44. Suppose it is said, 'Might it not be the case that if I were to *have* the Jonesian experience which the theory enables me to *infer* is a ϕ-state, I would *introspect* it as a ψ-state?' But this question, it is clear, merely repeats the supposition under examination and gives no additional reason for supposing it to be meaningful, given that the theory is adequate.

45. To make the same point in a different way, the supposition in question is equivalent to supposing that it could ever be reasonable to adopt a theory as 'the final word' in which the basic postulates are stipulated to hold for all space–time regions save one privileged location for which there is postulated a complete and systematic interchange of the roles of a certain set of states defined in the theory. Of course, at any given stage of scientific development, we may have reason to suppose that certain space–time regions are privileged and carry with them a more or less drastic reversal of the usual course of nature. And we may, at any stage, have to put up with similar anomalies in our theories. But surely it could never be reasonable to accept as a final and satisfactory explanation of empirical fact a theory in which such anomalies appear. Still less could it be reasonable to a theory containing such anomalies when the empirical material is free of them. Thus, while the concept of such anomalies contains no self-contradiction, the assumption that a reasonable theory could contain them *is* self-contradictory, and it seems proper to call the supposition of theoretically undetectable anomalies of this kind meaningless, or, in the material mode of speech, to say that we know that such anomalies do not exist.

Parallel: If it could never be reasonable to say 'Here is an event without a cause' (as opposed to 'Let's stop looking for the cause,

338

we're getting nowhere'), might this not be put by saying 'It is necessary that every event has a cause' or 'We know that every event has a cause'?

MATERIAL MOVES IN THE EMPIRICAL LANGUAGE

46. Against the background of all these considerations, the reasons for saying that the role of observation predicates involves material moves as well as formal moves and language entry transitions are seen to be compelling. The fundamental observation predicates are predicates pertaining to physical objects located in space and time. To learn the use of observation predicates, we must not only be put by our teachers in standard conditions and conditioned to respond —e.g. to red objects with 'red'—but we must learn to recognize that the circumstances are standard. In other words, the language of observation is learned as a whole; we do not have any of it until, crudely and schematically, perhaps, we have it all. We acquire the ability to use colour words along with the ability to speak of physical objects located in space and time (and hence to make the material moves characteristic of geometrical words), and to classify circumstances of perception in terms of other observation predicates. The use of observation predicates, when they have achieved their status as such, and are no longer mere isolated conditioned responses, involves the ability to draw inferences in accordance with principles of the form 'In circumstances C_i an object looks red if and only if it is red', 'In circumstances C_j an object looks blue if and only if it is green', etc. To have a battery of principles of this kind is to know what it is for things to have colours. (And I have not mentioned the material moves which characterize colour words as a family of mutually incompatible predicates.) I am able to 'see at a glance' that something is red only because I have a conceptual picture of myself as being in a situation consisting of such and such objects thusly located in Space and Time, a picture which I am constantly checking and revising, a picture any part of which, and any principle of which, can be put in jeopardy—but which cannot be put in jeopardy all at once.

LANGUAGE AND ACTION

47. But if the charge that our conception of language as a game is 'overly syntactical' because it neglects the 'semantical dimension of meaning' can be overcome by a proper analysis of the nature and function of the rubric '". . ." means —', there remains the more

penetrating accusation of the pragmatist. He argues that to conceive of a language as a game in which linguistic counters are manipulated according to a certain syntax is to run the danger of overlooking an essential feature of languages—that they enable language-users to find their way around in the world, and satisfy their needs.

48. And if we were to point out that we had already made a gesture in this direction by recognizing language entry and language departure transitions as parts of the game, he would doubtless reply that it is not a sufficient account of the connection between *language* and *living in a world* to recognize that people respond to red objects with 'I see red' and (given hunger) to 'this is an edible object' by eating. After all, we are not always in the presence of edible objects, and is not language (in our broad sense in which 'language' is equivalent to 'conceptual structure') the instrument which enables us to go from *this* which we see to *that* which we can eat? When all is said and done, should we not join the pragmatist in saying that in any non-trivial sense of this term, the 'meaning' of a term lies in its role as an instrument in the organism's transactions with its environment?

49. Now I would argue that Pragmatism, with its stress on language (or the conceptual) as an instrument, has had hold of a most important insight—an insight, however, which the pragmatist has tended to misconceive as an *analysis* of 'means' and 'is true'. For it is a category mistake (in Ryle's useful terminology) to offer a definition of 'S means p' or 'S is true' in terms of the role of S as an instrument in problem solving behaviour. On the other hand, if the pragmatist's claim is reformulated as the thesis that the language we use has a much more intimate connection with conduct than we have yet suggested, and that this connection is intrinsic to its structure as language, rather than a 'use' to which it 'happens' to be put, then Pragmatism assumes its proper stature as a revolutionary step in Western philosophy.

50. One pillar on which the conduct guiding role of language rests is, of course, its character as embodying convictions as to the ways of things. It was pointed out above that our understanding of the laws of nature resides in what we have called the material moves (inferences) of our language, that is to say, those moves whereby we go from one sentence to another which is not a logically analytic consequence of it. It is by virtue of such a move that we go, let us suppose, from the sentence 'Here is smoke' to 'Near by is fire'. But the *linguistic* move from 'Here is smoke' to 'Near by is fire' does not get us from the smoke to the fire, and if such moves were all we had in the way of linguistic moves, language would not be an instrument for action. Putting the point bluntly, an organism which 'knew the

340

laws of nature' might be able to move around in the world, but it could not move around *in the light of its knowledge* (i.e. act intelligently) unless it used a language *relating to conduct*, which tied in with its assertions and inferences relating to matters of fact. Action can be guided by language (thought) only in so far as language contains as an integral part a sub-language built around action words, words for various kinds of *doing*.

51. This is not the occasion for a detailed discussion of the 'logic' of action words. What is important for our present purposes is that the linguistic move from 'Here is smoke' to 'Yonder is fire' can guide conduct only because there are also such moves as that from 'Yonder is fire' to 'Going yonder is going to fire'. Of course, it is *per accidens* that *going yonder* is, on a particular occasion, *going to fire*. On the other hand, there are 'essential' relations among actions. Thus, one action may be *analytically* a part of another action. And if we take both relationships into account, we see that one action may be *per accidens* a part of another action, by being *per accidens* an action which is a part of that action. Thus, actions which are motions of the agent's body (e.g. waving the hand) can be *per accidens* parts of actions the successful accomplishment of which involves goings-on which are *not* motions of the agent's body (e.g. paying a debt). Indeed, there could be no performance of actions of the latter type unless there were 'basic actions', actions which are motions of the agent's body, to be, *per accidens*, parts of them.

52. We shall round off the above remarks on the relation of thinking to doing after we have further explored the doing involved in thinking. Let us get this exploration under way by turning our attention to rule *obeying* behaviour.

PLAYING THE SYNTACTICAL GAME

53. We have already noted that rule obeying behaviour involves a distinction between game and metagame, the former, or 'object game', being played according to certain rules which themselves are positions in the metagame. Furthermore, we have emphasized that in an object game played as rule obeying behaviour, not only do the moves exemplify positions specified by the rules (for this is also true of mere pattern governed behaviour where even though a rule exists the playing organism has not learned to play it) but also the rules themselves are engaged in the genesis of the moves. The moves occur (in part, and in a sense demanding analysis) *because of* the rules.

54. Fortunately, our discussion of language games has put us in a position to clarify the manner in which rules are involved in rule

obeying behaviour. To begin with, we note that typically a rule sentence enjoins that such and such be done in such and such circumstances. (Of course, not all sentences in a rule language do this; 'one may do A in C' is also a sentence in the language of rules.) Thus rules contain words for mentioning circumstances and for enjoining actions. In the latter respect they contain action words ('hit', 'put', 'run') in contexts such as '. . .!' or '. . . ought to . . .'.

55. Now since the games in which rules occur are language games, it occurs to us that the categories of language entry and language departure transitions may throw light on the nature of rule obeying behaviour. Thus, we might start by trying the following formulations. Words which mention the positions of a game (position words) are, we might say, the 'observation words' of a rule language. In addition to their syntactical role in the rule language, they occur in sentences which come to be occupied as the result of a language entry transition into the rule language, in which transition the stimulus is a situation of the kind meant by the position words. 'Action enjoining contexts', on the other hand, are the 'motivating expressions' of the rule language. In addition to their syntactical role in the rule language, they occur in sentences the occupying of which is the stimulus for a language departure transition out of the rule language to a response which is [remember that both 'observation sentence' and 'motivating expression' are, in Ryle's sense of the phrase, 'achievements words'] an action of the kind mentioned in the motivating context. Thus we might give the following as an example:

Example: I am looking at a chessboard set up in a certain way. This acts as stimulus for the language entry transition into the rule language position '. . . and my king is checked by his bishop'. I then make the move in the rule language via the auxiliary position 'If one's king is checked by a bishop interpose a pawn!' (needless to say, I am taking liberties with the game) or '. . . one *is to* interpose a pawn' or '. . . one should interpose a pawn' to 'Sellars, interpose a pawn!' (or correspondingly on the alternative formulations of the auxiliary sentence). The latter is a motivating position in the rule language, and I make the language departure transition from the rule language to the action (in the chess game) of interposing a pawn.[1]

56. Instead of commenting directly on the above line of thought,

---

[1] (Added 1963) The interpretation of language departure transitions in terms of self-addressed imperatives is ultimately unsatisfactory, though it doesn't do too much damage to the point I was trying to make. A more adequate account of 'shall' and 'ought' is given in 'Imperatives, Intentions and the Logic of "Ought"', *Methodos*, 8, 1956. This paper is reprinted with substantial alterations in *Morality and the Language of Conduct*, edited by George Nakhnikian and Hector Castañeda, Wayne State University Press (Detroit, Michigan) 1963.

I shall beat about the neighbouring bushes. In the first place attention must be called to the differences between

'bishop'	and 'piece of wood of such and such shape'.
'My bishop is checking his king'	and 'There is an open diagonal space between this white piece of wood and that red piece of wood.'
'Interpose a pawn!'	and 'Place this piece of wood between those two!'

Clearly the expressions on the left-hand side belong to the rule language of chess. And clearly the ability to respond to an object of a certain size and shape *as a bishop*[1] presupposes the ability to respond to it as an object of that size and shape. But it should not be inferred that 'bishop' is 'shorthand' for 'wood of such and such size and shape' or even for 'object of such and such size and shape *used in chess*'. 'Bishop' is a counter in the rule language game and participates in linguistic moves in which the first of the two longer expressions does not, while the second of the longer expressions is a description which, whatever its other shortcomings, presupposes the language of chess rules and can scarcely be a definition of 'bishop' as a term belonging to it. Nor should it be supposed that to respond to a situation as a bishop checking a king is to respond to it *first* by an observation sentence *not* belonging to the rule language—thus, 'this is such and such a piece of wood thus and so situated with respect to another piece of wood'—and *then* to respond to this sentence in turn by a *language entry transition* into the rule language. For this would make the word 'bishop' a metalinguistic word (it is, of course, a meta*game* word) which mentions the words 'such and such a piece of wood' and not the piece of wood itself. For the language entry transition category to be relevant to all, 'this is a bishop checking a king' must be a response to a chessboard arrangement, and not to *words* describing the arrangement.

57. If we are to use the 'language entry transition' category, we must say that having acquired the ability to respond to a chessboard arrangement as objects of such and such shapes in such and such arrangements, we then learn to respond to the same situation by a game entry transition into the rule language of chess. Similarly in the

---

[1] Roughly, to say of Jones that he responds to *x as a* ϕ, at least in this kind of context, implies that his response contains a mention of ϕ; that is, an element which *means* ϕ. Thus, when I say of Schmidt that he responds to this piece of wood as a bishop, I am implying that his response contains an element which means *bishop*. This element is, presumably, the German word 'Bischof'.

case of the 'move' words as well as the 'piece' and 'position' words. Thus I might learn to respond to the move-enjoining sentence 'Sellars, advance your king's pawn!' as I would to 'Sellars, shove this piece of wood two squares forward!'

58. But while this *might* be the description of learning to apply the rule language game (given that I have learned the moves within the rule language game—its syntax), it would make the connection between expressions such as 'bishop', 'check', etc., in chess language and the expressions in everyday language which we use to describe pieces of wood, shapes, sizes, and arrangements much more 'external' than we think it to be. For surely it is more plausible to suppose that the piece, position, and move words of chess are, in the process of learning chess language, built on to everyday language by *moves* relating, for example, 'x is a bishop' to 'x is a ♝-shaped piece of wood', or by means of auxiliary sentences, for example, 'x is a bishop if and only if x is a ♝-shaped piece of wood'. In other words, chess words gain 'descriptive meaning' by virtue of *syntactical relations* to 'everyday' words.

59. Yet these syntactical relations do not give a complete interchange ability to, for example, 'x is a bishop' and 'x is a ♝-shaped piece of wood' for the former has a syntax in chess language which the latter does not—a syntax by which it is related to action-enjoining contexts, and hence, it may be, to such normative words as 'ought', 'permitted', 'may', etc., with their characteristic grammar, or to imperative devices the logical syntax of which has been given less attention by philosophers.[1] To be sure, we could say that non-chess words correlated with chess words acquire normative meaning by virtue of these syntactical relations with chess words having normative meaning. But one of the consequences of having a special chess language is that it is only when we are in the 'chess-playing frame of mind' that these syntactical connections become operative. Non-chess words do have a chess meaning, but only in chess-playing contexts, when the system of learned habits with respect to chess moves and chess language moves is mobilized and called into play. Notice also that the language of chess, by virtue of its special vocabulary, has a certain autonomy with respect to the everyday language in which it becomes embedded. Thus, 'piece' words might be syntactically related to expressions mentioning various shapes of wood in New York, and to expressions mentioning different makes of cars in Texas—pawns being Fords, the king a Cadillac, squares counties—and yet the game be 'the same'.

[1] For a thorough treatment of this topic, see Hector Castaneda, *The Logical Structure of Moral Reasoning*, a Ph.D. thesis submitted to the Faculty of the Graduate School at the University of Minnesota, April, 1954.

60. If we apply these considerations to the case of those rule languages which are syntactical metalanguages, we get something like the following: A syntactical metalanguage (ML) is a rule language, the entry into which is from situations which are positions in the game for which it is the rules (OL), and the departure from which is the being motivated (by motivating contexts in ML) to make moves in OL. Thus it contains expressions for situations and moves in the OL game, as well as rule sentences involving these expressions. Now, we might be inclined to represent this as in diagram A. But this

METALANGUAGE: ' "red" '   'Move$_1$!'

OBJECT-LANGUAGE: 'red'——————————————→?
                                                        Move$_1$

WORLD OF FACT:
                        a red patch

Key:
————→ intra-game move
～～～→ language entry
--------→ language departure   DIAGRAM A

clearly won't do as it stands. An arrow going from the expression meaning the word 'red' as a pattern in OL to the expression meaning the word ' "red" ' as a pattern in ML can scarcely have the same sense as an arrow going from the expression referring to a *particular* red patch to the expression meaning the word 'red' as a pattern in OL (where it stands for the language entry transition). Thus, even though there is a relationship between OL and ML which would properly be represented by something like the above diagram, some modifications must be introduced.

61. To build a more adequate representation, we must first note that just as chess language contains the word 'bishop' which is correlated (in different ways) with (*a*) ♗-shaped pieces of wood, and (*b*) the expression ' ♗-shaped piece of wood', without itself containing either wood of any shape or the word 'wood'—so a syntactical ML can contain an expression appropriately correlated with (*a*) the sound *redd* as used in OL game playing contexts, and (*b*) the expression 'the sound *redd*' without itself containing either the sound *redd* or the

345

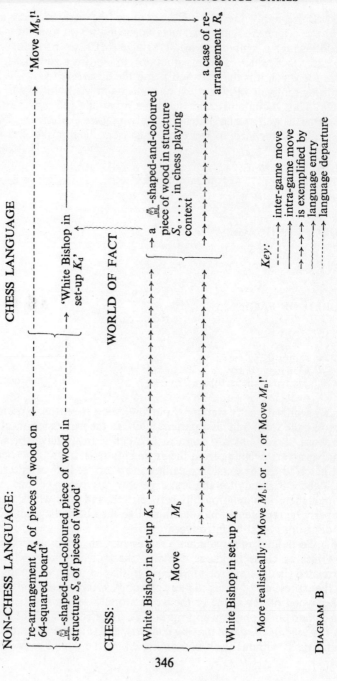

CHESS LANGUAGE

NON-CHESS LANGUAGE:

'Move M_b!'[1]

'White Bishop in set-up K_d'

a case of re-arrangement R_a

'a $♗$-shaped-and-coloured piece of wood in structure S_c..., in chess playing context

're-arrangement R_a of pieces of wood on 64-squared board'

$♗$-shaped-and-coloured piece of wood in structure S_c of pieces of wood'

WORLD OF FACT

CHESS:

White Bishop in set-up K_d

Move M_b

White Bishop in set-up K_e

[1] More realistically: 'Move M_b!. or ... or Move M_n!'

Key:
----→ inter-game move
——→ intra-game move
→ → → → is exemplified by
↝↝↝↝ language entry
........→ language departure

DIAGRAM B

346

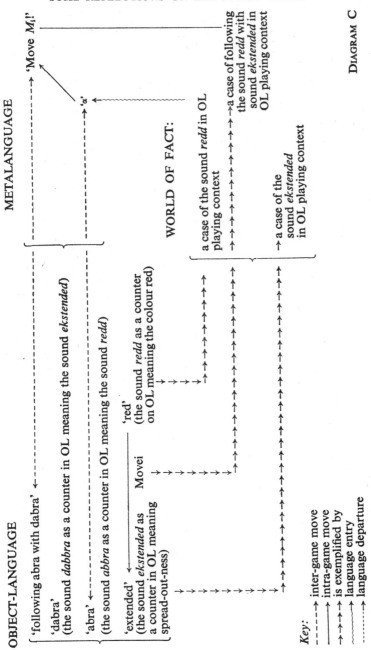

DIAGRAM C

347

word '*redd*'. Thus, the ML expression meaning the word 'red' might be 'α'. This expression would be a point of entry into ML, as 'bishop' is a point of entry into chess language. Now, we saw that the chess rule game gains application by being built on to non-chess language (thus making a more inclusive game). The chess word 'bishop' is correlated in this inclusive game by a syntactical move with the non-chess expression '♗-shaped piece of wood'—though not in Texas—and is also correlated with ♗-shaped pieces of wood (in chess playing contexts) in a language entry transition (the ♗-shaped pieces of wood are seen *as bishops*) A parallel situation obtains in the case of the syntactical metalanguage we are considering. Suppose that the OL word for the sound *redd* is 'abra'; then we may diagram the chess language and metalanguage cases as in diagrams B and C.

62. Just as the term 'bishop' as it occurs in the language of both Texas and ordinary chess can be correctly said to have a common meaning—indeed to mean the bishop role, embodied in the one case by pieces of wood, and in the other by, say, Pontiacs, a role which Frenchmen would refer to as *le rôle de l'évêque*—so 'α', on the above assumptions, can correctly be said to mean a certain linguistic role, a role which is embodied in different linguistic materials—in English by the sound *redd*, and in German by the sound *roat*.[1]

63. Notice that the non-rule language in which the positions and moves specified by the rule language ML are described is identical with (it need only be translatable into, as when Germans brood metalinguistically about English) OL, the game for which ML is the rule game, whereas in the case of chess, the non-chess language in which pieces of wood are described is obviously not identical with the game of chess, the game for which chess language is the rule game. We must beware of putting this by saying that ML is part of the language game for which it is the rules. We can, however, say that just as chess language is built on to non-chess language to make a

---

[1] For a discussion of linguistic roles thus conceived, see my 'Quotation Marks, Sentences and Propositions' in Volume X of the *Philosophy and Phenomenological Research*, 1950, pp. 515–25; also 'The Identity of Linguistic Expressions and the Paradox of Analysis' in Volume I of the *Philosophical Studies*, 1950, pp. 24–31. In the former paper, pp. 519ff., I distinguished between the 'pragmatic' and the 'syntactical' use of quotation marks, using single quotes to distinguish the latter. In their 'syntactical' use—I would prefer a different terminology now—quotation marks form the names of what I called 'pure linguistic functions'. Thus the expression ' "Truman is in Washington" ' names a pure linguistic function, or linguistic role, which is embodied in English and French by different strings of vocables and printables. Notice that according to this use of single quotes,

Jones said 'Truman is in Washington'

translates into French as

Jones a dit 'Truman est à Washington'.

more inclusive language game, so syntactical language is built on to non-syntactical language to make a more inclusive language game. That the inclusive game permits the effective formulation of rules the obedience to which is the playing of the less inclusive game, whereas the inclusive language game, in the case of chess, permits the effective formulation of rules the obeying of which is the playing, not of the less inclusive game, but of the game of chess, loses it air of paradox, once it is remembered that when the rules of non-syntactical English are formulated in German, the parallel with chess is restored. And it is scarcely cause for puzzle or paradox that non-syntactical German (on which the German builds ML) is translatable into non-syntactical English.

64. But it is not the purpose of this chapter to follow up all the important and difficult topics involved in clarifying the status of metalanguages and the nature of the meta-meta-. . . .-hierarchy. Our concern is with the most general implications of the conception of a language as a game. Let us therefore turn to a second comment on the analysis proposed in 51. Let us note that it must not be supposed that in order to play a game at the level of rule *obeying* behaviour, one must first learn to play it at the level of mere pattern governed behaviour. As we have pointed out before, not all learning to play games can be learning to obey rules, but given that one has learned a language adequate to the purpose, one can learn to play (e.g. chess or poker directly as a mode of rule obeying behaviour). By 'a language adequate to the purpose' I mean, for example, that one must be able to respond to certain pieces of cardboard as having ten diamond-shaped spots printed on it, before one can learn to apply the rule language of poker. Learning to play a game at the rule obeying level does presuppose that the patterns and activities involved belong to the organism's repertoire of available discriminations and manipulations. Notice also that the vocabulary and syntax of action enjoining contexts is, to a large extent, common to the rule languages of the many games we play, a fact which facilitates the learning of new games.

65. In the third place, it should be emphasized that the phrase 'rule obeying behaviour' is not restricted in its application to behaviour in which one makes moves in a game via making moves in its rule metagame. There is a sense in which it is quite legitimate to say that Jones is obeying the rules of chess, even though he is not actually making moves in the rule language, and yet to deny that Smith, who has learned to play merely at the level of pattern governed behaviour and hence is also not making moves in the metagame, is obeying rules. For there are many true subjunctive statements we could make about Jones and the rule language which we could not make about

Smith. In this chapter, however, I have limited my discussion of rule obeying to the more pedestrian cases, oversimplifying in order to focus attention on fundamentals. For a sensitive and illuminating account of the complex logical devices built into ordinary language about human behaviour, the reader is referred to Gilbert Ryle's *The Concept of Mind*.

MOTIVATING CONTEXTS AND THE CONCEPT OF OBLIGATION

66. It is time that something more was said about language-departure transitions or action-enjoining contexts. To begin with, it should be emphasized that while action words occur in motivating contexts such as '. . . ought to . . .', sentences containing action words may motivate without containing a motivating context. Thus, given a certain organic state (hunger), if I occupy the position 'there is an edible object within my grasp', I may proceed to grasp the object with my hand and eat it. In such cases we speak of acting 'on impulse'. In the case of more reflective action, we may speak of action 'from desire' or 'from pathological love' (Kant) as contrasted with acting 'from a sense of duty'.

67. Learning the use of normative expressions involves not only learning the intralinguistic moves or 'logical grammar' of these expressions, but also acquiring the tendency to make the transition from occupying the position 'I ought now to do A' to the doing of A. This motivating role of 'ought' in the first person present is essential to the 'meaning' of 'ought'. That is to say, it could not be true of a word that 'it means *ought*' unless this word had motivating force in the language to which it belongs. It is a necessary truth that people tend to do what they think they ought to do, for it is a necessary truth that people who occupy a linguistic position which means *I ought to do A now*, tend to do A. If they did not, the position they occupy could not mean *I ought to do A now*.

68. The motivating role of 'ought' has often been misconstrued. In the first place, those who recognize that the role is 'essential to the meaning of "ought"' sometimes conclude that 'ought' has motivational *rather than* conceptual meaning. This, of course, is a radical mistake which has its primary source in the 'matrimonial' or 'bow and arrow' theory of meaning criticized in the previous chapter '"*Soll*" means *ought*' is exactly as legitimate as '"*rot*" means *red*' and '"*und*" means *and*'. 'There is something which "*soll*" means' is exactly as legitimate as 'There is something which "*rot*" means', and '"ought" means a *prescriptive* property of states of affairs of the form x does A in circumstances C' is exactly as legitimate as '"red" means a *descriptive*, indeed, observable property of physical objects' and

' "necessary" means a *modal* property of states of affairs of the form x *is* $A \supset x$ *is* B'.

69. Of course, if 'ought' played no *syntactical* role, then it could, at best, be a mere trigger or spur, and no genuine concept. But the fact that it is not an observation word, nor definable in terms of such, and is therefore neither directly nor indirectly related to the world by means of conditioned responses of the language-entry type, would only point to the conclusion that 'ought' is a pseudo concept if we suppose that in the case of non-logical words, ' "..." means —' speaks of this kind of relation to the world. It is this mistake which has led philosophers to suppose that the 'logic' of 'ought' must be a pseudo logic, a masquerade.

70. Singular normatives are 'implicitly universal'. As a rough approximation we may say that in some sense of 'implies', 'Jones ought to do A in C' implies 'Everybody ought to do A in C'. Of course A (the action) and C (the circumstances) must be properly specified. 'Jones ought to fetch a glass of water when Cynthia cries' does not imply, 'Everybody ought to fetch a glass of water when Cynthia cries.' Perhaps it is sufficient to say that a person who says 'Jones ought to do thus and so in these circumstances' commits himself to backing up this statement by giving a reason of the form 'the circumstances are of kind C, and to do thus and so in C is to do A, and everybody ought to do A in C'.

71. Now it is often thought that the motivational force of 'ought' is that of imperatives. This is a mistake which not only misinterprets 'ought' but imperatives as well. In its most plausible form, the idea is that normatives are a subclass of imperatives, those, namely, which signallize a commitment to corresponding universal imperatives. Thus, 'You ought to do thus and so' is compared to 'Do thou thus and so!' where the archaic 'Do thou' signallizes a commitment to back up the imperative by saying something of the form 'the circumstances are of kind C, and to do thus and so in C is to do A, and everybody, do ye A in C!' But while this account does justice to the universality implicit in 'You ought to do thus and so', it commits a fatal logical error when it seeks to explicate the normative character of the statement in terms of imperative discourse. For instead of normative discourse being a form of imperative discourse, the latter presupposes normative discourse and does not exist outside it.

72. The parallel of 'commanding' and 'asking' with 'promising' is instructive. Promising is a performance which creates a presumptive prima facie obligation to do A on the part of the person who says 'I promise to do A'. It creates the obligation by virtue of the fact that we recognize a moral rule which can, for our purposes, be formulated as follows: 'If x properly says "I promise to do A" to y,

then x ought to do A.' In the absence of this rule, there would be no such thing as promising. A person who said that moral principles have authority because we have implicitly or explicitly promised to obey them would show that he simply does not understand what promising is.

73. Now commanding, like promising, is an institution. Issuing a command within one's authority creates a presumptive prima facie obligation on the part of the recipient to do the action commanded. Promising is a performance which binds *oneself*. Commanding is a performance which binds *others*. And commanding, like promising, has created obligations only because, like promising, it rests on a principle—in this case, 'If x properly says "Do A!" to y, then y ought to do A.' The word 'properly' reminds us that the authority of one person to command or tell another person to do various kinds of things is a function of the relationships which obtain between them, e.g. general–colonel, parent–child, friend–friend, or certain more ephemeral relationships in which people are thrown by the way of the world. In the absence of a relationship which makes a certain command appropriate, the recipient can correctly say, 'Who are you to tell me to do that!' The idea that moral principles are 'really' commands is as absurd as the idea that they are 'really' promises.

74. We have seen that in order for a language to contain singular normatives, it must contain universal normatives among its primitive sentences. These universal normatives will be of two kinds: (*a*) *unrestricted*, e.g. '*Everybody* ought to keep their properly made promises'; (*b*) *restricted*, e.g. 'All *chess players* ought to . . .' or 'All members of the armed forces ought to . . .', or 'All users of ML ought to . . .', where the obligations are laid down, so to speak, for playing a special game, rather than for the general game of living. Notice that there is a sense in which to acknowledge that an individual anthropoid is *somebody* is to include it within the scope of those to whom he has duties and against whom he has rights. A tribal morality is tribal not because it differs from the morality of other tribes, but because in its unrestricted norms, 'Everybody' simply means 'all of *us*'.[1]

INDUCTION

75. We must now confront a challenge which has been dogging our heels since our brief discussion of material moves and the laws of nature in sections 25–29 above. 'According to your account,' the challenge begins, 'our consciousness of the ways of things is a matter of the "material moves" of the language game in which we speak

---

[1] The interpretation of ethical statements which is sketched in these sections is developed at length in the essay referred to in footnote 1, p. 342.

about the world. In other words, you claim that to know that all occasions of kind A are occasions of kind B is a matter of one's language containing the move from "x is A" to "x is B". It is along these lines that you account for the fact that we back up our assertion that an occasion is of kind B by *giving a reason*, namely that it is of kind A. On the other hand, when you describe the process whereby we come to adopt the language of which this move is a part, you give an *anthropological*, a (very schematic) *causal* account of how languages come to be used, and, presumably changed, in which you stress evolutionary analogies and cite the language of the beehive. Do you not imply that there is no such thing as *giving a reason* for (or against) the decision to include a certain material move in the syntactical structure of one's language?' This challenge takes us to the very heart of an issue central to modern philosophy since Hume, namely, the reason-ability of our 'beliefs' in (particular) laws of nature.

76. The mention of Hume inspires another critic to brandish quite a different cudgel. 'By making the material moves in which an empirical predicate participates constitutive of its being the predicate it is, as the moves of a bishop constitute its being a bishop, are you not, in effect, joining the ranks of those long scattered legions who thought that to *have* (clear) *concepts* is to *know causes*? But in your nominalistic version, in which natural selection takes the place of divine *illuminatio* as reality's dominion over human concepts, different peoples with different languages would "know" different causes. There would be as many "truths" as languages . . . in short, no truth at all!'

77. Now it must be granted that as soon as an attempt is made to rephrase our discussion in terms of 'understanding' and 'knowing', not to mention 'meaning' and 'truth', one begins to feel acutely uncomfortable. Thus, suppose we sought to express what we have hitherto formulated as

(i) 'All A is B' is unconditionally assertable (in L)

or

(ii) 'All A is B' (in L) corresponds to the material move from 'x is A' to 'x is B' which holds in L

by saying

(iii) 'All A is B' (in L) is true *ex vi terminorum*.

Clearly, we would be on the threshold of paradox. For suppose that there are two groups of language users, G-1 and G-2, using languages L-1 and L-2 respectively. And suppose that L-1 and L-2 are radically different in that they involve two different systems of material moves —that is, they cannot be regarded as different embodiments of the same 'pieces' and 'positions', as automobiles and counties on the one hand, and pieces of ivory and wooden squares on the other, can be alternative embodiments of the pieces and positions of chess. In short, L-1 and L-2 are not mutually translatable. Now, if we were to adopt mode of formulation (iii), we should have to say that each of these languages contained a set of universal sentences which were not only 'lawlike' but *true*, indeed, true *ex vi terminorum*. And if G-2 abandoned L-2, acquiring some other language in its place, we should have to say that it was abandoning a set of true lawlike sentences about the world. And even though in doing so it was acquiring another set of true lawlike sentences, can it ever be *reasonable* to abandon true sentences?

78. But while we may legitimately conclude from this that it is often inappropriate to use mode of formulation (iii) where (i) and (ii) are appropriate, it would be a mistake to suppose that (iii) is never correct. In general, when I commit myself to

(iv) S is a true sentence (of L)

I am committing myself to asserting either S itself (if I am a user of L) or a translation of S into the language I do use. Thus, if the position sketched in this chapter is sound, it is only if I myself use L, or a language which stands to L as chess played with Cadillacs for *kings* and counties as *squares* stands to chess embodied in more usual materials, that I can make a correct use of (iii). Consequently, it could not be correct for me to say that G-2 switched from one set of *true* lawlike sentences to another, nor to say of my group that it has switched from one set of true lawlike sentences to another (unless I 'relativise' the notion of truth as true in W [the world of L], true in W' [the world of L'], etc.—as opposed to true of *this* world).

79. A closely related point concerns such expressions as 'Jones knows that all A is B' or 'They knew that all A is B'. It should be clear in the light of the above (given the general epistemological orientation of this chapter) that a correct use by me of either of these sentences presupposes that in the one case Jones, and in the other case 'they' use either the same language which I myself speak, or a language which is 'another embodiment of the same game'. Where this condition is not fulfilled, we must abandon indirect discourse and make explicit reference to the language used by the individual or group of which we are speaking.

80. We have already pointed out that statements of the form

'. . .' means — (in L)

are incorrectly assimilated to relation statements. They do not say of an expression (in L) and an entity that they stand in the 'meaning relation'. They belong to semantical discourse, which is no more describing discourse than is prescriptive discourse. They convey, but do not assert, the information that '. . .' plays the role in L which '—' plays in the language in which the semantical statement occurs. Thus, if the argument of this chapter is correct, it can only be correct to make statements of the form

(v) 'β' means B (in L)

where the language (say L′) which one is using as a metalanguage (and which therefore contains the appropriate semantical vocabulary) is, in its non-semantical part, to which 'B' belongs, another embodiment of the same game—i.e. the same system of formal and material moves—as L, to which 'β' belongs. And a statement of this form is *true*, if and only if 'β' stands to 'B' as another embodiment of the same 'piece'.

81. Everyone would admit that the notion of a language which enables one to state matters of fact but does not permit argument, explanation, in short *reason-giving*, in accordance with the principles of *formal logic*, is a chimera. It is essential to the understanding of scientific reasoning to realize that the notion of a language which enables one to state empirical matters of fact but contains no material moves is equally chimerical. The classical 'fiction' of an inductive leap which takes its point of departure from an observation base undefiled by any notion as to how things hang together is not a fiction but an absurdity. The problem is not 'Is it reasonable to include material moves in our language?' but rather '*Which* material moves is it reasonable to include?'

82. Thus, there is no such thing as a problem of induction if one means by this a problem of how to justify the leap from the safe ground of the mere description of particular situations, to the problematical heights of asserting lawlike sentences and offering explanations. The sceptics' notion that any move beyond a language which provides only for the tautologous transformation of observation statements is a 'venture of faith' is sheer nonsense. An understanding of the role of material moves in the working of a language is the key to the rationale of scientific method. And since, as we have seen, this role can be characterized both as constituting the concepts of the language and as providing for inferences, explanations, and reasons relating to statements formulated in terms of these concepts, it is clear that to be in a position to ask the question 'Is it ever reasonable to assert one matter of fact on the basis of another matter of fact?' is to be in a position to answer with an unequivocal 'yes!'

83. Thus, once we realize that the problem is not 'Is it reasonable

to include material moves in our language?' but rather '*Which* material moves is it reasonable to include?' we also see that the problem is not 'Is it reasonable to give "explanations" of matters of fact?' but '*Which* explanations of matters of fact is it reasonable to give?' It comes home to us that the problem concerns the grounds on which a decision to use—that is, to teach ourselves—*this* language rather than *that*, can be justified. And to play the language game in which we can be confronted by the need for such a decision, is to know what would constitute a good reason for making it in one way rather than another.

84. Viewed from within a *used* conceptual framework, with a sufficiently rich metalinguistic apparatus, observations belong to the *ordo rerum*. It is only when we reflect on the nature of a decision to change conceptual frames that it strikes us anew that the making of an observation is the impact of the nonconceptual on the conceptual. The *metalinguistic* position 'U (meaning *that-p*) was an observation utterance', which entails 'p was the case', rests on no privileged access to the world. A sufficiently rich conceptual frame enables the one who uses it to recite the story of its achievements and to support with reasons the claim that they *are* achievements. *But reasons are always positions within a frame.* We may conclude that x was an observation judgement; but observation judgements are not conclusions.

85. But this means, of course, that no giving of reasons for adopting a language game can appeal to premises outside all language games. The *data* of the positivist must join the *illuminatio* of Augustine. In other words, instead of justifying nomologicals by an appeal to observation statements the predicates of which would have conceptual meaning independently of any commitment to laws, the problem is rather that of deciding *which* conceptual meaning our observation vocabulary is to have, our aim being so to manipulate the three basic components of a world picture: (*a*) observed objects and events, (*b*) unobserved objects and events, and (*c*) nomological connections, so as to achieve a world picture with a maximum of 'explanatory coherence'. In this reshuffle, no item is sacred. On the other hand, it is obviously reasonable to preserve the achievement status of as many observation claims as possible, for the more we preserve, the more the world picture we select is 'based on observational evidence'.[1]

86. The difference between observation predicates and theoretical constructs is not that the former have a conceptual status independent of material moves (implicit definition), whereas the latter are implicitly defined predicates in a system which is 'interpreted' by a 'dictionary' which ties certain expressions in the theory with empirical

[1] Cf. footnote 2, p. 293 in Chapter 9.

constructs. Rather, the conceptual status of theoretical and non-theoretical expressions alike is a matter of material (as well as formal) moves.

87. When we adopt a theoretical sub-language, we characteristically hold it at arm's length. That is to say, instead of simply enriching our non-theoretical ('background') language with new material moves relating existing terms to a new vocabulary, as we should if we simply decided to take—and taught ourselves to take—'gas' and 'congeries of molecules' as synonymous, we put raisable drawbridges 'co-ordinating' (moves) between the theoretical and the non-theoretical vocabularies. We use these drawbridges when we play the scientific game—compare the move from 'x is wood of such and such shape' to 'x is a knight' in chess-playing contexts—and their status can only be understood in the light of the total rationale of the scientific enterprise. The co-ordinating moves (inferences) which connect an island of theory with the highways of non-theoretical discourse on the mainland (themselves by no means immune to revision) must not be confused with the language entry transitions (*not* inferences) which give observation words their observation status.

88. But philosophically more interesting are those cases in which we decide to introduce new material moves into *non-theoretical* discourse. Thus, suppose that 'ϕ' and 'ψ' are empirical constructs and that their conceptual meaning is constituted, as we have argued, by their role in a network of material (and formal) moves. Suppose that these moves do not include the move from 'x is ϕ' to 'x is ψ'. Now suppose that we begin to discover (using this frame) that many ϕ's are ψ and that we discover no exceptions. At this stage the sentence 'All ϕ's are ψ' looms as an 'hypothesis', *by which is meant that it has a problematical status with respect to the categories of explanation.* In terms of these categories we look to a resolution of this problematical situation along one of the following lines.

(*a*) We discover that we can derive 'All ϕ's are ψ' from already accepted nomologicals. (Compare the development of early geometry.)

(*b*) We discover that we can derive 'If C, then all ϕ's are ψ' from already accepted nomologicals, where C is a circumstance we know to obtain.

(*c*) We decide to adopt—and teach ourselves—the material move from 'x is ϕ' to 'x is ψ'. In other words, we accept 'All ϕ's are ψ' as an unconditionally assertable sentence of L, and reflect this decision by using the modal sentence 'ϕ's are *necessarily* ψ'. This constitutes, of course, an enrichment of the conceptual meanings of 'ϕ' and 'ψ'.

357

89. But it may be long before we arrive at a *decision*, and in the interim (always supposing that no exceptions turn up), we will say 'It is probable that all ϕ is ψ'. The important thing is to realize that instead of 'probable hypothesis' or 'mere inductive generalization' being a *terminal* category, it is an interim category. And if we were to say (as it is often sensible to say) 'It is probable that ϕ's are necessarily ψ', we should be giving notice that we expected a resolution of the problematic situation along the lines of either (*a*) or (*c*) above.

INDEX

359

International Library of Philosophy & Scientific Method

Editor: Ted Honderich
Advisory Editor: Bernard Williams

List of titles, page two

International Library of Psychology Philosophy & Scientific Method

Editor: C K Ogden

List of titles, page six

ROUTLEDGE AND KEGAN PAUL LTD
68 Carter Lane London EC4

International Library of Philosophy and Scientific Method
(Demy 8vo)

Allen, R. E. (Ed.)
Studies in Plato's Metaphysics
Contributors: J. L. Ackrill, R. E. Allen, R. S. Bluck, H. F. Cherniss, F. M.
Cornford, R. C. Cross, P. T. Geach, R. Hackforth, W. F. Hicken, A. C. Lloyd,
G. R. Morrow, G. E. L. Owen, G. Ryle, W. G. Runciman, G. Vlastos
464 pp. 1965. (2nd Impression 1967.) 70s.

Armstrong, D. M.
Perception and the Physical World
208 pp. 1961. (3rd Impression 1966.) 25s.
A Materialist Theory of the Mind
376 pp. 1967. about 45s.

Bambrough, Renford (Ed.)
New Essays on Plato and Aristotle
Contributors: J. L. Ackrill, G. E. M. Anscombe, Renford Bambrough,
R. M. Hare, D. M. MacKinnon, G. E. L. Owen, G. Ryle, G. Vlastos
184 pp. 1965. (2nd Impression 1967.) 28s.

Barry, Brian
Political Argument
382 pp. 1965. 50s.

Bird, Graham
Kant's Theory of Knowledge:
An Outline of One Central Argument in the *Critique of Pure Reason*
220 pp. 1962. (2nd Impression 1965.) 28s.

Brentano, Franz
The True and the Evident
Edited and narrated by Professor R. Chisholm
218 pp. 1965. 40s.

Broad, C. D.
Lectures on Psychical Research
Incorporating the Perrott Lectures given in Cambridge University in 1959
and 1960
461 pp. 1962. (2nd Impression 1966.) 56s.

Crombie, I. M.
An Examination of Plato's Doctrine
I. Plato on Man and Society
408 pp. 1962. (2nd Impression 1966.) 42s.
II. Plato on Knowledge and Reality
583 pp. 1963. (2nd Impression 1967.) 63s.

Day, John Patrick
Inductive Probability
352 pp. 1961. 40s.

2

International Library of Philosophy and Scientific Method
(Demy 8vo)

Edel, Abraham
Method in Ethical Theory
379 pp. 1963. 32s.

Flew, Anthony
Hume's Philosophy of Belief
A Study of his First "Inquiry"
296 pp. 1961. (2nd Impression 1966.) 30s.

Fogelin, Robert J.
Evidence and Meaning
Studies in Analytical Philosophy
200 pp. 1967. 25s.

Gale, Richard
The Language of Time
256 pp. 1967. about 30s.

Goldman, Lucien
The Hidden God
A Study of Tragic Vision in the *Pensées* of Pascal and the Tragedies of
Racine. Translated from the French by Philip Thody
424 pp. 1964. 70s.

Hamlyn, D. W.
Sensation and Perception
A History of the Philosophy of Perception
222 pp. 1961. (3rd Impression 1967.) 25s.

Kemp, J.
Reason, Action and Morality
216 pp. 1964. 30s.

Körner, Stephan
Experience and Theory
An Essay in the Philosophy of Science
272 pp. 1966. 45s.

Lazerowitz, Morris
Studies in Metaphilosophy
276 pp. 1964. 35s.

Linsky, Leonard
Referring
152 pp. 1967. about 28s.

Merleau-Ponty, M.
Phenomenology of Perception
Translated from the French by Colin Smith
487 pp. 1962. (4th Impression 1967.) 56s.

3

International Library of Philosophy and Scientific Method
(Demy 8vo)

Wittgenstein, Ludwig
Tractatus Logico-Philosophicus
The German text of the *Logisch-Philosophische Abhandlung* with a new translation by D. F. Pears and B. F. McGuinness. Introduction by Bertrand Russell
188 pp. 1961. (3rd Impression 1966.) 21s.

Wright, Georg Henrik Von
Norm and Action
A Logical Enquiry. The Gifford Lectures
232 pp. 1963. (2nd Impression 1964.) 32s.

The Varieties of Goodness
The Gifford Lectures
236 pp. 1963. (3rd Impression 1966.) 28s.

Zinkernagel, Peter
Conditions for Description
Translated from the Danish by Olaf Lindum
272 pp. 1962. 37s. 6d.

International Library of Psychology, Philosophy, and Scientific Method
(Demy 8vo)

PHILOSOPHY

Anton, John Peter
Aristotle's Theory of Contrariety
276 pp. 1957. 25s.

Bentham, J.
The Theory of Fictions
Introduction by C. K. Ogden
214 pp. 1932. 30s.

Black, Max
The Nature of Mathematics
A Critical Survey
242 pp. 1933. (5th Impression 1965.) 28s.

Bluck, R. S.
Plato's Phaedo
A Translation with Introduction, Notes and Appendices
226 pp. 1955. 21s.

Broad, C. D.
Scientific Thought
556 pp. 1923. (4th Impression 1952.) 40s.

Five Types of Ethical Theory
322 pp. 1930. (9th Impression 1967.) 30s.

The Mind and Its Place in Nature
694 pp. 1925. (7th Impression 1962.) 55s. See also Lean, Martin

Buchler, Justus (Ed.)
The Philosophy of Peirce
Selected Writings
412 pp. 1940. (3rd Impression 1956.) 35s.

Burtt, E. A.
The Metaphysical Foundations of Modern Physical Science
A Historical and Critical Essay
364 pp. 2nd (revised) edition 1932. (5th Impression 1964.) 35s.

6

International Library of Psychology, Philosophy, and Scientific Method
(Demy 8vo)

Carnap, Rudolf
The Logical Syntax of Language
Translated from the German by Amethe Smeaton
376 pp. 1937. (7th Impression 1967.) 40s.

Chwistek, Leon
The Limits of Science
Outline of Logic and of the Methodology of the Exact Sciences
With Introduction and Appendix by Helen Charlotte Brodie
414 pp. 2nd edition 1949. 32s.

Cornford, F. M.
Plato's Theory of Knowledge
The Theaetetus and Sophist of Plato
Translated with a running commentary
358 pp. 1935. (7th Impression 1967.) 28s.

Plato's Cosmology
The Timaeus of Plato
Translated with a running commentary
402 pp. Frontispiece. 1937. (5th Impression 1966.) 45s.

Plato and Parmenides
Parmenides' *Way of Truth* and Plato's *Parmenides*
Translated with a running commentary
280 pp 1939 (5th Impression 1964.) 32s.

Crawshay-Williams, Rupert
Methods and Criteria of Reasoning
An Inquiry into the Structure of Controversy
312 pp. 1957. 32s.

Fritz, Charles A.
Bertrand Russell's Construction of the External World
252 pp. 1952. 30s.

Hulme, T. E.
Speculations
Essays on Humanism and the Philosophy of Art
Edited by Herbert Read. Foreword and Frontispiece by Jacob Epstein
296 pp. 2nd edition 1936. (6th Impression 1965.) 32s.

Lange, Frederick Albert
The History of Materialism
And Criticism of its Present Importance
With an Introduction by Bertrand Russell, F.R.S. Translated from the German
by Ernest Chester Thomas
1,146 pp. 1925. (3rd Impression 1957.) 70s.

International Library of Psychology, Philosophy, and Scientific Method
(Demy 8vo)

Lazerowitz, Morris
The Structure of Metaphysics
With a Foreword by John Wisdom
262 pp. 1955. (2nd Impression 1963.) 30s.

Lean, Martin
Sense-Perception and Matter
A Critical Analysis of C. D. Broad's Theory of Perception
234 pp. 1953. 25s.

Lodge, Rupert C.
Plato's Theory of Art
332 pp. 1953. 25s.

The Philosophy of Plato
366 pp. 1956. 32s.

Mannheim, Karl
Ideology and Utopia
An Introduction to the Sociology of Knowledge
With a Preface by Louis Wirth. Translated from the German by Louis Wirth and Edward Shils
360 pp. 1954. (2nd Impression 1966.) 30s.

Moore, G. E.
Philosophical Studies
360 pp. 1922. (6th Impression 1965.) 35s. See also Ramsey, F. P.

Ogden, C. K., and Richards, I. A.
The Meaning of Meaning
A Study of the Influence of Language upon Thought and of the Science of Symbolism
With supplementary essays by B. Malinowski and F. G. Crookshank
394 pp. 10th Edition 1949. (6th Impression 1967.) 32s.
See also Bentham, J.

Peirce, Charles, *see* Buchler, J.

Ramsey, Frank Plumpton
The Foundations of Mathematics and other Logical Essays
Edited by R. B. Braithwaite. Preface by G. E. Moore
318 pp. 1931. (4th Impression 1965.) 35s.

Richards, I. A.
Principles of Literary Criticism
312 pp. 2nd edition. 1926. (17th Impression 1966.) 30s.

Mencius on the Mind. Experiments in Multiple Definition
190 pp. 1932. (2nd Impression 1964.) 28s.

Russell, Bertrand, *see* Fritz C. A.; Lange, F. A.; Wittgenstein, L.

International Library of Psychology, Philosophy, and Scientific Method
(Demy 8vo)

Smart, Ninian
Reasons and Faiths
An Investigation of Religious Discourse, Christian and Non-Christian
230 pp. 1958. (2nd Impression 1965.) 28s.

Vaihinger, H.
The Philosophy of As If
A System of the Theoretical, Practical and Religious Fictions of Mankind
Translated by C. K. Ogden
428 pp. 2nd edition 1935. (4th Impression 1965.) 45s.

Wittgenstein, Ludwig
Tractatus Logico-Philosophicus
With an Introduction by Bertrand Russell, F.R.S., German text with an English translation en regard
216 pp. 1922. (9th Impression 1962.) 21s.
For the Pears-McGuinness translation—*see page 5*

Wright, Georg Henrik von
Logical Studies
214 pp. 1957. (2nd Impression 1967.) 28s.

Zeller, Eduard
Outlines of the History of Greek Philosophy
Revised by Dr. Wilhelm Nestle. Translated from the German by L. R. Palmer
248 pp. 13th (revised) edition 1931. (5th Impression 1963.) 28s.

PSYCHOLOGY

Adler, Alfred
The Practice and Theory of Individual Psychology
Translated by P. Radin
368 pp. 2nd (revised) edition 1929. (8th Impression 1964.) 30s.

Eng, Helga
The Psychology of Children's Drawings
From the First Stroke to the Coloured Drawing
240 pp. 8 colour plates. 139 figures. 2nd edition 1954. (3rd Impression 1966.) 40s.

Jung, C. G.
Psychological Types
or The Psychology of Individuation
Translated from the German and with a Preface by H. Godwin Baynes
696 pp. 1923. (12th Impression 1964.) 45s.

International Library of Psychology, Philosophy, and Scientific Method
(Demy 8vo)

Koffka, Kurt
The Growth of the Mind
An Introduction to Child-Psychology
Translated from the German by Robert Morris Ogden
456 pp. 16 figures. 2nd edition (revised) 1928. (6th Impression 1965.) 45s.
Principles of Gestalt Psychology
740 pp. 112 figures. 39 tables. 1935. (5th Impression 1962.) 60s.

Malinowski, Bronislaw
Crime and Custom in Savage Society
152 pp. 6 plates. 1926. (8th Impression 1966.) 21s.
Sex and Repression in Savage Society
290 pp. 1927. (4th Impression 1953.) 28s.
See also Ogden, C. K.

Murphy, Gardner
An Historical Introduction to Modern Psychology
488 pp. 5th edition (revised) 1949. (6th Impression 1967.) 40s.

Paget, R.
Human Speech
Some Observations, Experiments, and Conclusions as to the Nature,
Origin, Purpose and Possible Improvement of Human Speech
374 pp. 5 plates. 1930. (2nd Impression 1963.) 42s.

Petermann, Bruno
The Gestalt Theory and the Problem of Configuration
Translated from the German by Meyer Fortes
364 pp. 20 figures. 1932. (2nd Impression 1950.) 25s.

Piaget, Jean
The Language and Thought of the Child
Preface by E. Claparède. Translated from the French by Marjorie Gabain
*220 pp. 3rd edition (revised and enlarged) 1959. (3rd Impression 1966.)
30s.*

Judgment and Reasoning in the Child
Translated from the French by Marjorie Warden
276 pp. 1928 (4th Impression 1966.) 28s.

The Child's Conception of the World
Translated from the French by Joan and Andrew Tomlinson
408 pp. 1929. (4th Impression 1964.) 40s.

International Library of Psychology, Philosophy, and Scientific Method *(Demy 8vo)*

Piaget, Jean *(continued)*
The Child's Conception of Physical Causality
Translated from the French by Marjorie Gabain
(3rd Impression 1965.) 30s.

The Moral Judgment of the Child
Translated from the French by Marjorie Gabain
438 pp. 1932. (4th Impression 1965.) 35s.

The Psychology of Intelligence
Translated from the French by Malcolm Piercy and D. E. Berlyne
198 pp. 1950. (4th Impression 1964.) 18s.

The Child's Conception of Number
Translated from the French by C. Gattegno and F. M. Hodgson
266 pp. 1952. (3rd Impression 1964.) 25s.

The Origin of Intelligence in the Child
Translated from the French by Margaret Cook
448 pp. 1953. (2nd Impression 1966.) 42s.

The Child's Conception of Geometry
In collaboration with Bärbel Inhelder and Alina Szeminska. Translated from the French by E. A. Lunzer
428 pp. 1960. (2nd Impression 1966.) 45s.

Piaget, Jean and Inhelder, Bärbel
The Child's Conception of Space
Translated from the French by F. J. Langdon and J. L. Lunzer
512 pp. 29 figures. 1956 (3rd Impression 1967.) 42s.

Roback, A. A.
The Psychology of Character
With a Survey of Personality in General
786 pp. 3rd edition (revised and enlarged 1952.) 50s.

Smythies, J. R.
Analysis of Perception
With a Preface by Sir Russell Brain, Bt.
162 pp. 1956. 21s.

van der Hoop, J. H.
Character and the Unconscious
A Critical Exposition of the Psychology of Freud and Jung
Translated from the German by Elizabeth Trevelyan
240 pp. 1923. (2nd Impression 1950.) 20s.

Woodger, J. H.
Biological Principles
508 pp. 1929. (Reissued with a new Introduction 1966.) 60s.

867 PRINTED BY HEADLEY BROTHERS LTD 109 KINGSWAY LONDON WC2 AND ASHFORD KENT